RIMSKY-KORSAKOV AND HIS WORLD

# RIMSKY-KORSAKOV
## AND HIS WORLD

EDITED BY
MARINA FROLOVA-WALKER

PRINCETON UNIVERSITY PRESS
PRINCETON AND OXFORD

Copyright © 2018 by Princeton University Press

Published by Princeton University Press, 41 William Street,
Princeton, New Jersey 08540
In the United Kingdom: Princeton University Press,
6 Oxford Street, Woodstock, Oxfordshire OX20 1TR
press.princeton.edu

All Rights Reserved

For permissions/credits, see page xiii

Library of Congress Control Number: 2018940955

Cloth ISBN: 978-0-691-182704
Paper ISBN: 978-0-691-182711

British Library Cataloging-in-Publication Data is available

This publication has been produced by the Bard College Publications Office:
Mary Smith, Director
Irene Zedlacher, Project Director
Karen Walker Spencer, Designer
Text edited by Paul De Angelis and Erin Clermont
Music typeset by Don Giller

This publication has been underwritten in part by grants from
Roger and Helen Alcaly and from the Dragan Plamenac Endowment of the
American Musicological Society, funded in part by the National Endowment
for the Humanities and the Andrew W. Mellon Foundation.

Printed on acid-free paper. ∞

Printed in the United States of America.

1 3 5 7 9 10 8 6 4 2

# Contents

Preface and Acknowledgments — vii

Permissions and Credits — xiii

### CORRESPONDENCE

The Professor and the Sea Princess: Letters of Nikolai Rimsky-Korsakov and Nadezhda Zabela-Vrubel — 3
EDITED BY MARINA FROLOVA-WALKER
TRANSLATED BY JONATHAN WALKER

### OPERAS IN CONTEXT

Rimsky-Korsakov, *Snegurochka*, and Populism — 63
EMILY FREY

"You, Mozart, Aren't Worthy of Yourself": Aesthetic Discontents of Rimsky-Korsakov's *Mozart and Salieri* — 97
ANNA NISNEVICH

### ORIENTALISM AND *THE GOLDEN COCKEREL*

Nikolai Rimsky-Korsakov and His Orient — 145
ADALYAT ISSIYEVA

*The Golden Cockerel*, Censored and Uncensored — 177
SIMON MORRISON

Staging Defeat: *The Golden Cockerel* and the Russo-Japanese War — 197
MARINA FROLOVA-WALKER

COLLEAGUES AND DISCIPLES

St. Petersburg Conservatory and the Beginnings           223
of Russian Musicology
OLGA PANTELEEVA

How Stravinsky Stopped Being a Rimsky-Korsakov Pupil     249
YAROSLAV TIMOFEEV
TRANSLATED BY JONATHAN WALKER

Stylistic Turbulence: The Experience of the              277
Rimsky-Korsakov School
LIDIA ADER
TRANSLATED BY JONATHAN WALKER

AFTERWORD

In Search of Beauty: Autocracy, Music, and Painting in   301
Rimsky-Korsakov's Russia
LEON BOTSTEIN

Index                                                    355

Notes on the Contributors                                365

# Preface and Acknowledgments

In the summer of 2003, I found myself taking a group of British music lovers on an educational tour of St. Petersburg. One of the main attractions on the schedule was Nikolai Rimsky-Korsakov's apartment on Zagorodny Avenue, where the composer's long fur-tipped coat was hanging up over a little table where Stravinsky's calling card lay, while in the study, two large writing desks allowed the composer and his wife, Nadezhda, to face each other as they wrote. I had always been impressed by the authenticity of the place, which looks as if Rimsky-Korsakov might step back in through the door at any moment. But one of the tourists was clearly disappointed. She was startled that there was nothing to be seen but a kind of professorial respectability. What had she expected? Her description of the kind of dwelling the composer *should* have occupied was a multicolored palace, something along the lines of Leon Bakst's set for the ballet *Sheherazade*. Rimsky-Korsakov had only written a symphonic poem, but Sergei Diaghilev had used it as a ballet score in Paris after the composer's death, and he added an orgy and a massacre, provoking Nadezhda to protest. Perhaps the tourist also thought that Rimsky-Korsakov would stagger from orgy to massacre to orgy. This brought home to me the gulf between the Russian image of Rimsky-Korsakov—a respectable professor with a colorful imagination—as compared to the Western image, which has been shaped largely by a lurid balletic reinterpretation of *Sheherazade* that would have outraged its composer.

The genre on which Rimsky-Korsakov staked his reputation was opera, and he contributed fifteen works to the repertoire. About half of these are well established in the repertoire of Russian opera companies, but in the West, only *The Golden Cockerel* makes frequent appearances, some of the others are occasionally performed, and the rest are unknown. The success of the *Cockerel*, the strangest of Rimsky-Korsakov's operas, is also due to Diaghilev's bold adaptation: his 1914 *Cockerel* was again staged as a ballet, with the singers and their words put on the same level as the orchestral writing. At the beginning of the twentieth century, Western audiences did not yet know Russian opera, and Western companies were not prepared to take them on. The finances of Diaghilev's enterprise were usually precarious, and his artists were Russian, so translated versions were not an option at this stage. He realized that he needed to shift Russian texts to the background, before an opera could win a hearing abroad. A century has passed since then, and given that his operas are still little known outside Russia, Western audiences have been unable to grasp his true stature. This, in turn, means that there is nothing that impels them to seek out his non-operatic works: there are dozens of wonderful songs, chamber music, and various orchestral pieces beyond *Sheherazade*.

Richard Taruskin encapsulated the problem of Rimsky-Korsakov in the West: his works "can be divided into two groups: the unknown and the overplayed. They are not of equal size. The overplayed category consists, by my count, of exactly five pieces."[1] These five he lists as follows: "The Flight of the Bumble Bee" (an extract from the opera *The Tale of Tsar Saltan*), "The Song of India" (sung by the Hindu Trader in the opera *Sadko*), and then three "symphonic warhorses": *Sheherazade*, the *Capriccio espagnol*, and the *Russian Easter Overture*. Taruskin demonstrates that this has skewed Rimsky-Korsakov's reception in the West, where he is seen merely as a purveyor of entertaining trifles, not as a serious composer with a very substantial oeuvre. Western musicology had hitherto ignored Rimsky-Korsakov, but Taruskin's pioneering article explains why they should change their attitude, not least because Stravinsky (who certainly does interest Western musicologists) cannot be accounted for without serious distortions unless his enormous debt to his teacher, Rimsky-Korsakov, is included, and not just for superficially similar early works like *The Firebird*, but for his principles of pitch organization, which stem from the older composer's innovations and theoretical discoveries. But even if Taruskin managed to awaken some musicological interest in Rimsky-Korsakov, it will take much time and effort to shift the attitude of Western performers and their public.

In this context, the Bard Music Festival "Rimsky-Korsakov and His World," held in the summer of 2018, is a unique and exciting event that will reveal much of the composer's music that is still unknown to the West. This volume is published in association with the festival and is designed to acquaint readers with the most interesting and thought-provoking new research on Rimsky-Korsakov, including work from established and rising scholars, and from inside and outside Russia.

The volume begins with documentary materials, for the first time offering the Anglophone reader translations of the rich correspondence between Rimsky-Korsakov and the soprano Nadezhda Zabela-Vrubel, who was his muse between 1898 and 1904. Rimsky-Korsakov was a prolific correspondent, and most of his exchanges with musical colleagues have been published in Russian and thoroughly researched.

But this particular correspondence stands apart from the rest, because of the strong currents of emotion running just below the surface. It was selected for this volume for two purposes: it has much to tell us about how Rimsky-Korsakov dealt with the performers and theater management involved in productions of his operas, but it also gives us a unique insight into the composer's inner world which he kept hidden under the unruffled surface of his respectable professorial existence. Rimsky-Korsakov's biography contains nothing that could shock or fuel gossip: as a young naval officer, he traveled round the globe, but he settled down into a quiet family existence, far from the alcoholism that dogged several of his fellow composers. We might style him a workaholic today, but this is only a humorous pretense that such behavior is a vice or an addiction. The romanticized public image of artists is greatly enhanced by an early death or by great suffering, whether uninvited or self-inflicted, mental or physi-cal. The public is less interested in a composer who is a family man with a successful career and a long and healthy existence. The correspondence between Rimsky-Korsakov and Zabela should do much to humanize Rimsky-Korsakov, softening his image. There is nothing scandalous, but there is much that is touching and even poignant.

A conscious effort has been made in this volume to bring Rimsky-Korsakov's operatic output into the foreground. The cultural context of his operas is inexhaustibly rich, and the resulting picture allows us to see the composer as a public intellectual as well as an artist, responding to a variety of political and aesthetic impulses of his time in a way that is more often associated with literary figures. For any scholar immersed in Rimsky-Korsakov's work, the interpretation of his operas is always an enjoyable and fruitful undertaking. Emily Frey's essay on *The Snow Maiden* is a reconsideration of this opera in the political context of the era, namely within a particular branch of 1870s populism that extolled "harmonious communal ritual, agrarian prehistory, [and] the development of individual feeling." By contrast, Anna Nisnevich uses Rimsky-Korsakov's opera *Mozart and Salieri*, a watershed work that inaugurated his "late" period, as a lens through which she observes and analyses Rimsky-Korsakov's creative crisis. As she explains, he attempted to renew his style by means of a more spontaneous and melodic approach that would clear away the "Salierism" he diagnosed in his music.

A trio of articles about Rimsky-Korsakov's last opera, *The Golden Cockerel*, demonstrates how rich this work is, since far from converging on a consensus, each essay illuminates a very different aspect. Adalyat Issiyeva sets the opera in the context of the composer's Orientalism, looking at its musical sources and more generally at the complexity of influences at work on an artist working in the capital of a Russian Empire that directed much of its energy and ingenuity to the task of keeping its Asian territories under control. Simon Morrison's essay addresses two contrasting aspects of the opera: its political provocativeness, which leads to a censorship saga, but also the attraction of the music and the mystery of the story, which takes us outside of the political sphere. Using the aesthetic notion of *enchantment*, Morrison places the opera in the context of Symbolist and "decadent" currents in the culture of the time, and shows how these were still relevant in the 2012 production by the choreographer Alexei Ratmansky. My own addition to this forum on the *Cockerel* seeks to read the opera as a pointed political satire, prompted and shaped by the concrete events of the Russo-Japanese War. Here Rimsky-Korsakov appears as politically radical, and returns to the idioms (and clichés) of the Russian Style, not in a spirit of nostalgia, but with the aim of inverting and mocking his previous values, and also mocking the Russian state, whose hubris had led to a humiliating defeat.

The next group of articles addresses Rimsky-Korsakov in the context of his pedagogical activities and his school of composers. Olga Panteleeva sets the scene by writing about St. Petersburg Conservatory, arguing that under Rimsky-Korsakov, music theory was seen as the handmaiden to composition, which hindered the institutionalization of historical musicology. Yaroslav Timofeev focuses on a dramatic moment in the life of Stravinsky when he was forced to choose between loyalty to the memory of his beloved teacher Rimsky-Korsakov on the one hand, and his new loyalty, both commercial and artistic, to Diaghilev on the other hand—a choice, in effect, between St. Petersburg and Paris. Matters were brought to a head by the preparation of a new edition of *Khovanshchina* that was to be used for an "authentic" Paris production of the opera in 1913 in rivalry with the version prepared by Rimsky-Korsakov. Lidia Ader traces the fate of Rimsky-Korsakov's legacy in the Soviet Union of the 1920s and 1930s, when composition teaching (along with most aspects of life) became a bone of ideological contention. Her article allows us to understand how far-reaching Rimsky-Korsakov's principles of composition proved to be, forming a solid foundation that was built on by loyal members of his compositional school over the next two generations, through favorable and unfavorable ideological swings.

Leon Botstein's essay closes the volume with a broad consideration of Rimsky-Korsakov in the context of Russian politics, philosophy, and aesthetics in the nineteenth and early twentieth centuries, drawing some persuasive parallels between the development of Russian music and Russian painting. This book would never have come into existence without the Bard Music Festival, which is a unique enterprise that unites performers and scholars each year in an exploration of a single composer. I have been privileged to attend and participate in several Bard festivals over the years, and I have always been thrilled by the scale of the events and the vision behind them. Many thanks are therefore due to the president of Bard College, Leon Botstein, who stands at the festival's helm. In the case of this book, I have been working most closely with Botstein's co-artistic director Christopher Gibbs, and the project benefited much from his guidance every step of the way. In the actual preparation of the book, I would like first to thank all of the contributors, most of whom conducted new research at my request and who showed much good will throughout the very thorough editing process. The volume itself was lovingly put together by Paul De Angelis, who made great efforts to see the big picture in each essay, while still training his eagle eye on minute details. I am immensely grateful to him for his professionalism and for his patience. Erin Clermont, the copy editor, kept all of us on our toes, and Irene Zedlacher, a person of many talents and many roles, lent her perceptive eye to the final polishing of the book. Karen Spencer skillfully set the words and images into the finished layout, and Don Giller set the music examples. Finally, I would like to thank Jonathan Walker, who, besides providing fine translations of the Russian sources and of the Russian-language contributions to the volume, was always on call for my queries on both content and style and who was able to cover my back on more than one occasion. Battling out the finer points of the Russo-Japanese War with him also left an indelible imprint on my own essay in this book.

## NOTES

1. Richard Taruskin, "Catching Up with Rimsky-Korsakov," *Music Theory Spectrum* 33/2 (Fall 2011): 169–185, at 169.

# Permissions and Credits

The following institutions and copyright holders have graciously provided the images for illustrations as mentioned here:

In "The Professor and the Sea Princess": The State Russian Museum, St. Petersburg, Russia for Figure 1, Nadezhda Zabela-Vrubel with her husband, Mikhail Vrubel; Tretyakov Gallery, Moscow, Russia/Bridgeman Images for Figure 2, *The Swan Princess*; State Russian Museum, St. Petersberg, Russia/Bridgeman Images for Figure 3, Portrait of Nadezhda Zabela-Vrubel among the birch trees.

In "Nikolai Rimsky-Korsakov and His Orient": Boris Yeltsin Presidential Library, St. Petersburg, Moscow for Figure 1, Pyotr Badmaev; Beinecke Library, Yale University for Figure 2, Ivan Bilibin, "Tsar Pea," cover of magazine *Zhupel*, 1906 (also used in "*The Golden Cockerel*, Censored and Uncensored").

In "*The Golden Cockerel*, Censored and Uncensored": Beinecke Library, Yale University for Figure 1, Ivan Bilibin, "Tsar Pea," cover of magazine *Zhupel*, 1906; American Ballet Theatre for Figure 3, the photograph by Fabrizio Ferri of Skylar Brandt and Duncan Lyle in *The Golden Cockerel*.

In "Staging Defeat": British Library, London, UK © British Library Board/Bridgeman Images for Figure 1, *We'll Just Sit Looking Out to Sea and Wait for the Weather*; Hamburg, Kunsthalle, © Alfred Kubin/DACS, akg-images for Figure 2, Alfred Kubin (1877–1959), *Das Grausen* (The Horror), drawing from 1902; Library of Congress Prints and Photographs Division, Washington, D.C. for Figure 3, Japanese wartime woodblock by Kobayashi Kiyochika (1847–1915); State Central Museum of Contemporary History of Russia, Moscow, Russia for Figure 4, "Let's see how they manage without the eagle . . ."

In "St. Petersburg Conservatory and the Beginnings of Russian Musicology": National Library of Russia, St. Petersburg, Russia for both Figure 1, Liveri (Liberio) Antonovich Sacchetti, and Figure 2, Nikolai Fyodorovich Findeisen.

In "How Stravinsky Stopped Being a Rimsky-Korsakov Pupil": The Paul Sacher Foundation, Basel, Switzerland, for Examples 1 through 7, Stravinsky manuscript sketches of revisions to Musorgsky's *Kovanshchina*.

In "In Search of Beauty": Tretyakov Gallery, Moscow, Russia/Bridgeman Images for Figure 1, Karl Briullov, *The Siege of Pskov* (1837); Figure 2, Alexander Ivanov, *The Appearance of Christ Before the People* (1837–57); Figure 5, Vasili Vereschagin, *Defeated, Requiem* (1879); and Figure 6, Viktor Vasnetsov, *The Snow Maiden* (1899); Musee d'Orsay, Paris, France/Bridgeman Images for Figure 3, Nicolai Ge, *Crucifixion* (ca. 1892); State Russian Museum, St. Petersberg, Russia/Bridgeman Images for both Figure 4, Ilya Repin, *Barge Haulers on the Volga* (1870–73), and Figure 7, Mikhail Vrubel, *The Six-Winged Seraph* (1904).

Also, Figure 1 in "'You, Mozart, Aren't Worthy of Yourself'—of Vasili Shkafer as Mozart and Fyodor Chaliapin as Salieri in the 1898 MPO production of *Mozart and Salieri*—is taken from Fedor Chaliapin, *A Story About Life* (Perm Publishing House, 1966).

The authors, editors, and publisher have made every effort to trace holders of copyright. They much regret if any inadvertent omissions have been made.

# Correspondence

# The Professor and the Sea Princess: Letters of Nikolai Rimsky-Korsakov and Nadezhda Zabela-Vrubel

### EDITED BY MARINA FROLOVA-WALKER
### TRANSLATED BY JONATHAN WALKER

> I am still filled, my dear, dear friend,
> Filled with your visage, filled with you! . .
> It is as if a light-winged angel
> Descended to converse with me.
>
> Leaving the angel at the threshold
> Of holy heaven, now alone,
> I gather some angelic feathers
> Shed by rainbow wings . . .
>
> —Apollon Maykov (1852),
> set by Rimsky-Korsakov as No. 4 of his Opus 50 songs
> and dedicated to Nadezhda Zabela-Vrubel

"I am rather dry by nature," confessed Rimsky-Korsakov in one of his letters.[1] This is indeed the prevailing impression we are likely to draw from his biographies, or even from his own memoirs. We know so much about the externals of his life, and yet the inner man somehow eludes us, obscured by his professorial image: a kindly but reserved man, with a positive outlook on life, dignified and of impeccable morals. The contrast with the wild biographies of Musorgsky and Tchaikovsky allows us to suppose that Rimsky-Korsakov was really rather ordinary, even a little dreary.

---

1. Maykov's Russian original of the epigraph above is as follows: Yeshcho ya poln, o drug moy milïy, / Tvoim yavlen'yem, poln toboy!. ./ Kak budto angel legkokrïlïy / Sletal besedovat' so mnoy, / I, provodiv yego v preddver'ye svyatïkh nebes, ya bez nego / Sbirayu vïpavshiye per'ya / Iz krïl'yev raduzhnïkh yego...

The selection from his correspondence with the soprano Nadezhda Zabela-Vrubel (1868–1913) that is presented here offers us a glimpse into the composer's inner world that cannot be found in other sources.[2] He first heard Zabela sing in late 1897, when she performed as the Sea Princess in his opera *Sadko*, and from that moment on, she became his muse, prompting him to create soprano parts specifically for her, in one opera after another. The context of this artistic relationship is Savva Mamontov's Moscow Private Opera (hereafter MPO), where Zabela was one of the leading soloists.[3] For several years, this opera company devoted itself to the operatic oeuvre of Rimsky-Korsakov, providing him with a reliable vehicle for bringing his music to the public as soon as it was written. The performances were not always musically perfect, but great care was lavished on the visual aspects, since Mamontov was equally a patron of the most interesting painters of the day. One of these was Mikhail Vrubel, Zabela's husband, who was a visionary innovator in painting, but also firmly embedded in the culture of applied art, often producing costumes and sets for the MPO.[4] He also made several striking portraits of his wife in her Rimsky-Korsakov roles, most famously as the Swan Princess from *The Tale of Tsar Saltan* (1900), or the Sea Princess from *Sadko* (1898). Eschewing naturalism, Vrubel tried to evoke the magic of an operatic moment animated by Zabela's voice, encapsulating the qualities that held Rimsky-Korsakov captive in the later years of his life.

Rimsky-Korsakov's collaboration with the MPO began after the Mariinsky turned down the opportunity to launch *Sadko*. The Mariinsky was, quite literally, the court theater, and Nicholas II did not find the opera engaging enough.[5] The composer took this snub badly, and when his friend Semyon

---

2. All 189 extant letters in Russian were published in N. A. Rimskiy-Korsakov, *Perepiska s N. I. Zabeloy-Vrubel*, ed. by L. G. Barsova (Moscow: Kompozitor, 2008). The letters translated here were drawn from this source.

3. The railway tycoon and philanthropist Savva Mamontov created the company in 1885, originally on his own estate, Abramtsevo. The company's prestige rose significantly in the mid-1890s, when Chaliapin joined, and Rachmaninov became a resident conductor—at this stage, they performed in the Solodovnikov Theatre, in the center of Moscow. After Mamontov was jailed for embezzlement in 1899, the company was put on a new financial footing as the Society for Private Opera (*Tovarishchestvo Chastnoy Operï*) until 1904. Rimsky-Korsakov and Zabela were both investors in the Society. For clarity, though, we will refer to both entities as the "Moscow Private Opera," using the abbreviation MPO.

4. Vrubel was the designer for Rimsky-Korsakov's *Mozart and Salieri*, *The Tsar's Bride*, and *The Tale of Tsar Saltan* at the MPO, as well as operas by Cui and Kalinnikov.

5. *Stranitsï zhizni N. A. Rimskogo-Korsakova: Letopis' zhizni i tvorchestva*, ed. A. A. Orlova, vol. 3 (Leningrad: Muzïka, 1972), 90. The Mariinsky in St. Petersburg and the Bolshoi in Moscow were the two Imperial stages, both operating under the direct control of the Imperial Court. It was nothing out of the ordinary for interested members of the royal family to decide whether a particular opera should be approved or rejected.

Figure 1. Nadezhda Zabela-Vrubel with her husband, Mikhail Vrubel.

Kruglikov[6] suggested that he offer *Sadko* to the MPO, he took action. He had, it is true, heard about some unsatisfactory orchestral playing when this company first produced an opera of his (*The Maid of Pskov*, in 1896). But this was not enough to put him off, especially since it enabled him, as he said, "to spite you-know-who."[7] Kruglikov duly brokered the deal.

Rimsky-Korsakov was unable to attend the MPO's premiere of *Sadko*, but he was present at the third performance, given on 30 December 1897.[8] Noting that the musical aspects were generally lacking in polish, he nevertheless singled out Anton Sekar-Rozhansky[9] and Zabela for praise; they played the roles of Sadko and the Sea Princess, respectively. He also recorded the fact that Zabela was the wife of Mikhail Vrubel, whose sets he also enjoyed. He went to meet Zabela personally in the intermission.[10] The opera was clearly a public success, and Rimsky-Korsakov, overcoming his characteristic modesty, enjoyed being feted by Mamontov and the troupe.

---

6. Semyon Kruglikov (1851–1910) was a Russian music critic, a pupil and friend of Rimsky-Korsakov's. In the 1890s, he served as a consultant for the Moscow Private Opera.

7. *Stranitsï*, 3:100.

8. All the dates in this publication are given according to the "old style," the Julian calendar, which ran twelve days behind the Gregorian calendar in the nineteenth century, and thirteen days in the twentieth.

9. Anton Sekar-Rozhansky (1863–1953), tenor, was one of the most distinguished soloists at the Moscow Private Opera, and particularly remembered for performances in the title role of *Sadko*.

10. *Stranitsï*, 3:114.

He attended one more performance, where Chaliapin sang the Venetian Guest. Zabela now fascinated him, and Rimsky-Korsakov decided that she was the ideal performer for the Sea Princess.[11]

Mamontov, fired up by the success of *Sadko*, immediately launched a production of *May Night*, and after only a month's preparation, this reached the stage in early February 1898. Rimsky-Korsakov, in turn, was inspired to revive a long-abandoned project, a prequel (he called it a Prologue) to his very first opera, *The Maid of Pskov*, under the title *The Boyarinya Vera Sheloga*. It is highly probable that he had already seen how Zabela would fit into the new opera, since he was aware that she had previously taken the role of Olga in the MPO's production of *The Maid of Pskov*.

Always ready to exploit a good opportunity, Mamontov asked Rimsky-Korsakov to conduct *Sadko* in St. Petersburg in the MPO's forthcoming tour, and once he had agreed, more of his works were added to the program. The MPO arrived in late February, and over the next two months staged no less than four Rimsky-Korsakov operas in the Conservatory's Grand Hall: *Sadko*, *The Maid of Pskov*, *May Night*, and *The Snow Maiden*. While rehearsing *Sadko* with Zabela, Rimsky-Korsakov was carried away in a flight of enthusiasm: "I am not the only one robbed of his senses by the Sea Princess. All honor and glory to her!"[12] Rimsky-Korsakov also had Zabela in mind for *The Snow Maiden*'s title role, and rehearsed it with her very thoroughly. Mamontov, however, had other ideas, and cast Alevtina Paskhalova[13] in the role, leading to a serious rift with Rimsky-Korsakov, who heard Paskhalova's first performance and declared that it was "poor." He then refused to conduct the second performance of *The Snow Maiden*, and vowed that he would not even attend any other events in the festival. Mamontov decided that he had allowed matters to deteriorate too far, and reversed his decision, allowing Zabela to take over from Paskhalova. She then sang in the third performance of *The Snow Maiden*, after minimal rehearsal with the rest of the cast. Much of the credit must go to Kruglikov, who worked hard behind the scenes to smooth things over, although Mamontov and Rimsky-Korsakov were never on a friendly footing again, and treated each other with caution.

During this intense period, Rimsky-Korsakov neglected his Conservatory duties and experienced a surge of emotion that led him to present Zabela

---

11. Ibid., 3:115.
12. Ibid., 3:121.
13. Alevtina Paskhalova (1875–1953) was recruited to the MPO by Mamontov himself, and still sang for the company at this stage; she left the following year (1899), and toured widely, eventually pursuing an international career and recording several discs of Russian romances.

with a vocal score of his new opera, *Christmas Eve*, carrying the following inscription: "To the poetic and musical Olga, Pannochka, Snow Maiden and Volkhova: Nadezhda Ivanovna Zabela, with the devoted composer's request that she add Oxana to these, N. Rimsky-Korsakov, 22 April 1898, St. Petersburg."[14] He spent the summer months at work on a new opera that would suit her talents well, *The Tsar's Bride*, which he intended from the outset for the MPO, overlooking, for Zabela's sake, the recent friction with Mamontov.

Such is the back story that brings us up to the very first letter of their correspondence. This, and the following two letters in the selection, can all be understood in light of the events just described.

In October of 1898, Rimsky-Korsakov traveled to Moscow for the rehearsals of *Christmas Eve* at the Bolshoi, and used the opportunity to refresh his association with the MPO. At the theater, he attended a dress rehearsal of *Sadko*. He was also invited to Mamontov's home for a very lengthy soirée, where he heard a rendition of his operas *Mozart and Salieri* and *Sheloga* (the latter twice, allowing him to hear both Sofya Gladkaya[15] and Zabela in the role of Vera), rounded off with dinner.[16] All this attention, art, and bonhomie left him feeling elated, and inspired to write more operas, as he tells Zabela in Letter 4.

Letters 4–10 refer to a concert at the Russian Musical Society (19 December 1898), where Zabela sang extracts from *Sheloga* and *The Tsar's Bride*. Vrubel, in a letter, tried to persuade Rimsky-Korsakov to make arrangements for a complete concert performance of *Sheloga*,[17] but knowing that Mamontov was not even happy with performances of extracts before the stage premiere, Rimsky-Korsakov declined. His artistic relationship with the couple was of mutual benefit: just as Rimsky-Korsakov's later operas (and several songs) were inspired by Zabela, Vrubel was inspired by Rimsky-Korsakov's operas, and his work on the sets and costumes was a labor of love that far outstripped the bare requirements of Mamontov's commission. As he said, he was so immersed in Rimsky-Korsakov's fairy-tale world that he wished to stay there,[18] and so we find that world reflected in many of his paintings and sculptures from these years.

In the end, the Russian Music Society concert received disappointing press, especially from the newspaper *Novoye vremya* (New Era).[19] Nevertheless,

---

14. *Stranitsï*, 3:132–33.
15. Sofya Gladkaya (married name Kedrova, 1875–1965), Russian lyrical soprano, and a singer at the MPO.
16. *Stranitsï*, 3:148.
17. Ibid.
18. Ibid., 3:134.
19. Ibid., 3:162.

Rimsky-Korsakov began to lobby the Mariinsky to hire Zabela, although without any discernible result (Letter 10). His next visit to Moscow ran from late 1898 into the new year, and the score he carried on his journey revealed his main purpose: he could now reveal *The Tsar's Bride*, a new departure in his operatic work, and written to showcase Zabela. Vrubel was certainly flattered that an opera had been written expressly for his wife, but he also worried that "such signs of respect for Nadezhda's talents and achievements only serves to make a jealous Directorate treat her with greater severity and neglect."[20] Whether or not these concerns had much basis in reality, Zabela evidently shared them, since the subject of unfair treatment does indeed feature prominently in Zabela's next letters to Rimsky-Korsakov, and he patiently indulges all her complaints.

Looking in more general terms at the correspondence in 1898 and 1899, we find the most intense and revealing letters here: they are full of warmth and subtle flirtation, punctuated by examples of Rimsky-Korsakov's characteristic self-deprecating humor. There are endearing tokens of intimacy, such as Rimsky-Korsakov's requests that Zabela stay in the key of A major, their key of spring. But the same letters also provide us with musical insights into Rimsky-Korsakov's creative practices and anxieties, and cast light on his relationship with the MPO and the pitfalls of opera production in Russia at the turn of century.

In the spring of 1899, the MPO paid another visit to St. Petersburg, and Rimsky-Korsakov dominated their program once again, with *Sheloga*, *Sadko*, *Mozart and Salieri*, *The Maid of Pskov*, together with Musorgsky's *Boris Godunov* (a version by Rimsky-Korsakov, soon to become the standard version of this opera under Diaghilev). By the end of the tour, Rimsky-Korsakov was planning a further opera with a prominent role for Zabela, namely *The Tale of Tsar Saltan* (containing the famous bumblebee interlude).

*The Tsar's Bride* had to wait until the autumn to see its premiere, with the MPO's production closely supervised by Rimsky-Korsakov, and featuring Zabela in the role of Marfa. At this stage in the correspondence, we find Rimsky-Korsakov returning again and again to a defense of the *Bride*, obviously stung by the critics, who failed to appreciate the simpler and more lyrical style the composer had chosen for this work. For the public, the *Bride* was a huge success, and Rimsky-Korsakov could have satisfied himself with this if it were not for deeper issues lurking in the background. The problem was not just with the critics: even his closest friends saw the *Bride* as a blatant betrayal of the "progressive" principles that had been formulated by Rimsky-Korsakov himself and his colleagues of the

---

20. Vrubel's letter to his sister, ibid., 3:165.

Kuchka back in the 1860s, and developed ever since. These principles most prominently included dramatic realism and a focus on declamation (in opposition to bel canto lyricism). In general, all operatic convention was treated with suspicion. The *Bride* was inevitably seen as a repudiation of all that the Kuchka had stood for and, worst of all, a repudiation by its most prolific representative (not only for his own operas, but for his completions and revisions of Musorgsky and Borodin). Even Rimsky-Korsakov's own wife, Nadezhda Nikolayevna, saw the *Bride* in these terms, as we know from the withering account of the opera in a letter she sent to their son Andrei.[21] She was a musician herself, and had formerly composed; she had been closely and enthusiastically involved with the work of the Kuchka, and with all her husband's previous productions, so her hostility to the *Bride* cannot be written off as the mere symptom of a marital tiff. In his subsequent letters to Zabela, Rimsky-Korsakov's unease is focused on a recurring comparison between the *Bride* and *Saltan* as the representatives of his new and old styles, and now it is Zabela's turn to indulge him as he gives vent to his interior struggles.

Early in 1900, Rimsky-Korsakov returned to Moscow, still carried along by public acclaim for the *Bride*, which spilled over into new opportunities for the composer. He wrote an extra aria for Sekar-Rozhansky, in the role of Lykov, thereby confirming his new commitment to opera as, above all, a collaborative art between composers and singers (the Kuchka had always regarded this as one of the vices of Italian opera). This might well be regarded as the pinnacle of his involvement with the MPO, since his public success would soon bring him back into the gravitational pull of the Imperial theaters. In January 1900, he received the curious but very welcome news that the Tsar had reversed his earlier decision on *Sadko*, and now required its performance at the Mariinsky. We might well say

---

21. In her letter, Mme. Rimsky-Korsakov's description reads thus: "I would place this opera far below the level of *Sadko*, and on the whole, it is the least successful of your father's operas. In the first place, I don't particularly like Mey's drama, and the form it takes in the libretto is still less satisfactory. Secondly, I have little sympathy for this return to the old operatic forms of *A Life for the Tsar*, especially when they are applied to this entirely dramatic plot, since they hobble the dramatic action. Third and last, even if we were to let these forms pass, they would still need to be justified by wonderful music to compensate for the lack of movement—but this is precisely what's lacking. To my mind, all these duets, trios, quartets, and sextets are musically quite banal, no more than acceptable. Admittedly, you can detect the hand of a master at work, all the parts are put together very well, and it does indeed make pleasant listening. But unfortunately, there wasn't a single moment when the opera convinced me that it had any power, or any capacity to astonish. Your father, on the contrary, is delighted, as is everyone else (so they say, at any rate). This left me sounding the only discord in the midst of so much smooth harmony." Ibid., 3:193.

that Rimsky-Korsakov's strategy of the "counter-snub" had worked: his studied avoidance of the Imperial theaters eventually led the directors to realize that they needed him after all. He also received a "strange" invitation, as he told Zabela, to have his "new opera" staged by the Imperial theaters—except that he had not even planned, let alone written any new opera.[22] His state of bemusement was brief, and he made plans for his first *grand opéra*, titled *Servilia*, a project that was obviously far beyond the MPO's resources and abilities. He had not abandoned the MPO, which was given *Saltan* in preference to the Bolshoi, but he was now determined to see his work return to the stage of the Mariinsky.

The *Bride*, in the meantime, had begun spreading to other theaters across the country. Rimsky-Korsakov enjoyed a new production by the Tsereteli company in St. Petersburg, with Maria Insarova as Marfa, whom he found "wonderful."[23] This throwaway comment was not received well by Zabela, jealous of her place in his affections as a composer, and Rimsky-Korsakov had to tread carefully whenever he mentioned Insarova thereafter (Letters 14 and 18). This little sign of Rimsky-Korsakov's disloyalty, as Zabela saw it, showed that the high flowering of their artistic partnership was over, and Letter 19, full of very intense, if veiled emotion, is the last of its kind. The pace of the correspondence then slackens, although there is still another central role for Zabela, namely the Tsarevna in *Kashchei the Immortal*, premiered at the close of 1902. Later in the same year, we see the onset of Vrubel's mental illness, which soon led to his final decline, and there was now a baby to care for, so Zabela's attention was necessarily transferred to these domestic problems, although she managed to maintain her career. She suffered much: Vrubel sometimes had violent breakdowns, which were a danger to Zabela, and he was eventually taken to a sanatorium; in the midst of this turmoil, her baby son died at the age of eighteen months. Weathering these storms, she continued to pursue and even advance her career, securing a post at the Mariinsky (where Rimsky-Korsakov was still lobbying in her favor), bringing her to St. Petersburg in 1904. She remained a soloist with the Mariinsky until 1911.

Perhaps the artistic partnership could have adjusted to the new circumstances, but instead it petered out, even if their personal relations remained amicable. In September 1904, Rimsky-Korsakov heard Zabela perform at the Mariinsky (as Margarita in Gounod's *Faust*) and wrote to

---

22. Ibid., 3:216.
23. Ibid., 3:211. Maria Insarova (1866–?), soprano, sang with many private opera companies throughout Russia. In St. Petersburg and in Kharkov she sang with the Tsereteli company.

his wife that "she sang well, but her voice is too weak for the Mariinsky Theatre." During the intermission, he had a chance to speak to Vrubel (who was enjoying a period of remission), and "found him changed and looking older, but speaking 'quite normally.'"[24] A few days later, he heard Zabela again in *Sadko*, and reported that her performance "is undoubtedly very fine, but she has developed a mannerism, a forced open tone for lower notes, which I didn't like and told her so."[25] Now outside the more intimate environment of the MPO, which had suited Zabela's voice perfectly, she could no longer hope for a central role in any further Rimsky-Korsakov opera, a painful truth that was tacitly understood by both of them. She admits that much as she enjoyed singing through Fevroniya's part in *Kitezh* (which demands almost Wagnerian strength), she realizes that it was not written with her in mind, and that she wasn't suited to delivering it from the grand stage. Instead, she humbly asks Rimsky-Korsakov to see that she is cast in the much more modest role of Sirin, one of the paradise birds in the opera's transcendent finale. This turned out to be the final chapter of their partnership, allowing her, for the last time, to inhabit the realm of the fantastic that they had cultivated together. Outside of her operatic performances, some later events deserve mention: in early 1905, Zabela sang the aria from *Servilia* (discussed in Letter 18) in concert,[26] and one year later gave another concert performance of two Rimsky-Korsakov songs with orchestra ("Midsummer Night's Dream" and "The Nymph"), with great success.[27] She also put in the occasional appearance at Rimsky-Korsakov's musical soirées, where she would sing some of his pieces, together with others written by his composition pupils.

In his operas, Rimsky-Korsakov liked to pair more earth-bound women, dramatic and passionate, with other female roles that were ethereal and otherworldly, and so the Sea Princess in *Sadko* is a foil to Sadko's wife, Lyubava, the Snow Maiden to the feisty Kupava, and the innocent unwitting victim Marfa to the tormented and malign Lyubasha. Zabela proved to be a perfect embodiment of these fairy-tale women and fantastic creatures. As a woman in real life, she also remained for Rimsky-Korsakov a beautiful fantasy, fragile and unattainable. As his muse, she was pivotal in Rimsky-Korsakov's decision to break with his former declamatory aesthetic. He showed inclinations toward this aesthetic shift in some songs that predate their first meeting, but it was Zabela who effectively

---

24. Ibid., 3:344.
25. Ibid., 3:345.
26. *Stranitsï zhizni N. A. Rimskogo-Korsakova: Letopis' zhizni i tvorchestva*, ed. A. A. Orlova, vol. 4 (Leningrad: Muzïka, 1973), 6.
27. Ibid., 4:99.

gave him the confidence to transfer this to a grand public statement, his designedly conventional and melodic *Tsar's Bride*. He told Zabela at the time that he hoped the *Bride* would draw other Russian composers into its wake "even though at present they think it is backward" (Letter 15). As his life drew to a close a decade after his first encounter with Zabela, he doubted whether he should ever have departed from his artistic path, and doubted even the artistic worth of the *Bride*. Perhaps it was just the product of an aging composer's chaste infatuation for a younger woman, an interesting, if not major singer, wrapped up in the mystique of her husband's costumes, stage sets, and paintings. If posterity has a say in the matter, his delightful melodic tribute to Zabela is vindicated: the *Bride* remains a favorite on the Russian stage to the present day.

## 1. Rimsky-Korsakov to Zabela-Vrubel

29 April 1898, St. Petersburg

Most respected and most kind Nadezhda Ivanovna,
I am sending you my Romances Op. 50, and apart from yours,[28] I think you might also make use of No. 1, "The Maiden and the Sun." You are forbidden to peek at them yet, and the same applies to *Christmas Eve*, because you really must have a good rest over the summer and gather fresh strength for the autumn. According to rumors doing the rounds here, the Moscow Opera will not be coming to St. Petersburg in the autumn. That would be very sad, because in St. Petersburg everyone often remembers a talented Volkhova princess, Olga Ivanovna, or rather Yuryevna, etc.[29]

Be healthy and merry: in *la majeur*.[30]
My wife sends her greetings.
Yours, N. R-Korsakov

---

28. Rimsky-Korsakov refers here to the song No. 1, Op. 50, which he dedicated to Zabela. The lyric is by Apollon Maykov, and the full text can be found in the epigraph of this essay.

29. Rimsky-Korsakov is referring to roles played by Zabela in his operas: Volkhova (the Sea Princess) in *Sadko*, and Olga in *The Maid of Pskov*. The two patronymics Rimsky-Korsakov gives for Olga reflect the vexed question of Ivan the Terrible's paternity, on which the plot turns.

30. The key of A major, which Rimsky-Korsakov saw as the key of spring (see Letter 5 for further elaboration).

## 2. Zabela-Vrubel to Rimsky-Korsakov

31 August 1898, Moscow

Most respected Nikolai Andreyevich,
You wished us to inform you when we are back in Moscow, and I hurry to use this chance in order to converse with you.

We only arrived in Moscow a few days ago, but we've already managed to see Savva Ivanovich [Mamontov] and even went with him to Lyubatovich's estate,[31] which is two hours' journey from here. We only arrived back yesterday, and my head is still full of *Mozart and Salieri*, which was performed there by Chaliapin. He sang both the bass and tenor parts, since Shkafer[32] wasn't there, and he sang wonderfully, while Rachmaninov was marvelous as an accompanist. I have rarely experienced such pleasure: the music is so graceful and touching, and yet also so clever, if you'll allow me to say so. There was much discussion of how to produce the opera: my husband immediately drew the costumes, and at dinner, we drank to the success of *Mozart and Salieri*, which I do not doubt in the least (its success, I mean). Although it is a very subtle piece, the public should be able to understand it, especially since everyone knows the Pushkin.

We now have five new sopranos in our company, so although there are still five mezzos, we have nine sopranos altogether now, and I jokingly suggested to Savva Ivanovich that he should recommend another three, so that we could have twelve in all.[33]

Tsvetkova[34] will be singing in *The Maid of Pskov*, but *Sadko* and also perhaps *May Night* will remain mine, and I will even be singing at the opening night of the season, in *Sadko* (the date is not yet known, because the Solodovnikov Theatre is not ready).[35] On top of that, we will all be wearing new costumes that are much more eye-catching—"what more could I wish for," so it is not surprising that I am in *la maj*. During the summer, I learned Oxana's role [in *Christmas Eve*] for my own pleasure, and also (I don't know whether I should be telling you this) Kupava's role [in *The Snow Maiden*]. I don't think

---

31. Tatyana Lyubatovich (1859–1932), a distinguished mezzo-soprano who sang with the MPO at the same time as Zabela. See also Letter 12.

32. Vasili Petrovich Shkafer (1867–1937) was a Russian tenor who sang the role of Mozart in the MPO's premiere of *Mozart and Salieri*, 18 November 1898.

33. This is probably a reference to the twelve sopranos required to play the maidens in Rimsky-Korsakov's *May Night*.

34. Elena Yakovlevna Tsvetkova (1871–1929), dramatic soprano, sang for several private opera companies in Moscow, and also played some individual roles at the Bolshoi.

35. The MPO rented the Solodovnikov Theatre building on Dmitrovka Street, which today houses the Moscow Operetta Theatre.

they'll give me the Snow Maiden, but my Kupava sounded very well in the summer, and when you think about it, Kupava's situation is not so much dramatic as naively comical, so perhaps a lyrical soprano [like Zabela] could sing her part. But I must admit that if Tsvetkova sings the Snow Maiden and I sing Kupava, the result won't be very interesting, since our voices are too much alike.

They considered starting the St. Petersburg season earlier, and I would have liked that, but nothing came of it, hence our stay in Moscow, and my only comfort is that you will visit us in October. Because you do need to come here: at *Christmas Eve*, we'll have *Mozart and Salieri*.[36]

I've reread this letter now and I'm not entirely happy with it: I somehow didn't manage to convey my enthusiasm for *Mozart and Salieri* (as it happens, I was so overwhelmed that I feel my very being has been enhanced by it), and instead of that, I've written to you about the costumes, which will be of little interest to you. Even so, I will send you this letter, hoping for your eternal kindness and condescension.

Our address is the same until October: Bratanovsky's house in Sukharevo-Sadovaya. My husband has been composing a letter to you in his mind the whole summer and is very embarrassed that he still hasn't managed to write it, so he would like to repay the debt through his fervent participation in the production of *Mozart [and Salieri]*.

My heartfelt greetings. Also convey my sincere greetings to Nadezhda Nikolayevna and Sofya Nikolayevna.

Devotedly yours,<br>Nadezhda Vrubel

## 3. Rimsky-Korsakov to Zabela-Vrubel

10 September 1898, St. Petersburg

Most respected Nadezhda Ivanovna,
Your spring letter was forwarded to me in the country, and the autumn letter I found in my apartment in Petersburg on our return, which was not until the 8th of September, hence my very tardy reply. I am very grateful to you for both letters—which are expansive and engaging in

---

36. Zabela-Vrubel's joke here refers in turn to the Bolshoi's production of *Christmas Eve* and the MPO production of *Mozart and Salieri*.

equal measure, while mine are brief and devoid of interest. You always have a good stock of news, while I have none. This time I received conflicting reports from the same city [Moscow]: you are now telling me that your Opera will *not* be coming to St. Petersburg (which saddens me), while Kruglikov, on the other hand, had told me that the Moscow Private Opera *will* be in St. Petersburg all October, which pleased us all to hear. I suspect, though, that your report is more likely to be correct, so I feel quite upset.

I'm glad you liked *Mozart and Salieri*, but I don't believe the public has any need for it, and I don't even see why they should be expected to like it. As for the fact that the plot has been drawn from Pushkin, I can't see much significance in this: everyone knows Pushkin's name, and feel they owe him a certain dutiful respect, but they don't know Pushkin's work beyond a few popular favorites. According to Kruglikov, S. I. [Mamontov] wants to stage the Prologue (to *The Maid of Pskov*), *The Boyarinya Vera Sheloga*, and also *Mozart*.

During the summer, I managed to finish (in draft) the whole of a new opera, *The Tsar's Bride*, and I polished and orchestrated two acts (out of four). I think the soprano part of Marfa should suit you. I'm quite certain that you'll make a good job of Kupava, but will they give you the part? It would be good if S. I. was to allocate the Sea Princess exclusively to you, but I suspect that once again, he might have you and Antonova[37] alternating in the role, and that wouldn't please me one bit.

Perhaps, when I come to Moscow, I might be able to hear you in *Sadko* (in your new costume), but I am worried about the rehearsals: both the orchestra and the choir are new, and even the conductors are new, so how will it all come together?

In Moscow, the Russian Symphony Concert that I'm conducting [in the series of concerts under this name] will take place on the 17th of October, and I will have come a week beforehand for the rehearsals. I don't know whether I'll be able to listen to *Christmas Eve* during that time—most likely not. I am not particularly anxious to hear it anyway. Alongside this letter, I am sending you five of my latest songs and two duets, one of which you heard when you visited us.

I am sincerely grateful to Mikhail Aleksadrovich [Vrubel] for his great efforts over the *Mozart and Salieri* costumes. From your statement that you are feeling in *la majeur*, I conclude that you are in good health, since

---

37. Varvara Antonova, soprano, sang at the MPO from 1896, often cast in the same roles as Zabela: Vokhova, Pannochka, Margarita in *Faust*, Micaëla in *Carmen*, etc.

*la majeur* is not compatible with sickness. I want you to stay in that key (with permitted modulations to *re* and *mi majeur* only).

So, in all probability, I will see you soon in Moscow.

Devotedly yours, N. R-Korsakov

P.S. Greetings from all of my family.

## 4. Rimsky-Korsakov to Zabela-Vrubel

22 October 1898,<br>St. Petersburg

Respected and most kind Nadezhda Ivanovna,
Today, for a change, I will be writing you a long letter. You will read a lyrical part first, and then the business part. The lyrical is as follows. During my stay in Moscow prior to the concert, I was oppressed by gloom, tiredness, and anxiety. But on Sunday, they began to take care of me properly, and even spoil me a little: Savva Ivanych saw to my needs, so did Kruglikov, and also a nice lady who was sitting next to me at dinner. In short, everyone looked after me and I felt a change within myself that you noticed, too. This is what it means for a composer to be vain, fame-seeking, and so on.

While I was on the train, then just after my arrival in St. Petersburg, and, for that matter, just a moment ago, I've wanted to compose, to compose another ten operas, five hundred songs, and so on. But if I take a long hard look at myself, I must conclude that this is a false desire, and that I am actually too tired and should not be composing at all: firstly, because it will be harmful to me; and secondly, because nothing decent will come of it, because I will just start repeating myself and produce a diluted version of all my old things. So then: Lent and abstention, and in the meantime, I need to finish orchestrating *The Tsar's Bride*, which has already tired me out, and is going to tire me out even more. My good cheer is deceptive, and the cause is artistic vanity. I am rather shy by nature, so floral wreaths and applause only embarrass me—I really can't say I like them much; but what I *do* love, I must confess, is to hear my own pieces. I also confess that I love to be taken care of properly by pleasant, straightforward people. Well, enough of the lyrical, or you'll just stop reading soon.

On to business, then. Tomorrow, I will send you a parcel containing the score of *Boyarinya Sheloga* and also the manuscript of Marfa's aria (from

Act 2) [from *The Tsar's Bride*]. Do please look it over (the aria, I mean) and check whether it suits your voice and whether it pleases your heart. While I was writing *The Tsar's Bride*, I admit that I had you and your voice in mind. Don't show it to anyone; but if you find someone to accompany you, then you can sing it to Savva Ivanovich and Kruglikov. Write and tell me if you are prepared to sing it at one of the Russian Symphony Concerts in St. Petersburg, and if you are, then how it can be arranged and when. I could place you either in the second concert (19 December) or in the fourth (6 March). It would be more convenient for me to put you in the second concert, but will they let you go, and would you yourself actually want to come to St. Petersburg at the height of the opera season? Both of these concerts will be held on Saturdays, so you would need to leave on Wednesday in order to be here on Thursday night to sing the aria with piano, then on Friday you would sing it during the last orchestra rehearsal, and on Saturday there will be the concert; finally, you would be able to depart on Sunday, leaving us to collect your feathers (as it says in one of my songs).[38] Will Savva Ivanovich let you go, and who should be the first to tell him—you or me? This has to be handled diplomatically. If the 19th of December is no good for you, then you could sing it at the March concert; if Moscow Private Opera is going to be here, that will certainly smooth everything out for you, and I will arrange the program accordingly. But it would be good if I could know now, because I will have to arrange a performance of some fragments from *Ratcliffe*,[39] which requires three soloists, so it depends on our arrangements whether they will be singing in the second or the fourth concert. I do hope that Savva Ivanovich will make the right decision and come to the concert in which you sing the aria, and then Marfa's part will be yours not merely at my insistence but by natural right, in a manner of speaking. Apart from the aria, I hope you wouldn't mind singing a few songs on your second appearance—whether they are mine or someone else's is entirely up to you.

Do please give me a reply to all my questions soon, and then tell me how the production of *The Boyarinya Sheloga* has fared. How much I'd like to hear *you* on stage in this piece!—but I felt it would have been awkward to insist on that when I was with Savva Ivanovich in Moscow, since we had just settled our differences, so to speak, during his visit. And I forgot to ask Savva Ivanovich whether Olga's and Vera's parts will be sung by the same singer on the same night. Please tell me whatever you might know about that. I would also be pleased if you could let me know how

---

38. Rimsky-Korsakov is referring to his song Op. 50, No. 4, to a text by Apollon Maykov featuring an angel who sheds feathers. The text is given in the epigraph to this essay.

39. *William Ratcliffe* (1869), an opera by César Cui.

the performance of *Christmas Eve* goes, and to hear about your general impression of it if you do manage to see it.

I've ended up writing such a long letter that I really must draw it to a close now. Greetings to your artist husband, who spoils me with his kind remarks. I didn't even manage to speak to him properly, just as I didn't have the chance to hear you performing my songs. I wish you good health, and ask you to stay in the key of *la majeur* . . .

Devotedly yours,<br>N. Rimsky-Korsakov

P.S. Greetings from my wife and Sonya.

### 5. Rimsky-Korsakov to Zabela-Vrubel

28 October 1898, St. Petersburg

My dear and most respected Nadezhda Ivanovna,
Thank you for agreeing to come by the 19th of December. I don't foresee any changes at present. But if it would be better and more pleasant for you to come at Lent, when the opera is in St. Petersburg, and if a trip to St. Petersburg in December would be inconvenient (although you do like the city), then for goodness' sake please just tell me, and I'll happily move you to March—although March is so far away, and God only knows what might happen before then. But I repeat: I could put you in the fourth concert. Must I write to Savva Ivanovich about you, and ask him personally, even though he has already promised you can come?

I'm very much looking forward to your reply about the aria. At first, I set out boldly, composing with confidence, because I think I know your voice, and I was designing the aria and indeed Marfa's entire role just for you. But then when it came down to it, I began to worry that perhaps you wouldn't like it after all. As far as your second appearance in the concert is concerned, your reply didn't tell me whether you would be singing my songs or someone else's, since all you said was that we would choose them together. Don't be shy to say so if you think there will be too much R-K, and in that case sing something by another composer, as long as it's good and it's Russian. Although if you *do* end up choosing another composer, I'll be a little jealous and I'll say to you, "You keep singing composer X"—in the same way that you told me [Madame] Runge[40] was always singing at my place (when in fact she's never sung to me). Both are equally unfair.

It wasn't until today that I finally managed to press on with the orchestration of *The Tsar's Bride*, because I had a lot of business matters to get out of the way first. Once I finish orchestrating your aria from the last act, I'll send you the manuscript. You must have noticed that the aria is copied out in my own hand; I told you that I would give the task to Sonya,[41] but I copied it myself because I felt I simply *had* to do so, since you were looking after me so well at S. I.'s dinner, and served me several dishes with your own fair hand. Now, as to whether I'm feeling in the key of *la-maj.*, which is what you hoped for me, I must tell you that I'll only go as far as *mi♭ majeur.*—which isn't bad either, but *la maj.* doesn't suit a man of my age. It's a key of youth and spring—not early spring, with its ice and little puddles, but the spring well underway, when the lilacs are in bloom and the meadows covered with flowers; it is the key of dawn, not the first glimmers, but the sky in the east when it's already crimson and gold. How did I do there as a decadent? — *La maj.* and the picturesque imaginings? This time, the second part of my letter has turned out to be lyrical, and so I expect you to write me a business letter in the epic style, about *Christmas Eve* and other things.

Devotedly yours,<br>N. R-Korsakov

P.S. Nadezhda Nikolayevna is keeping well, and she was pleased to hear that you were asking for her, and sends you her greetings [a bow]. My greetings also to Mikhail Aleksandrovich.

### 6. From Zabela-Vrubel to Rimsky-Korsakov

28 October 1898, Moscow

Most respected Nikolai Andreyevich,
I expect you've already heard that *Christmas Eve* [at the Bolshoi] was a success, but I don't mind giving you the good news again. The audience loved it, and their interest never flagged. There were curtain calls for the performers after every act, and after Act 2, there was a real storm of applause,

---

40. Alexandra Runge-Semyonova (1868–1939) was a soprano at the Mariinsky Opera.
41. Diminutive form of "Sofya," Rimsky-Korsakov's eldest daughter (1875–1943).

with people demanding to see the composer. They were sorry to hear (and I particularly regretted) that the composer was not actually in Moscow. The performance was very good; it's a pleasure to hear a large orchestra that plays well together, and an even greater pleasure to sing with such an orchestra. The choruses were excellent, and the scene with the carols was encored. Sionitskaya[42] does indeed, as she aptly put it, remind me of a dancing elephant, but she still displayed a lot of talent in her role, with excellent phrasing, and just the kind of coquetry that you find among country girls—still, her high notes could have been more attractive. Donskoy[43] also sings quite well, and pleases the ear at first, but then you find yourself losing patience until eventually you want to shout out: "Come on, sing with full force!" It's as if he has a voice made of cotton wool that can never be sonorous; he encored his song at Solokha's, but in my opinion, the duet in the final act was just a failure: Donskoy couldn't really be heard, and Sionitskaya's top notes were not at all attractive. Since Uspensky[44] (as the Deacon) delivered his phrases in a very comic manner, but also with surprisingly deft intonation, he had the audience rolling in the aisles, which you rarely see in opera. The peasant women's duet (one had a purple nose, the other was normal) went very well, and there were noisy calls for an encore, which for some reason never actually took place. The others were just okay. All the basses—Vlasov, Trezvinsky, and Borisoglebsky[45]—seemed to be performing for a funeral, not in an opera, and you could well imagine them as priests. My personal favorite is the orchestral theme of falling stars, as my husband and I named it, which is heard several times in the prelude to the opera, and many more times during the action.

I am very grateful to you for sending me the Aria [from *The Tsar's Bride*] and the Prologue [*Boyarinya Vera Sheloga*], and also, yet again for the inscription (you spoil me). The Adagio of the Aria is incredibly beautiful, good for presenting a singer's voice in the best light; I'm now singing it every day, in

---

42. Maria Deisha-Sionitskaya (1859–1932), dramatic soprano, was one of the most prominent singers of the time; she performed at both the Mariinsky (before 1891) and the Bolshoi (1892–1908).

43. Lavrenty Donskoy (1857/8?–1917) was the Bolshoi's leading tenor from 1883 to 1904.

44. Alexander Uspensky (1859–1920), tenor, sang at the Bolshoi from 1890 to 1920, and was particularly successful in character roles, such as the Deacon in *Christmas Eve* or Misail in *Boris Godunov*.

45. Stepan Vlasov (1854–1919), bass, sang at the Bolshoi, often alternating in the same roles as Chaliapin; Stepan Trezvinsky (1860–1942), Russian *basso profondo*, sang at the Bolshoi from 1889 to 1928; Sergei Borisoglebsky (1863–1927), an Italian-trained baritone, sang at the Mariinsky from 1892 to 1895 and at the Bolshoi from 1895 to 1902. Zabela refers here to their common background in church choral singing (although this might not be true of Vlasov).

the morning and again at night, and I want to achieve a perfect cantabile, goodness only knows whether I'll succeed, but I have a very strong desire to perfect myself. In the Più lento, if you don't mind, I'll move some words around a little. For example, the syllable "yu" in "uteshayuchis'" would be easier to sing on the C first, moving onto the A afterward, instead of starting it straightaway on the A; otherwise the A comes out with a glissando before it, and the same goes for the other words I had in mind....

Our opera house still hasn't opened. They are rehearsing various operas. *Carmen*, for example, which was never good for the box office, and I'm taking the role of Micaëla for some reason, even though we have a bevy of young singers thirsting for that role. Instead, they're given the roles of Tatiana and Margarita, while I mysteriously end up with Micaëla. They're waiting for Tsvetkova to recover so that *The Maid of Pskov* can go ahead. I heard *Mozart* twice with the orchestra and I really wasn't happy with their performance: the orchestra is quite lifeless, and their Requiem was barely audible, and the choir is either singing too loudly and out of tune, or so quietly that it can't be heard; Shkafer sings off-key and expresses nothing. I am not sure it's right for me to tell you all this, since it will just upset you, but I thought the piece should either be performed superbly, with thorough preparation, or else left alone.

In general, the end of my letter came out in the minor. Do please forgive me, but it's the tension while I'm waiting for the opera that's causing me so much upset, and this makes me see everything in darker hues.

Do please write to me, maybe not right now, but at some stage, to tell me what songs you think I should sing at the concert.

I shake your hand, and please pass my greetings on to all of yours.

Devotedly yours,<br>N. Vrubel

### 7. From Rimsky-Korsakov to Zabela-Vrubel

25 November 1898, St. Petersburg

My delightful Sea Princess, dear Nadezhda Ivanovna,
I received your two letters: one in A minor, another in A major. First, I really must tell you to drop your formal "most respected," and just call me Nikolai Andreyevich, or whatever you like. And next, I'd like to let you know that the warmth and sincerity of your second letter really moved me,

and apart from that, it is so full of your youthful artistic spirit that you can hardly claim A major doesn't suit you, as you told me in one of your letters.

Thank you for everything you told me about *Sadko*—I am very happy that it's a success, and my only regret is that your voice doesn't carry to where I am. It was you yourself, of course, who composed the Sea Princess: your singing and acting created the image I have of you, an image that will always stay in my mind. Madame Van Zandt[46] (I am slightly intimidated by celebrities) will sing my duet well, it goes without saying, but she won't be able to compete with you.

I finished the orchestration of *The Tsar's Bride* yesterday, down to the last full stop. . . . I'm not feeling tired just yet, but that's because I'm still up in the clouds, but when I come back to earth, I'll fall apart. Still, I should manage to pull myself together again afterward. Composers are like hopeless alcoholics: all you need to do is keep away from composition and you'll be fine—but no, you can't keep away from it, and hope to stave off old age just so that you can keep writing. This really makes me fearful. Anatoly [Lyadov] said recently that those who are afraid to grow old are not old yet. I certainly hope so! I just have trouble believing it.

I sent you the Aria by recorded delivery, so I hope it has reached you: let it be a house-warming gift for your new home. At the same time, I've written to Savva Ivanovich, asking him to let us have the pleasure of your company on the 19th of December. This is what I wrote to him: "I would like her to perform a small aria from *The Tsar's Bride*, because I composed this aria for her (later, when you manage to stage *The Tsar's Bride*, can I hope for your support?) Apart from the *Tsar's Bride* aria, she will also sing Vera Sheloga's Tale, in concert, and it would be both interesting and useful for me to hear this scena again over here before the Moscow Private Opera comes during Lent."

I added the following: "I know that my request is a little bold, but I cannot restrain myself, because the role of Marfa is so closely tied to N. I.'s [Zabela's] voice and performing manner that I really would prefer not to have any other singer present this aria in concert." I am quoting verbatim, just so that you know how things stand. I look forward to Savva Ivanovich's reply.

Now a few words about your first letter. It is in A minor, and it therefore upset me, and my family felt the same when I conveyed the contents to them. This systematic neglect of an artiste of your stature is really quite shocking. It can't be accounted for by any ill will toward you, but perhaps it's just that the others are benefiting from waves of sympathy; still, this

---

46. Marie van Zandt (1858–1919), an American soprano with a varied international career. She toured Russia several times.

tidal swell comes and goes, as it did with Paskhalova,[47] for example. The same will happen to Stavitskaya.[48] Stavitskaya's name in big letters—well, what a surprise! All the same, this won't actually make you feel any better about things. Instead, find consolation in art itself, in music, which will never neglect you, but offers itself up to your talents. Believe me, these overrated celebrities cannot be at peace with themselves.

In *Sadko*, you sang in front of a full house—I can't give you any guarantee of this in a Russian Symphony Concert. I'm worried that during your absence from Moscow, the MPO might put on *Sadko* or something—without you. And then you'll be unhappy that you'd exchanged a full house for a merely respectable attendance. The admirers of the Sea Princess will be delighted to welcome you here, but there aren't enough of them to fill the hall. I'm waiting for your decision on the program so that I can start copying the orchestral parts for the concert. Do tell me about *Mozart and Salieri*—but give me "the whole truth and only the truth," as they say in *The Maid of Pskov*.[49] You'll have heard by now about the rehearsals of *Sheloga*. After this tiring sermon I am getting irritated again, and so I shall bring this letter to a close. Stay healthy, be young and merry:

Devotedly yours, N. R-Korsakov

P.S. Greetings to your husband.

---

47. Alevtina Paskhalova was the singer Zabela replaced after the dispute between Rimsky-Korsakov and Mamontov.

48. Anna Stavitskaya, soprano, sang at the MPO from 1899 to 1890. Rimsky-Korsakov was proven right about the transience of her fame, and she failed to leave any other significant trace in operatic history.

49. The quotation is from *The Maid of Pskov*, Act 3, scene 2, in the dialogue between Olga and Ivan the Terrible.

## 8. From Zabela-Vrubel to Rimsky-Korsakov

26 November 1898, Moscow

My dear and most respected Nikolai Andreyevich,
You were asking me to reply as soon as possible, so I've made my mind up and I'll sing Marfa's second aria as an encore, starting at Figure 203, as you advised. I only managed to play through it, of course; I liked its soulful melody, but I haven't sung it yet, so I don't know whether I'll manage very well. Generally speaking, I never sing anything well the first time around, so I have to play through a new piece for myself several times until I've familiarized myself with it, and even then I only dare to sing it with considerable trepidation. As for "The Nymph,"[50] I will sing it at your house if there is time, because I can only take a little time off.

Yesterday, *Mozart and Salieri* was playing here, but the house was nowhere near full, because [Gluck's] *Orpheus* scared off the public as usual. The impact *Mozart and Salieri* made was something along these lines: the gallery and the claque in general was rather bemused, unsure whether it was anything they should worry about, while in the stalls, it was quite the opposite, and they applauded energetically—I heard many people say flattering things about it, and some even expressed real delight. I was sitting next to Savva Ivanovich and we enjoyed it all together: the piece makes a most graceful impression and it went rather well. This Chaliapin is blessed with the ability to phrase so wonderfully: it sounds as if his phrasing has its own commas, semicolons, and exclamation marks, but all of it falls within the limits of the written score, without any changes. Shkafer, to his own surprise, was not at all bad, and his expression was certainly pleasing although his intonation faltered a couple of times; the orchestra, of course, was rather weak, and the pianist we have here is better passed over: he even played wrong notes, and his tone was poor. Now Savva Ivanovich wants to put on *Mozart* on Sundays, coupled with *May Night*, in order to bring in the public. This is so sweet of him—I'm really grateful. I'm also grateful to him that I will be singing the Sea Princess tonight; I hardly dare think ahead to the day when Antonova will take the role, but no doubt that will eventually happen.

I shake your hand and send a bow to you and yours.

N. Vrubel

---

50. Rimsky-Korsakov's song dedicated to Zabela. The autograph manuscript he inscribed for her is dated 25 May 1898.

### 9. Rimsky-Korsakov to Zabela-Vrubel

7 December 1898, St. Petersburg

Dear Nadezhda Ivanovna,
What does all this mean—that you're in an A-minor mood? Why doubt yourself? What kind of things did Plotnikov[51] say to you?—"your breathing is no good, and the aria is too high for you"! I do not, I simply do not believe that your breathing is no good, and if the aria is really too high, I can only despair of my ability to grasp the qualities of your voice, which I love so much. Perhaps I've really become "old and naughty" like the Miller in *Rusalka*,[52] and "I need to be looked after." In my head, it was as if I could hear you singing the [Sea] Princess and the Snow Maiden, and so I could equally well imagine you singing Marfa, but now it turns out that I can hear and understand nothing. This simply cannot be true! Plotnikov might be a good musician, but he just makes you confused. If you haven't mastered the last aria, then don't sing it, and for goodness' sake don't be afraid of the first one. I am sure that we will all be full of admiration for you over here, and you are just talking a lot of old nonsense. Retune yourself in A major quickly, abandon all your doubts and come over here to sing Vera [the Prologue from *Sheloga*] and Marfa's first aria, and some songs of your choosing as encores....

Now, for more on the aria: the adagio tempo (which is the only thing that might worry you) is about ♩ = 44 (♪ = 88); but you can take it slightly faster if this will be more comfortable for you, and perhaps it may even turn out better that way. Because before you can actually hear a piece in performance, it's very difficult to establish the tempo with any precision. For goodness' sake, then, modulate into A major, and if you can't do that in Moscow, come quickly to St. Petersburg, and we'll retune you—I remember you mentioning that St. Petersburg has a good effect on you. Some more on the aria: I can't imagine that the Nadezhda Ivanovna who sang her way through the Snow Maiden's final melting hasn't been able to manage this aria.

Yesterday, I was very glad to receive a poster of Mikhail Aleksandrovich's painting.[53] I like it very much and it's sitting on my desk at this moment.

---

51. Plotnikov was the pianist who accompanied Zabela in her rehearsal of Marfa's Aria; she had described his criticisms in the letter to which Rimsky-Korsakov is now replying.

52. An opera by Dargomyzhsky.

53. The identity of the Vrubel painting here is unclear; *Morning* (1897) was recent, and compatible with Rimsky-Korsakov's description.

When I look at it, the desire to compose an opera from the world of Russian fairy tale takes hold of me again. It has neither Sadko nor the Snow Maiden in it, but it reminds me of them for some reason, and it gives me much pleasure looking at it.

... I await your reply to my letter, with an indication of your day of arrival. I hope it won't be later than Wednesday. You can be frank with me. In recent years, I've been trying to live and act in such a way that I don't have any secrets from anyone, and when I happen to learn of other people's secrets, I know how to keep them. And I am very attracted by sincerity and warmth in other people, perhaps because I myself am rather dry by nature.

I look forward to seeing you soon, and to your next letter before that. Be cheerful, stay in good health and pass my greetings to your husband along with my thoughts on his picture.

Devotedly yours, N. Rimsky-Korsakov

P.S. Why on earth does Savva Ivanovich like to put singers like Koltsov on stage, when they're so wet behind the ears?!

### 10. Rimsky-Korsakov to Zabela-Vrubel

21 December 1898, St. Petersburg

Dear Nadezhda Ivanovna,
The concert has passed, you have left and somehow life has become boring, and besides, I have a niggling suspicion that the concert might not have done you any good. Your public was grateful, of course, but there is no point in waiting for any well-deserved praise from the critics. Just to spite me, or to spite the Russian Symphonic Concerts, the critics would hold back their praise, or write something negative, or perhaps keep their silence altogether. Today the *Novoye vremya* printed the following: "We are surprised that the composer, conducting the orchestra himself, could be satisfied by such a limp and colourless interpretation, which does not support the work but destroys it. Even the delightful (?!) Lullaby[54] was drained of color under the composer's baton."

---

54. The Lullaby referred to was an extract from *Sheloga* that Zabela sang separately (see Letter 7).

There isn't a single word about your performance of the aria from *The Tsar's Bride*: not a word about the fact that you had to give two encores. They also inform us that "the vocal performers" were given baskets of flowers. How do you like that? I'm not even going to bother reading the articles in the *St. Petersburg Gazette*, and I would advise you not to check them either. In the other papers, there is nothing to be found. I am sending you two programs of the concert as a memento (we forgot about them during the concert, and I only read them today). For my part, I will tell you privately that I am not happy with the orchestration of the Lullaby, which could have been better, and it rather spoiled the impression given by your wonderful voice and your delightful singing. The other parts of *Sheloga* I consider really quite successful as accompaniments, and I think the aria from *The Tsar's Bride* is very successful in this respect.

I must say it once again: you gave this composer the greatest pleasure by your singing and the part of Marfa is now in your complete possession. This composer is also very happy that it seems "The Nymph" is suitable for you, by general acclaim, and that means that he was not mistaken when he dedicated it to you.

Before my (hoped-for) departure for Moscow, I will communicate the matters we have discussed to the powers-that-be in the theater directorate.[55]

Could you please let me know about the repertoire of the Moscow Private Opera during the forthcoming holidays, starting with 31 December. I am writing to Kruglikov about this as well, but he isn't very reliable, and I don't want to disturb Savva Ivanovich with this matter. Could you also perhaps find out something about the impression that *Vera Sheloga* made on the Moscow public?

Be healthy and cheerful and put together a lyrical repertoire for concerts. And don't forget your

devoted<br>N. R.-Korsakov.

P.S. Greetings from mine.
Sending a bow—a deep bow to your husband. Have you managed to rest after the journey and after all the St. Petersburg hustle and bustle in general?

---

55. Rimsky-Korsakov was assisting Zabela in her inquiries about transferring to the Mariinsky Opera.

## 11. Rimsky-Korsakov to Zabela-Vrubel

14 November 1899, St. Petersburg

Dear Nadezhda Ivanovna,

Today I will be relatively brief, because I'm very busy. I received your previous letter, which was addressed to 59, Sadovaya—I'm glad it didn't go astray, because there were some nice things in it. You are so absent-minded! But fortunately it was re-directed by the post office.

Thank you for your information about *The Tsar's Bride* and *May Night*. I'm pleased to see that you're continuing to have success, and as for Rozenov[56] and the others who find your tempi too slow, don't pay any attention. Also pay no attention to the fact that Rostovtseva[57] is praised beyond her just desserts.

I must tell you that the critics have become confused recently, the same as the public. Composers are to blame that both groups no longer understand singing. In everything, they have been striving for dramatism, naturalism, and other -isms. The singing is only of concern now for the followers of Italian opera, but they have been neglecting the musical content and all kinds of truth in stagecraft, which is scant consolation. In *The Tsar's Bride*, it has been possible for true singing to make a return, and the critics were lost. They praised your singing, but they can't grasp that the singing provides everything: dramatism, stage-worthiness—everything that's needed from an opera. The critics say: "It was just singing," but they don't understand that this is the most difficult thing to bring off, and that it embraces everything else. If you find that you've been able to apply your talent to my pieces, then I will tell you too that no one has sung my soprano parts better than you (and I don't expect ever to hear them better). And if it so happened that I wrote all of them except for Marfa before I met you, and I managed to please you even so, then that's just fate. Why did you choose to sing my songs "Captivated by the Rose" and "Quiet Evening"?[58] Because you told me that you don't know my old songs. One day, do please perform the song I dedicated to you (as a kind of advance before "The Nymph")—I think it's fine, and you sing it marvelously. I am glad that you sang the aria from *The Maid of Pskov*. You sing that wonderfully, but I suspect that as a program choice it was

---

56. Emily Rozenov (1861–1935), Moscow pianist and music critic.
57. Alexandra Rostovtseva (1872–1941), mezzo-soprano, singer at the MPO. Sang the role of Lyubasha in the MPO production of *The Tsar's Bride*.
58. "A Nightingale, Captivated by a Rose" ("Plenivshis' rozoy, solovey") is a song from Rimsky-Korsakov's Op. 2, and "Quiet Evening" ("Tikho vecher dogorayet") from his Op. 4.

influenced by Kerzin.[59] *The Maid of Pskov* and the old songs—those match his "progressive" tastes. Although when I was revising *The Maid of Pskov* in the '90s, I also took pains over the singing, and that has probably displeased many people. I regret that I have never heard you in Pannochka [from *May Night*]. You tell me that Rostovtseva is getting better; give her some lessons—she needs it. Recently Miss Bunakova visited me and sang Lyubasha [from *The Tsar's Bride*]. She has a good voice and she sings it reasonably well, apart from some slight problems of intonation, but even so, she's much weaker than Rostovtseva.

In the Prague and Brussels concerts, the program will be purely instrumental (I haven't yet worked it out). But in Prague there will also be a chamber concert with some of my songs and duets (although no operatic excerpts). Which songs, I don't yet know—I sent them a selection from which they can choose. Also, in Prague, they'll be performing *May Night* for me.

Over the past few days, I've been working on *Saltan*. If Moscow Private Opera is still functioning next season, then of course I'll give them *Saltan* if they want it, because there's no hope of seeing it on the Imperial stages. The role of the Swan will be yours, of course: who else could I possibly hope for? I send a bow to your husband. What do they say about his *Satyr*? Nadezhda Nikolayevna sends a bow. Be healthy and do more singing, and don't forget to write to me sometimes about this or that.

Your N. R.-Korsakov.

P.S. I promised I'd be brief, but this has turned out a long one.

### 12. Rimsky-Korsakov to Zabela-Vrubel

3 December 1899, St. Petersburg

Dear Nadezhda Ivanovna,

The existence of *Tsar Saltan* is a secret no more. I saw Malinin[60] yesterday, and somehow he had discovered that I have a new opera. He asked me

---

59. Arkady Kerzin (1856–1914), Russian lawyer and promoter of Russian music. Together with his pianist wife, he formed a circle to promote Russian music, and in particular, the Kuchka, from whose "progressivism" Rimsky-Korsakov had now defected.

60. Mikhail Malinin (1853–1919), a baritone at the MPO and one of its directors. He was married to Tatyana Lyubatovich, the sister of Klavdiya Vinter, another director of the MPO. See also Letter 2.

to give it to Moscow Private Opera with a view to staging it this season, in February. I told him everything, i.e., the plot and the staging requirements, but refused to give it to him for the current season because 1) there is too little time for me to finish orchestrating the last act; 2) it would all have to be done in too much of a hurry in any case; 3) the opera cannot be published as early as February, and that would mean I will lose my publisher, because then it will be too late; 4) *Tsar Saltan* would actually be more useful for the Moscow Private Opera next season, because at least they will then have a major new work. In the end, I promised to reserve *Saltan* for Moscow Private Opera and gave them some instructions with regard to the casting: the Swan Princess will of course be you, Tsaritsa Militrisa will be Tsvetkova, Saltan will be Mutin, Guidon will be Sekar,[61] and the Old Man will be Shkafer. I haven't got any ideas about the others yet. I can't interfere in the set design and staging, and although I've spoken to Mikhail Aleksandrovich [Vrubel] about it, I'm letting them (the Directors) do as they see fit all the same. I've never touched this side of things and don't intend to do so, and I do hope that dearest Mikhail Aleksandrovich will not be angry with me. By the time of the production, Savva Ivanovich might be released already and perhaps he will take the reins, to some extent at least, and then it will be completely his business. As for the musical side—that's another matter altogether. If they don't follow my casting instructions, the opera simply won't run. The existence of *Saltan* will be revealed to the public tomorrow, since tomorrow is the Second Russian Symphony Concert, and we are going to play a suite under the name *Pictures for the Tale of Tsar Saltan*, i.e., the preludes to Acts 1 and 2 and to the final scene, and there will be a note in the program that these pictures are instrumental numbers from the completed opera *The Tale of Tsar Saltan*.

Today there was the last rehearsal—I am happy with how it has all come out. Yesterday's rehearsal was attended by Malinin. Some day, when you have the time, why don't you invite Kruglikov to your house, with an accompanist like Rachmaninov, for example, and try out the only fragment you have, except don't sing it in public—let them wait until next year, especially since this fragment ends rather abruptly and isn't really very substantial. In the next letter, I will send you the program for the Russian Symphony Concert. So don't refuse to sing the Swan—I hope that this role will show off your voice, but I'm worried that it will not automatically become a hit, compared to Marfa, and it will perhaps

---

61. Nikolai Mutin (1868–1909), basso profondo, was a soloist at the MPO, as was Anton Sekar-Rozhansky (see introduction).

be something more like the Sea Princess. Don't reproach me for that: it doesn't happen every time.

> Keep in good health and be cheerful.
> Your N. R-Korsakov

A bow to your husband. Nadezhda Nikolayevna sends you her greetings. Yanovsky sent me some of his pieces, but I haven't looked at them yet—no time.

## 13. Rimsky-Korsakov to Zabela-Vrubel

15 January 1900, St. Petersburg

Dear Nadezhda Ivanovna,
I was happy to receive your letter yesterday. It seems we wrote each other a letter on the same day. I do admit that I love getting your letters, but don't be in any great hurry to answer the previous one, so that our correspondence can keep to some sort of order, otherwise our letters will pass each other in transit, somewhere in Bologoye.

You've made me very happy by the fact that you are going to sing the Sea Princess again, because it saddens me that with every new role, fate leads you to abandon the previous ones. I cannot imagine any Sea Princess other than you, even though Iretskaya told me a few days ago that Gladkaya is very good in the role (she has this information from somewhere). I said I knew nothing about it, but that Gladkaya was indeed a great Domna Saburova.[62] Actually, I was mistaken when I said that I couldn't imagine any Sea Princess other than you; regrettably, I *can* imagine Antonova, but I picture that negatively. I was saddened to see in your letter that ticket sales at the Opera have fallen. That is very bad indeed. Benefit concerts (presumably even in a token sense) are the product of wishful thinking, and can't be sustained in the long run. How can they possibly fail to pay you your wages? And what resources will they draw on to pay them later? Is it possible that Moscow Private Opera is on the road

---

62. Natalia Iretskaya (1843–1922), singer and singing teacher. She was the teacher of Zabela, and also of Sofya Gladkaya, who made her successful debut in the role of Domna Saburova (a secondary character in *The Tsar's Bride*) at the MPO, and from 1900 sang at the Mariinsky.

to ruin? Then where will *Saltan* play next year? I am treating the Paris enterprise[63] with some skepticism: it will be very expensive and beyond [their] resources, and I'm afraid it will be too much of a responsibility. It needs to be *done well* and would they actually manage that? . . .

While I will probably write an orchestral piece after *Saltan*, I am drawn to opera again, so I've been obtaining various books for my perusal in search of a new plot, although I haven't started reading them just yet, since I haven't the time I need to finish writing *Saltan* first. I'm very tired, but I'm afraid to rest, because I'm worried that if I take a little break from composition, I'll never be able to take it up again. And if that were to happen, degradation will immediately set in, followed swiftly by the end. As it happens, I am not afraid of the end when it comes, but I am dreadfully afraid of an old age spent in idleness. This is why I am consumed by feverish activity, which many, including you yourself, might easily mistake for energy and vitality. I am simply the rambler who keeps on walking, afraid to sit down, because he knows that if he ever does so, he'll never make it to his destination. Or maybe the reason for all this activity is a weakness of the will that has reached pathological levels. But I'll write about that some other time.

But for now, stay healthy, be cheerful, and don't forget about me. A bow for Mikhail Aleksandrovich.
P.S. Nadezhda Nikolayevna is sending her greetings.
I didn't reply to Kruglikov because I haven't got round to it, and because I don't really have anything to say to him.

### 14. Rimsky-Korsakov to Zabela-Vrubel

23 January 1900, St. Petersburg

Dear Nadezhda Ivanovna,
Yesterday, Prince Volkonsky informed me by letter that *Sadko* will run next season at the Mariinsky. I paid him a visit today in order to give him my thanks. It turns out that the repertoire has already been presented to the Emperor and the production of *Sadko* was approved by underlining in red pencil (they usually stroke out items in green). The conversation switched to the general nature of the production and performers, and I

---

63. It was possible that the MPO planned to stage one of Rimsky-Korsakov's operas in Paris.

mentioned to him that they will not be able to find a Sea Princess like the one at Moscow Private Opera (I believe you've made her acquaintance). It's useful for him to know this. He told me that closed debuts take place the week after Easter, and that there will be two sopranos, two mezzos, two tenors, and even two basses. Just who these are he didn't tell me. Did Monakhov-Yershov[64] tell you anything on the way back?

During our conversation, Diaghilev arrived, and started talking about *The Tsar's Bride*, which he had heard in Moscow; he kept singing your praises, by the way, and I, of course, agreed with him. Even so, I have my doubts that anything will materialize from this, but who knows? You must already have read what Findeisen has written about you in *The Musical Gazette*, with three photo portraits. He really waxed lyrical; still, I think his article has come too late. All of this would have been very good if it had been written before *The Tsar's Bride*, but now he really ought to devote a substantial lyrical soliloquy to it—although, since he hasn't actually heard it, he had to restrict himself to a passing mention. Additionally, I found that the whole article, although it contains things which are very much true, smacks of foreign-style advertising patter. Does it strike you the same way? In the same issue, did you read a dispatch from Kharkov about *The Tsar's Bride*? It's obvious that it's not going well there, and that Miss Insarova's[65] main talent is being a clothes-horse for her costume. It seems that the opera has not been received well. And perhaps it's because of the performance, since they like it in Moscow. I find that this opera often receives unfair treatment, as if I should limit myself to writing music in the fantastic manner. Routine and conservative attitudes are everywhere in the ascendant. In the past, it was *de rigueur* to praise me for orchestration, now the done thing is to praise me for the fantastic, and no one dares to take [my music] simply for what it is.

On Wednesday, Glazunov will be traveling to Moscow, and I have written to Shkafer to ask him whether *The Tsar's Bride* could be performed on either Thursday, Friday, or Monday, so that he would be able to hear it (his ballet *Raymonda* is playing on Sunday, which is the reason for his journey to Moscow). You haven't answered my question: has permission been granted for *Kalashnikov* to be staged?[66] For that matter, you haven't

---

64. The Mariinsky's administrator.
65. Rimsky-Korsakov has noticed that Zabela is jealous of Insarova, and attempts to deflect this with a derogatory comment about the latter.
66. Anton Rubinstein's opera *The Merchant Kalashnikov* (1880) had two performances at the Mariinsky before it was withdrawn by the censor, because of concerns over its execution scene. It was staged by the MPO in 1901.

told me anything at all about Mikhail Aleksandrovich's portrait, or about your joint portrait.

I have finished my *Saltan* and I'm now awaiting your congratulations. There is still much work to be done: the publication, i.e., all the preparation for printing, revision, proofing etc. In music, this all takes a long time and a lot of effort. Yastrebtsev greeted the completion of *Saltan* with much greater delight than when I finished *The Tsar's Bride*: that's how he puts limits on my art. I've told him almost nothing about *The Tsar's Bride* or about you as Marfa. After my first trip, there was a moment when—*in general terms*—I started to praise the performance of *The Tsar's Bride* (I hadn't yet mentioned you), only to be told that I was too indulgent. I fell silent and refused to tell them any more, and to all the questions I just said: "Go yourself and listen." Write to me. May you be healthy and stay in A major.

Nadezhda Nikolayevna sends a bow. And what of *The Demon*?

Yours, N. R-Korsakov

## 15. Rimsky-Korsakov to Zabela-Vrubel

17 May 1900, St. Petersburg

Dear Nadezhda Ivanovna,
This letter is likely to catch you still in Moscow, and if not— it will be rerouted to you in the country. I gave Bessel[67] your address, and arranged with him that the vocal score of *Saltan* would be sent to you as soon as it's ready; that will probably be toward the end of June, since they are currently waiting for the proofs, which will take us through to 1 June, and afterward, another three weeks will be needed for the printing. You will receive the vocal score minus the title page, since I'll bring that to you myself in the autumn when I'm in Moscow, when I'll add an inscription. Simultaneously with your copy, they'll send the copies to the Directors of the Private Opera, which they'll relay to the other soloists, whereas you'll receive yours directly.

All this time, I've been dreadfully busy preparing the proofs of *Saltan* for copying and printing, and I'm now very tired. I had to revise various things and finish off the orchestration. At the same time, I've been sent

---

67. Vasili Bessel (1843–1907) was a prominent Russian music publisher.

the proofs of the vocal score and the libretto. You wouldn't believe how difficult it is to come back to something that has already been written and seemingly finished, but which actually required a lot of extra work. During the process, I had a good chance to look at my work critically, and I can tell you frankly that I consider *Saltan* to be weaker and less emotionally powerful than The Tsar's Bride. I picture *Saltan* as a kind of painting by numbers, while *The Tsar's Bride* was executed freehand. From another point of view, *Saltan* is a return to *The Snow Maiden* and *Sadko* (the first of these is by far the most attractive), while *The Tsar's Bride* is something quite new and original for me. I am surprised that so many respected musicians refuse to see this. Many, without even hearing *Saltan*, are bestowing advance praise upon it at the expense of *The Tsar's Bride*, just because in their minds it's already settled that my speciality is fantastic music, so they won't let me have dramatic music. How can they fail to understand that *The Tsar's Bride* was prefigured in a series of studies, like my forty or fifty songs and also my *Mozart and Salieri*? Taken together, these works wrought a substantial change in my style of writing, and the most perfect incarnation of this new style—to date—is *The Tsar's Bride*. Could my lot really just be the portrayal of monsters, whether of the sea, of the earth, or reptiles? *The Tsar's Bride* is not fantastic in the least, while *The Snow Maiden* certainly is, but both of them are very human and soulful, unlike *Sadko* and *Saltan*. (*But no one is supposed to know my personal thoughts about "Saltan." Let them praise it.*) To conclude: out of all my operas, I love *The Snow Maiden* and *The Tsar's Bride* best. The first of these is not under attack, and the second I will defend, but when I have to keep silent, I will indeed shut up, but in high dudgeon.

My dearest Marfa Vasilyevna,[68] I hope you too will stand up for *The Tsar's Bride*. I noticed that many who were at first against it (whether from rumor or from their own knowledge), but who then heard it two or three times, began to develop an attachment for it. Those who have only heard it once apparently haven't understood it, and perhaps there is indeed something that resists easy comprehension—maybe it's not as straightforward as it seems. But my delusions of grandeur stretch so far that I imagine that *The Tsar's Bride* will have a great influence on other Russian composers, even though at present they think it is backward. These are the thoughts wandering across my mind, and in fact my mind is wandering like never before, and I simply can't concentrate and start something new, which upsets me a lot. May you be healthy and merry. We are all

---

68. Rimsky-Korsakov here addresses Zabela by the name of her character in *The Tsar's Bride*.

in St. Petersburg until 2 June, after which we are leaving for the Black Forest or the Vosges—we're not yet sure where exactly.

A bow from me to Mikhail Aleksandrovich. Nadezhda Nikolayevna sends her greetings.

Yours, N. R-Korsakov

### 16. Rimsky-Korsakov to Zabela-Vrubel

30 September 1900, St. Petersburg

Dear Nadezhda Ivanovna,
There is no point in asking someone who has no ear for his opinion and advice on music. For my part, I am a person who has no *eye*. So don't ask for my opinion and advice on matters pictorial and visual. I understand nothing of them. Once I offered you my opinion on the headdress in the last act of *The Tsar's Bride*—and failed dismally. But if you still want to know how I imagine the costume of the Swan-bird and its transformation, I will only make a few general points: it actually has to look like a bird, and above all, it must be beautiful. It is indeed hard to eclipse God's light, but it would be easy for you to eclipse the heavenly bodies of the fantastic world with your voice, and you always do that, especially to my eyes, because you know how much I love your voice and your singing. Coming back to the visual aspects, I must say that at the moment of your transformation I'd like an electric star to light up on your head, and a moon to light up among your braids, definitely a crescent moon. So don't begrudge me for making you carry a battery or an accumulator on your person—I don't know what to call it, but some kind of device for that purpose.[69]

Of course the star and the moon cannot eclipse the light, but from the moment of your transformation, we need you, your surroundings, and everyone around you to be flooded by bright electric light from above. To facilitate the transformation from bird into princess, I have written two-or-so measures of music for the purpose, when the stage must be in complete darkness (as indicated in the vocal score). During these bars, it will be easy to change from the bird costume to the princess costume: the wings will fall off, the braid with the crescent moon will unravel, and so on. Just as in *Faust*,

---

69. Rimsky-Korsakov is perhaps indulging in a little absurd humor here.

Figure 2. Mikhail Vrubel, *The Swan Princess*, 1900.

where his costume is changed in a moment without even a musical theme to assist. I also think that the Swan should not be too realistically bird-like—a hint will suffice. I also think that blond hair (but not strawberry blond) would be more in keeping with the image of the Swan Princess; this would suit better than black, although this isn't really any of my business. I await an invitation from the Directors and the rehearsal timetable.

I've just read Kruglikov's article. I won't say anything about it until I see you. I looked at *Assya*[70] in the vocal score and I didn't like it. The characters of Assya, Gagin, and NN may be rather better than the others, who are very poorly done, but that's saying very little. It's all quite bland, the singing is either deficient or just not there, the vocal melodies are unclear and amount to nothing more than little snatches made up of chord tones or else doubling the accompanying phrases. Why does Assya have to shout rather than sing the words "You've driven into the moonlight! You broke it!" What a strange affair! And this Mr. NN is also strange: he never introduces himself to Gagin.[71] We'll talk about it when we see each other.

Be healthy, cheerful, and merry.

Yours, N. R-Korsakov<br>A bow to Mikhail Aleksandrovich.

### 17. Rimsky-Korsakov to Zabela-Vrubel

7 October 1900, St. Petersburg

Dear Nadezhda Ivanovna,
I was planning to write to you today in the hope that this would somehow conjure up the arrival of your letter—I mean that just as my letter will be on its way to Moscow, yours will be coming from Moscow to St. Petersburg (as you see, I am becoming superstitious in my old age). But your letter actually did arrive before I started, so I'm now writing this letter immediately after receiving yours (this lets me off the hook—I don't need to

---

70. An opera by Mikhail Ippolitov-Ivanov (1859–1935), premiered by the MPO on 11 October 1900.

71. The strangeness Rimsky-Korsakov mentions here is a feature of the opera rather than the Turgenev original.

become superstitious now). I hoped to hear some news about *Saltan* from you, and so I did. Here, now, is what I wanted to tell you. This morning, César Cui came and asked me for your address, saying that he wanted to invite you to sing in November, in one of the Russian Music Society concerts. In particular, he hoped you would sing Marfa's Aria, as I was happy to hear, of course. So I did indeed give him your address, and I'm telling you about it now so that you can have an immediate answer at the ready when you receive a letter with an invitation from him (from Cui, that is). I cannot give you any guarantee, of course, that Caesar [*sic*] will actually stick to his plans, because he does have a tendency to change his mind, so his words don't always translate into actions. But I'm telling you what I heard, and I do rather think that he wouldn't have expressed such an intention to me without actually intending to see it through, not least because I haven't been telling him anything about you since the last time.[72]

I'm pleased to hear that the part of the Swan is to your tastes, and indeed *Saltan* as a whole. I didn't say that this opera would just be a rehash of *The Snow Maiden* or *Sadko*, but even so, I firmly believe that I've managed to say something new in *The Tsar's Bride*. *Saltan*, on the other hand, has a familiar ring to it, which is why it's more to the liking of those who admire my art (Kruglikov, for example), since they don't need to evaluate anything afresh. The price of my fairy-tale works has been settled, and there is no need for me to justify them, which makes things easier. Why is it that almost every critic writing about *The Tsar's Bride* says something like this: "Marfa and her closing scene are liable to bring tears to the eyes" (Note: the opera increases in interest as it goes along), but then he will conclude that this opera is musically weaker than any of my others? Isn't this a lot of nonsense? Still, I will tell you more about this when we see each other, because a letter can only go so far. I also hope that this letter of mine will be the last before my departure for Moscow (in the same sense of "hope" as in your letter).[73]

So keep in good health then, a bow to your husband, and I'll see you soon in Moscow. And then *you* might decide to come to St. Petersburg.

Yours, N. R-Korsakov

---

72. By "last time" Rimsky-Korsakov is most likely referring to a previous performance of hers for the Russian Music Society.

73. Rimsky-Korsakov means that they will see each other very soon, not that they will neglect writing to each other.

## 18. Rimsky-Korsakov to Zabela-Vrubel

6 November 1900, St. Petersburg

Dear Nadezhda Ivanovna,

I am sending you the aria. Have a look at it and tell me whether you like it, and do please sing it to me in St. Petersburg, but take care that no one sees the score in your hands. I even took the precaution of omitting the title, but the name *Servilia* is mentioned in the text, so they could easily guess. Obviously, this doesn't have to be concealed from Mikhail Aleksandrovich. I think it will suit your voice well, even though it doesn't offer any of your delightful top notes—the aria couldn't really accommodate *pianissimo* this time.

Have you read *Servilia*? If not, then do please read it: it's in the same volume of [Lev] Mey's [dramas] as *The Maid of Pskov* and *The Tsar's Bride*. When you read it, you'll find the complete text of the aria there (in Act 3), and in fact the whole scene in my opera reads just the same as in Mey. When you come to St. Petersburg, don't trouble yourself to bring the parts and the score of Marfa's Aria: I have arranged for the Russian Musical Society to purchase this material in advance of your arrival, especially since Nápravník,[74] cautious as ever, wants to go through the accompaniment with the orchestra before you come. And perhaps the Moscow Private Opera schedule, with a little luck, may allow you to arrive on Thursday instead of Friday, and then you'd be able to stay an extra day in P-burg, which would be nice.

I'm disappointed to see that many of the singers in *Saltan* have been replaced, but I hope—depending on the rest of the repertoire—that this will only be a brief temporary measure. I'm still worried that *Saltan* will suffer from being performed too often early on. Do please give me the details in your reply: how many times did it run, what kind of audience did it have, who performed, and how well, etc. Has Insarova joined the Private Opera? If Klavdiya Spiridonovna [Vinter][75] was against inviting her, then who were the men who accepted her? Perhaps Ippolitov-Ivanov and Solodovnikov?[76] I do sympathize with you, of course, and I myself

---

74. Eduard Nápravník (1839–1916), Czech-Russian composer and chief conductor at the Bolshoi Theater for almost fifty years (1869–1916).

75. Klavdiya Vinter (née Lyubatovich), was the official director of the MPO in 1896–99, and sister of the singer Tatyana Lyubatovich.

76. Gavrila Solodovnikov (1826–1901), Russian merchant, real-estate owner, and philanthropist. He financed the construction of the theater that the Private Opera rented in the center of Moscow (the Solovodnikov Theater, now Operetta Theater) and was one of the directorate of the MPO. Ippolitov-Ivanov was the chief conductor at the MPO at the time.

don't see why she should be invited, but I think that the hysteria among the sopranos is really too much—beyond anything justifiable. Tsvetkova should not have pulled out of [Tchaikovsky's] *The Maid of Orleans*! What has *The Maid of Orleans* got to do with anything?[77] I doubt very much that Insarova could harm you—or Tsvetkova, for that matter. Are you really sure she is going to overshadow you because of all her (exaggerated) talents and critical success? As for her fawning ways with the critics, here's something I know about her: when she was in St. Petersburg, Ivanov was insisting that she must sing in his *Zabava*,[78] but Insarova turned him down (quite rightly, I thought), but because of this, she was always ignored by the *Novoye vremya*, even though she was a success with the public. These are the facts. You don't like it when I defend Insarova, but trust me: much of what her colleagues say about her is exaggerated, and sometimes a complete fabrication. What I personally know about her is backed up by what I hear from the conductor Suk,[79] and from others at the same theater. But can one ever trust all those theatrical tales and rumors? Anyway, that's enough on Insarova—I don't want to upset you, especially when all my advice is that you should take a calmer approach to things. You know your own worth, after all, so have faith that others will appreciate you, and that if Lipaev,[80] or suchlike, decides to give you a hostile review in *The Musical Gazette*, so much the worse for him. Kashkin, for example, understands you. All the same, Kashkin overpraises me while quibbling a little over the plot of *Saltan*—he's wrong there, because without that plot, he wouldn't have any of the music that he likes so much.

It's tedious to talk, or even think about the company's shares[81]—I also dislike all that, but I meant something different when I asked for your opinion on what I had done. Doesn't a composer need his freedom? And the shares do tend to keep him tied up. Let him be loved, and let his works be staged for the sake of his music—not because he is a shareholder

---

77. The precise reference is unclear, but Rimsky-Korsakov is generally indulging Zabela as she recounts her various professional crises.

78. *Zabava Putyatishna* is an opera by the composer and critic Mikhail Ivanov (1849–1927).

79. Vyacheslav (Václav) Suk (1861–1933), Russian conductor of Czech extraction. He conducted several private opera troupes and Rimsky-Korsakov praised the orchestral sound he drew from his musicians. He went on to become chief conductor of the Bolshoi Theatre, and was generally considered the most distinguished Russian conductor of the period.

80. Ivan Lipaev (1865–1942), Russian music critic and trombonist.

81. Rimsky-Korsakov and Zabela had both become investors in the MPO after Mamontov had to relinquish control due to his incarceration. From 1899 to 1904, the MPO became the Society for Private Opera (*Tovarishchestvo Chastnoy Ooperï*), and run as a co-operative with shares held by several members of the troupe.

in the troupe. Am I right? And how is Mikhail Aleksandrovich? Is he busy with set designs, or has he got back to his paintings? A bow to him from me. Stay healthy and keep calm. I await your reply.

Yours, N. Rimsky-Korsakov

### 19. Rimsky-Korsakov to Zabela-Vrubel

12 November 1900, St. Petersburg

Dear Nadezhda Ivanovna,
Yesterday, I received your letter at last. Its arrival made me happy, because I've been uneasy about something over the past few days,[82] but even so, the contents of your letter upset me.

My letter will be slightly disordered, because I feel somehow distracted. Please don't take it amiss. I was saddened by your phrase: "I neither want to love nor hate anything." I really must insist that you stop looking at things this way. It is impossible not to love anything, and with your talent, you *must* love art—I think that you simply cannot fail to love. You should love the art of music in general, and I ask you especially not to fall out of love with my music. You should also love your wonderful voice, and you really shouldn't tire it out so much. You have sung twelve times in sixteen days—this is far too much. And my own pieces featured twice on those twelve occasions. I particularly don't want my own works to be the cause of fatigue and harm to your voice, the voice I love so much. That would truly burden my soul. I know that as an artist, you are jealous of your roles, but if *Saltan* is played too much, then you really ought to insist on a double. I'm not sure who should do that, but maybe Veretennikova? If this means *Saltan* won't sound quite so good from time to time, then so be it, but you will be able to get some rest. I'm sure that Sekar is soon going to have himself replaced with a double. The only thing is that all the doubles should perform together. Never mind if the opera is sometimes less successful, never mind if it sometimes brings in less at the box office, because *you* will then be able to rest. The best option, naturally, would be fewer performances of *Saltan*, which would remove the need for a second cast and leave you fresh at the same time. You also need to preserve the freshness of your voice for St. Petersburg.

---

82. Rimsky-Korsakov used a colorful Russian idiom here: "The cats have been scratching my soul."

When will they finally stage *The Enchantress* [by Tchaikovsky] instead of my *Saltan*? You tire yourself out, but why allow yourself to be upset and fretful on top of that? Thank you for actually *boasting* to me about your performance as Marfa. This made me very happy indeed, since it means that things really *must* have gone well. I wish you had a photo taken of yourself in your newly invented hairstyle, because when would I ever get a chance to see it otherwise? And when will you be photographed as the Swan? It's never too late to perfect your art, and if the critics don't understand this, do not get upset.[83] I noticed it before, and told you that the text in your singing can be particularly well heard this year—so it seems to me. I don't think you actually paid any attention to what I said then,[84] but I think that my observation is correct. This is very important for opera and for music in general. Your husband isn't being fair to you when he says that your Swan still needs further polish. I think it's a highly finished product. Now for a little comic relief: Glazunov didn't go to Moscow—that's a fact.

Mr. X of St. Petersburg has turned out to be as thick as two short planks, and your attempt to register disapproval will be in vain. Have you guessed, by any chance, who I believe this Mr. X to be? I think he's none other than the *Novoye vremya* critic Ivanov. Have you read his article of 6 November? Do please read it. He gave everyone in the Moscow Private Opera a drubbing, apart from his praises for you and me alone. Ha, what are we like! Read what he says about "the *prima* of the theater, Madame Zabelo." He's so hopeless that he not only messed up your name, but also mixed up the roles of Saltan and Guidon [Saltan's son]. We've never groomed him, but now you see he's praising us. At the same time, he praised Shkafer, Vekov, and Levandovsky, but he obviously has something against the institution [the MPO].

Well, my dear Nadezhda Ivanovna, I'm afraid I am very, very cross with you. How can you possibly be having intonation problems? You've such a good ear and voice that this is just impossible. If *you* find my aria [from *Servilia*] difficult in this regard, then what will the other sopranos say? And if I wrote unmusical leaps for the voice in the manner of Wagner, then I would have to reprimand myself, but I didn't do anything like that. So just what is it that you find difficult? The interval of A♯ to A♮.

---

83. Here, Rimsky-Korsakov is not implying that Zabela needs to perfect her art more, rather that the critics should appreciate Zabela's latest refinements.

84. Mikhail Levandovsky was a bass at the MPO. Vekov was presumably another soloist.

Yes, that would have been difficult if there hadn't been a G

at the word "why," and so forth . . .

Practice this passage (until the change to five sharps) by taking the low F♯ in the left hand, putting everything else in the right—this won't be difficult for you. Practice the passage by playing these chords in the left hand:

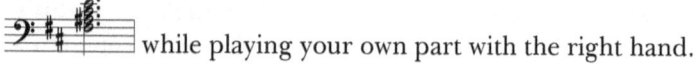 while playing your own part with the right hand.

I am sure this will only take you five minutes to learn. Actually, you've [probably] learned it already and you're just being unfair with yourself: or perhaps now that you've fallen out of love with everything in the world, you've fallen out of love with my music, even if you don't despise it. Don't be cross at my jokes (I'm only speaking partly in jest).

I sincerely wish that you'd cheer up, but you'll need to stop tiring yourself out first. Save your voice. I don't dare ask you to be in A major, as I used to, but please at least try to be in F♯ major—in the key of the aria, that is. What am I saying!—if you're tired, you shouldn't practice it at all. At some later stage, when things improve, you can sing the aria just for me, but in St. Petersburg, you can sing Marfa's Aria instead. I very much look forward to this, as I look forward to your arrival *tout court*. Do keep writing to me.

Yours, N. Rimsky-Korsakov<br>N.N. sends a bow.

I will explain this riddle when we see each other.

## 20. Rimsky-Korsakov to Zabela-Vrubel

6 March 1901, St. Petersburg

Dear Nadezhda Ivanovna,

If my letters have been infrequent of late, it's only because I'm very busy. Firstly, I think I've become lazier, or less mobile, let's say, because of my age (I am 57 today)—actually, that's already the second reason. Besides, I must admit that I'm very worried about what's going on in St. Petersburg, and also to an even larger extent in Moscow, where you are.[85] Although the events have no direct bearing on me or my family, they've deprived me of all tranquility, and I'm now just trying to keep a firm hold on my work and to keep my mind on artistic matters. But I also have my doubts about what the future holds for art, and these things put me in a bad mood, which is not conducive to composition—although at the same time, composition is what normally calms my nerves. And so, I finished Act 2 of *Servilia*—that is, I've completed the full score and will soon carry on with the rest. When I retire from all this and just rest on my laurels, can I abandon the life of an artist and just lead a normal human life: reading, going for walks, attending theater? On the one hand, I keep wondering whether there's any purpose in continuing to work if in the future, although perhaps not immediately, I foresee the demise of professional art, and the rise to power of folk art, with all those balalaikas, concertinas, and rowdy songs. On the other hand, I may still be able to make a good contribution to the art that is so dear to my heart, and in that case, I ought to continue and compose more of my "swan songs." But then perhaps these contributions of mine are worth little, perhaps even nothing? At times I feel a surge of pride and self-satisfaction, and I'm flushed with admiration for my own work. Last night, for example, I was proofreading the full score of *Saltan*, currently with the printer, and I got up to the Swan aria. And I thought, "Look how clever and poetic I was then! And how pretty." (I mean the music, of course). I've told you that for me, my pieces always evoke something from the irrecoverable past—that's just my personal foible. While I'm looking at that aria, I also remember what a wonderful and poetic Swan you are, and the beautiful and quite incredible atmosphere of that moment all comes back to me. By the way, what reason could you possibly have to think I was telling fibs in my previous letter, when I was talking about you in the role of Volkhova?

---

85. Rimsky-Korsakov is most likely referring to the student riots that took place in Moscow and other Russian cities after a Moscow State University student assassinated the minister of education, Nikolai Bogolepov.

Did I ever say that your voice is better than Bolskaya's?[86] (Although, I *do* prefer yours.) Did I ever actually say that Bolskaya doesn't sing as well as you? No, I never said that.

I'll say it again: Bolskaya's singing is wonderful in that role. She has an excellent voice that is more powerful than yours (I doubt that your voice would project like that in the Mariinsky). Altogether, she presents herself well. I am really very pleased with her, in fact. The only thing I claimed was that the Volkhova who lives on Lubyansky Lane[87] was more poetic, and I've no wish to take that back.

I keep forgetting to ask you: are Chaliapin and Mikhail Aleksandrovich on better terms now, or are things still just as bad? . . .

Tell something about yourself, about your husband, repertoire, my operas. And please write more often—don't follow my bad example.

Yours, N. R-Korsakov
N. Nik. sends her greetings.

### 21. Rimsky-Korsakov to Zabela-Vrubel

9 July 1901, Krapachukha[88]

Dear Nadezhda Ivanovna,
I feel very guilty that I've taken so long to reply to your letter. When I received it, I saw that you asked me whether I was working on a new opera yet, and I couldn't really give you an answer. But now I can tell you that I have indeed begun work on a new one.[89] The plot is in the fantastic genre, in an over-the-top way, but I don't want to tell you what it is yet; and as I've asked before, please don't tell anyone even the bare facts. You find my level of activity unnatural.[90] But is it *supernatural* or *going against nature*? I do hope it's the first, but I have trouble believing that. The most

---

86. Bolskaya, née Adelaida Yulianovna (Adela Bolska, 1863–1930), Russian lyrical soprano of Polish extraction, was trained in Italy and sang at the Bolshoi under the name Skompskaya before her marriage. After a break, she resumed her career at the Mariinsky under the name Bolskaya, where she sang until 1918.

87. Lubyansky Lane was Zabela's Moscow address.

88. Krapachukha was an estate not far from Novgorod, where the Rimsky-Korsakovs rented a summer residence.

89. *Kashchei the Immortal*, which premiered at the MPO in 1902.

90. Rimsky-Korsakov is referring to Zabela's letter of 19 June 1901, in which she says that he would have to draw on some "supernatural" strength to start yet another opera in the heat of the summer.

likely thing, actually, is that it's merely *natural*, because if I were to stop composing, what am I going to do, and who will have any need for me? And does it really make any difference whether I keep composing operas or compose something else instead?

This time, the new opera will be small-scale, in two acts (and four scenes). If I can get the whole thing drafted over the summer, I'll be very happy. I could then deal with the orchestration in the winter, ever mindful of the fact that I'm still actually doing something. And then a couple more operas beyond this one—that would suffice.

I was also hoping to start an opera with a plot taken from Homer's *Odyssey*, but the libretto hasn't materialized yet, and I'll probably limit myself to a symphonic poem based on the same episode.[91] . . .

Keep well and be happy. Greetings to your husband.

Yours, N. R-Korsakov . . .

### 22. Rimsky-Korsakov to Zabela-Vrubel

14 August 1901 (Krapachukha)

Dear Nadezhda Ivanovna,
You ask me how my work is going this summer. My reply must be that I'm not pleased with this year's summer, because I've achieved little. I only managed to complete a draft of the opera's first scene, and now I'm orchestrating it. I've also written a piece that's half orchestral, half vocal: the prelude-cantata *From Homer*—in other words, a little sketch from the *Odyssey*. The orchestral beginning portrays a storm, which takes Odysseus off course; as it calms down, singing can be heard, and there is a trio for female voices with a female choir, sung to the words: "From the darkness, the child of morning, Dawn, arose." If I ever *do* begin an opera on a plot from the *Odyssey*, this will serve as the introductory number. The storm will sound in the orchestra before the curtain is raised, and the trio with the choir would be the voices of the dryads, greeting the dawn in an olive grove on the island where Odysseus has been carried by the storm.

I ask you not to breath a word about this operatic project for the time being, because it might never come to fruition. For now, it is just the prelude-cantata *From Homer*—a concert piece, and nothing more.

---

91. The eventual result was the Prelude-Cantata *From Homer*, Op. 60.

You are saying that I shouldn't give *Servilia* to the Moscow Private Opera—and I won't. Firstly, because the published score won't be ready any time soon, and secondly, because I'd like to hear it on the Imperial stage first [the Mariinsky]. Both Count Volkonsky and Telyakovsky[92] wanted me to present a new opera on the Imperial stage, so it's my duty to respond to the Directors by offering them *Servilia*. It follows that it could only run on a private stage after the Imperial production, or if the Imperial Directors turn it down, which I really don't think is going to happen. The production of *The Maid of Pskov* on the Moscow Imperial stage [the Bolshoi] was planned for the beginning of the season, and that's why I'll probably need to visit Moscow at the end of September or the beginning of October. . . .

Keep well and be cheerful. If you decide to write, do note that I'll still be in Krapachukha until early September.

Yours,
N. R-Korsakov

P.S. A bow to your husband.

### 23. Zabela-Vrubel to Rimsky-Korsakov

7 March 1902, Moscow

Dear Nikolai Andreyevich,
I've received *Servilia*, and I'm very grateful, but I haven't yet had a chance to look at it, and at present, I'm very upset and burdened in various ways, above all by my husband's nervous illness. This is really all I can think about, and I'm afraid I must sound quite incoherent, so please forgive me that I won't write anything more today; all I wanted to do was tell you that I've received *Servilia*.

Yours, N. Vrubel

---

92. Vladimir Telyakovsky (1860–1924), head of the Directorate of the Imperial Theaters, 1898–1917.

## 24. Zabela-Vrubel to Rimsky-Korsakov

28 March 1902 (Moscow)

Dear Nikolai Andreyevich,

It will be very difficult to give you a brief account of everything that's going on here and all the things that have happened to me recently. In St. Petersburg, all my friends and relatives found Mikhail Aleksandrovich's state of health so alarming that they managed to have him seen by the psychiatrist Bekhterev,[93] who diagnosed his illness as the onset of a serious psychiatric condition. M. A. returned to Moscow afterward, and remained in the same state of agitation: he rushed around the city all day, spending money as if there were no tomorrow, borrowed funds from everyone, and got into such a temper that on a couple of occasions, he raised his hand as if he was going to hit me, and reproached me in coarse language. One time he even tried to attack me with a knife; I asked my sister and cousin to come down from St. Petersburg, as well as M. A.'s relatives, and yesterday the psychiatrists had a meeting and arrived at a conclusion that differed from Bekhterev's. They didn't find any psychiatric problem, and think it's only a matter of neurasthenia or a loss of control, so he ought not to be hospitalized, but they were trying to convince him to take cures or rest in the countryside, if possible. It's out of the question, of course—he won't hear of it. It really is hard to imagine what will happen now, because it's completely impossible to live with him now, and if *he* doesn't leave, then it must be *me* who leaves, no matter how difficult that will be with a small baby in my care. I want to finish the season somehow—my singing career is becoming ever more important these days [as a family income].

So this is the disaster that has befallen me. I'm keeping this brief, because it's painful for me to expand on these matters, but since you obviously have some sympathy for me, I wanted to write to you frankly and without hiding anything.

Yours, N. Vrubel[94]

---

93. Vladimir Mikhailovich Bekhterev (1857–1927), distinguished Russian psychologist and psychiatrist, founder of the St. Petersburg Institute for Psychoneurology (1907).

94. We do not know how Rimsky-Korsakov reacted to Zabela's unhappy situation, because his reply to this letter has not survived. From Zabela's following letters, we can deduce that the exchange continued, but there are no extant letters on Rimsky-Korsakov's side between March and September. Zabela might have destroyed the letters later, or they might simply have been misplaced and lost.

## 25. Rimsky-Korsakov to Zabela-Vrubel

2 December 1902 (St. Petersburg)

Dear Nadezhda Ivanovna,

I didn't send a reply to your last letter, because I thought that I was soon going to set out from Moscow and would shortly see you. But my trip has been pushed back further and further—they're [the Moscow Private Opera] having problems of some sort with *Kashchei*. I also had some altercations (fairly amicable, but still . . . ) with Mikhail Mikhailovich[95] when trying to cast the role of Burya-Bogatyr; it seems that it isn't flashy enough for Trubin[96] or for any of the other basses, because they've turned the part down. Likewise, there are no other takers for the role of Domna Saburova [in *The Tsar's Bride*], which Gladkaya[97] has been singing.[98] Flashy arias, of course, are the main thing a premier soloist wants from a role, or someone who has pretensions to becoming a premier soloist. For them, respect for art or respect for the composer's name are neither here nor there, *and*, for that matter, the public as a whole has little respect for a composer, no matter how much important work he's produced over the years. (Do you agree? I changed topic with the deftness of a regular *feuilletoniste*.)

My *Servilia* was given here, not just once, but six times in all, as part of the subscription series, and then last Friday, it was finally shown to non-subscribers. I was aware that the criticisms emanating from the *Novoye vremya* and other papers would have made the public less eager to fill up the Mariinsky Opera, and I thought that maybe the first few rows of the belle-étage would have been rather empty. However, not only the belle-étage, but also the first circle and the second circle were completely empty, while the third was half-empty, and even the balcony only had seats taken here and there. This is the worst I've ever seen: the public simply wasn't interested. The public put its trust in the authority of talentless hacks, while putting no trust at all in my good name. If the Directorate is so foolish as to present *Servilia* again, it will be in my absence. I'd really rather stop making appearances before the public at performances of my own operas, and I'll focus on rehearsals instead. All those bouquets for the composer while the curtain is raised, the applause of the artistes and the choir, have become

---

95. Mikhail Mikhailovich Ippolitov-Ivanov.
96. Vladimir Nikolayevich Trubin (1861?–1931?), Russian baritone and later bass, sang at the MPO from 1898 to 1904, and at the Zimin Private Opera from 1905. He sang the roles of the Varangian Guest in *Sadko* and the title role in *Saltan*.
97. Gladkaya had moved to the Mariinsky in 1900.
98. In other words, the MPO has no other singers to alternate with Gladkaya.

so routine that they're now given for anyone—I don't think this sits well with my head of gray hair (as declared in *Servilia*). Why am I telling you all this? Just because I like to have these conversations with you. And on that note—until soon, I hope. Keep well.

Yours, N. R-Korsakov

### 26. Rimsky-Korsakov to Zabela-Vrubel

30 December 1902, St. Petersburg

Dear Nadezhda Ivanovna and superb Tsarevna![99]
I have just received your very sweet letter. Aside from the fact that you're a wonderful person and a wonderful singer, you sometimes reveal another lovely facet of your personality, and you've revealed it this time in this sweet letter of yours. A happy New Year to you, keep well and be cheerful! Beyond that, don't abandon the roles you sing in my operas, and don't abandon the Tsarevna's part either—it would be better if no one else sang it, since then we won't have to suffer any more of Kruglikov's remarks.

At the end of January, I'm hoping to visit Moscow for a couple of days so that I can attend the premiere of *Dobrynya Nikitich*[100] at the Bolshoi— I'm very eager to hear it. Please try to arrange everything so that I can see *Kashchei* as well, either the day before or the day after, since I'd really enjoy hearing it again. I trust that this won't be too awkward for you, because the public really *does* like *Kashchei*, as you've been telling me. Don't trouble yourself to send me a page from *Kashchei*, because I can easily sign it for you when I'm in Moscow. And while I'm around, I'll also give Kruglikov a piece of my mind on your account. I can assure you that he has no real reason for goading you, and he doesn't even know himself why he does it. In any case, this isn't right, and once I've explained everything to him, he'll stop—sincerely, I mean, and not just to pacify me.

I'm feeling quite well at present, in good spirits, and that's because I'm composing something again. Why I was in such poor spirits while visiting Moscow I really can't say—now that I'm older, I sometimes have bouts of ill temper. I'm often cross, jealous, and at odds with myself—in a word, I suffer attacks of megalomania together with a persecution mania. Moscow has approved of *Kashchei*, the critics bestowed their praise on me, so did

---

99. This is a reference to Zabela as the Tsarevna in *Kashchei the Immortal*.
100. An opera by Grechaninov.

the musicians, and the public also came out in strength, but it's as if none of this is quite enough. I *do* very much want to enjoy public repute, but I want this to come from some ideal public of my imaginings. As for the real public, I can't say that I like them a great deal. But all of this is riven by contradictions, and it's hard to resolve them. Kruglikov is pinning all his hopes on me as if I were still a young man: may his words come true!

I would like to write two more operas: to finish one, and to start and finish another.[101] Both are rather large affairs, and after them, I'll be ready for my dressing gown or for my coffin. I do hope I still have enough left in me to see these two operas through to the end.

The [St. Petersburg] Private Opera presented *Saltan* here, but I attended neither the rehearsals nor the performances because I prefer to give Baskin a wide berth[102] (he's their artistic director). They say it isn't going at all well, and Madame Plotnikova is especially poor as the Swan.

Your news of Mikhail Aleksandrovich's improvement truly gladdens me, and I do hope he is now firmly on the way to recovery.

Yours, N. R-Korsakov . . .

### 27. Zabela-Vrubel to Rimsky-Korsakov

14 March 1903, Moscow

Dear Nikolai Andreyevich,
You've fallen silent for some reason—I've had no letters from you, and heard nothing about you. Up here, we've had plenty to worry about. Solodovnikov suddenly refused to rent the theater out to us, leaving us stranded, and we're now trying to create some sort of life raft, so to speak. The latest plan is to rent the Imperial New Theatre and move the whole troupe there; this struck me as pure fantasizing, but those who are more knowledgeable say that it's certainly not out of the question. But even if this *is* the eventual outcome, using the New Theatre will reduce our profits compared to the Solodovnikov Theatre, not to mention the fact that there would also be opera at the Solodovnikov,[103] and apart from that,

---

101. These were *Pan Voyevoda* (1903), which he had already begun, and *The Invisible City of Kitezh* (1904). At this stage, he had not anticipated writing *The Golden Cockerel*.

102. Vladimir Sergeyevich Baskin (1855–1919), Russian playwright and music/theater critic.

103. Solodovnikov was now renting out his theater to a different opera company.

we have rivalry from the Mamontov Opera at the Hermitage, and from another company at the Aquarium.[104] So as you can see, our investments in the Moscow Private Opera could well go down the drain and we'd have to consider leaving Moscow. In that event, I have some small hope of being hired by Kiev, and I'd want to try for the St. Petersburg Private Opera, since everyone who was employed there remembers it fondly and says that it's a solid business. I also hear that Guidi,[105] the owner, is a wealthy man with a real love for Russian music, so he's most unlikely to abandon the business any time soon. Relocating would, of course, only be possible and of any practical interest if they offered good money, otherwise there'd be no point in setting out on this course—it would otherwise be better just to hang on in Moscow, do nothing and hope for the best.

Mikhail Aleksandrovich is now in the Crimea, and sending me melancholy letters: it is rather cold there, and his state of mind doesn't seem to be improving.

And what about you? What are you up to, and what have you composed?—you've probably finished another opera by now.

My greetings,
Yours, N. Vrubel

## 28. Rimsky-Korsakov to Zabela-Vrubel

15 March 1903, St. Petersburg

Dear Nadezhda Ivanovna,

I stand guilty as accused: I still hadn't answered your previous letter when today your second letter arrived. All this time, I've been meaning to write to you and ask about the affairs of the [Private Opera] Society (since we've heard nothing good from that quarter), but your latest letter already contains all the answers I needed. It is indeed very sad if the opera of the Solodovnikov Theatre, of happy memory, is now set to collapse. I like the idea of renting a new theater and continuing with the enterprise there, but four private opera houses in Moscow is just too much! Three of them would end up failing, if not all four. It generally seems to be the case that private opera companies are unsustainable in Russia. In Kharkov

---

104. The Hermitage Garden and Aquarium Garden were theater venues in Moscow.
105. Carlo (Karl Osipovich) Guidi was the manager of the St. Petersburg Private Opera.

and in Tiflis, nothing is happening where opera is concerned, whereas in Odessa, Italian opera dominates the scene. All is quiet in Kazan, too, and there's no point listing any other places. Can it really be that the private opera business is wilting before it could come into full bloom? From a distance, you seem to have a very rosy view of the St. Petersburg Private Opera. The troupe is actually not so great, it has not been well rehearsed, the conductors are only average, and attendance at barely acceptable levels. I'm of the opinion that, in reality, Guidi is completely indifferent to the arts in Russia, and that he's just seeing to his own interests, trying out various approaches. He knows absolutely nothing about music, and placed a most unsavory character in charge of artistic decisions and repertory, namely Baskin, the music critic of the *St. Petersburg Gazette*. And it was under such conditions that they presented *Saltan*. I declared that if they ever wanted to see me at the rehearsals, they'd have to get rid of Baskin first. This they had no wish to do, so I simply stayed away from all the rehearsals and performances. Next season, if they choose to stage another opera of mine, I'm going to impose such severe conditions that they'll almost certainly back off.

I'm very sad to hear your news about Mikhail Aleksandrovich; his state of mind is important, but time is needed too—let's hope that spring will be better for him, and that his spirits will brighten then, and he'll start working as he used to. What are you planning for the summer?

I wasn't writing to you because I was very busy. At the moment, I'm working on two pieces simultaneously, although I'm a bit worried that I'll spread myself too thinly and won't manage to finish either of them—the end is not in sight yet. One of these is an opera, *The Invisible City of Kitezh*, a tale that comes from beyond the Volga. This is actually an old idea of mine. It's in three acts with a prologue. Regarding Vasilenko's *Kitezh*, by the way, do tell me how things turned out in the end.[106] Why was it postponed? Has it actually been premiered yet? What is it like on stage? (I don't really expect anything of it: it's more a cantata than an opera). I work a lot, but I can't manage to progress as fast as I used to—I'll be hitting 59 on the 6th of March!

Keep well. Thank you for not forgetting me and not being cross with me. So don't forget me and don't be cross!

Yours, N. R-Korsakov . . .

---

106. Sergei Vasilenko's dramatic cantata *A Tale of the Great City of Kitezh and the Quiet Lake of Svetloyar* was his graduation work, premiered in a concert performance in March 1902, and first staged in 1903 by the MPO. Rimsky-Korsakov knew the work, and was worried that it had already taken the same subject matter as his own projected version of *Kitezh*.

### 29. Zabela-Vrubel to Rimsky-Korsakov

10 July 1904, Moscow
Petrovsky Park, Tram-line 2
Petukhov's dacha

Dear Nikolai Andreyevich,
I promised to update you in case my engagement with the Imperial Stage came through, and now it has. I received the contract yesterday: I've been invited to St. Petersburg for one year, and I'll be paid 3,600 rubles, which is not a great sum, but certainly better than nothing (you, with your usual pessimism, didn't even think they would offer me that much). I'm spending the summer at the dacha in Petrovsky Park, near Moscow, because Mikhail Aleksandrovich is at the nearby sanatorium. His health is much improved, and you might even dare to say that he's well again. He spends most of the time with me at the dacha, and works a lot—he's painting a portrait of me. The weather is the only drawback, together with the very noticeable dampness of Petrovsky Park, so it's my hope that I'll be able to finish the summer in warmer climes so that I can get back into form for the coming season. It's still quite uncertain whether they'll actually give me anything [substantial] to sing; you, of course, will say "no, they won't."

Please pass on my greetings to Nadezhda Nikolayevna. I hope you are in excellent health and good spirits.

N. Vrubel

### 30. Rimsky-Korsakov to Zabela-Vrubel

14 July 1904, Vechasha

Dear Nadezhda Ivanovna, I'm so very pleased for you.
I don't know how this came about. Perhaps someone with real influence stepped in to assist your application on this occasion. But if your success with the Mariinsky didn't require any such pressure from above, I'll be just as happy with that, because of my own tiny contribution to the affair—although it would be incredible if that was the cause.[107] I'm also

---

107. Rimsky-Korsakov had repeatedly tried to cajole the directors to hire Zabela, but he was politely rebuffed on each occasion. This is why he has trouble believing that his interventions could have been a significant factor in Zabela's success, and so he speculates instead that someone with much greater influence might have leaned on the directors. He is trying to be modest in his claims for himself, rather than insinuating that Zabela didn't merit her post at the Mariinsky. See Rimskiy-Korsakov, *Perepiska s N. I. Zabeloy-Vrubel'*, 298n1.

very glad that Mikhail Aleksandrovich is now better. God grant that his recovery should be permanent, rather than just a temporary reprieve like the last time. Let us live in hope. Is his portrait of you turning out well? Such work is very important for him at the moment. Please pass on my greetings to him, if that will please him. Petrovsky Park, Tram No. 2 (!!). How very civilized! Over here in Vechasha, we have Lake Pesno, Lake Nyukh, Sherega and Polosy villages, the Lozi estate, and so on.[108] I love Vechasha so very much. This is where I wrote *Christmas Eve*, *The Tsar's Bride*, *Sadko*, and *Tsar Saltan*. And I hope to finish my current opera [*Kitezh*] here as well. A pity that the weather is so poor, although I hear it's worse with you: tornados, hurricanes, typhoons, etc.

Keep well and be cheerful. Greetings from N. N.

Yours, N. R-Korsakov

### 31. Zabela-Vrubel to Rimsky-Korsakov

31 March 1905, St. Petersburg

Dear Nikolai Andreyevich,
I still haven't managed to meet up with you, and I would like to say that what you did has won my sympathy and admiration, which seems to be growing day by day rather than diminishing. I am truly outraged with the Directors.[109] I expect you've already heard that my husband's illness has returned, and this time, I don't foresee any recovery; I've descended into a terrible fatalistic gloom.

I hope to see you soon and send you my greetings, asking that you add me to the number of your ardent supporters.

N. Vrubel

---

108. Here, Rimsky-Korsakov is savoring the archaic and exotic-sounding place names around his summer retreat.

109. This is a reaction to Rimsky-Korsakov's resignation from the Conservatory in solidarity with students who had been expelled for their part in seditious public demonstrations.

Figure 3. Mikhail Vrubel, portrait of Nadezhda Zabela-Vrubel among the birch trees, 1904.

## 32. Zabela-Vrubel to Rimsky-Korsakov

27 April 1906, St. Petersburg

Dear Nikolai Andreyevich,

Thank you so much for bringing me *Kitezh*. I'm playing through it now, and I'm hugely excited, just as I always am when reading something that's new and very good, especially if it's one of your pieces.

The role of Fevroniya is probably designed for some very distinguished singer at the Mariinsky, but it does happen to fit my voice rather well, although I understand that it is one thing to sing it in the drawing room, and quite another to deliver it from the stage of the Mariinsky. But please don't forget me when you're casting. Do please grant me the role of Sirin [a bird of paradise]—you must agree that I've beaten all records where fish and birds are concerned. In any case, whether you like it or not, I'll be singing Fevroniya—I mean singing her arias and duets in concert here and there. They sound so good that I'm sure I'll find a place.

As for your song "A Midsummer Night's Dream," I thought you should know that I've tried it out a semitone and a tone lower, but haven't been able to reach a decision yet: it all depends whether I'm on form, and sometimes it comes out well even when I sing it at pitch. If you're interested, perhaps you could listen to me singing it in different keys, in which case do please choose a convenient time, whether at your place or mine, and quite soon, if possible, before I have to leave for Moscow (I've been invited to give a concert at the Sokolniki Circle around the beginning of May, but I don't have the exact date yet).

With that, good-bye, together with my greetings and thanks.

Yours, N. Vrubel

P.S. It's such a pity that Sirin has so little to sing. And what kind of voice is needed for the Ghost?

# Operas in Context

# Rimsky-Korsakov, *Snegurochka*, and Populism

## EMILY FREY

It is the misfortune of any *enfant terrible* to mature into an *adulte agréable*, and that is precisely what Rimsky-Korsakov did in the 1870s. He began his career as a self-styled avant-gardist and became—in an ill-advised review of 1869—a defender of the new against the now-"impossible" forms of old opera.[1] The projects Rimsky chose in his kuchkist years were highly ambitious in both an aesthetic and a conceptual sense. Like *Boris Godunov*, his roommate Musorgsky's first complete essay in the genre, Rimsky's inaugural opera was a grand historical pageant that actually had something to say about historiography. *Pskovitanka* (1872) imagines the events that brought independent Pskov under the centralizing authority of Ivan the Terrible—and, as Richard Taruskin has argued, it is an opera not just set in but explicitly about history. Rimsky's Ivan is a world-historical individual whose will is aligned with the nation's historical destiny. His bloody behavior (well, not too bloody in Rimsky-Korsakov's version of events) is justified in the opera on the grounds of necessary historical progress, an interpretation that resonated strongly with the views of contemporary liberal historians such as Sergei Solovyov. These resonances were deliberate: Rimsky and his colleagues, Taruskin writes, "viewed themselves in the period around 1870 . . . not as 'mere' musicians but as participants and contributors to their country's seething intellectual life."[2]

In this context, Rimsky-Korsakov's subsequent development as a composer can only appear an abandonment of that lofty purpose. In 1871, the youngest kuchkist joined the enemy ranks of the St. Petersburg Conservatory, launching an ambitious program to educate himself in just those classical forms he had scorned two years before. This aesthetic shift was paralleled by a conceptual one: Rimsky's operas of the later 1870s would deal not with politically sensitive topics like the inevitable progress of Russian history but with timeless and seemingly toothless subjects drawn from fantasy and folklore. Though *Pskovityanka*, written in 1871–72, and

*Snegurochka*, written eight years later, both end with the redemptive death of a teenage girl, the reconciliation of opposing parties, and an apotheotic final chorus, Hegel and Solovyov are nowhere to be found in the later work. Set in a hazy and half-mythical prehistory, *Snegurochka* juxtaposes its characters' fates with the changing seasons, not the clash and progress of nations. In his memoirs, Rimsky characterized *Snegurochka* as indeed marking a retreat from the intellectual concerns that had captivated him only a few years earlier:

> I had first read [Alexander Ostrovsky's] *Snyegoorochka* in 1874 or thereabouts, when it had just appeared in print. At that reading I had liked it but little; the kingdom of the Byeryendyeys [*sic*] had appeared queer to me. Why? Were the ideals of the sixties still alive in me, or did the demands, current in the seventies, that subject matter be taken from so-called *life* hold me in their grip? Or had Moussorgsky's naturalism carried me away in its current? Probably all three together. . . . During the winter of 1879–80, when I reread *Snyegoorochka*, its wonderful, poetic beauty had become evident to me.[3]

Rimsky's memoirs (written, it bears mentioning, during the aestheticist ferment of the Silver Age) portray his newfound appreciation for Ostrovsky's play *Snegurochka* as a victory of aesthetics over intellectual considerations: "wonderful, poetic beauty" had trumped "the ideals of the sixties." The timelessness of poetic beauty, rather than the timeliness of contemporary thought, apparently constituted *Snegurochka*'s appeal for Rimsky-Korsakov. Perhaps appropriately, then, scholars have rarely sought connections between *Snegurochka* and the literary, intellectual, and social life of contemporary Russia, characterizing Rimsky's post-kuchkist works more often with a rhetoric of escape. Taruskin writes of Rimsky's later operas: "In the stringent conditions that followed the liberal Tsar's [Alexander II's] assassination [in 1881] and that obtained throughout the reigns of Alexander III and Nicholas II, the safest course was a retreat into fantasy."[4]

Undoubtedly so, but Rimsky-Korsakov's "retreat" began several years before the assassination of Alexander II, and the particular direction it took was no escapist idiosyncrasy. The subject matter of *Snegurochka*—the mythology of the ancient Slavs, the life of the peasant village—was eminently fashionable among literary and intellectual circles by the winter of 1879–80, when Russia was in full thrall of a movement known as *narodnichestvo* (populism). The previous twenty years had seen the rise of ethnography as an academic pursuit, and studies of the Russian folk and their beliefs were published by the likes of Alexander Afanasev, Ivan Sakharov, Pavel Shein, and Alexander Tereshchenko, all writers Rimsky read in the years preceding his work on *Snegurochka*.[5] Russia's thick journals of the seventies, meanwhile, brimmed with articles by populist thinkers like Nikolai Mikhailovsky and stories about village life by writers such as Gleb Uspensky and Nikolai Zlatovratsky. These authors were born, like Rimsky, in the first five years of the 1840s, and they shared the composer's leftward politics. For them the peasant village, and especially the peasant village of the past, represented an alternative to a present blighted by autocracy and industrialization—and, perhaps, a model for an egalitarian Russian society of the future.

*Snegurochka* offers few such quixotic delusions. The connections between the opera and the contemporary populist movement are worth pursuing, however, for Rimsky-Korsakov's operatic engagement with the civic and intellectual issues of contemporary Russia did not end in 1872 with *Pskovitanka*; *Snegurochka*, for all its apparent timelessness, reflects in striking ways the preoccupations of its era. But those preoccupations had changed. The populist movement had cut its teeth with a series of articles undermining the vision of history that motivates Rimsky's first opera, in which human suffering is justified in the name of inevitable historical progress. By the end of the 1870s, necessity and nation-states were out. Folk and feeling were in.

## Nikolai Mikhailovsky and the Populist Ideal

As all followers of twenty-first century politics know, populism is a vexingly capacious term. It has been applied to almost the entire spectrum of the political left in mid- and late nineteenth-century Russia, from Westernizers like Belinsky to nihilists like Pisarev to Jacobins like Tkachev. Here I want to restrict it to a narrow historical meaning, referring to a political and intellectual movement that originated in Russia in the late 1860s, flourished in the 1870s, and waned after the assassination of Alexander II in 1881. Like any such movement, it was rife with complexities and contradictions. For a start, it owed intellectual debts to both conservative Slavophiles and the socialist Westernizer Alexander Herzen. Broadly speaking, however, populism advocated for a kind of agrarian

· 65 ·

socialism based on the principles of Proudhon rather than Marx, the latter's works having just begun to trickle into Russia in the 1870s.[6] Compared with their better-known predecessors, such "men of the sixties" as Chernyshevsky, Dobroliubov, and Pisarev, the 1870s generation evinced a distrust for the universal applicability of scientific laws, a greater interest in subjectivity and individuality, and a preference for social over political reform. James Billington, a historian of the movement, characterized populist thinkers as attempting to find a "middle way" between the extreme ideologies of the period—revolutionary terrorism on the one hand and reactionary pan-Slavism on the other.[7]

This middle way demanded a reevaluation of some of the more radical elements of 1860s thought. (Rimsky-Korsakov was not the only Russian to reconsider his former hardline stances during the seventies; if the sixties are known in Russian as the Era of Great Reforms, the seventies are better termed the Era of Great Rethought.) The populists believed that humanity was the baby their radical predecessors had thrown out with the tsarist bathwater. Too eager to remake Russian society based on rational socialist principles, the men of the sixties had over-relied on scientific and impersonal models. In doing away with the evils of autocracy, the populists argued, Russia did not need to institute a new tyranny by imagining human relationships and human behavior to be the products of scientific laws. History, they boldly proclaimed, was not a natural science, and the populists raced to debunk all theories of history they held to be deterministic and inhumane. These included theories that saw history as following a course of natural, inevitable progress (like Solovyov's, embodied in Rimsky's early opera *Pskovityanka*), as being impervious to individual human effort (like Tolstoy's, expounded in the infamous second epilogue to *War and Peace*), or as encompassing a Darwinian struggle for survival among competing groups (like Pisarev's, expressed in the 1864 essay "Progress in the Animal and Plant Worlds").[8]

In his *Historical Letters* of 1869–70, Pyotr Lavrov (1823–1900), a professor of mathematics who dabbled in socialist politics, attacked the notion of historical progress on ethical grounds.[9] His most famous essay from that collection, "The Cost of Progress," is a direct rebuttal to the idea that historical destiny justifies great human suffering. The current state of Russian society, in which an educated elite had the means and the leisure to sit by the samovar and discuss the current state of Russian society, had come at a horrifying human cost—a cost for which that educated elite was very much on the hook. "Each generation is answerable to posterity . . . for what it *could have* done but did not do," wrote Lavrov:

> Thus in light of the verdict of posterity we, too, shall have to answer certain questions. How much of the evil contained in the process to which we give the high-sounding title of "historical progress" is unavoidable and natural? To what extent did our ancestors—who provided us, the civilized minority, with the chance to enjoy the advantages of this progress—needlessly increase and prolong the sufferings and toil of the majority which has never enjoyed the advantages of progress? In what instances may the responsibility for this evil also fall upon us, in the eyes of future generations?[10]

For Lavrov "progress" is a dodge; the notion of historical necessity did not, and could not, discharge the enormous debt the educated elite owed to the suffering masses. Rather than dull their consciences with the morphine of inevitability, the educated classes (whom Lavrov called "critically thinking individuals") had an ethical imperative to spread truth, science, art, and morality—to transform Russian culture with the fruits of that education for which the masses had paid so dearly.[11]

Lavrov's *Letters* electrified Russian youths from Kherson to Kazan.[12] Their author, however, had escaped to the West following his 1868 political exile, and would spend the rest of his life publishing from Paris and Zurich. Within Russia, the most influential thinker of the populist movement was Nikolai Mikhailovsky (1842–1904), a social and literary critic who published his own critique of progress in an essay aptly titled "What Is Progress?" (*Chto takoe progress?*). This work appeared contemporaneously with *Historical Letters* and went even further in arguing that progress could not be defined in Hegelian-Solovyovian terms. Mikhailovsky measured progress, rather, by what he called "the struggle for individuality" (*bor'ba za individual'nost'*)—a term formulated in seeming rebuttal to the Darwinian "struggle for existence" (*bor'ba za sushchestvovanie*).[13] By this Mikhailovsky had in mind the development and consummation of the individual human personality, an item the men of the sixties had also thought to be governed by natural laws.[14] (For Mikhailovsky, by contrast, the personality was "holy and inviolable," for "it alone feels, thinks, and suffers.")[15] Not only did the notion of inevitable historical progress threaten to crush individuality, Mikhailovsky asserted, but the development of the modern nation-state—the ultimate goal of Hegel's and Solovyov's teleologies—was antithetical to the development of the individual. The division of labor was an essential component of the modern European economy, as complex social organization allowed for an outstanding increase in productivity. But the complexity of a society appeared to Mikhailovsky inversely related to the complexity of its individual members. Instead of being "integral," self-sufficient personalities (*tselostnïye lichnosti*), individuals in a specialist economy became fragmentary selves, simple cogs to be "integrated" into a complex capitalist machine. Mikhailovsky wrote:

> To the question we have posed—what is progress?—we answer: Progress is the gradual approach to the integral individual, to the fullest possible and the most diversified division of labor among man's organs and the least possible division of labor among men. Everything that impedes this advance is immoral, unjust, pernicious, and unreasonable. Everything that diminishes the heterogeneity of society and thereby increases the heterogeneity of its members is moral, just, reasonable, and beneficial."[16]

What had been for Solovyov the ideal of progress thus became for Mikhailovsky the very image of decline.

And so, argued Mikhailovsky, the recent influx of capitalism in the wake of Alexander II's Great Reforms did not represent a step forward in Russia's historical evolution. Western capitalism was the product of a fragmented, "eccentric" worldview, and it was therefore not to be imitated if Russia were to seek "progress" as Mikhailovsky defined it.[17] There was a healthier social model closer to home: the ancient, but now endangered, ecosystem of the peasant village, where division of labor was minimal and "integral" personalities in abundance.[18] Industrialization, expanding at a fever pitch during the 1870s, posed a grave threat to this ancient idyll, disrupting traditional agricultural practices and making possible the rapid spread of "eccentric" ideas. Perhaps the disease of modernity had already taken root. As the decade wore on, Mikhailovsky like many of his contemporaries proved susceptible to what Richard Wortman has called "the crisis of populism": the clash of ideals and realities resulting from the intelligentsia's failed "movement to the people" of 1874–75.[19] In those years, young populists shipped out en masse to provincial villages, hoping both to learn the peasantry's bucolic virtues and to evangelize the gospel of contemporary socialism. But the people turned out to be not quite the unspoiled noble savages of the intelligentsia's imagination. They were conservative, suspicious of outsiders, and deeply devoted to the tsar; the movement ended in arrests by the thousands, as many peasants were only too happy to turn over these quixotic rabble-rousers to the authorities. As for the villages themselves, they appeared to the interlopers shockingly bleak and brutal, hardly the proto-socialist Arcadias the populists had envisioned.

Mikhailovsky's solution to this problem was a restrospectivism that was ever-increasing. The critic projected his ideal back in time, training his rose-colored glasses less on the contemporary peasant commune (which perhaps had already been corrupted by capitalist greed) than on the village of the hazy and distant past. In "On Schiller and Many Other Things" (1876), Mikhailovsky once again undermined the popular "progressive" view of history and declared, with Schiller: "Our ideal is behind us."[20] Mikhailovsky's statements about the German poet might be taken as his own historicist credo:

> Amid that amazing confusion of concepts that the majority of our educated society is now experiencing, there has developed some sort of strange idea of the confluence of freedom, democratic principles, and progress with the actual, incremental movement of history. I'm not talking about those completely absurd people who rejoice over every step of history just because it's still a step. But even far more prudent people are prone to think that on the whole, minus a few random deviations, history continuously allows the triumph of freedom, democratic ideas, progress. Count Lev Tolstoy says quite rightly that this has *never* been proven by anyone, but everyone accepts it as the truth. . . . I think, therefore, that many readers will be confused when they read, for example, these words of Schiller: "In the child we see fundamentals and purpose; in ourselves we see the execution, and the latter is always infinitely far from the former. That is why for us the child is the embodiment of the ideal . . . " ("On Naïve and Sentimental Poetry"). It should be noted that, according to the general meaning of the article and the direct instructions made earlier, that "rural customs and the morals of primitive society" should be inserted in that quotation next to "the child." Thus, it turns out that Schiller says almost exactly the same thing as Tolstoy: our ideal is not ahead of us, but behind us—in the child, in the folk, in the past.[21]

"Progress," as Mikhailovsky defined it in his humanistic way, was not inevitable; it had to be fought for and passionately defended. Therefore it was also not inevitable that the current moment was the best, most "advanced" time in history. Mikhailovsky's ideal future was based on an idealized past, a past he connected with harmonious social feeling and the triumph of the individual personality. He and his like-minded contemporaries were nostalgic futurists—or, as Lenin put it less kindly, a generation of mealy-mouthed Januses, "looking with one face to the past and the other to the future."[22]

And Mikhailovsky's like-minded contemporaries were many. In the 1870s, Billington writes, "the Russian intelligentsia was united as it had never been before by a deep common faith" in populism, which had redefined progress in terms of the development of the "thinking, feeling, suffering" personality and the attainment of just, cooperative social relations.[23] Mikhailovsky's dacha at Gatchina was frequented by members of St. Petersburg's leading artistic circles, including the painter Ilya Repin and the cellist Karl Davydov, Rimsky-Korsakov's boss at the St. Petersburg Conservatory. With Mikhailovsky as chief critic, *Otechestvennye zapiski* (Notes from the Fatherland) became the mouthpiece of Russian populism and the most important journal of the era. Turgenev, Dostoevsky, and Tolstoy—writers of very different political stripes who had had complicated relationships to the socialist left of the 1860s—all published their works in that journal in the succeeding decade. More important for our purposes, so did Alexander Ostrovsky, the playwright who would furnish Rimsky-Korsakov the material for his fairy-tale opera of 1880.

## Nostalgic Utopia

*Otechestvennïye zapiski* was the first place Ostrovsky chose to shop his new drama in the spring of 1873. It was a logical choice, given that he had already published several of his plays in it and, as he later wrote to the editor, Nikolai Nekrasov, he felt "a full and deep sympathy" for the populist journal and its mission.[24] But Nekrasov's reaction to *Snegurochka* was cool; he sent Ostrovsky a terse reply offering the playwright a much lower than usual fee for the new work. Hurt, Ostrovsky withdrew *Snegurochka* and published it in *Vestnik Evropï* instead. The episode did not sour Ostrovsky on *Otechestvennïye zapiski*, however; he wrote to Nekrasov that the populist journal would remain his top choice for future publications.[25]

*Snegurochka*'s plot is based on a Russian tale found in Afanasev's 1855 collection of Russian folktales as well as several other sources.[26] The story unfolds in prehistory, in a half-mythical kingdom ruled by the benevolent Tsar Berendey. For fifteen years the Berendeyans have suffered cold and sunless weather, owing to a feud between the sun god Yarilo and Ded Moroz, the god of winter (usually portrayed as an avuncular Santa

Claus-like figure, but here rather, well, frostier). Caught between the dueling deities is Moroz's innocent but coldhearted daughter Snegurochka, who has been captivated by the plaintive songs of the shepherd Lel. Her entry into the village of Berendey causes turmoil; setting eyes on her, the traveling merchant Mizgir jilts his fiancée Kupava in spectacular fashion. Snegurochka begs her mother (Spring Beauty) to grant her the power to love, and her mother does so, admonishing Snegurochka to stay out of the sun. Being fifteen, Snegurochka immediately falls in love with the smitten Mizgir and disregards her mother's advice. The sun's rays strike her heart and she melts, prompting Mizgir to throw himself into the sea. Tsar Berendey exhorts the villagers not to grieve, for the lovers' sacrifice has put an end to the plague of cold. Throughout the play, the passage of time is marked by the villagers' succession of ceremonial songs, which accompanies the seasonal cycle from Maslenitsa (Shrovetide) to Kupala (midsummer).

Nekrasov's ambivalence to such a scenario was not entirely unfathomable. While academic studies of folklore were highly popular at the time, the fashion in drama and fiction was for pageants based on cruel episodes from Russia's tsarist history or realistic treatments of contemporary topics. (Recall among Rimsky-Korsakov's reasons for his early indifference to *Snegurochka* the "demands, current in the seventies, that subject matter be taken from so-called *life*.")[27] Folk subjects, whether treated with vinegar (emphasizing the corrosive effects of autocracy and capitalism) or with sugar (emphasizing the folk's innate goodness and closeness to nature) were no exceptions; the works of both the vinegary Gleb Uspensky and the saccharine Nikolai Zlatovratsky dealt with conditions in the contemporary, post-Reform Era countryside rather than the prehistoric past. To attempt, as Ostrovsky did in *Snegurochka*, to forge fiction from folklore was, in the dramatist's own words, a "new direction"—one that left many Russians, Nekrasov and Rimsky-Korsakov among them, perplexed.[28]

By the 1870s, Ostrovsky had become known as a playwright with a nasty streak; the main works by which he had made his not-inconsiderable reputation were stinging indictments of contemporary Russian society. In *Snegurochka*, however, Ostrovsky retracted his claws. The fictional village of Berendey is notably fairer, kinder, and more humane than the often-savage societies depicted in Ostrovsky's dramas about modern life. Perfect social equity does not yet reign among the Berendeyans—there are rich and poor villagers, and Snegurochka's adoptive parents are forever scheming to get more money—but social divisions are not the point of this play, and their effects on village life are minimal. Also, though Ostrovsky's earlier dramas were most famous for their depictions of capricious and dimwitted domestic tyrants, a character type still known in Russia by the Ostrovskian appellation *samodur*, in *Snegurochka* the playwright offered a supremely enlightened ruler.[29] If the *samodur* wields the power but not the title of the autocrat, the leader of the Berendeyans does the opposite: Berendey is called tsar, but his dominion is severely circumscribed. He commands a village, not an empire, and his power is bounded both by the rule of law—he holds open trials, attended by all—and by nature. He is intimately sympathetic to his subjects, fretting with his boyar Bermyata over the people's well-being and responding to Kupava's seemingly pedestrian romantic complaints with kindness and solicitude. Cruelty, the coin of the realm under the *samodur*, is a capital crime among the Berendeyans. Or at least it would be: Tsar Berendey declares that Mizgir's unfeeling treatment of Kupava "deserves the death penalty, but our legal code has no such bloody laws."[30] The worst punishment Berendey can muster is exile—and even then, the tsar mercifully commutes Mizgir's sentence just moments after he pronounces it. Compared with the "dark kingdoms" of Ostrovsky's merchant dramas, *Snegurochka*'s ancient village is a social and political ideal; "rural customs and the morals of the primitive world" (to put it Mikhailovskianly) are portrayed as markedly better than those of the modern capitalist class. The world of Ostrovsky's *Snegurochka* is a nostalgic utopia.[31]

Nostalgia for a lost bucolic idyll also played a role in Rimsky-Korsakov's eventual attraction to *Snegurochka*. The backward-looking impulse that struck Ostrovsky, Mikhailovsky, and so much of the Russian intelligentsia during the 1870s did not leave the composer unmoved. Inspired, perhaps, by the study of Bach and Cherubini his new post at the conservatory had necessitated, Rimsky-Korsakov worked his professorial red pen on *Pskovityanka*, the opera he had written as a tradition-scorning kuchkist only a few years before.[32] At the same time, he prepared new editions of Mikhail Glinka's two operas, *A Life for the Tsar* (1836) and *Ruslan and Lyudmila* (1842).[33] Concurrent with these editorial efforts was Rimsky-Korsakov's work on a collection of Russian folksongs, which he compiled through interviews with his acquaintances. Then followed two operas on folk themes: *May Night* (1879), based on a Gogol story that depicts Russian peasant life and customs, and *Snegurochka*. Rimsky-Korsakov wrote in his memoirs that the impetus for those operas had come, in part, from his work on the folksong collection. He had been most captivated by the category of songs he called "ceremonial," which accompanied communal activity; these included game songs, "calendar songs" marking seasonal events, and dances like the *khorovod* (which Rimsky linked to summer celebrations), as well as more obviously "ceremonial" songs connected with events such as wedding rituals. In his memoirs, Rimsky described these songs, and the agrarian way of life they reflected, with more than a hint of aristocratic nostalgia:

> In my reminiscences of 1876-7 [he meant 1875-76] I spoke of my enthusiasm for the poetry of pagan worship—an enthusiasm that had originated in my work on ceremonial songs. That enthusiasm had not cooled even now [in 1878]; on the contrary . . . it led to a series of fantastic operas in which the worship of the sun and of sun-gods was introduced. . . . Though sun-worship had entirely faded before the light of Christianity . . . the whole cycle of ceremonial songs and games to this very day rests on the ancient pagan sun-worship which lives unconsciously in the people. The people, as a nation, sing their ceremonial songs by force of habit and custom, neither understanding nor suspecting what really underlies these ceremonies and games. Today, however, the last vestiges of ancient song and, with them, all signs of ancient pantheism are evidently vanishing.[34]

Ceremonial songs, Rimsky believed, were the most unmediated of all types of folksongs; they were an aural point of contact with an ancient and venerable past whose last traces were threatened by modernity. These songs, which showed human beings acting in harmony both with one another and with the cycle of seasons, were for Rimsky the bearers of a vanishing cultural ideal. At the time of writing *Snegurochka*, he later recalled, "There was no better theme in the world for me . . . there was no better kingdom than the kingdom of the Byeryendyeys and their wonderful ruler; there was no better view of the world and religion than the worship of Yarilo-Sun."[35]

In *Snegurochka*, Rimsky found a perfect vehicle for his newfound interest in ceremonial songs and the harmonious worldview they disclosed. Ostrovsky, a fellow connoisseur and collector of folklore, had already incorporated several such songs into the structure of his play.[36] Rimsky-Korsakov's procedures in crafting a libretto from Ostrovsky's drama were typical, even exemplary, of Russian approaches to operatic adaptation during the 1870s. He acted as his own librettist, adapting the text directly from the original source—as did the composers of fully half of all Russian operas written during the decade.[37] In cutting Ostrovsky's play down to manageable operatic size, Rimsky operated under the principle of omission rather than paraphrase: he did not include all of Ostrovsky's text, but the text he included was all, or nearly all, Ostrovsky's. (This "fastidious retention of texts," Taruskin writes, makes *Snegurochka* "every bit as entitled as Dargomyzhsky's *Stone Guest* or Musorgsky's *Marriage*—those pillars of 'realism'—to be classified as a 'sung play.'")[38] To the surprise of Ostrovsky, who would have had little idea of Rimsky's interest in them, Rimsky-Korsakov retained all of the ceremonial scenes from the original play.[39] Moreover, he distinguished these numbers musically from the rest of the opera by setting them to genuine folk tunes. Many of *Snegurochka*'s folksiest-sounding passages, Rimsky noted tetchily in his memoirs, are not in fact artifacts but new pieces "successfully composed in folk-spirit."[40] The communal, ceremonial numbers, however—the birds' game song, the Maslenitsa choruses, the wedding ritual, the ceremonial folk dances in Act 3, and the millet-sowing chorus—are based on authentic folksongs from the collections of Lvov-Prach, Stakhovich, Balakirev, and Rimsky-Korsakov himself. Preserved largely intact, and swathed in genuine musical artifacts, the ceremonial songs in *Snegurochka* assume great thematic significance. They unite human experience with the seasonal cycle, emphasizing the collective sympathy of human beings with one another and with nature—and narrate this utopian ideal in the authentistic language of pagan antiquity.

Russian historical dramas of the late 1860s had tended to focus on pasts that were worse than the present—the Russia of ruthless tyrants and scheming pretenders, of Ivan the Terrible and Boris Godunov, of widespread starvation and suffering masses. Ostrovsky and Rimsky-Korsakov had both contributed to this trend at the time: Ostrovsky with works like *The Pretender Dmitri and Vasili Shuisky* (1866) and *Tushino* (1867), both set during the Time of Troubles, and Rimsky-Korsakov with *Pskovityanka* (1872), set during the reign of Ivan the Terrible. In an era of extreme *art engagé*, these bloody tsar-and-boyar dramas worked by means of historical analogy. By depicting the horrors of the past, one implicitly criticized the present, in hope of bringing about a brighter and more equitable future. The 1870s, a decade of accelerated industrialization and metastatic capitalism, saw a shift in the way many Russian writers and artists oriented themselves toward the past. The past that most captivated the populists was that of the ancient village, not sixteenth-century Moscow, and this bucolic prehistory was interesting precisely because it was *not* analogous to the present. It was better—more humane, more cooperative, and more egalitarian than the Russia that currently ached from the growing pains of modernization. The utopian future in which the populists so fervently believed involved not just a transcendence of, but also a return to, the past. The *Snegurochka*s of Ostrovsky and Rimsky-Korsakov offer perhaps the clearest representations in art of the populist notion of the ideal past, depicting the prehistoric village as a site of social cooperation and humane politics.

In one respect the opera outdid its prototype in portraying the village of Berendey as a model of human sympathy. Flying in the face of all operatic precedent, Rimsky-Korsakov cast *Snegurochka*'s Tsar Berendey—a man so old his gray beard reaches his waist—not as a dignified and weighty bass but as a sensitive lyric tenor.[41] Mikhail Vasilyev, the tenor who originated the role, was the Mariinsky's go-to "lover" at the time; he also created the roles of Prince Sinodal in Rubinstein's *Demon*, Andrei in Tchaikovsky's *Mazepa*, and Vladimir in Borodin's *Prince Igor*. He would have been an obvious choice for Mizgir, the bold foreign trader for whom the teenage heroine eventually falls. But Rimsky-Korsakov subverted vocal tradition, casting a baritone as young lover, a tenor as tsar, and Fyodor Stravinsky, the Mariinsky's talented bass, in the bit part of Ded Moroz.[42] This voice typing, unprecedented as it is, seems nonetheless appropriate: Berendey, the supremely sympathetic ruler of an idealized Russian village, sings with the voice of feeling, not that of authority.

## Once More, with Feeling

"Feeling," however, was a quality Ostrovsky's village—like most utopias—lacked. Harmony and goodwill may prevail among the happy Berendeyans, but complex psychology does not. Gerald Abraham once wrote that Rimsky-Korsakov's fantastic opera *The Tale of Tsar Saltan* (1900) is populated by "puppet-characters [who] are too remote for us to sympathise with,"[43] but that description is even better applied to Ostrovsky's *Snegurochka*. The play's early critics often diagnosed *Snegurochka* with the same disease that afflicts its heroine: a cold heart. "What kind of drama can there be," asked a correspondent for the St. Petersburg journal *Golos*, "when the main heroine has no heart, when she lacks all that, in common parlance, must exist in the human heart, upon whose expression drama depends?"[44] Snegurochka, an emotionally deficient interloper whose presence disrupts the peaceful life of the village, never exerts more than feeble pressure on the heartstrings; the only character who does is Kupava, the village girl whose mercurial fiancé prefers his female companions modest rather than passionate. If, as the writer in *Golos* asserted, such a state of affairs could not do for drama, it could surely do even less for opera, and

Rimsky-Korsakov worked hard to ameliorate the problem. Even while preserving Ostrovsky's words, Rimsky overhauled *Snegurochka*'s fictional universe, minimizing the heroine's failings and magnifying her feelings.

Song being slower than speech, the adaptation of a full-length play to an opera libretto almost always involves compression. Ostrovsky's *Snegurochka* contains an assortment of subplots involving the social life of the peasant village: the romantic mishaps of the village youths, the stock marital squabbling of Snegurochka's adoptive parents, and the amorous pursuits of one Elena Prekrasnaya, a boyar's wife who orchestrates a sylvan tryst with Lel. These plots, and most of the characters they implicated, were obvious candidates for amputation. Rimsky's libretto subsumed the individual village youths into the chorus, abridged the roles of Bobyl and Bobylikha, and left poor Elena Prekrasnaya to seek her extramarital adventures in non-operatic realms. The cuts made for a much more focused narrative—and, of course, a more manageable roster of singers to hire. They also had a profound influence on the title character, changing fundamentally her relationship to the village. In Ostrovsky, Snegurochka is always figured as an outsider among the Berendeyans, and her difference from the villagers is frequently noted.[45] Moreover, she poses an imminent threat to village life, for Mizgir is not the only rustic roué to throw over his girlfriend in pursuit of her. Early in the play, Bobyl chides his adopted daughter: "And our young men have lost their minds: in hoardes, in herds they madly fling themselves at you. They've left their fiancées, they've quarreled and fought because of you."[46] This situation is a major source of conflict in the play. Of the village girls, only Kupava does not ostracize Snegurochka, which makes Mizgir's abandonment of the former for the latter sting all the more.[47] Later, when Tsar Berendey mentions his plan to mollify Yarilo by holding a mass wedding ceremony, the boyar Bermyata tells him that it is impossible as all the village couples have parted ways over Snegurochka.[48] The disruptions her presence has caused are "unheard of among the honorable Berendeyans,"[49] and they threaten to estrange the village still more from Yarilo, who prefers his subjects safely encoupled. By scaling back the minor characters, then, Rimsky-Korsakov removed nearly all traces of Snegurochka's "outsider" status. While the soprano Snegurochka still cannot understand the village girls' romantic behavior, she is never explicitly ostracized, as she is in the play. More important, we do not see the opera's village boys desert their girlfriends en masse over Snegurochka.[50] Mizgir's actions thus appear all the more heinous, and Kupava's heartbreak all the more poignant, for their breakup comes as a shock. Compared to her dramatic predecessor, the operatic Snegurochka causes little harm to village life. Her only crime is her frosty genetics.

Even Snegurochka's frostiness is limited, however; in transferring to the opera stage, the heroine's personality underwent a bit of de-icing. Act 1 of Ostrovsky's play shows Snegurochka arguing with her adoptive father; she tells him he has only his own laziness to blame for his poverty, and he, hinting that he regrets adopting her, blasts her severity. To this, Snegurochka replies that she is not severe, only bashful. Rimsky removed almost all hint of this conflict, portraying the relationship between adoptive parents and daughter as generally amicable, even if the peasant pair still hope to profit by marrying off Snegurochka to a rich man. Likewise, Rimsky excised most of Ostrovsky's references to Snegurochka's emotional deficiencies. Her "coldness" in the play extends not only to her personal relationships, but also to her ability to appreciate the significance of ritual. In Act 3, Kupava accuses Snegurochka of blankly going through the motions of Kupala Day preparations, being more concerned with her appearance than the solemnity of the holiday: "Snegurochka, what kind of way is this to meet the rising of Yarilo-Sun? . . . Your apron and your new fur slippers are your only concern; like a stupid child, you delight in your own attire."[51] These observations reinforce the fact that Ostrovsky's Snegurochka is a misfit who disturbs and even threatens the social and religious life of the village. Rimsky's heroine never hears this reproach, for indeed she does not deserve it. She participates actively in village rituals, even singing a descant in "Ay vo pole lipen'ka," the *khorovod* in Act 3. Whatever her ignorance of romantic love, Rimsky's Snegurochka is "cold" to neither interpersonal dynamics nor communal rituals.

Both of the tendencies noted above—Rimsky-Korsakov's dissolution of the conflicts between Snegurochka and the villagers and his softening of the title character's emotional deficits—are evident in his abridgement of Snegurochka's Act 1 monologue, delivered after Lel carelessly crumples the flower she has given him. Rimsky's selective cuts to Ostrovsky's text (shown in Table 1) demonstrate the different social and emotional circumstances navigated by the operatic snow maiden, as compared with her prototype.

The libretto completely reaccentuates the monologue, even while treating Ostrovsky's text literalistically. Rimsky-Korsakov removes most of the social context of Snegurochka's speech: his heroine does not comment on the village girls' unabashed behavior, nor react indignantly to their laughter, nor find it "painful and sad" to see them happy with Lel. What is "painful and sad" to the soprano is the emotion itself—vexation—rather than the cause of it. And, significantly, Rimsky's heroine does not

Table 1. Snegurochka's monologue and arietta.
Deleted text appears in italics.

| Ostrovsky (Act 1, scene 4) | Rimsky-Korsakov (Act 1) |
|---|---|
| How painful it is here! How heavy my heart has become! | How painful it is here! How heavy my heart has become! |
| The flower Lel crumpled *and cast aside* has fallen on my heart | The flower Lel crumpled has fallen on my heart |
| Like a heavy insult, like a stone. *And I, as if also rejected and cast aside, withered under his mocking words.* The shepherd | Like a heavy insult, like a stone.

The shepherd |
| Runs to others, for they are more agreeable, | Runs to others, for they are more agreeable, |
| Their laughter more resonant, their speech warmer; | Their laughter more resonant, their speech warmer. |
| *They're more amenable to kisses,* | |
| *They put their arms around his shoulders and look* | |
| *Boldly and directly into his eyes, in front of everyone,* | |
| *They swoon in his embraces.* | |
| *There's joy and happiness there.* | |
| *(She listens.)* | |
| *Well! Laughter!* | |
| And here I stand, nearly weeping from grief, | And here I stand, nearly weeping from grief, |
| *Vexed,* for Lel has left me. | For Lel has left me. |
| *And who could blame him? Wherever it's merriest,* | |
| *That's where his heart is drawn. He's right,* | |
| Handsome Lel. Run to where you are loved, | Handsome Lel. Run to where you are loved, |
| Seek love; you're worthy of it. | Seek love; you're worthy of it. |
| *Snegurochka's heart, cold to everyone,* | |
| *Does not beat with love even for you.* | |
| But why is this painful to me? Why does vexation | But why is this painful to me? Why does vexation |
| Constrain my breast? Why is it painful and sad | Constrain my breast, painfully and sadly? |
| *To look at you, to look at your happiness,* | |
| *Happy girlfriends of the shepherd?* | |
| Father Moroz, you've hurt Snegurochka. | Father Moroz, you've hurt Snegurochka. |
| But *I'll set things right: from among the trifles,* | |
| *Pretty beads, and cheap rings* | |
| *Of* Mother Spring I'll take *a pinch,* | But I'll take a pinch of Mother Spring's |
| A little pinch of heart-warmth, | heart-warmth, |
| So my heart will warm up, even if just a little. | So my heart will warm up, even if just a little. |

describe her own heart as "cold to everyone," not "beat[ing] with love even for [Lel]." The opening melody of the arietta is based on a theme Lel plays on his shepherd's pipe (see Examples 1 and 2), suggesting more directly than her words just how deep an impression Lel has made on her. The focus in the arietta, unlike the monologue, is squarely on what Snegurochka *does* feel, not what she doesn't.

Example 1. Lel's pipe theme.

Example 2. Snegurochka's arietta.

What Snegurochka feels, moreover, is aired at far greater length in the opera than it is in the play. The progress of her feelings is limned in a series of arias and ariettas that unfold across the work. Focusing on the heroine's inner emotions rather than a complicated system of subplots was a natural thing for an opera composer to do, particularly in a Russia enthralled by the psychological prose of Tolstoy and Dostoevsky. But there was a problem for a composer as dedicated to textual preservation as Rimsky-Korsakov: Ostrovsky's snow maiden is not a particularly self-revealing character. Other than the lines she delivers as she melts, the monologue quoted above is her only extended lyric moment in the play. Rimsky called on a variety of means to solve this problem. In Act 3, he repurposed Ostrovsky's text, engineering an arioso out of what had been a dialogue. After yet another disappointment by Lel, Ostrovsky's Snegurochka confronts the shepherd, accusing him of offending an orphan. (Lel, being made of flintier stuff than Gilbert and Sullivan's pirate king, responds rather obtusely.) Rimsky-Korsakov recast this dialogue as a solo arioso delivered to an absent Lel—shifting the emphasis, once again, from interpersonal conflict to inner feeling. (See Table 2 below.) Elsewhere, Rimsky-Korsakov turned relatively compact and inexpressive speeches into arias by repeating text and amplifying the emotional content through music. The two such arias Snegurochka sings in the prologue are written in contrasting musical styles, suggesting a greater emotional range—and a *far* greater capacity for passion—than

Table 2. Dialogue and arioso. Discrepancies appear in italics.

| Ostrovsky (Act 3, scene 2) | Rimsky-Korsakov (Act 3) |
|---|---|
| Snegurochka<br>Are you not sorry<br>For hurting an orphan so?<br><br>Lel<br>*I don't know<br>What you find hurtful.*<br><br>Snegurochka<br>*How is that?*<br>Is Snegurochka a beauty *or not*?<br><br>Lel<br>A beauty.<br><br>Snegurochka<br>And yet you've chosen Kupava,<br>You've led her to the tsar, you've kissed her.<br>Perhaps Kupava is better than Snegurochka?<br>*There's the insult; you cannot forget it.*<br><br>[...]<br><br>Snegurochka<br>*Forget about the past*, darling Lel!<br>Love me a little, just you wait,<br>Snegurochka herself will love you.<br>Lead me to see the tsar's tents<br>And take me to meet the sun as your girlfriend! | Snegurochka<br>*Darling Lel*, are you not sorry<br>For so hurting *Snegurochka*, an orphan?<br><br><br><br><br><br><br>Is Snegurochka a beauty?<br><br><br>A beauty!<br><br><br>And yet you've chosen Kupava,<br>You've led her to the tsar, you've kissed her.<br>O, perhaps Kupava is better than Snegurochka!<br><br><br><br><br>Darling Lel, *love me*, love me a little;<br>Just you wait,<br>Snegurochka herself will love you.<br>Lead me to see the tsar's tents<br>And take me to meet the sun as your girlfriend! |

her cold heart would seem to admit. The first aria, "To go raspberry-picking," a brisk and chipper *allegretto capriccioso* in E major, presents a childlike, fairy-tale heroine straight out of Ostrovsky. The second, "I've heard the singing of the larks," is the very opposite in style, a D-minor *larghetto* full of long, arched, legato phrases and chromatic yearning. Right up until the last word, "melt," this second aria's text has been innocent enough, comparing Lel's songs favorably to those of various birds. But that longing, aching, unmistakably sensuous melody, accompanied

Example 3. Snegurochka's aria ("S podruzhkami po yagodu khodit'"), opening bars.

Example 4. Snegurochka's arietta ("Slĭkhala ia, slĭkhala"), opening bars.

by the Dionysian oboe, underscores Snegurochka's internal and decidedly un-childlike reaction to those songs. It is not for nothing that her parents recoil: how cold can Snegurochka's heart really be if she can sing such a steamy tune? (See Examples 3 and 4.)

Snegurochka's "love-death" at the end of the opera will reprise this sultry melody from the prologue, first in the violin and then in the voice.[52] (See Example 4.) Though Ostrovsky's text does not literally repeat at this moment, the musical quotation makes for a fitting thematic reference, as the early arietta describes figurative melting—"You listen [to Lel's songs], and you melt!"—and the final aria shows Snegurochka literally doing so. The prologue arietta is not the only reminiscence to appear in Snegurochka's "melting" aria, however; as in *Tristan und Isolde,* Snegurochka's version of the Liebestod incorporates material from both the prologue and the love duet, which she and Mizgir sing at the beginning of Act 4. In this second instance, the reminiscence is a purely Rimskian invention, because Ostrovsky's text for Snegurochka's final speech contains no such recollection. Indeed, Ostrovsky's play does not contain the text that underlies this melody at all—"O, my dear, I'm yours, I'm yours!"—either in the love scene or in the finale. At this moment, Rimsky-Korsakov briefly abandons the literal approach he has followed throughout the opera, inserting his own text in order to make this musical reminiscence work. (See Examples 5 and 6.) Juxtaposing the music from the prologue with that from the love duet, Snegurochka's final aria telegraphs an internal, emotional process that we have watched unfold throughout the opera. Although the plot has constantly insisted that Snegurochka cannot feel, her music, summarized and synthesized here in this aria, has constantly insisted otherwise. Her personal faults discharged, her difference from the villagers all but erased, and her feelings magnified and foregrounded, this daughter of Frost and Spring becomes the most human character in the opera. Snegurochka's final aria, the apotheosis of her intensely human experience, is affecting in a way the corresponding passage in Ostrovsky could never hope to be. "[Snegurochka's] little love-death," writes Taruskin, "is among the most touching pages in the repertory."[53]

*Snegurochka* does not quite end with the heroine's death, however. After Snegurochka melts, Mizgir rushes into the sea, Tsar Berendey announces the end of wintry weather, and the chorus sings Yarilo's praises in 11/4 time. The moral of Ostrovsky's "Spring Fairy Tale" was nearly identical to that of Rimsky's first opera, *Pskovityanka*—just as Pskov must yield to Moscow, so must winter yield to summer. The death of the snow maiden, like that of Olga, the maid of Pskov, is justified by necessity, for the progress of nature is no less sure than that of history. But neither Olga Ivanovna nor Ostrovsky's snow maiden had sung a love-death. Ostrovsky's Snegurochka was ever a stranger in paradise, an inexpressive threat to the Berendeyans' nostalgic utopia. In the play, Tsar Berendey's line after her death ("Snegurochka's

Example 5. Love duet.

Example 6a. Final aria; reprise of Snegurochka's arietta from the prologue.

Example 6b. Final aria; reprise of love duet theme.

sad end . . . cannot trouble us . . . for with her miraculous end, Frost's interference has ceased") is merely a statement of fact. In the opera the tsar's remarks—coming, as they do, on the heels of one of the most remarkable arias in all of Russian opera—appear uncharacteristically heartless. Of *course* Snegurochka's sad end troubles us. The Soviet musicologist Boris Asafyev wrote:

> If in the opera Tsar Berendey, as a hierophant and priest of the god of the Sun, announces that neither the sad passing of Snow-Maiden nor the demise of Mizgir should disturb anyone; and if the magnificent ritualized final chorus praises mightily the coming of the spring, all of this will still not deceive the listener: the mournful tale of the life and death of the girlish Snow-Maiden . . . cannot fail to produce such a deep and lasting impression, so that no sort of triumphant ritual and no amount of conviction that all comes to pass as it must and is taking its proper place can convince us as to the justice in the Sun's retribution, of the necessity of the summer's coming. . . . We *grieve* for Snow-Maiden.[54]

Abram Gozenpud pithily concurs: "Nothing following the death of Snegurochka can compare with this arioso."[55] Ostrovsky's finale had asserted the justice of a fixed, deterministic system; Rimsky-Korsakov's shifted the emphasis to feeling. The change was fitting: after all, in an opera that has been called dramatically "dead,"[56] in which human events are tied to the natural cycle of seasons rather than the forward motion of history, Snegurochka's emotional development—her "struggle for individuality," her desire to experience *all* of human feeling—constitutes the only form of what might be called "progress."

In his adaptation of *Snegurochka*, Rimsky-Korsakov united an idealized vision of the past with the progress of private, inner feeling. The connection between the peasant village and individual (rather than collective or national) feeling was hardly an inevitable one. Glinka's heroic villager Ivan Susanin had been a self-abnegating representative of his class and nation; in *The Rite of Spring* the prehistoric village is a profoundly *anti*-psychological place. But the little cluster of themes *Snegurochka* presents—harmonious communal ritual, agrarian prehistory, the development of individual feeling—is a veritable cocktail of 1870s populism, as expressed by the movement's most important thinker, Nikolai Mikhailovsky. Modest Musorgsky, Rimsky-Korsakov's eternal antipode, is the Russian composer to whom the label "populist" is more often applied, but the overwhelming aroma of fatalism and futility that pervades his *Khovanshchina* is the very furthest thing from a populist worldview according to the nineteenth-century meaning of the term. Musorgsky's opera *Marriage*, brazenly innovative and quasi-scientific in its use of speech rhythms, was perhaps the quintessential musical product of the 1860s. But Rimsky-Korsakov's *Snegurochka*—utopian, nostalgic, and sympathetic—reflects far more closely the thinking and the preoccupations of Russian society in the next decade.

## A Man of the Seventies

Mikhailovsky's biography shares certain contours with Rimsky-Korsakov's. The critic and the composer were born sixteen months apart to military families in provincial towns; both moved to Petersburg as teenagers and called that city home for the rest of their lives; both became members, and then elder statesmen, of prominent artistic and intellectual circles within the city. Both, too, died of angina in the first decade of the twentieth century—an era that would not be kind to the reputation of either. Rimsky-Korsakov would become, in Taruskin's only mild hyperbole, "perhaps the most underrated composer of all time," a craftsman known for doing "trivial things superlatively well."[57] As for Mikhailovsky, his influence at the end of his life may be observed—and his subsequent obscurity explained—by the fact that Lenin began his career by attacking him. Lenin's first major foray into print was a lengthy diatribe against Mikhailovsky titled *What the "Friends of the People" Are and How They Fight Against the Social Democrats* (1894), which accused the populist writer of, among other things, "giv[ing] us nothing but examples of bourgeois banality."[58] (The word *bourgeois*, incidentally, is not an infrequent fixture among criticism of Rimsky-Korsakov.) Twenty years later, Lenin was still at it: "The tenth anniversary of the death of N. K. Mikhailovsky (who died on 28 January 1904) was marked by a spate of laudatory articles . . . but one cannot help protesting against the flagrant distortion of the truth and the corruption of proletarian class-consciousness when attempts are made to pass Mikhailovsky off as a socialist. . . . Mikhailovsky's views were *bourgeois-democratic* views veiled by quasi-socialist phrases. Such were his 'progress formula,' his 'struggle for individuality' theory and so on."[59] At the heart of Lenin's critique is a polemic about the nature of socialism, for the kind Mikhailovsky had advocated—incremental and non-revolutionary, concerned with the subjective and individual over the objective and collective, agrarian and nostalgic rather than industrial and futuristic—was antithetical, and threatening, to Lenin's socialist ideal.

What of Rimsky-Korsakov's own politics? A lifelong partisan of the left, he became a reluctant symbol of resistance during the 1905 revolution, when he temporarily lost his position at the conservatory after writing a letter in support of the striking students. Liberal Petersburgers flocked to V. F. Komissarzhevskaya's private theater, where Rimsky-Korsakov's *Kashchei the Immortal (An Autumn Fairy Tale)*—which conspicuously echoes *Snegurochka (A Spring Fairy Tale)* in both plot and subtitle—was read as an anti-tsarist parable.[60] Rimsky-Korsakov, who had foreseen no such interpretation, found his lionization as revolutionary hero embarrassing and overblown, though he did remark to his would-be Boswell, Vasili Yastrebtsev, that his political views of late had become a "vivid red."[61] Even at that stormy time, there is reason to think that Rimsky-Korsakov's preferred ruddy hue probably ran more toward Mikhailovskian burgundy than Leninish scarlet. No revolutionary by nature, he had at first tried to forestall the conservatory strikes by acting as a liaison between the students and the administration. In early 1906 he hosted a lecture by Razumnik Ivanov-Razumnik, a disciple of Mikhailovsky's and a friend of Andrei Rimsky-Korsakov, the composer's son.[62] But in general, Rimsky-Korsakov was highly circumspect about his views on topics other than music. His memoirs are invaluable in so many ways, but their title—*My Musical Life*—is accurate; they give little hint of Rimsky-Korsakov the private individual. As his bemused reaction to the reception of *Kashchei* shows, there is a special kind of folly in confusing art with politics, and likewise in assuming that a work of art must reflect the sincerely held views of its creator. Rimsky left no record of his thoughts on the populist movement, nor any indication that he had even read Lavrov or Mikhailovsky—though he was an avid reader and they would have been difficult to miss. He certainly did not share the delusions of the most starry-eyed populists, who believed their utopian ideals not only could, but imminently would, become reality. "The Berendeyans," he remarked to Yastrebtsev many years later, "may make a worthwhile theme for music, but if such people existed in reality, what nonsense that would be."[63] Nonsense, perhaps, is an inevitable component of any utopia.

Nevertheless, the unmistakably "populist" flavor of *Snegurochka* might give us cause to reevaluate two common and contradictory images of Rimsky-Korsakov. The first is that of Rimsky as the ultimate trivialist, a purveyor of picturesque fairy tales and music-box exotica that had nothing to do with the social and intellectual concerns of nineteenth-century Russian life. This image of the composer has a lengthy history in the West.

"Though the music is the loveliest of picture-books," wrote the American critic Paul Rosenfeld in 1918, "it is nothing more. It is as if Rimsky-Korsakov had ignored the other and larger functions of his art, and been content to have his music only picturesque and colorful; as if the childish Czar in 'Le Coq d'Or,' who desires only to lie abed all day, eat delicate food, and listen to the fairy tales of his nurse, had been something of a portrait of its composer."[64] This aesthete with Oblomovitis could hardly be further from the vision offered by the Soviet musicologist Abram Gozenpud, who characterized Rimsky-Korsakov as an inveterate "man of the sixties." Contesting Rimsky-Korsakov's claims that his interest in *Snegurochka* marked a retreat from the "ideals of the sixties," Gozenpud writes: "If we accept that Rimsky-Korsakov could be attracted to Ostrovsky's play only after abandoning the ideals of the sixties, then we must . . . count all of the composer's works of the succeeding period as somehow foreign to the tradition of the 'mighty kuchka.' . . . The ideas of the sixties, the principles of realism and the creative example of Musorgsky never lost their magnetic significance for Rimsky-Korsakov."[65] The American historian Lynn Sargeant has written more recently: "Rimsky-Korsakov was a true *shestidesyatnik*—a man of the sixties."[66]

The period known as the sixties, which spanned the years 1855 to 1866, was dominated by uncompromising rhetoric, the rejection of tradition, an unwavering faith in objective scientific laws, and the absolute primacy of utility over aesthetics. Rimsky-Korsakov, the youngest kuchkist by half a decade, was eleven years old when the sixties began. The decade that proved most formative for him would be the next one, a time when Russians struggled to reconcile the traditional with the innovative, the scientific with the subjective, the real with the beautiful. These dynamics would play out in Rimsky-Korsakov's creative endeavors for the rest of his life. For he was a true *semidesyatnik*—Russian music's most characteristic man of the seventies.

# NOTES

1. Nikolay Rimskiy-Korsakov, *Polnoye sobraniye sochineniy*, vol. 2 (Moscow: Muzgiz, 1963), 14–15. Rimsky's uncharacteristically scathing review of Eduard Nápravník's opera *Nizhegorodtsï* forever spoiled his relationship with Nápravník—who had just been appointed chief conductor of the Mariinsky and would oversee the premieres of Rimsky's first five operas.

2. Richard Taruskin, *Opera and Drama in Russia as Preached and Practiced in the 1860s* (Ann Arbor: UMI Research Press, 1981), 200.

3. Nikolay Rimsky-Korsakov, *My Musical Life*, ed. Carl Van Vechten, trans. Judah A. Joffe (New York: Alfred A. Knopf, 1942), 228.

4. Richard Taruskin, *Defining Russia Musically: Historical and Hermeneutical Essays* (Princeton: Princeton University Press, 1997), 84.

5. Rimsky's autobiography reports that in 1875–76, "I read some descriptions and essays on this [ceremonial] side of folk-life by Sakharov, Tereshchenko, Sheyn, and Afanasev, for instance; was captivated by the poetic side of the cult of sun-worship, and sought its survivals and echoes in both the tunes and the words of the songs." Rimsky-Korsakov, *My Musical Life*, 165–66.

6. James Billington sums up the main tenets distinguishing Proudhon's socialism from Marx's: "1. The belief that the final appeal for socialism must be based on subjective choice and moral ideals rather than objective necessity and material facts. 2. The conviction that socialism opposed the institution of the state and should not work through political institutions even as a temporary expedient." James H. Billington, *Mikhailovsky and Russian Populism* (Oxford: Clarendon Press, 1958), 65. For a discussion of Proudhon's influence on Russian populist thought, see Billington, *Fire in the Minds of Men: Origins of the Revolutionary Faith*, 2nd ed. (New Brunswick and London: Transaction, 1980), 303–6.

7. See the chapter "A Social Philosophy," in Billington, *Mikhailovsky and Russian Populism*, 42–52.

8. "In a word," wrote Pisarev, "organic life is unthinkable without the constant, every-minute destruction of living beings. Organic life is an eternal struggle between living beings. . . . This struggle cannot stop for even a moment, for every step in life is an act of struggle." Dmitriy Ivanovich Pisarev, "Progress v mire zhivotnïkh i rasteniy," in *Polnoye sobranie sochineniy i pisem v dvenadtsati tomakh*, vol. 6 (Moscow: Nauka, 2003), 35. Populists such as Nikolai Nozhin (trained as a biologist!) and Nikolai Mikhailovsky rejected what they saw as the overextension of Darwin's theories, placing their emphasis on cooperation (the Proudhonian idea of *mutualité*) rather than competition and struggle. For a history of Darwin reception in Russia, see James Allen Rogers, "The Russian Populists' Response to Darwin," *Slavic Review* 22/3 (September 1963): 456–68; and Daniel P. Todes, *Darwin Without Malthus: The Struggle for Existence in Russian Evolutionary Thought* (New York and Oxford: Oxford University Press, 1989).

9. For a critical biography of Lavrov, see Philip Pomper, *Peter Lavrov and the Russian Revolutionary Movement* (Chicago: University of Chicago Press, 1972).

10. Peter Lavrov, *Historical Letters*, trans. James P. Scanlan (Berkeley and Los Angeles: University of California Press, 1967), 135–36.

11. This approaches the main point of contention of a famous debate of the 1870s between the followers of Lavrov, who believed that revolution had to be a gradual process, preceded and prepared for by the spread of education, and those of Mikhail Bakunin, who believed that revolution should be instigated immediately as the people did not need enlightening about their own interests. For more on this topic, see Franco Venturi, *Roots of Revolution: A History of the Populist and Socialist Movements in Nineteenth-Century Russia*, trans. Francis Haskell (London: Weidenfeld & Nicolson, 1960), 565–67.

12. The future revolutionary Nikolai Rusanov recalled his youthful encounter with Lavrov's *Historical Letters*: "At one time we had been attracted to Pisarev, who told us of the great utility of the natural sciences in making a 'thinking realist' out of men. . . . And suddenly [Lavrov's] little book tells us that there are other things besides the natural sciences. . . . There are the people, the hungry masses, worn out by labor, the working people who themselves support the whole edifice of civilization solely to make it possible for us to study frog. . . . Henceforth our lives must belong wholly to the masses, and only by dedicating all our strength to the triumph of social justice could we appear anything but fraudulent bankrupts before our country and before all mankind." Cited in Joseph Frank, *Dostoevsky: The Mantle of the Prophet, 1871–1881* (Princeton: Princeton University Press, 2002), 69–70.

13. The term "struggle for individuality" comes from Mikhailovsky's 1875 essay of the same name, which like most of Mikhailovsky's works has not been translated into English. See "Bor'ba za individual'nost'," in Nikolay Konstantinovich Mikhaylovskiy, *Geroi i tolpa: Izbrannïye trudï po sotsiologii v dvukh tomakh*, ed. V. V. Kozlovskiy, vol. 2 (St. Petersburg: Aleteyia, 1998), 229–67. Mikhailovsky developed his ideas on personality still further in 1877's "Letters on Truth and Falsehood" (*Pis'ma o pravde i nepravde*) and 1878's "The Utopia of Renan and the Theory of Personality of Duehring" (*Utopiya Renana i teoriya avtonomii lichnosti Dyuringa*). For a discussion of these works, see Billington, *Mikhailovsky and Russian Populism*, 97.

14. See esp. Chernyshevsky's "The Anthropological Principle in Philosophy," in *Selected Philosophical Essays* (Moscow: Foreign Languages Publishing House, 1953), 49–135.

15. Quoted in Billington, *Mikhailovsky and Russian Populism*, 97.

16. Nikolay Mikhailovsky, "What Is Progress?" in James M. Edie, James P. Scanlan, and Mary-Barbara Zeldin, eds., *Russian Philosophy* (Knoxville: University of Tennessee Press, 1976), 2:187.

17. Mikhailovsky, anti-Hegelian in so many other respects, still divided history into three stages: the "objectively anthropocentric," the "eccentric," and the "subjectively anthropocentric." The first stage represented a good type of society at a low level of development (for example, the Russian peasant village), the second a poor type of society at a high level of development (the Europe of Darwin and Offenbach), and the third a good type of society at a high level of development (the ideal Russian society of the future). There was little sense of teleology to this vision; he believed that movement from one stage to the next was not inevitable and that a society could (and in Russia's case should) move directly from the "objectively anthropocentric" to the "subjectively anthropocentric" phase without any "eccentric detours." See "Teoriya Darvina i obshchestvennaya nauka," in Nikolay Konstantinovich Mikhaylovskiy, *Sochineniya N. K. Mikhaylovskogo* (St. Petersburg: B. M. Vol'f, 1896), 1:165–348.

18. The tinge of Slavophilia is unmistakable here—but the harmonious and egalitarian ethos of the idealized peasant village was put to different purposes by Mikhailovsky, who saw in it an embryo of socialism, and the Slavophiles and "men of the soil" (*pochvenniki*) of earlier decades, who saw in it a model of Christian virtue and love of tsar, the embodiment of God on earth.

19. Richard Wortman, *The Crisis of Russian Populism* (Cambridge and New York: Cambridge University Press, 1967).

20. N. K. Mikhaylovskiy, "O Shillere i o mnogom drugom," in *Sochineniya N. K. Mikhaylovskogo* (St. Petersburg: B.M. Vol'f, 1897), 3:709–738; quote from 722.

21. Ibid., 720–21.

22. Vladimir Ily'ich Lenin, *Collected Works*, vol. 1 (Moscow: Foreign Languages Publishing House, 1963), 501.

23. Billington, *Mikhailovsky and Russian Populism*, 82.

24. In Nikolay Alekseyevich Nekrasov, *Perepiska N. A. Nekrasova*, ed. N. M. Fortunatov, G. V. Krasnov, and V. A. Viktorovich, vol. 2 (Moscow: Khudozhestvennaya literatura, 1987), 130.

25. The entire exchange between Ostrovsky and Nekrasov regarding *Snegurochka* can be found in ibid., 2:129–32.

26. Two versions of the Snegurochka tale appear in Afanasev's *Russkiye narodnïye skazki*. In his dissertation on *Snegurochka*, Gregory Halbe identifies two other published sources of the snow maiden tale that were likely known to Ostrovsky: the first a version published in the journal *Moskvityanin*, on whose board Ostrovsky served as editor, and the other in a collection by M. Maksimovich, a book that was owned by both Ostrovsky and Rimsky-Korsakov. See Gregory A. Halbe, "Music, Drama and Folklore in Nikolai Rimsky-Korsakov's Opera *Snegurochka* [Snowmaiden]" (PhD diss., Ohio State University, 2004), 43.

27. Rimsky-Korsakov, *My Musical Life*, 228.

28. Abram Gozenpud notes that Ostrovsky was not the only Russian artist whose folklore-based works were received with ambivalence in the 1870s: "The creative embodiment of folkloric themes did not take root immediately or easily in Russian art. It is enough to recall the failures of Repin (the painting *Sadko*, 1876) or of A. K. Tolstoy (the popular ballad of the same name). By the end of the 1870s and beginning of the 1880s, artistic interpretations of Russian folklore had accumulated in the nation's art." Abram Gozenpud, *N. A. Rimskiy-Korsakov: Temï i idei yego opernogo tvorchestva* (Moscow: Gosudarstvennoye muzïkal'noye izdatel'stvo, 1957), 46.

29. To opera fans, the most familiar representative of the *samodur* type may be Boris Izmailov, the tyrannical father-in-law in Shostakovich's *Lady Macbeth of Mtsensk*. Shostakovich based his opera on an 1865 novella by Nikolai Leskov, but it was Ostrovsky who had made the type famous in his plays of the 1850s. The nineteenth-century Russian critic Nikolai Dobrolyubov discussed the *samodur* at length in his seminal articles on Ostrovsky. See "Tyomnoye tsarstvo" (1859) and "Luch sveta v tyomnom tsarstve" (1860), in Nikolay Aleksandrovich Dobrolyubov, *Russkiye klassiki: Izbrannïye literaturno-kriticheskiye stat'yi*, ed. Yu.G. Oksman (Moscow: Izdatel'stvo Nauka, 1970), 70–188 and 231-300. To Dobrolyubov, samodurism was both the root and the hallmark of the "dark kingdom" that was contemporary life among the Russian merchant class.

30. "Dostoyna smertnoy kazni / vina yego; no v nashem ulozhen'ye / krovavïkh net zakonov."

31. V. A. Koshelev has recently described the world of *Snegurochka* as a "prehistoric future" (*doistoricheskoye budushcheye*), a term that nicely captures the simultaneous dynamics of nostalgia and messianism that characterize both Ostrovsky's play and 1870s thought more generally. Koshelev argues that the "Russian utopia" of the Berendey village does not meet Rousseauian standards of a utopia, given that socioeconomic equality in the village is not absolute. See Vyacheslav Anatolyevich Koshelev, "Budushcheye 'do istorii': *Snegurochka* A. N. Ostrovskogo," in *Budushcheye kak syuzhet*, ed. S. A. Vasily'eva et al. (Tver': Izdatel'stvo Marinï Batasovoy, 2014), 222–31. I'd argue that the more apt comparison is not with the eighteenth-century Genevan but with Ostrovsky himself: *Snegurochka*'s "prehistoric future" is immeasurably more equitable and humane than the contemporary Russia of Ostrovsky's earlier works.

32. This revision was not a success—Taruskin writes of it that "pedant definitely had upper hand over master"—and Rimsky would revise this work again, and again, in later decades. The standard performing edition is now the fourth, completed in 1901. Richard Taruskin, "The Case for Rimsky-Korsakov," in *On Russian Music* (Berkeley and Los Angeles: University of California Press, 2008), 168.

33. This intimate acquaintance with Glinka left obvious marks on *Snegurochka*, not least in the unconventional voice typing, which pairs a chirpy soubrette with a baritone

and a throatier lyric soprano with an alto *en travesti*, just as Glinka had done in *Ruslan*. Though the role of Snegurochka has long been the province of Liudmila-like soubrettes and coloraturas, the original Snegurochka, Feodosia Velinskaia, was described as having a heavier and more powerful voice. See Juliet Forshaw, "Dangerous Tenors, Heroic Basses, and Non-Ingénues: Singers and the Envoicing of Social Values in Russian Opera, 1836–1905," (PhD diss., Columbia University, 2014), 207n75. However, Rimsky-Korsakov's vocal writing for the character—fast-moving and staccato, with a high tessitura and frequent high Bs—suggests that he had a lighter, more "Glinkan" voice in mind. Snegurochka's vocal line looks much less like that of the role Rimsky wrote for Velinskaia in 1879's *May Night* (the wailing mermaid Pannochka) than those he later wrote for the coloratura Nadezhda Zabela in his operas of the Silver Age, such as Marfa in *The Tsar's Bride* and the Swan Princess in *The Tale of Tsar Saltan*.

34. Rimsky-Korsakov, *My Musical Life*, 207–8.

35. Ibid., 228.

36. Tchaikovsky provided the incidental music for the Moscow production of *Snegurochka* in 1874, though Rimsky-Korsakov neither attended that production nor, apparently, consulted Tchaikovsky's score while composing his own *Snegurochka*. This would not be the last time Rimsky-Korsakov pilfered an operatic plot from his Moscow rival. Rimsky's *Christmas Eve*, which he began composing not long after Tchaikovsky's death, was based on the Gogol story that had served as the basis of Tchaikovsky's *Vakula the Smith* (and its revised version, *Cherevichki*).

37. The vogue for self-fashioned librettos was not limited to the former members of the Kuchka; even Tchaikovsky tried his hand at libretto adaptation with 1879's *The Maid of Orleans*. The process was a painful one, as he wrote to Nadezhda von Meck: "I am very well pleased with my musical work [on *The Maid of Orleans*]. As regards the literary side of it, I believe it will cost me some days of my life. I cannot describe how it exhausts me. How many penholders I gnaw to pieces before a few lines grow perfect! How often I jump up in sheer despair because I cannot find a rhyme, or the metre goes wrong, or because I have absolutely no notion of what this or that character would say at a particular moment!" Tchaikovsky to von Meck, January 1879, in Modeste Tchaikovsky, *The Life & Letters of Peter Ilich Tchaikovsky*, ed. Rosa Newmarch (London: J. Lane, 1906), 331.

38. Richard Taruskin, "*Snow Maiden, The*," *Grove Music Online*, n.d. http://www.oxfordmusiconline.com/grovemusic/view/10.1093/gmo/9781561592630.001.0001/omo-9781561592630-e-5000009827.

39. The critic Semyon Kruglikov, a former student of Rimsky-Korsakov's who delivered the libretto and vocal score of *Snegurochka* to Ostrovsky, wrote to his teacher of Ostrovsky's surprise that the Maslenitsa effigy, a part of the Shrovetide ritual, had made it into the opera. Kruglikov to Rimsky-Korsakov, 3 November 1880, in Nikolay Andreyevich Rimskiy-Korsakov, *Polnoye sobraniye sochineniy: Literaturnïye proizvedeniya i perepiska*, vol. 8a (Moscow: Gosudarstvennoye Muzïkal'noe Izdatel'stvo, 1981), 57.

40. Rimsky-Korsakov, *My Musical Life*, 238. Rimsky discusses his use of folk and other borrowed material, such as bird calls in ibid., 236–38. Nina Bachinskaya has published a more thorough account in *Narodnïye pesni v tvorchestve russkikh kompozitorov*, ed. E. V. Gippius (Moscow: Muzgiz, 1962). Beyond the ceremonial numbers and a few isolated phrases here and there, the only other place in which *Snegurochka* quotes folk music is in the horn calls of the shepherd Lel.

41. In Russian opera, to my knowledge, the only other tenor role that combines advanced age with advanced rank is that of Kashchei from Rimsky's own *Kashchei the Immortal* (1902), a work whose subtitle "An Autumn Fairy Tale" seems a deliberate reference to *Snegurochka*'s own "A Spring Fairy Tale." At the outsets of their respective operas, both Berendey and Kashchei are the immortal rulers of gloomy kingdoms, and so the voice

typing in the later opera may well be a reference to that in the earlier one. Kashchei, a familiar villain from Russian fairy tales, quickly proves the benevolent Berendey's evil twin.

42. Had Rimsky wanted a lower voice for the tsar, Stravinsky could have easily (and economically) pulled double duty as Ded Moroz and Berendey, for the former appears only in the prologue and the latter not until Act 2. As for Mizgir, Rimsky-Korsakov certainly had justification for denying him the tenor voice that would seem to be his birthright. Mizgir quickly distinguishes himself as perhaps the most unattractive "lover" in all of opera: he betrays one woman and attempts to possess another by force, despite knowing nothing of the latter but her beauty. In Rimsky's later *Tsar's Bride* (1899), this very same behavior earns Grigory Gryaznoy an antihero's mantle—and even Gryaznoy, the brutal henchman (*oprichnik*) of Ivan the Terrible, expresses pity on seeing the tears of the woman he has abandoned. Mizgir, however, has only insults for his cast-off fiancée. Later, when Snegurochka declares her love and begs him to carry her away from the sun's fatal rays, Mizgir refuses with this rather incredible declaration: "You're used to governing submissive hearts, but I am no boy. I am ready to love and to command: stay!" Unlike with Snegurochka, Rimsky-Korsakov made little attempt to mitigate the rougher qualities of Ostrovsky's Mizgir. Perhaps he was beyond mitigation—Mizgir is an *oprichnik* in a merchant's cloak.

43. Gerald Abraham, *On Russian Music* (London: William Reeves, 1939), 127.

44. Quoted in Nikolay Pavlovich Kashin, "Snegurochka: Vesennyaya skazka v 4-kh deystvyakh s prologom (opyt izucheniya)," in *A. S. Pushkin, A. N. Ostrovskiy, zapadniki i slavyanofilï*, ed. N. L. Meshcheryakov, Sbornik IV (Moscow: Sotsial'no-ekonomicheskoye izdatel'stvo, 1939), 97.

45. For example, early in the play, Kupava's father flatly remarks that "Snegurochka doesn't resemble our women and girls" (Ne pokhozha / Snegurochka na nashikh bab i devok). Act 1, scene 1.

46. "A parni nashi / S uma soshli; oravami, stadami / Bez pamyati kidalis' za toboj, / Pokinuli nevest, perebranilis', / Peredralis' iz-za tebya." Act 1, scene 1.

47. While Kupava's first words to Snegurochka, "Snegurochka, you're standing all alone, poor thing!" (Snegurochka, odna stoish', bednyazhka!), are identical in the opera and the play, the reasons for her loneliness are different. In the opera, she is standing alone because Lel has just run off, whereas in the play, she is alone because the village youths have been arguing over the boys' infatuation with her. Act 1, scene 5.

48. Act 2, scene 1.

49. "Takogo dela / Ne slïkhano u chestnïkh berendeyev." Act 2, scene 8.

50. In the opera, the only mention of this situation is in a fleeting reference by Bermyata in Act 2: "The boys have all fought over her, and the brides-to-be have lashed out at their fiancés." But as we do not hear these lines until after Mizgir has left Kupava (in the play, the village couples' breakups are mentioned throughout Act 1), and as we have seen no other evidence that multiple couples have parted ways over Snegurochka, it is easy to interpret Bermyata's remarks as a reference to Mizgir and Kupava, magnified through hearsay.

51. "Snegurochka, da chem zhe / Vstrecha' tebe voskhod Yarila-Solntsa? / . . . i zapon, i kotï / Novyokhon'ki,—tebe odna zabota / Kak glupomu rebyonku, lyubova'sya / Na svoy naryad." Act 3, scene 7.

52. Marfa's concluding scene from 1899's *The Tsar's Bride*—a descendant of Snegurochka's "love-death" that is even more stunning than its predecessor—repeats this device, with a solo instrument (in this case, the clarinet) "singing" the melody of the heroine's first aria.

53. Taruskin, *On Russian Music*, 177.

54. Boris Asafyev, *Symphonic Etudes: Portraits of Russian Operas and Ballets*, ed. and trans. David Haas (Lanham, MD, Toronto, and Plymouth, UK: Scarecrow Press, 2008), 64.

55. Gozenpud, *N. A. Rimskiy-Korsakov: Temï i idei yego opernogo tvorchestva*, 47.

56. Rimsky-Korsakov recalled that when he submitted *Snegurochka* to the Imperial Theatres Directorate for consideration, "Nápravník hemmed and hawed for a long time, but said in the end that, owing to the absence of dramatic action, this was a 'dead' opera and could not be successful; however, he had nothing against its being produced." Rimsky-Korsakov, *My Musical Life*, 250.

57. Taruskin, *On Russian Music*, 166, 177.

58. Lenin, *Collected Works*, 1963, 1:155.

59. Vladimir Ily'ich Lenin, *Collected Works*, vol. 20 (Moscow: Foreign Languages Publishing House, 1972), 117–18.

60. For more on these events, see Lynn M. Sargeant, *Harmony and Discord: Music and the Transformation of Russian Cultural Life* (New York: Oxford University Press, 2011), 237–50.

61. V. V. Yastrebtsev, *Reminiscences of Rimsky-Korsakov*, ed. and trans. Florence Jonas (New York: Columbia University Press, 1985), 351.

62. Ibid., 383.

63. Quoted in Gozenpud, *N. A. Rimskiy-Korsakov: Temï i idei yego opernogo tvorchestva*, 47.

64. Paul Rosenfeld, "Rimsky-Korsakov," *The Dial* 64 (1918): 279.

65. Gozenpud, *N. A. Rimskiy-Korsakov: Temï i idei yego opernogo tvorchestva*, 44.

66. Sargeant, *Harmony and Discord: Music and the Transformation of Russian Cultural Life*, 243.

# "You, Mozart, Aren't Worthy of Yourself": Aesthetic Discontents of Rimsky-Korsakov's *Mozart and Salieri*

ANNA NISNEVICH

*To the memory of Wye J. Allanbrook*

"The news printed in newspapers that I have written 39 romances and the opera *Mozart and Salieri* is completely fake," Nikolai Rimsky-Korsakov wrote to his friend music critic Semyon Kruglikov in September 1897 apropos his creative production that summer. "For I have written 40 romances, 2 vocal duets, *Mozart and Salieri*, the cantata *Svitezianka* for soprano, tenor and choir with orchestra, and, on top of it, a trio for piano, violin and cello."[1] This victorious, tongue-in-cheek passage has backed many a scholarly claim about the flourishing of Rimsky-Korsakov's creativity in the late 1890s as a result of the final, definitive integration of the composer's artistic and academic personae.[2] Well ensconced institutionally yet once again full of creative vigor, the fifty-three-year-old Rimsky-Korsakov emerges in these accounts as reaching the prime of his life—or what he would later identify in his memoir as the start of his "third period," a sure proof (in the best tradition of the three-period romantic biography) of creative maturity.[3]

The scholars are less certain, however, about the merits of the first major substantiation of this creative surge, Rimsky-Korsakov's opera *Mozart and Salieri*, after Alexander Pushkin's 1830 "little tragedy." Tense, aphoristic, thick with psychological contrast rather than making the most of the drawn-out mirth (more customary for the composer), and dealing with denizens of Western music history instead of dwellers of Russian mythology, this one-act wonder has long been treated as an aberration in Rimsky-Korsakov's rich operatic output. Staunchly labeled an "experiment"—owing perhaps as much to the opera's genealogy as to the composer's own designation in his later memoir—his *Mozart* figures even in differing scholarly narratives as perched uneasily between the spirited nationalist(-realist) works of Rimsky-Korsakov's Kuchka period and the searching eclectic oeuvre of his fin-de-siècle phase.[4] Indeed (as those stories go), this nearly word-by-word setting of Pushkin's brief blank-verse drama is well in tune with Russian musical realists' 1860s experiments in the genre dubbed by Modest Musorgsky as *opéra dialogué*, a through-composed musical approximation of a preexistent literary text of proven value. But the persistence in *Mozart* of dotingly, studiously resuscitated eighteenth-century musical styles also points to a resolute break with the Kuchka's ideals of empirical truth, difference, and spontaneity. Aesthetically speaking, this work invites historical readings just as readily as it subverts them.

Musicologists tend to disagree on the precise import of this incongruence. Branding *Mozart* a "progeny" of the Kuchka's once-radical genre, Richard Taruskin, for instance, charges the opera with promoting "an academically tinctured distillate" that "impoverish[es] the genre to the point of futility"—thus sounding, as it were, a death knell for Russian musical reformism.[5] Marina Frolova-Walker, on the contrary, hails "the stirrings of Rimsky-Korsakov's neoclassical ambitions" as a welcome deliverance from the "rusty chains" of the Kuchka's now-stale realism and nationalism.[6] In his more recent *History of Russian Music*, Francis Maes circumvents the contradiction by placing *Mozart* in the section handily titled "Continuation of, and Detachment from, the *Kuchka* Ideal."[7] But whatever the adjudication, its grounds stay largely the same: that this opera succeeds in catching the scholarly eye only as a critical link in a chain of stylistic and ideational transformations—either as an exhauster of one artistic stance or as a foreshadower of another.[8]

But having a slot in style-historical lineage explains little about *Mozart*'s strangeness or the opera's role in kindling the fire strong enough to sustain the last, most productive decade of Rimsky-Korsakov's creative life. A different kind of optics might also be needed to tackle this work's peculiarity, one allowing for angles other than those of genre and national style.[9] This essay probes one such field of vision: *Mozart*'s place in Rimsky-Korsakov's conflicted thought on giftedness and creativity. Engaging with Pushkin's by-then already well-known literary dramatization of the myth of Salieri's envy and subsequent poisoning of Mozart, the composer joined in a debate that went beyond musical factionalism or matters of operatic technique. For, to choose to take on the lines that rendered Salieri a self-appointed high priest of music resentful of Mozart's effortless composition meant to try to wrestle with such big existential questions as the purpose of artistry, the paths of ingenuity, and, perhaps most important, the limits of an artist's moral compass. With *Mozart* Rimsky-Korsakov was compelled to interrogate directly, for the first (and last) time in his life, in the aural flesh, the very core of his professional being, and so query the very grounds of composerly worthiness.[10] A closer look at the terms of that interrogation might yield a finer grasp of how the aging composer, caught in a vortex of professional as well as social crises, succeeded in turning his anxieties into a steady stream of creative production.

## Mozart's Worth

A few lines into Pushkin's "little tragedy" *Mozart and Salieri*, Salieri, having mused on his great love for music, his learnedness, and his hard-earned fame, confesses—to himself and so to the reader—his own deep, toe-curling envy. He is repulsed by his emotion, but sickened even more by what he sees as the undue allocation of artistic facility. "Where is justice," he asks grandiloquently, "when holy gift, eternal genius / is given not to reward the burning love, self-sacrifice, hard work and zealous prayer / but lights instead the head of a madman, / a shallow idler? Oh Mozart, Mozart!" With these last words Mozart enters, as if called up by Salieri's exasperated inquest. "Aha!" he shouts. "You saw me! / And I was hoping to treat you to an unexpected joke."[11]

Salieri's meetings with Mozart in the play's two scenes only strengthen his paradoxical conviction that the all-too-earthly composer is not worthy of his own heavenly music. Pitted against the ever-brooding Salieri, Pushkin's Mozart is largely bereft of self-reflection, neither soliloquizing nor taking a lead in conversation. His task is mostly to respond, refract Salieri's thoughts, words, and deeds, whether offsetting Salieri's affected "Oh!" with a plain "Aha!" or sharing a worry that foretells the outcome of Salieri's dark ruse. Hardly articulate, this Mozart is even less arty. He readily punctures Salieri's ecstatic "You, Mozart, are a god, and you don't even know it—/ I know, I!" with "Bah, really? This may be so, / but my divinity is getting hungry." This guileless declaration seems to confirm Salieri's view of Mozart as skin-deep, but it also articulates anew Salieri's own profundity. Grasping for the ultimate in aesthetics, little by little Salieri persuades himself that he owns it. Set on a collision course with Mozart's unadorned, jesting vitality, his high-priestly ambition is about to crash.

For hidden behind Pushkin's succinct stage directions is the crucial part of Mozart's role, hardly graspable through mere reading: twice "he plays." The first scene involves a piano improvisation preceded by Mozart's muddled explanation and followed by Salieri's rapturous praise. An excerpt from the Requiem, which Mozart plays to Salieri right after having drunk the poisoned wine, provides the second scene's unheard climax. It is only through Mozart's soft surprise at Salieri's astonishment ("Are you weeping?" he mutters) that we can catch a trace of this impossible music, at once celebrating and mourning its soon-to-be-dead maker. Rather than emitting sound, the auditory void absorbs the shock of recognition. It leaves Salieri both victorious and unfulfilled; thinking worthiness to hinge on a correlation between holy gift and individual virtue, he is caught in his own argument. In the play's final verse, he recaps Mozart's earlier quip, oddly resonant with his belief: "Isn't it true that genius and villainy are two things incompatible?" Now the paradox has sunk in. "What if he is right and I am no genius?" Salieri queries. Having come full circle in self-questioning and self-affirmation, he is left where he started, tortured by doubt, shame, and now possibly guilt.[12]

Its historical inauthenticity aside, Pushkin's play entered Russian cultural consciousness as a major feat, "a great and profound tragedy" that, in the tone-setting words of the prominent critic Vissarion Belinsky, spoke to "the essence as well as mutual relationships of a genius and a talent."[13] "As a mind, a consciousness," Belinsky wrote in 1843, Pushkin's "Salieri is far above [Pushkin's] Mozart, but as a might, a sheer fount of creative energy, he is nothing before [Mozart]."[14] In the next few decades, as the play's lines reemerged in all kinds of public discourse and took on lives of their own, much critical ink was spilled on tackling Belinsky's lopsided dichotomy.[15] Various commentators, fired up by (and further fueling) the already enflamed cult of Mozart in Russia, drew on Pushkin's text to form a shared image of the worthiest kind of high artist.[16] That image, of a sincere, gullible man best observed through a comparison with his strong-willed and cunning counterpart, was as much a reflection of the broader romantic notion of genius as it was of the Mozart myth shaping up overseas.[17] But if Belinsky never quizzed the morality (while admitting the superiority) of Pushkin's Mozart, taking this hero's apparent nonchalance as a dramatic device serving to accentuate his nemesis's angst and resolve, later Russian interpreters discerned correlations between this Mozart's personal qualities and his holy gifts.

More than a few turn-of-the-twentieth-century critics sensed a higher design in this Mozart's lightness of being.[18] It was precisely Mozart's playfulness, his "inspired whimsy," argued philosopher Yuli Aikhenvald, that made him a perfect receptacle of heavenly grace.[19] Philologist Dmitri Ovsianiko-Kulikovsky saw in Mozart's nonchalance a sign of "supreme inner freedom," a sturdy shield, as it were, from the pressures of the social world and thus from the pangs of such "social passions" as envy, avarice, or ill will. This freedom, he explained, sustained Mozart's artistic facility, whereas Salieri's unfreedom, his commitment to his profession alone made *his* music flawed. Unburdened by spite, truly catholic in his appreciation of the world at large, this Mozart couldn't help but reciprocate. His unselfish voraciousness propelled his unmatched creativity, transforming him into that marvel called "a true genius." And who could have been more perceptive about this correlation than Pushkin, himself surely Mozart's closest of kin?[20]

Seeing Mozart and Pushkin as built in the same image became these readings' perhaps most common thread. Two equally radiant makers of art, both prematurely dead, each by the hand of a treacherous friend—even if, in Mozart's case, this was an unsubstantiated rumor—made this shared plot of martyrdom too tempting an analogy not to be passed on. As Monika Greenleaf has suggested, Pushkin himself was also complicit in teaching the Russian public to read his life and art through the lens of Mozart's Christological myth. His *Mozart*, she argues, dramatized the then-nascent cultural practice "by which—to use [Pushkin's] favorite phrase—'inexplicable art' would be reprocessed into readily legible genius."[21] His Salieri the murderer was as indispensable as his Salieri the glorifier because Mozart, with his "unruly creative flow," ought to have been "sacrifice[d] in order to be reborn as a sublime national heritage."[22] Only when guzzled up by the public and abstracted by the burgeoning throng of exegetes—that is, only by ceasing to be a discrete body and becoming a recognizable and unifying plenitude—could this Mozart, whether fictional or historical, persist for posterity as a conduit of the divine. But to extend Greenleaf's analogy, the divine-human transmittance worked both ways, and by the century's end Russia's original Mozart lore had been overlaid with the more recent Pushkin mythology—famously formulated by Dostoevsky as the Russian poet's unmatched, uniquely indigenous gift of "universal responsiveness."[23] That protean gift, having to do with Pushkin's equally sensitive poetic treatment of themes and peoples from diverse lands, spoke first and foremost to the redeeming power of empathy. Reflected back onto Pushkin's Mozart, this familiarly hallowed capacity flaunted the perfect composer as someone who could be as generous a receiver as he was a giver. "Pushkin himself was, of course, a Mozart," an early twentieth-century critic would ascertain, because "[he] always responded like an echo to sounds of contemporaneity."[24] Like many others, that interpreter sought—and found—the crux of creative inspiration in the artist's gullibility, the sort of basic receptiveness that could fittingly be relayed by a keen "Aha!"

It may not then have been a coincidence that it was Mozart's "Aha!" that drew Rimsky-Korsakov to Pushkin's "little tragedy" in the summer of

1897. He started to sketch his future opera with this first Mozart-Salieri exchange, the lively scene playing well into what he felt was the beginning of a new phase of his artistic biography.[25] The milestone involved trying his hand in expressive vocalization by churning out, "one by one," dozens of romances whose "melody germinated before any accompaniment" and "flowed freely" as if "composing itself as it followed the curvatures of the text."[26] Previously, as Rimsky-Korsakov would later explain in his memoir, his songs had perhaps been too cerebral, their melodies more of a function of preplanned instrumental design than a response to poetic cadence or the words' emotional thrust. Now he felt he was delivering more instinctively "true vocal music," one subsisting on poetry while also idiomatically tied to the human voice.[27] Pushkin's play with its prominent characters and proverbial turns of phrase, seemed perfect as a vehicle for applying his newly gained faculty on a larger scale.

As scholars have noted, Rimsky-Korsakov's fresh interest in spontaneous composition had a competitive edge. To set to music an entire play by Pushkin meant to tackle the legacy of the original undertaking of this kind: Alexander Dargomyzhsky's 1860s opera *The Stone Guest*, a word-by-word setting of another famed "little tragedy." That aria-less, recitative- and arioso-driven work was meant deliberately to exemplify an aesthetic of "dramatic truth"—a new, bold kind of musical earnestness, and soon a cornerstone of the Kuchka's realist mission. Although it would remain unfinished by the author, *The Stone Guest* inspired several Kuchka projects, Musorgsky's opera *Boris Godunov* (1868–74) becoming its perhaps highest-flying (although already remote) legatee. But just as the perennial maverick Musorgsky was testing out ever-peculiar forms of declamation to convey his characters' unparaphrasable human traits, his friend Rimsky-Korsakov, a fledgling professor, was drawn to shared, already tested forms of musical communication. Growing ever more distant from the undisciplined experiments of his youth, he would attain mastery by, among other things, soaking up a broad range of music's proven techniques.[28] His return to the cradle of unruliness in 1897, long after his youthful circle's demise, must itself have been a bit of a coup.

Rimsky-Korsakov gives a hint of his venture's deliberateness in his memoir, noting modestly that if "in its manner" his take on Pushkin did "approach Dargomyzhsky's *Stone Guest*," its "form and modulation scheme were nevertheless not as fortuitous as those of Dargomyzhsky's opera."[29] Marina Frolova-Walker has traced the tension behind this "nevertheless" to an old trauma, the composer's discontent with being perceived by diehard Kuchka buffs as too much of a purist to rival in deep, instinctive originality his Kuchka comrade Musorgsky.[30] A few months before he embarked on his *Mozart*, that wound would be poked again when the arch-kuchkist critic Vladimir Stasov blasted Rimsky-Korsakov's latest project, a thorough revision of Musorgsky's opera *Boris Godunov*, for the very thing the revision was meant to accomplish. What Rimsky-Korsakov had plotted as improvement—smoothing out prickly harmonies, tidying unkempt recitative—Stasov perceived as mutilation, a mistreatment by a musician simply insensitive to the habits that lent the original most of its preciousness.[31] The reviser could hardly agree with the critic, but the charge of insensitivity must have stung, for Rimsky-Korsakov had spent years learning to impersonate musically (what he deemed a better version of) his late friend.[32]

That pain was likely exacerbated by another disgrace, the refusal of the Imperial Theaters to stage Rimsky-Korsakov's own newest opera, *Sadko*. The shocking, unprecedented snub came in January 1897, soon after the Theaters' administration had received several letters from season subscribers asking to pull Rimsky-Korsakov's currently running showpiece, *The Christmas Eve*, and offer instead something "less boring."[33] The tsar himself seems to have shared in the sentiment; as Ivan Vsevolozhsky, the director of the Imperial Theaters, regretfully informed the composer, Nicholas II personally crossed out *Sadko* from the list of next season's hopefuls after hearing that it was similar in style to Rimsky-Korsakov's previous works. "Let the Directorate find something more entertaining," the autocrat purportedly said.[34] The merrier fare approved for the following year included Tchaikovsky's *Oprichnik* and Mozart's *Don Giovanni* (among other works).

Thus suddenly finding himself wedged between the Scylla of kuchkist ire and the Charybdis of public indifference, Rimsky-Korsakov was pressed, once again, to reevaluate his métier. He had experienced feelings of inadequacy before; indeed, for a while his career progressed in fits of compulsive self-bettering.[35] But if at that time getting a good handle on yet another technique opened a wider horizon of musical possibility, his latest failings seemed to call for a different kind of fix. And whereas after Stasov's flare-up Rimsky-Korsakov could still jokingly think of devising, as a retort, an ultra-"realistic" version of Rossini's famed slander aria *La calumnia*, utilizing "a real dynamite blast on [these] words: 'and provokes an explosion,'"[36] the dispiriting news about *Sadko* brought about a far gloomier stance. "Maybe my latest works are just lacking in inspiration," the composer complained to his friend and chronographer Vasili Yastrebtsev in the winter of 1897.[37] This uncharacteristically blunt claim bared an insecurity no longer of the purely professional kind. Was there a grain of truth in the scolding of the ever-clueless Stasov? What if *The Christmas Eve*'s alleged frostiness indeed stymied the pleasure of the Mariinsky's fickle crowd?

Rimsky-Korsakov's engrossment that spring in free vocalization of beloved poetry was thence at heart an activity to coax inspiration, both a response to his latest plight and an as yet untried bid for self-assurance. Letting the melodies of his new romances unfurl as if on their own, nourished by text before any conception would take hold of composition, the composer plied his habitual modus operandi by revising his creative algorithm. His new habits expressly harked back to the free arioso of *The Stone Guest*, and his decision to set another Pushkin "little tragedy" seemed to many cronies to yield a perfect complement to the kuchka classic. If only his choice, by now foreseeable, had not been *Mozart and Salieri*. Not only did this Pushkin, zeroing in on mysteries of inspiration, ring much too close to home to occasion merely a dedicated nod to the ur-kuchkist method, but taking on *this* classic also meant to devote special effort to staging a Mozart hardly transmittable through Dargomyzhskian speech-song.

This paradox is already evident in the scene of the first Mozart-Salieri encounter, with which Rimsky-Korsakov started his opera. Setting Salieri's haughty "Oh, Mozart, Mozart!" (the high point of a gradually escalating soliloquy) as a melodic peak, and making Mozart's casual "Aha! You saw [me]" reflect the inflections of colloquial speech, the composer tangibly displayed his allegiance to the Dargomyzhskian (and Musorgskian) sort of vocal plasticity, one at once accentuating and abstracting different shapes of speaking (Example 1a).

But setting speaking was only the first, even if now crucial, leg of a multi-stage compositional process. As the author would later detail in his memoir, "The initial composition was purely voice-driven. . . . The accompaniment, quite complex, came afterward, but even that part as firstly sketched was much different from the final orchestral score."[38] Letting the initial shapes of his new work sprout instinctively, Rimsky-Korsakov would in due course put them through the refinery of his rich technique—thus dissenting not only in praxis but also in ideology from his *Mozart*'s supposed kuchkist prototype. In the full score, his Mozart's arrival onstage is both a wink and a swipe at the word-based musical creed: before having uttered a single syllable, Rimsky-Korsakov's Mozart has already emerged in the orchestra. Salieri's spectacular groan, it turns out, has been partaking of a stretched-out cadence that resolves, with Mozart's entrance, into a lively gush of sixteenths, the entire succession reminiscent of the slow-fast pattern of an eighteenth-century Italian overture (Example 1b).

In the full score, then, the freedom of spontaneity was qualified by the freedom of mastery, and not just any mastery but a quasi-Mozartean kind of compositional prowess. Rimsky-Korsakov's uncommon turn to that classic could be sensibly read as yet another of his opera's realist traits, a period garb as serviceable in a stage work about Mozart as, for instance, Ukrainian songs had been in *The Christmas Eve* set in a Ukrainian village. Here, however, what might have proven a fitting vignette—and Pushkin's source play with its provisional soundtrack even supplied exact spots to feature Mozartean sound—resisted enclosure. Rather, as if in concurrence with other Pushkin interpreters of the time, Rimsky-Korsakov's Mozart succeeded literally in looming larger than his timid, carefully circumscribed literary forebear. His friendly "Aha!" activated an entire still-functioning system of musical conviviality, lighting up a wholly different path to the regeneration of inspiration.

## An Aesthetics of Responsiveness

It is indeed next to impossible to miss the persistence of eighteenth-century musical styles in *Mozart and Salieri*. Even before the curtain goes up, a sarabande, its regal melody convoyed by slithering chromaticisms as if on loan from an *aria seria*, welcomes the listener to the rarefied world of wigs and farthingales. The frothy buffa passages of Mozart's entrance are tirelessly paraphrased to back up Mozart's jokes, the first of which is his gleeful greeting to a blind street violinist whom he then asks to play "something from Mozart." The violinist does, screeching out "Batti, batti" from *Don Giovanni*. Even the opera's orchestra is trimmed to conjure up a pre-Beethovenian kind of aural transparency. Yet the two protagonists (not unexpectedly, given their strikingly different verbal shapes) have unequal shares in this quasi-Mozartean economy. Salieri's imperious soliloquies may set in motion an assortment of aptly antiqued musical signs, such as the same sarabande that comes to prop Salieri's invocations of fame and glory, but it is his speaking that governs his part. Rimsky-Korsakov saves heightened declamation for depicting Salieri's perspicuity, and Salieri's broodings, his sudden jumps from anguish to awe, also mobilize more contemporaneous musical analogues—from intricate modulations to "realistic" dramatic outbursts. This Salieri may have a strong voice and even stronger will, but he has no style; his musical physiognomy sticks out of his supposed setting. Rimsky-Korsakov's Mozart, on the other hand, is all (diversely *galant*) style. Not only does he emerge enmeshed in an overture that is all but his own; most of his utterances are also tied to Mozartean stylistic tics: here a zesty cadence, there an appoggiatura on the verge of distress. And of course he plays his own music. Giving in to the temptation nested in Pushkin's text, Rimsky-Korsakov, with a good student's zeal, fashions the ephemeral improvisation that Pushkin's Mozart

Example 1a. Rimsky-Korsakov, *Mozart and Salieri*, vocal parts, "Aha!"

silently performs for his Salieri. Finally, taking up the poet's suggestion of the Requiem as the soundtrack of Mozart's last supper, the composer lets a fragment of the real thing lead to the opera's denouement.

Although this Mozart-Salieri dichotomy has been noted and variously glossed by scholars, most exegetes cannot help but engage in figuring out who wins the alleged battle of wits: the self-conscious (melo)dramatic Salieri or the utterly musical Mozart. The verdicts are rarely nonpartisan, for name tagging already pegs the winner (it's Mozart!), his nemesis praised insomuch as his inner drama succeeds as a spectacular, poignant foil to Mozart's far-and-wide charm.[39] Purveying Mozart as either the center of the opera's concentric construction (Aleksei Kandinsky), a credible emblem of "music itself" (Marina Rakhmanova), or an epitome, together with Pushkin, of the art "that transcends the costs of its genesis" (Caryl Emerson), commentators let on that, although Rimsky-Korsakov may certainly feel for (and even identify with) Salieri, history has shown who must prevail.[40] But however incisive their readings, they preach to the choir, the post-musical "museization" (and post-neoclassicism) crowd. Their—our— Mozart suffuses the everyday of classical music, recurring with routine frequency in school, media, and concert programs, just as he is safely stored away akin to the precious crown jewels fixed behind bullet-proof glass for distanced regard. He is no longer debated as a viable model for continuing creativity, a source (even potential) of still-extant stock.

Example 1b. "Aha!" with accompaniment, in piano reduction.

But circa 1897 this was hardly the case. As Leon Botstein has shown in relation to German musical thought, the decades on either side of the turn of the twentieth century saw "the culmination of more than a century of struggle over the soul and meaning of Mozart."[41] The climactic spike of attention to the eighteenth-century classic—a persistent, although limited, repertorial staple from Berlin to St. Petersburg to New York—worked to offset a crisis, "a deeper mistrust during the fin de siècle of the aesthetic direction being taken by living composers, above all those who continued to take their inspiration from Wagner."[42] Hailed by turns as a saintly naïf and a great sage, a finest maker of absolute music and a keenest capturer of emotions, the fin-de-siècle Mozart banded together the most unlikely playmates, from hardcore formalists to even some Wagnerians who now sought validation by digging for deeper historical roots. This motley self-styled progeny shared an apprehension that the progress that had once been so prized had gone, and kept going, awry. The increasingly frequent talk of decadence and demise translated into charges of musical formlessness, harmonic absurdity, orchestral glut—the kinds of excess that baldly frustrated (or, in stand-pat terms, corrupted) the habits of the general listener. The ostensibly wieldy, orderly Mozart was called up to serve as an antidote, even if (at least at first) less as a model to be emulated than as a yardstick by which to indict.

The cogency with which Mozart the music and Mozart the man had by then been fused into a single conceptual body made this yardstick particularly apt; as though the wholesome product bore out the integrity of the producer. This slippage—the marrow of aesthetic reactionism—allowed one to impute an artwork's behavior to both its maker and its devotees. (Thus, if Guido Adler could assert in his 1906 speech to middle schoolers that the genre diversity of Mozart's music testified to its author's "ethical universalism," it went without saying that appreciating this music's "perfect integration of form and content" amounted to being good boys and girls—and vice versa.)[43] But the blurring of lines between creation and creativity could also entail an affordance: an invitation to living, and thriving, as though by and through art's rules. The range of possibilities held by the aestheticist impulse had in fact already begun to be tested by the early modernist breed, including those who would come to define Russia's so-called Silver Age. The propensity for the art-life fusion among the fin-de-siècle Russian artistic and intellectual elite owed much to what the cultural historian Irina Paperno has diagnosed as an acute case of "aesthetic utopianism," the condition first striking the literary cohort that (like Rimsky-Korsakov) had been formed on the positivist social-activist ideals of the 1860s but was now facing the crisis of social alienation and mistrust.⁴⁴ By tapping afresh into their creative potential, these and later utopians, inspired largely by the ecumenical thought of the philosopher Vladimir Soloviev, sought not merely to resist what they sensed as a pre-apocalyptic ferment, but to configure the impending apocalypse to their own terms.⁴⁵

Rimsky-Korsakov is seldom perceived as kin to such markedly mysticist undertakings, perhaps the only exception being his penultimate opera *The Legend of the Invisible City of Kitezh and the Maiden Fevroniya* (1905), which veritably stages (an overcoming of) an apocalypse. Here, the Russian medieval city of Kitezh faces and loses to ruthless foreign invaders, but is miraculously transfigured into a heavenly burg (now glimpsed only as a lakeside reflection) in the wake of its deadly defeat. The emissary of the miraculous is the forest-raised sibylline beauty Fevroniya, the opera's central martyr and its saving grace. Sustained by her deep, untaught sapience, her compassion for every living thing she happens upon—her "natural gift that is higher and more valuable than anything else," in Rimsky-Korsakov's own explication—marks her as a savior.⁴⁶ Her gift, conveyed by her music's unique ability to meld with, and mend, the others' tones, lets her percolate through and so unite—musically, and thus both materially and metaphysically—all the opera's discrepant realms: forest, city, even the invaders' camp, and the heavenly burg. (Through their partaking of the resultant cosmic plenitude, Kitezh's good ones are redeemed, and its only bad one, marked out by his deafness to Fevroniya's attempts at harmony, is expelled.) That very same gift is encoded in the opera's music at large. Mobilizing and melding diverse stylistic realms—from stately Orthodox chant to lyrical Russian folksong to shapely Glinkian dramaticism to Musorgskian recitative to Wagnerian orchestral needlework—the opera heroicizes (though also starkly circumscribes) its own harmonious heterogeneity.⁴⁷ The legend itself of *The Legend*, as it were, amasses ecumenical agency; through their reenergizing synthesis, its many threads and planes are directed to transubstantiate into a single multiplicitous being with continuing resonance. Art becomes life, and Fevroniya, in Richard Taruskin's deft formulation, becomes "an apostle of pantheism,"⁴⁸ her tale transformed into the living gospel that joins together and inspirits her operatic community, her opera, her composer, and (potentially) her keen listeners.

But before Fevroniya there was Mozart. Indeed, Mozart surfaces in Rimsky-Korsakov's public thought in the early 1890s as a rescuer, a conceivable remedy to what the composer lamented as the musical world on the verge of apocalypse, "the eve of the end."⁴⁹ Facing a deep crisis of consciousness as he witnessed what looked like the distinct devitalization of his artistic milieu (his professional woes intensified by personal catastrophes, the deaths of several loved ones), Rimsky-Korsakov temporarily stopped writing new music. He turned instead to taking stock of his prior creative activity, at first fashioning yet-newer revisions of his first opera *The Maid of Pskov* and his early "symphonic picture" *Sadko* (the works he deemed his flawed juvenilia). Soon, however, perhaps discomfited by his own urge to contain his past infelicities within carefully tidied up scores, he immersed himself in broader self-reflection. As he would later note in his memoir (begun in earnest during this period of creative hiatus), his "obsession with writing a self-critique," with finding a place for himself in some larger scheme of things, compelled him to start pondering the grounds of musical creativity at large.[50] He embarked on an aesthetic treatise, seeking helpful formulations in recent philosophical texts but also drawing on his vast teaching experience, in hope of divining an ideal biography of musical giftedness—the kind of living that would neither breed the need to revisit one's oeuvre with a correcting pen nor push one to the limits of the musically possible. His earliest disquisition, dated 9 August 1892, was titled "Mozart and Glinka."[51]

Mozart became *Mozart*, Rimsky-Korsakov argued, on account of his phenomenal musical receptivity. Born "with that miraculous natural architectonic hearing and that natural logic of musical unfolding which need no formal schooling but develop and strengthen in living musical practice," Mozart never missed a chance to apply (and so further nurse) his multidimensional gift, from an early age and in the widest range of professional contexts.[52] "Where did Mozart gather patterns for his techniques and his forms? [His music's] seriousness and textural variety were the bequest of his German musical surroundings, S. Bach, Fried. Bach, Haydn, and Handel," whereas "Italian opera composers of the era of virtuosity were his teachers in nonchalance, melodiousness, and formal freedom. . . . Everything vital for his growth he absorbed with the strength of a genius, someone all-grasping and all-understanding, someone mastering everything he needs."[53] If opening his ears to diverse ways of doing music was Mozart's first step toward immortality, his glory was sealed by a massive return on his many debts. Out of all that "living textbook material" Mozart not only effected something decidedly his own, but his lithe, affable "music of varied moods"—the heterogeneous "free style" as opposed to the strict, single-affect-driven music of the previous era—also came to lay the groundwork for much of nineteenth-century sound art.[54] As an apotheosis of giftedness, Mozart's manifold, infinitely gainful creative life, impressed in his music, offered a gold standard of composerly existence. In all likelihood, anyone in possession of substantial musical talent who seized on each opportunity to develop by engaging in multiple musical acts might bring forth new brilliant sounds, and generate fresh, robust musical forms.

Such, for instance, was Mozart's Russian counterpart Mikhail Glinka, avowed Rimsky-Korsakov. Glinka, too, was blessed with a wondrous musical faculty that, although mobilized at a later age than Mozart's, led to the blooming of "a comparable genius." Although young Glinka was no fledgling professional but, conversely, a leisurely upper-cruster, or *barchuk*, his natural gift could not help but burst through. Glinka felt his first musical thrill and had his first public performance with his uncle's estate orchestra; in St. Petersburg, he became versed in a range of musical acts as "the life and soul of many a party"; his grand Italian tour offered many direct opportunities to "shed tears soaking up the charm of Italian melodiousness" as well as to learn singing. Finally, "several lessons with the Berlin contrapuntist [Siegfried] Dehn put in order everything [Glinka] had absorbed during his amateur life—and a great composer was minted."[55] True talent knew neither social nor formal-educational difference; its only imperative was submission to two major forces: its own natural drive and the vigor of surrounding socio-musical practices. "Mozart's marvelous, multifarious musical fabric resulted from his life as a professional, Glinka's—from his life as an amateur. But either path was that of an involved life, spirited practical activity.... Glinka ... may have produced very few works. But how fine they all are! There is nothing weak in them; everything is consummate and virtuosic."[56]

There was more to this argument than a (thin yet patent) attempt to inscribe Russian music into Western musical genealogies. Further on in his aesthetic texts, Rimsky-Korsakov's notion of Mozart's (and Glinka's) panoptic natural genius was put to work to redress the contemporaneous currents that he saw as threatening the vitality of musical art. One such current ran inside his own place of employment, the St. Petersburg Conservatory, in the guise of something seemingly innocent, even beneficent yet at closer inspection quite noxious: the curricular track of music theory, capped by theory of composition, which was growing ever more popular among the students. To Rimsky-Korsakov, mastering music primarily through theory—moreover, according to someone else's prepackaged design—just made no sense. (Never mind that he had recently authored a harmony textbook himself; his qualm bore on the systematic six-year course of study based, rather abstractly, on the gradual increase in complexity of musical forms and techniques.) If those "with talent for composition" were to flourish, he maintained, they would need a much different course, one not only "custom-tailored to every such student's gift" but also (*pace* Mozart) necessarily offering access to the full spectrum of the most recent ways of doing music. Meanwhile, those "with mediocre abilities," by nature unfit for composing yet endorsed institutionally as "theorists" and trained to fiddle with a fixed range of musical gear, could only produce simulacra—"colorless, lifeless, and ghostly fruit"—to the detriment of living-breathing musical art.[57] Ostensibly a critique of defunct infrastructure and outworn teaching methods, Rimsky-Korsakov's objection to theory as a métier was, however, far too strong to speak only to matters of education. "Music theorist is essentially an absurdity," he stressed all through his curricular musings, "the kind that ought not to exist." If Mozart embodied the pinnacle of musical being, "the phantasmal figure of theorist" stood lower even than the musical being's lowest point.[58]

The sweeping ontological angle of this verdict brings us closer to the conceptual underpinnings of Rimsky-Korsakov's aesthetic writ, and thus to the broader significance of his diligent appellation to ideas of naturalness, multiplicity, and involvement—all converging in his image of Mozart. On the lookout now for compatible thought, the composer found much resonance to his latest inklings in such unalike yet related empiricist tracts as August Wilhelm Ambros's *Die Grenzen der Musik und Poesie: Eine Studie zur Aesthetik der Tonkunst* (The Boundaries of Music and Poetry: An Etude in Musical Aesthetics), and George Henry Lewes's *A Biographical History of Philosophy* and *Problems of Life and Mind*, to which he returned time and again while plowing through his own essays.[59] From Ambros, Rimsky-Korsakov lifted the concept of music as the art of varied moods, or "attunements" (*Stimmungen* in German original, *nastroeniy* in Russian translation), and along with it the valuation of emotional flexibility as the core of music's liveness.[60] Whereas poetry, according to Ambros, worked by inducing diverse moods as responses to cunning narratives of the world's many facets, music furnished the already resultant affective forms of world-attunement, leaving it to the listener to fathom their possible meanings and paths. Music moved, that is, not merely by accessing the regions of human experience that could not have been reached by any other artistic means (a typical Romanticist creed), but in the very process of mapping these regions. The manifold Mozart served Ambros's argument as a perfect topographer of the sense-experience, his music purveying the stereoscopic "sphere of the soul-life" (*Gemütsleben*) through a "profusion of ideas, and modes and forms of expression."[61] Although in the broader (Hegelian) historical perspective the "emotional equilibrium" of Mozart's art would be superseded by Beethoven's messier (yet truer) self-reflective creations, Mozart remained the epitome of music's coming into "its own" at the end of the eighteenth century, with "its architectonic and its poetic aspects"—that is, its form and its content—"finally operating in total agreement."[62] Ambros's purposeful indistinction between music's life and Mozart's creativity signaled the common patrimony of the art and the man: within his study's mainly Hegelian framework, they were both similar realizations of the absolute spirit, arrived at in keeping with (and by way of) the victorious march of human history and necessarily bound by the shared consciousness (that is, the soul-life) of their epoch.

Rimsky-Korsakov may not have been fully swayed by Ambros's idealism, but, as his writings attest, he shared not only Ambros's emphasis on music's concretely experiential basis but also Ambros's trust in the larger-than-single-life source of artistic productivity. From this double standpoint, his strawman theorist, severed from the higher supply of ability by both his innate mediocrity and his learned disregard for living musical practices, was all but a traitor to music history. Even more treacherous were those highly gifted composers who had chosen to turn a deaf ear to the world and follow instead the ephemeral path of sheer speculation. At least this is how Rimsky-Korsakov characterized such musical reformists as Richard Wagner and Hector Berlioz, starting in his Mozart essay and carrying on in his next piece titled "Wagner and Dargomyzhsky" (24 August 1892), a pendant-cum-antithesis to "Mozart and Glinka." His anti-reformist wrath was informed by his newly shaped vision of the perfect composer, to which neither Wagner (nor Berlioz) nor Dargomyzhsky had been able to live up. (Incidentally, Rimsky-Korsakov never progressed on the Dargomyzhsky part of his essay, for that composer, the author of very few and rarely performed works, himself hardly lived up to the role of Wagner's counterpart.) What made Wagner flawed was not his dubious ideology, his formal iconoclasm or his harmonic radicalism; Rimsky-Korsakov's chief Wagner charge was monomania, the willful severance from the world and its riches. His entire Wagner essay was effectively an exercise in tabulating various aspects of lack of plurality: the lack of contrast ("Wagner . . . denied himself the powerful artistic means of diversity and juxtaposition"); of repose ("He built an edifice . . . comprised as if only of ladders, its few narrow plateaus too scarce to offer proper rest"); of memory ("Privileging the monotonous *elaborate* [*izïskannïy*] style . . . Wagner forgot about such great basics as the strict and free styles"); and ultimately of freedom ("The only possible progress [after Wagner] is by way of the *retreat* to the freedom of [classical] period structures . . . to a freer, more intuitive kind of creativity, one governed by the unconscious forces of imagination instead of canny calculation").[63]

In a word, Rimsky-Korsakov's Wagner was no Mozart, and therein lay his offense.

In addition to the apparent illogicality of such ruling, it might seem odd that the avowed rationalist Rimsky-Korsakov would find Wagner, the proven bard of the subliminal, lacking in "unconscious force." However, a brief scrutiny of the second critical catalyst of Rimsky-Korsakov's aesthetic cogitation, G. H. Lewes's positivist blend of philosophy, psychology, and physiology, helps clear the air not only around Rimsky-Korsakov's treatment of Wagner, but also concerning his take on Mozart in 1892 and 1897. The focus on the combination of inborn perceptiveness and continuous sensory activeness in Rimsky-Korsakov's depiction of his model composer can be traced to the key tenets of Lewes's widely read treatise *Problems of Life and Mind* (published in Russian as *Vosprosï o zhizni i dukhe*, or Questions of Life and Spirit).[64] At the center of Lewes's study lay the notion of sensibility—the organic quality that constituted human beings as living things and, as Lewes argued, proved the essential wholeness of the human subject against the traditional (Cartesian) view of mind (or soul) and body as ontologically distinct.[65] All human activity, Lewes stressed, was governed, directly or indirectly, by the work of the sensorium—a sort of meta-organ of responsiveness, variously distributed throughout the human organism—the brain being as much a function of sensory processes as the spinal cord. The difference between humans and other sensorily organized animals, however, was their double nature as biological and social beings. If biology was responsible for the initial aptitudes, "mechanisms of sensation," the varied and ever-changing "social medium" (itself a complex organism) made possible the development of specifically human cumulative "modes of sensibility": feelings, moods, imagings, and thoughts (self-aware perceptions). These, the products as well as further enablers of social interaction as the in-vivo relational give-and-take, constituted the engine of human evolution. In a striking reversal of Hegelian oneness, of the ever-unfolding absolute consciousness, Lewes posited multiplicity, the ever-diversifying "store of [sense-] experiences," as history's moving force.[66]

Rimsky-Korsakov likely agreed with Lewes's organicist accentuating of sensibility (this word, *chuvstvitel'nost'* in Russian, pervades his curricular writings as a key measure of his students' aptitude). He must have appreciated Lewes's claim that any true knowledge, as a symbiosis of "connate functions" and "acquired faculties," was a matter of social practicing. But perhaps most pertinent to Rimsky-Korsakov's notion of creativity was Lewes's assertion of the principally aggregative nature of individual experience. It was "the great human privilege to assimilate the experiences of others," Lewes maintained, portraying the individual not only as necessarily shaped by what Lewes called "the impersonal" (or interpersonal, in today's psycho-speak), but also as enhanced, indeed advantaged, by the interchange with/in the social environment.[67] The advantage involved developing the "intenser consciousness of a wider life" as a kind of "sympathetic imagination"—the dynamic affective bond with fellow humans through which the individual integrated into the larger social corps, and at the edge of which "the residual store" of shared social accoutrements sank beneath the level of acute individual awareness, "condens[ing] in intuitions" that made up the unconscious.[68] This trustworthy Victorian unconscious, unlike the Freudian trickster psyche (part of a later, and radically different, conceptual framework), calibrated selfhood to socialdom "for the sake of a foreseen general good."[69] A fine congruence between all these sentient planes could be attained only by a superior organism, one capable of generating ever newer intensities of sensation that "help[ed] to increase ... the store of experiences common to all."[70] Such, of course, was Rimsky-Korsakov's Mozart, now coming to light not merely as a model composer but as an exemplary human being thriving on the synergy of a keen sensibility and the great power to assimilate. And such a destiny was also probable, as Rimsky-Korsakov dreamed in 1892, for talented and properly managed conservatory students:

> Teach [them] to play and sing but don't exclude those willing from trying out other ways, and nothing will be out of their reach. Those in possession of the divine spark will start to improvise impromptus, nocturnes, romances, overtures, symphonies, cantatas, and operas—that is, they'll begin to compose. And this way music will transpire not only as the art of singing and playing, but also as the tonal art of conjuring moods in our imaginations. And that will be music worthy of *historical* and *aesthetic* exploration.[71]

In this vision, spontaneity occurred as a function of mastery, both aspects of creativity operating as reciprocal modes of sense-experience. By practicing myriad ways of doing the tonal art, Rimsky-Korsakov intimated, the gifted would join in and (sooner or later) upgrade the existing circuit of sentience, inevitably treading but also potentially paving the evolutionary road.

Within this framework, art formed a single (though not necessarily coextensive) continuum with the artist, both persisting simultaneously as recipients and catalysts of an extended natural process. In the context of this organicist argument the manifold, equilibrious Mozart-the-music evidenced the naturally harmonious Mozart-the-man, whereas the solipsistic strains of Wagner's music signaled an "anomalous being ... inherently lacking in musical as well as broadly artistic integrity."[72] For Rimsky-Korsakov, the self-indulgently lopsided Wagner was an antihero of music history merely masquerading as a progressivist, a textbook decadent—and so were his sybaritic legatees clustering on the wrong side of evolution.[73] Adding more fuel to Rimsky-Korsakov's distress, and possibly prompting his Wagner essay, was the continuing impact of Wagner's hypnotic, elaborate single-mindedness on musical youth—and perhaps most of all on Rimsky-Korsakov himself. By detailing Wagner's deficits, Rimsky-Korsakov toiled to dispel Wagner's metaphysical magic, exposing all aspects of Wagner's style other than his "incomparable, genius orchestration" as inorganically "ghostly" and even "necrotic" (*mertvennïe*)—sure aberrations in comparison with the "liveliness" and "plasticity" of the earlier music.

A similar vocabulary resurfaces in Rimsky-Korsakov's correspondence in the spring of 1897, five years after his first forays into the philosophy of creativity and in the thick of another crisis of composerly consciousness. Reflecting on his *Sadko* fiasco in a letter to his literary collaborator Vladimir Belsky (then sojourning in Munich), the composer bemoaned what he felt was his impending decline as the disease of the day, mixing assertions of his own frailty with visions of some "aging, etiolating musical pieces" standing (as it were) for modern music's general bleakness.[74] Belsky mostly concurred, complaining, too, about "the Wagnerian diet" of inelastic, formularized sound that he had had to live on while in Germany. But he mentioned "an unexpected recent aesthetic delight" that gave him a welcome "respite from [Wagner's] hounding leitmotifs" and altogether "mechanized creativity": a performance of Mozart's *Don Giovanni*, the opera "full of poetry, life and even drama."[75] Rimsky-Korsakov's animated response to this news (29 May 1897) gives a foretaste of his own Mozart project: "I am overjoyed that you have recognized the worth of *Don Giovanni*. It's time for Russian [musical] progressives to let go of their ersatz liberalism [that is, reformist bent] and understand that this is a genius piece and the *mother* of all operas."[76] As his forthcoming opera would corroborate, Rimsky-Korsakov was taking seriously his own suggestion of the progenitive nature of Mozart's art. His experiments with spontaneous vocalization had, in effect, already glimpsed the same general goal as his turn to the heterogeneous late-eighteenth-century style: to arrive at a natural (and thus endlessly extensible) process of sustaining his music's vitality by mobilizing the "residual store of common experiences." In the summer of 1897 Rimsky-Korsakov, it appears, was testing the evolutionary fitness of his own "sympathetic imagination."

The mixed, pliant music of Mozart's era, re-enlivened in Rimsky-Korsakov's *Mozart and Salieri*, made this venture possible in more than one way. Before all else, perhaps, that music, as a continually integral part of the living repertory, had already partaken of the molding of the contemporaneous listening subject: it still moved. From the maker's side, that music's basic articulatory logic—what Rimsky-Korsakov referred to in his Wagner essay as the free "period structure"—was likewise still in operation, condensing in many a composerly intuition as well as catechized in numerous textbooks. Far from being an abstract frame, moreover, that structure provided a dynamic model of sensorial engagement. The periodic syntax, an articulation of the dialogic, suasive poetics of tension and release, worked by rousing and balancing (via graded closures) perspicuous expressions of its own unfolding. Just as its effect hinged on the interplay of recognizable aural slivers of sense-experience—the "residual store" of songs, social dances, operatic, folk or churchly tunes—its formal tensility allowed for the accommodation of an ever-greater variety of musical modes of sensibility, a sustained gain indeed on the "intenser consciousness of a wider life." This sense of movement made Mozart's art akin to the Lewesian organism: as Wye J. Allanbrook formulated in her luminous study of stylistic paradigms of Mozart's time, the categorical proteanism of late eighteenth-century music—its "polyp aesthetics" of interaction, assimilation, and self-renewal—proved, over and over, the tight "connection between ways of moving and ways of being."[77] The constitutive power of social kinesthesis, vital at a time and place of looming social discombobulation, made one be as one moved (a composite of one's inter/actions); and musical acts, especially the sprightly mixed genre of opera buffa (such as *Don Giovanni*), took on that course of vitality.[78]

The Mozart of Rimsky-Korsakov's *Mozart* is as he moves, or what he does. Furthering the ontological premise of Pushkin's portrayal of the composer, Rimsky-Korsakov melds his Mozart with his opera's overall quasi-classicism, intermixing lifestyle and musical style. This Mozart does not just play his ditties, he lives them. The improvisation he performs in the first scene becomes the underlying sound of the second. His Requiem emerges, furtively yet unmistakably, long before Mozart starts playing an excerpt from it to Salieri. But Pushkin's script holds even broader intertextual provisions. As Mozart sits at the piano in the first scene, ready to extemporize on the "two-three thoughts" that came to him "last night," he images their fictive content:

> Now picture—whom?
> Let's say, me—a little younger;

Example 2a. Grave, second part of Rimsky-Korsakov's
Mozart's improvisation, a "sepulchral vision."

In love—not too much, but a little—
With a pretty girl, or a friend—let's say you—
I'm happy.... Suddenly: a grim sepulchral vision,
Swift darkness or something of the sort ...

This image is a shy encapsulation of the entire "little tragedy" of blithe Mozart/friend Salieri/lethal ruse, a wobbly sketch of Mozart's own impending plight. But for all that, it is also (or perhaps first) an impression of a specific, real operatic scene: the striking entrance, from beyond the grave, of *Don Giovanni*'s Commendatore. That very scene had inspired Pushkin's own take on the legend of Don Juan, *The Stone Guest*, an homage as well as a reworking of the Mozart-Da Ponte opera, and the source of Dargomyzhsky's maverick work. Pushkin's Don is more wistful and sincere than Mozart's, but even more vitally, he is a poet, Pushkin's alter ego; his conquests kindle his creative fire. And it is his "I'm happy"— an emphatic, thrice-repeated boasting of a requited love (preceding his required demise)—that Pushkin's Mozart echoes in his explication, just as surely as Rimsky-Korsakov's exultant, jumpy setting of that phrase echoes Dargomyzhsky's. The music of the following improvisation, however, still harks back to the Act 2 finale of *Don Giovanni*: the diminished sevenths and downward leaps of its "sepulchral vision" (intruding on the smooth periodicity of the improvisation's "happy" opening) face off against the real Mozart (Examples 2a and 2b).

Example 2b. Andante, Commendatore's entrance from Mozart's *Don Giovanni*, Act 2 finale, piano-vocal score.

For all that network of confirmed associations, the Grave of Rimsky-Korsakov still does not quite line up with Mozart's Andante, rhythmically, texturally, or procedurally. Yet it should not take long to descry other fitting antecedents of this specter: perhaps the dotted rhythms (and the intruding habits) of the Grave from Beethoven's *Pathétique*, or the forceful melodic plunge of the Grave that opens Chopin's "Funeral March" Sonata, or the awkward clangor of the Grave fashioned from that very Mozart by Liszt in his *Réminiscences de Don Juan*. Or, looking further back in history, the severe stateliness of all French overture Graves played and replayed by (among others) Bach and Handel—the affective disposition to which all consequent reiterations cannot help but direct. But Rimsky-Korsakov appears to be exactly after this kind of anamnesis: a concerted, cumulative imprint, at once precise and polyvalent, mobilizing at once entrained insight and a long line of music history as its experiential horizon. His specter, to extend the visual analogy, absorbs a range of prior incarnations to emit a boosted version of itself, one to appeal to and thus move most current listeners while at the same time capturing a recognizably far-off realm.

This symbiotic double function—of representing and affecting—pertains to almost everything Mozart in the opera, but it is denied to Salieri. At his most expressive, the obsessive Salieri falls off the eighteenth-century stylistic grid; and, inversely, the marks of his style-historical provenance—his sarabande patterns or the flashes of his polyphonic craft or the *galant* idiom that backs his single burst of studied whimsy—are too inflexibly representational to bid for sympathy. The opera's Mozart, on the other hand, *moves* as he moves. Not only does he help direct the large-scale musical locomotion as the key agent of closure, starting with the opera's first full cadence brought about by his first entrance.[79] He is also the key source of the opera's emotion, in a rather literal, material way. Although he is crafted out of heterogeneous musical bits, this Mozart is held together by one particular ligament linking all his constituents: the chromatic appoggiatura, a tangible token of what was sensed as "sensibility" in mid- to late eighteenth-century music, and a multivalent musical sign.[80] In Mozart's time, the half-step dyad expressed sorrow or condolence as effectively as it conveyed the *galant* grace (the interdependence of these inward and outward dispositions being explored, for instance, in Mozart's Symphony No. 40). In Rimsky-Korsakov, the slithering gesture percolates through, and thus unites, all the opera's varied spheres. The suave chromaticism of the introduction marks out *Mozart*'s general stylistic milieu while the orchestral swagger backing up Mozart's first-scene vocal lines parades his Giovanni-esque carriage. Salieri's acute Mozart-mania is also divulged by the appoggiatura—two falling chromatic dyads separated by a tritone (with the added harmonic suspension briefly projecting the augmented triad), their leitmotivic perseverance a fitting articulation of obsessiveness. This recherché figuration harks back to Dargomyzhsky (or rather Wagner) more readily than to Mozart; it intellectualizes, sublimates flair and yen. But the shifting stylistic vantage only adds to the opera's drama: combining the corporeality of the eighteenth-century gesture with the suggestiveness of the Romantic symbol, the appoggiatura now acts, and affects, as both an attribute of Mozart's style and a trace of his destiny. When in the second scene Mozart reveals his dark foreboding in a lyrical, Mozartized rendering of Salieri's leitmotif, his prescience is wrenching; it is primed to draw sympathetic response, mobilizing compassion as well as intelligence, mustering understanding.

That was it—the ideal Rimsky-Korsakov strived to attain: an all-understanding composer mustering understanding, working up sensibility. In his *Mozart* Rimsky-Korsakov summoned historical styles not to comment on history, but to confront the contemporaneity that appeared increasingly incapacitated by what he'd identified in 1892 as metaphysical excess,

Wagner's game, but what he was now coming to see as a more widespread ailment, "the indifference of taste" (*bezrazlichiye vkusa*)—the loss of familiar experiential connection, of active kinship between life and art.[81] His opera did not just celebrate the creator sympathetically aligned with his environment; it offered an object lesson in the proliferation of sentience. Its adroit interplay of tried-and-true styles and approaches (including the arioso-recitative, that vaunted kuchkist technique which by then had also become a matter of history) was designed to reactivate perceptiveness, to reawaken discernment—in a kind of Mozartean way. That Rimsky-Korsakov may have indeed come to fancy himself Mozart's heir in his last decade can be seen from a revealing entry in his diary in the spring of 1904, a joint declaration of musical faith and musical parentage:

> The period of *our* music—the free music with the interplay and interchange of varied moods, the music that enlists the full spectrum of diverse techniques and assumes multiple and interesting forms, the expressive music—started with Haydn and Mozart.[82]

Here, grouping Mozart together with Haydn, Rimsky-Korsakov was thinking historically rather than biographically, inscribing himself (and those he deemed his peers) into a distinct evolutionary line. But, listing in one breath moods, techniques, and forms as substantiations of expressiveness, he also evinced another kind of evolutionary thinking, one already inscribed in his 1897 opera: the proposition that feeling and mastering reinforced each other reciprocally in a kind of existential movement. Seven years and six operas after *Mozart*, and in the thick of working on his next opus—the stylistically ecumenical *Kitezh* with its empathetic Fevroniya—Rimsky-Korsakov kept on championing emotional intelligence as the definitive measure of talent, the grain of genius.

## *Mozart*'s Worth

But just how successful was Rimsky-Korsakov in transmitting this point with *Mozart*? The divergent responses to the opera's early performances seem to resist attempts at a coherent narrative, at least at first. According to Yastrebtsev, the first *Mozart* play-through in Rimsky-Korsakov's house on 5 November 1897 prompted some loud cheering from our kuchkist Stasov, thrilled by the opera's proficiency in Dargomyzhskian dramatic style. Recalling his past skepticism about Rimsky-Korsakov's ability to write "realistic" recitatives, Stasov publicly retracted his prior reproach—meanwhile paying no heed at all to the opera's "classicism."[83] ("There was much noise from Stasov," Rimsky-Korsakov wryly remarks on this act in his memoir, perhaps playing modest or simply expecting nothing else from the idea man.[84]) That noisy evening is periodically confused, and conflated in the scholarly (as well as popular) literature with another fabled home play-through, one in August 1898 near Moscow (and so sans Petersburgians Stasov and Rimsky-Korsakov), in which the young Fyodor Chaliapin sang-acted both parts, accompanied by the young Sergei Rachmaninoff.[85] The confusion is understandable: Stasov's thrill with the opera's dramaticism aligns so precisely with Chaliapin's soon-legendary dramatic gift that it is hard to imagine a different bass (in November 1897, Salieri was sung not by Chaliapin but by Mikhail Lunacharsky), let alone a specialist in lyrical songs and old-style oratorios rather than modern operas, as the source of Stasov's excitement.[86] But this ostensible disconnect only makes evident that the critic reacted more to the score than to its enactment, registering mainly the moments of formal resonance with his idea of righteous musical articulation. Ironically, for someone avowedly unconcerned with *mere* mastery, he responded with gusto to a familiarly potent technique.

The reaction of Rimsky-Korsakov's friend soprano Nadezhda Zabela to that other, August 1898 performance could not seem more different from Stasov's. Writing to the composer soon after seeing the Chaliapin-Rachmaninoff act, Zabela expressed her "rare delight" in terms not only far removed from Stasov's praise of the opera, but also hardly matching the standard accounts of Chaliapin's effect on his audiences. "The music of this piece is so graceful, moving, and at the same time, as it were, so intelligent," she gushed, as if unaware of the theatrical coup she had just witnessed.[87] Her choice of words suggests being taken precisely by the opera's Mozartean ambience while tuning out its (or rather Chaliapin's) high-drama bits. Yet even if her response accords better than Stasov's with what was arguably Rimsky-Korsakov's own conception of *Mozart*, like Stasov's it tells as much about the listener as it does about the opera. As Olga Haldey has shown, Zabela "viewed herself as a singer, rather than an actress" in the artistic environment that privileged acting over singing,[88] and her patent preference for the graceful over the thespian stemmed from that clash. The contentious environment was Savva Mamontov's Moscow Private Opera (MPO) where she worked—the troupe that would premiere *Mozart and Salieri* as well as five other Rimsky-Korsakov operas—and there Zabela would display her dissent (while still proving to be a good fit) by finding ample dramatic potential in her roles' musical, rather

Figure 1. Vasili Shkafer as Mozart (left) and Fyodor Chaliapin as Salieri (right) in the 1898 MPO production of *Mozart and Salieri*.

than scenic, articulation. Rimsky-Korsakov's *Mozart*, with its transparent yet pointed musical rhetoric, corroborated her creed. Like Stasov, she reveled in reclaiming the vigor of familiar techniques.

These responses answered, each in its own way, *Mozart*'s call for the reawakening of musical sensitivity. But of course both Stasov and Zabela had been on Rimsky-Korsakov's side all along: notwithstanding their specific stylistic allegiances they persisted in bearing out, in the press or on stage, the vitality of proven musical means. The techniques they favored were integral elements of their identity, parts of their personal and professional constitution. Yet even those not as invested in the musical practices that the opera coalesced also responded to it largely in vitalist terms. "Salieri's recitatives are crisp, sincere, true in feeling and varied moods. . . . [He] is as if alive—envious, resentful, penitent, weeping," raved the trombonist and music historian Ivan Lipaev in the *Russian Musical Gazette* after *Mozart*'s Moscow MPO premiere in November 1898.[89] "Mozart is shaped no less compellingly," the review went on. "His dialogues are now brimming with merriment and nonchalance, now full of languor and pain." This critic sensed no functional difference between the opera's Dargomyzhskian and Mozartean traits, hearing "sharp recitative," "beautiful, lithe cantilena," and "the stylish instrumentation . . . dictated by the character of the era" as equally forceful contributors to *Mozart*'s "precious fusion of music and poetry."[90] He celebrated the opera's symbiosis of feeling and form as the very effect of its stylistic congruence—thus coming remarkably close to catching Rimsky-Korsakov's aesthetic drift.[91]

But to sense the opera as a unified musical front could also turn damning. In his review in the same *Russian Musical Gazette* of *Mozart*'s St. Petersburg premiere (by the same MPO) in March 1899, the avid Wagnerian Evgeni Petrovsky rebuked Rimsky-Korsakov's latest piece for its failure to match musically the "deepest recesses of human soul" communicated in Pushkin. Petrovsky was making his case in terms strikingly resonant with Lipaev's, albeit with a reverse valuation:

> Opinions have been voiced about the beauty and sophistication of [the opera's] ostensibly "classical" style. . . . Ah, but a piece of paper should be enough to amuse oneself with subtleties of style and copycat *Kunststücke*; why take for such experiments living people with living souls, hearts, words and thoughts, why, in a word, exploit Pushkin's timeless characters that give us everything we ask for without unnecessary recitatives?[92]

At first blush, Petrovsky sounded much like the realism-driven kuchkists in the 1860s, only now even their recitative appeared too inept to convey "living people with living souls." But as his review went on, the readers learned that the living soul of, for instance, Pushkin's Salieri was "akin to Medusa's gaze . . . that kills because in it the woe of vice and darkness had found its highest form"; that is, they learned that Petrovsky's "living people" resembled Lipaev's "as-if-alive" protagonists as little as Schopenhauer's will resembled representation.[93] A professional devotee of Wagner's hypnotic reality (and never a music practitioner), this critic neither would nor could appreciate *Mozart*'s liveness. Rather than looking for empathetic experience, he longed to be lost in Medusa's gaze. His response realized Rimsky-Korsakov's worst nightmare by displaying the very "indifference of taste" that the composer so feared.[94] Far from the inability to tell one style from another, that indifference bespoke the refusal to perceive as valid the kinship between the wonted musical styles and the felt human lives.

As if to defy such assessment, another review of the opera's St. Petersburg performance, this time in the recently launched illustrated monthly *The World of Art*, focused specifically on the connectedness between having style and living life. The reviewer lauded Rimsky-Korsakov for bringing back "simple . . . and elegant form" in the wake of the long reign of reformist maximalism and "lucubration" (*elukubratsii*). He heard *Mozart* as righting a few wrongs of its predecessors by, among other means, achieving the formal cohesiveness that "Dargomyzhsky could not have dreamed about," or projecting Pushkin's crisp verse through the "lucid and economical harmonic syntax" that put to shame the "cheap effects" and "insufferable mannerisms" of latter-day Italian and German fare.[95] As he contrasted the elegance of Rimsky-Korsakov's music to the tawdriness of its antagonists, this critic imbued musical means with social-hierarchical value; his aesthetic judgment hinged on the adjudication of behavior, elevating Rimsky-Korsakov's perspicuous art expressly for not being crude or cringe-worthy—that is, for not being plebeian. By the same token (and perhaps by now expectedly), his review imputed the music's dignified conduct to its maker, praising both the opera and its composer for the "noble restraint and sense of proportion worthy of Pushkin himself!"[96] The critic thus claimed the similitude not only of musical style and lifestyle, but also of high art and high society—likening the lissome clarity of Mozart, Pushkin, and now Rimsky-Korsakov to the aristocratic refinement of the social elite. He knew firsthand what he purported: the critic's name was Gherman Larosh, and he had been a great friend of the late Pyotr Tchaikovsky, "the last of the court composers" (in Richard Taruskin's phrasing) and a man noteworthy precisely for "being elegant to his core" (in Larosh's own words).[97] Larosh, although never a close associate of Rimsky-Korsakov, sensed in his *Mozart* a kindred soul.

He had ample reasons to have that sensation. Acoustically, *Mozart*'s recitative-arioso took as much after Tchaikovskian cantilena, with its rounded phrasing and curvy tunelets echoed in the orchestra, as after Dargomyzhskian dramatic declamation, both approaches operating as the opposite, mutually balancing poles of the opera's range of vocal expression. Narratively, tracking obsession had also been one of Tchaikovsky's specialties, perhaps best demonstrated in his 1890 *The Queen of Spades* in the psychologized portrayal of Gherman, another Pushkinian antihero. (Not unlike Salieri, Gherman is characterized through a misalignment with his general aural environment.) But even without these junctures, Rimsky-Korsakov's turn to Mozart was resonant with the multiple turns to eighteenth-century music made by his late colleague. For Tchaikovsky had been the foremost Russian Mozartean. Not only did he promote Mozart by producing the performable, singing Russian translation of the libretto of *Le nozze di Figaro* (he planned, but never completed the same for *Don Giovanni*). Not only did he write homages to Mozart—directly, as with his orchestral suite *Mozartiana* or vocal quartet "Night" based on Mozart's concrete works, or indirectly, as in the pastoral *intermède* from *The Queen of Spades*, by summoning a cumulative likeness to late eighteenth-century sound. As Arkadi Klimovitsky has shown, Tchaikovsky also persistently channeled Mozart in more roundabout ways: through, for instance, the cheeky *buffo parlando* in the first movement of his Serenade for Strings, or the plaintive appoggiaturas saturating the opening of his *Eugene Onegin*—the willowy G-minor melody reliving, sometimes note-by-note, the opening of Mozart's Symphony No. 40.[98] Here the renewed Mozartean grace generated, in Klimovitsky's words, "the semantic halo... as a cultural-psychological mindset as well as a stylistic orientation," inviting one to partake of the keen yet self-aware sensibility of the "Russian manorial Mozart," the lustrous "classic" filtered through the lyricism of the early nineteenth-century Russian domestic romance.[99] This alloyed aural stance functioned as both a projector of aliveness and a means of distancing—a sort of cushion regulating the flow of sentiment, and helping to strike just the right balance between not enough and too much.[100]

Praising in his review *Mozart*'s elegance and sense of proportion, Larosh placed this opera beside Tchaikovsky's *Eugene Onegin*, the work he had singled out even before its 1879 premiere for the "naturally inspired melodiousness" and fine equilibrium of grace and warmth that showed its composer "freeing himself from the tumors of radicalism and sham realism" and "entering the radiant path paved by Mozart and Glinka."[101] These were just about the terms in which Rimsky-Korsakov explained his latest change of musical course in a letter to his friend Semyon Kruglikov in February 1898:

> The patchy surface . . . and the overabundance of dissonance . . . in modern decadent fare are undesirable things, and the public at large, when it asks for melody and simpler harmony, is right. It is not right when it demands vulgarity [*poshlost'*], but it seems that God has delivered me from such. I haven't surrendered to the public's tastes in this respect, and if I've tried to be closer to Glinka, it was because Glinka is always noble and elegant, in addition to other qualities of his genius. *To dumb yourself down* [*oprostit'sia*, literally, to make yourself a "simpleton"] is a poor and derogatory word, but to become simpler [*sdelat'sya proshche*], more natural and more open will not hurt but is even necessary, not only for

me but for everyone. There was a time in the 1860s . . . when most of Chopin's melodies were considered weak and worthless music; our dear Stasov still shudders when he hears the word *melody*, something they tried from time immemorial to replace with the term *theme*. Yet in the meantime the pure melody, which has come down to us from Mozart via Chopin and Glinka, lives on and must live on. Without it music's destiny is decadence.[102]

Here, like Larosh, Rimsky-Korsakov called up the triumvirate of melodiousness, naturalness, and nobility to take to task what he perceived as composerly cruelty on the one hand, and public crudeness on the other. Yet what for Larosh was a matter of leisurely (if acrimonious) observation, was for Rimsky-Korsakov the very stuff of his artistic being, and a matter of the continuation of music history. If he still looked to Mozart and Glinka as paragons of vitality whose torch ought to have been carried on, now he also clearly saw himself as the next key torchbearer. He would brave the rising tide of the "undesirable" and the "vulgar," wielding "pure melody" as the stronghold of virtue and verve. His pure melody was, of course, not some abstract euphonious ditty, but a concrete, lived-out act, the flowy fusion of the already conversable sounds re-created afresh in rhetorically potent ways. Necessarily "noble and elegant," and principally not a *theme*, that melody did not offer much to lucubrate about, but rather advanced a behavioral framework, a working likeness of dignified feeling and bearing—the beautiful cantilena (or dramatic oratory) ably maneuvering between the unnatural and the uncouth. Resisting the rise of "indifference of taste," it provided a measure of differentiation.

Adding Chopin to his exemplary twosome of Mozart and Glinka, Rimsky-Korsakov conjured up the refined, "endlessly poetic sound, after which any other music would seem heavy and rough," as he had characterized Chopin's aural stamp to Yastrebtsev.[103] His *Mozart*, however, evoked less of Chopin's legendary piano touch or cascading melodiousness than the assimilative, socially attuned sensibility of Tchaikovsky's operatic oeuvre. Even the aesthetic qualities that Rimsky-Korsakov campaigned for in his letter—seemly simplicity, a certain natural ease and broad-mindedness—easily call to mind the Tchaikovskian dialectic of propinquity and perspective, or what Taruskin has identified as Tchaikovsky's "politics of affirmation," his expert manipulation of active expressive codes, congruent with Mozart's tactics of sensorial engagement, and meant to appeal to, not attack or overwhelm, the musical palates of his urbane audiences.[104]

And yet Tchaikovsky—the great master of sympathy, and already a proverbial melodist—is nowhere to be found in the musical genealogies that Rimsky-Korsakov constructs for himself. But why? If Tchaikovsky was too close in time to be deemed a forebear, he was still a finest compeer, and it was he, after all, not Chopin, who fit amply both Rimsky-Korsakov's mold of a receptive, diversiform composer and his ideal of melody.

Why not Tchaikovsky in that letter? Rimsky-Korsakov surely was not unaware of the affinities sensed by Larosh, nor was he uninterested in Tchaikovsky as a role model. Yastrebtsev duly cites many instances of Rimsky-Korsakov discussing Tchaikovsky's exemplarity, including "a lengthy consideration" of Tchaikovsky's Mozartean "effortlessness of composition."[105] Notably, on the day that brought the news of (and consequently much mulling over) the Mariinsky's *Sadko* snub, Yastrebtsev also jots down: "[And then] we discussed . . . the score of *Eugene Onegin*."[106] In his own memoir, Rimsky-Korsakov is mostly silent about Tchaikovsky's style, but repeatedly professes his awe of Tchaikovsky's well-measured ease of communication. "He turned out to be a pleasant conversationalist and an amiable man who knew how to behave simply and how to speak as if always sincerely and genially," is how he describes fondly (even if somewhat incredulously) his first impression of his soon-to-be pal.[107] His letters, however, reveal a certain unease about Tchaikovsky's social charms. Having learned, for instance, that his Moscow colleague was contemplating a move to St. Petersburg, Rimsky-Korsakov complained to Kruglikov in June 1890: "If Tchaikovsky settles in St. Petersburg, a circle will form around him that will include Lyadov and Glazunov [Rimsky-Korsakov's favorite ex-pupils and now valued colleagues-friends]. . . . Tchaikovsky, with his innate *savoir-faire*, will enchant and captivate everyone, and will surround himself with the gifted."[108] The prospect of giving up his own treasured tribe to his worldlier friend might not have seemed too appealing. (As it happens, Tchaikovsky never moved to St. Petersburg, but he would charm away Lyadov and especially Glazunov all the same.) Lest a note of Rimsky-Korsakov's ambivalence toward Tchaikovsky turns into an insinuation of yet another Mozart-Salieri plot, however, a return to *Mozart*'s reception should clarify the aesthetic differences between the composers vis-à-vis their behavioral dispositions, and in so doing make one last point about the opera's worthiness.

Whether Rimsky-Korsakov ever read Larosh's plaudit is a matter of guesswork, but, thanks to Yastrebtsev, we know which assessment of his opera he valued the most. On 2 May 1899, the composer made a rare visit to Yastrebtsev especially to show him a review of *Mozart* in the *St. Petersburger Zeitung* by the music critic Emil Bormann—the only written response to the opera that would merit a lengthy direct quote in Yastrebtsev's *Reminiscences*, suggesting a deep resonance with the reviewee's own views.[109] There, praising *Mozart* as the latest scion in the distinguished line of Glinka's *Ruslan and Lyudmila* as well as Tchaikovsky's *Eugene Onegin* and *The Queen of Spades*—"the most genius, perhaps the only genius musical masterpieces on Pushkin's texts"—Bormann enthused:

> With what great simplicity did Rimsky-Korsakov put to work here his wonderful melodiousness, splendid technique, and truthfulness of expression. The latter made this genius composer turn to the Mozart-Beethovenian styles of harmony and modulation. He needed those to characterize the spirit of the time and [his heroes'] personalities, not just to present a clever exercise in the old style, as we may observe in Tchaikovsky. He [Rimsky-Korsakov] used the old material only to treat it in a modern way.[110]

As if having been privy (uncannily so) to Rimsky-Korsakov's own ruminations on simplicity, technique, and melody, the German-Russian critic pointed up his opera's symbiosis of form and feeling to proclaim Rimsky-Korsakov's turn to, and work with, late eighteenth-century music as the core of *Mozart*'s "truthfulness of expression." And yet for him the "period piece" succeeded not just because it looked back to Mozart (and, notably, to Beethoven), but because in it the ancient sound was filtered through the keen modern ear, proving the past as deeply ingrained in the present, and the present as already discernible in the past. Placing particular value on *Mozart*'s fusion of the current (the contemporary musical tongues) and the durable (the musical canon), the critic argued as though for the opera's historical invincibility. From that perspective, Rimsky-Korsakov's integrative way of handling the canon spelled reinvigoration, whereas Tchaikovsky's often expressly anachronistic use of Mozartean (or otherwise eighteenth-century) sonority looked like merely a clever exercise in the old style.

The discrepancy that Bormann sensed between Rimsky-Korsakov's Mozart as a blended part of the harmonious whole and Tchaikovsky's Mozart as an ill-fitting (if crafty) relic was far more than a matter of stylistic nuance. With his *Mozart*'s eighteenth-century musical fabric, Rimsky-Korsakov not only stepped on—and, according to Bormann, improved on—what had hitherto been almost exclusively Tchaikovskian territory; he also touched on the socio-cultural anxieties to which Tchaikovsky's Mozarteanism (still) spoke. Chief among these anxieties was the ambivalence about historical identity, widely shared among Russia's urbanized gentry (to which both Tchaikovsky and Rimsky-Korsakov belonged), which stemmed from the ongoing social situation: the peculiar persistence of the *ancien régime,* the eighteenth-century power structure, within an increasingly modernizing nineteenth-century culture. As the literary historian Luba Golburt has recently argued, this paradox, acutely perceived and responded to by many nineteenth-century authors starting with Pushkin, turned the eighteenth century into a constant, tantalizing vanishing point in the Russian cultural imagination.[111] As the originary era of both Russian absolutism and Russian modernity (a combination most pronounced during the reign of the enlightened monarch Catherine the Great [1762–1796], nearly coincident with Mozart's life span), the eighteenth century emerged as legible and opaque, having a strong hold over contemporaneity and quickly receding into the past, the begetter of historical consciousness and the resister of the juggernaut of history, an object of social critique and a metonym of aristocratic distinction.

Although both Tchaikovsky and Rimsky-Korsakov inherited and further participated in this conflicted economy, they also held different stakes in it. Indicative of these stakes were their takes on Mozart, an epitome of the musical eighteenth century, whose avid reception in nineteenth-century Russia (with, perhaps, the lone exception of the fledgling Kuchka) was allied with the strong feelings toward his era. Tchaikovsky's Mozart, whether hidden inside the domestic romance in *Eugene Onegin* or slyly sticking out of other music in *The Queen of Spades* (the instance that Bormann must have had in mind in his critique), emerged as a principally pre-Beethovenian phenomenon, projecting the rare, no-longer-emulatable sensibility possessing indescribable charm for nineteenth-century listeners. Rimsky-Korsakov's Mozart, however, with his consummate synthesis of form and content as well as his alleged influence on the succeeding generations, was largely assimilated to the image of the valiant, ever-current Beethoven. Put another way, Tchaikovsky's Mozart mostly pleased whereas Rimsky-Korsakov's Mozart mostly enlightened, and here lay the key behavioral differences between the two composers—the differences, in the broadest terms, between charm and grit, or between hedonism (opting for such a vital eighteenth-century value as the pursuit of happiness) and asceticism (holding to such a vital nineteenth-century notion as the idea of the greater good).[112] This is not to say that the composers' general haute-intelligentsia tastes radically diverged, or that they did not share a common (aristocratic) distaste for the coarse and the abstruse, or (least of all) that Rimsky-Korsakov did not write fetching, colorful music. Rather, the charm-grit distinction proves helpful in considering, one last time, Mozart/*Mozart*'s place in Rimsky-Korsakov's private crusade against the fin de siècle.

If, for Rimsky-Korsakov, Tchaikovsky's charm also had a darker side (besides working to lure away his associates), it would reveal itself in a certain nonchalance, the lightness of being in some sense not unlike that of Pushkin's Mozart. More than once would Yastrebtsev record Rimsky-Korsakov lamenting Tchaikovsky's squandering of his precious gift in works (particularly ballets) "slick on the surface yet awfully shallow musically," and thus "contribut[ing] to music's general decline."[113] But slickness and surface interest were of course the distinguishing features of the Tchaikovskian eighteenth century, reconstituted, for instance, in the play-within-the-play *intermède* in Act 2, scene 1 of *The Queen of Spades* precisely to deepen the sense of decline that was the opera's prevailing emotion. *The Queen of Spades*, broadly about the irretrievability of the secret ostensibly lodged inside the eighteenth-century body of an old Countess (once virtually a female Don Juan but now on the verge of becoming a ghostly Stone Guest), dealt in ciphers and surfaces, and thrived, as Simon Morrison has demonstrated, on the "transform[ation of] familiar, 'unambiguous' musical forms into unfamiliar 'ambiguous' ones."[114] It played on, by playing up, the ambivalence that its author shared with audiences about the interconnectedness of the Imperial past and the Imperial present. Here, Mozart as well as Mozart's French (that is, truer *ancien régime*) contemporary André Grétry were summoned to supply style-historical frame and charm, but also to illustrate, by being warped, chipped away at, and quite literally disembodied as the abstract nineteenth-century sounds swallowed the gestural eighteenth-century ones, their era's inescapable passing portending the passing of the world as Tchaikovsky's audiences would have known it. If that was an exercise in the old style, it was very clever, and prescient indeed. But if that was a vision of the apocalypse, it was blocked by its own exquisite opacity, stopped short of ever forecasting salvation.

Rimsky-Korsakov's *Mozart* tracked an almost directly opposite trajectory. Here, initially (save for the opera's prelude) mostly nineteenth-century sounds gave way little by little to mostly eighteenth-century musical flow. Using Tchaikovskian techniques of quotation and quasi-quotation, Rimsky-Korsakov, as it were, turned them inside out. Could his unobvious choice of Mozart's arietta "Batti, batti" as his opera's first embedded quotation garbled by an old blind violinist have been a calculated reference to the emphatic "qui bat, qui bat" from the Grétry arietta mangled by the old Countess in Act 2, scene 2 of *The Queen of Spades*? And if so, could his progressive Mozartization of his opera have been a rejoinder to Tchaikovsky's thorough symbolization of *his*? By echoing the bouncy shapes of "Batti, batti" in his own first-scene "stylization" of Mozart's improvisation (itself turning into the ambient sound of the second scene), by infusing his opera with expressive appoggiaturas (culminating in the performance of the first fourteen measures from Mozart's appoggiatura-strewn Requiem), Rimsky-Korsakov challenged the image of Mozart's music as a beautiful fairyland good mainly for serving as a utopian foil to some complex postlapsarian reality. By and through his opera, he celebrated Mozart's ongoing vitality that had already proved to withstand the vicissitudes of history far better than, say, the waning Russian aristocracy. Perhaps by restoring *to* time Tchaikovsky's express anachronism, Rimsky-Korsakov hoped to push back time's end.

But be that as it may, he still lived in the largely Tchaikovskian era. When Rimsky-Korsakov finally made his long-coveted return to the Imperial stage in the 1901–02 season, *Mozart and Salieri* was among his first works to be staged. The opera's reduced scale and its stylistic poise praised by Larosh, however, branded it as a better fit for an intimate theatrical venue than the big public stage. As a single, markedly elegant body, the chamber *Mozart* looked conspicuously like a courtly collectible, an *objet d'art* akin to a Fabergé egg or Tchaikovsky's rococo *intermède* (performed in *The Queen of Spades* in a home theater of some high aristocrat from the era of Catherine the Great). Or so at least reasoned the Directorate of the Imperial Theaters. On 22 February 1902, Rimsky-Korsakov's *Mozart* was performed in the recently reopened Winter Palace's private Hermitage Theater as a part of weekly royal entertainment. That evening, the opera was sandwiched between two other curios in eighteenth-century style. One was a comédie-vaudeville, *Les deux timides* by Eugène Labiche, the last French playwright of old-fashioned farces that poked fun at the mid-nineteenth-century *hommes bourgeois* still dreaming of becoming *gentilshommes*. Another, the ballet-pantomime *Le coeur de la marquise* (with music by Ernest Guiraud and choreography by Marius Petipa), harked back to the gilded rococo genre of *fête galantes*. The pantomime's charming sets and costumes were designed by Léon Bakst, a young protégé of the erstwhile editor of the *Yearbook of the Imperial Theaters* (and presently the editor of *The World of Art* that printed Larosh's encomium), Sergei Diaghilev. The issue of the *Yearbook* that reported on that evening at the Hermitage Theater also contained a translation of a recent French play about a gawky Jewish nouveau riche on the brink of buying his gentility through marriage to an impoverished duchess. A xenophobic mixture of mockery, fear, and disdain, that play was called *Décadence*.[115]

# NOTES

1. N. A. Rimskiy-Korsakov, *Polnoye sobraniye literaturnïkh proizvedeniy* (Moscow: Muzïka, 1982), vol. 8B, 19. Here Rimsky-Korsakov does not even mention a string quartet he also composed that summer, as well as a good handful of the preparatory kind of composerly work: the analyses of numerous Bach and Mozart pieces that he undertook in June and July. For these biographical details, see Aleksandra Orlova, *Stranitsï zhizni N. A. Rimskogo–Korsakova: letopis' zhizni i tvorchestva*, vol. 3: *1894–1904* (Leningrad: Muzïka, 1972).

2. Among the more substantial contributions are Richard Taruskin, *Opera and Drama in Russia as Preached and Practiced in the 1860s* (Rochester, NY: University of Rochester Press, 1993); Marina Frolova-Walker, "Nikolay Andreyevich Rimsky-Korsakov," in *The New Grove Dictionary of Music and Musicians*; Marina Rakhmanova, *Nikolay Andreyevich Rimskiy-Korsakov* (Moscow: Akademiya imeni Gnesinïkh, 1995); Evgeniya Chigaryova, "'Mozart i Sal'yeri' Rimskogo–Korsakova: Dialog epokh i stiley," in *Nikolay Andreyevich Rimskiy-Korsakov: K 150-letiyu so dnya rozhdeniya i 90-letiuy so dnya smerti*, ed. Aleksey Kandinskiy (Moscow: Izdatel'stvo Moskovskoy konservatorii, 2000).

3. See N. A. Rimskiy-Korsakov, *Letopis' moyei muzïkal'noi zhizni* (Chronicle of My Musical Life), 8th ed. (Moscow: Muzïka, 1980), 266–67.

4. See esp. Taruskin, *Opera and Drama in Russia*; and Rakhmanova, *Nikolay Andreyevich Rimskiy-Korsakov*.

5. Taruskin, *Opera and Drama in Russia*, 326.

6. Marina Frolova-Walker, *Russian Music and Nationalism from Glinka to Stalin* (New Haven: Yale University Press, 2007) 206–7.

7. Francis Maes, *A History of Russian Music from "Kamarinskaya" to "Babi Yar"* (Berkeley: University of California Press, 2002), 175–81.

8. Russian scholarship, however much its range of perspectives diverges from that of Western musicology, is nevertheless largely in concurrence with this general conceptualization of Rimsky-Korsakov's artistic legacy.

9. Marina Frolova-Walker goes beyond this general style-historical argument in her recent essay "Salieri's Revenge" (*Mozart y Salieri*, program booklet, Teatro Musical de Cámara, Madrid, 2017) by looking at Rimsky-Korsakov's *Mozart* as a carefully crafted response to a certain critical stance. My essay, though in agreement with that view, focuses on a somewhat different context. I thank Dr. Frolova-Walker for kindly sending me the manuscript of her essay.

10. This work's self-reflectiveness has been noted by many, but never figured as a focal point of academic inquest. Likewise, several authors suggested Rimsky-Korsakov's identification with either Salieri—thus portraying Rimsky-Korsakov as a well-trained yet less adventurous contemporary of the more talented Musorgsky or Borodin—or Mozart, as a true "classicist" who values beauty and harmony above all. For the former, see Taruskin and almost everyone else; for the latter, see Rakhmanova, who renders Mozart and Rimsky-Korsakov in the same image. Caryl Emerson suggests a fusion of the two figures. See her "Little Tragedies, Little Operas," in *Alexander Pushkin's Little Tragedies: The Poetics of Brevity*, ed. Svetlana Evdokimova (Madison: University of Wisconsin Press: 2003), 265–89.

11. A. S. Pushkin, "Motsart i Sal'yeri," in *Sobraniye sochineniy v desyati tomakh*, vol. 4 (Moscow: GIKhL, 1960), 321–32. All translations in this essay are mine, unless indicated otherwise.

12. It was the real Salieri's alleged confession of guilty conscience, reported in the press perpetuating the rumor of his poisoning of Mozart, that caught Pushkin's attention before he embarked on this "little tragedy." See M. P. Alekseyev, "Kommentarii k 'Motsartu i Sal'yeri,'" in A. S. Pushkin, *Polnoye sobraniye sochineniy* (Moscow and Leningrad: Izdatel'stvo Akademii Nauk, 1937), 7:543–44.

13. Vissarion Belinskiy, "Sochineniya Aleksandra Pushkina," in *Polnoye sobraniye sochineniy* (Moscow: Izdatel'stvo Akademii Nauk, 1955), 7:557–60.

14. Ibid.

15. Numerous expressions from Pushkin's *Mozart and Salieri* would detach from their source play to serve as punchlines in philosophical essays, feuilletons, and even personal correspondence. For a salient instance of the latter, see V. I. Dotsenko, "Motsart v vospriyatii Turgeneva," *Naukovi zapiski harkivs'kogo nacional'nogo pedagogichnogo universitetu* 1/4 (2013): 65–70. For the rich public afterlife of the play's themes and memes, see V. S. Nepomnyashchiy, ed., *"Motsart i Sal'yeri," tragediya Pushkina: Dvizheniye vo vremeni* (Moscow: Naslediye, 1997).

16. On the cult of Mozart in Russia, see especially Tamara Livanova, *Motsart v russkoy muzïkal'noy kul'ture* (Moscow: Gosudarstvennoye muzïkal'noye izdatel'stvo, 1956); and Monika Greenleaf, "Feasting on Genius," in Evdokimova, *Alexander Pushkin's Little Tragedies*, 172–90.

17. On the late nineteenth-century Mozart mythology in the West, see esp. Leon Botstein, "Aesthetics and Ideology in the Fin-de-Siècle Mozart Revival," *Current Musicology* 51 (1993): 5–25; William Stafford, *Mozart Myths: A Critical Reassessment* (Stanford, CA: Stanford University Press, 1991); John Daverio, "Mozart in the Nineteenth Century," in *The Cambridge Companion to Mozart*, ed. Simon P. Keefe (Cambridge: Cambridge University Press, 2003), 169–84; Mark Everist, *Mozart's Ghosts: Haunting the Halls of Musical Culture* (Oxford: Oxford University Press, 2010).

18. Among these close readers were St. Petersburg University professor Dmitri Ovsyaniko-Kulikovsky, literary critic Arkady Gornfeld, and philosopher Yuly Aikhenvald, all quoted in Nepomnyashchiy, *"Motsart i Sal'yeri," tragediya Pushkina*. These intellectuals circulated in the networks closely associated with Rimsky-Korsakov's own circles; a few of the younger regulars at Rimsky-Korsakov's jour-fixes were students or avid readers of the above authors.

19. Yuliy Aykhenvald, *Pushkin* (Moscow: Nauchnoye slovo, 1908), quoted in Nepomnyashchiy, *"Motsart i Sal'yeri," tragediya Pushkina*, 53.

20. Dmitriy Ovsyaniko-Kulikovskiy, *Pushkin* (Simferopol: Russkoye knigoizdatel'stvo v Krïmu, 1919), quoted in Nepomnyashchiy, *"Motsart i Sal'yeri," tragediya Pushkina*, 61–63.

21. Greenleaf, "Feasting on Genius," 187.

22. Ibid., 186.

23. Fyodor Dostoevsky, the 1880 speech at the unveiling of the Pushkin Moscow monument. See F. M. Dostoyevskiy, *Polnoye sobraniye sochineniy v 30 tomakh* (Leningrad: Nauka, 1972–90), 26:137–48. That Pushkin's "universal responsiveness" was a uniquely Russian trait—the punchline of the whole speech—would by the early twentieth century have come as a natural quality of a "national genius."

24. The "responsiveness" argument, voiced by, among others, the literary critic R. V. Ivanov-Razumnik, was requoted in Gornfeld's take on Pushkin's Mozart, a testament to the argument's weight at the time. Quoted in Nepomnyashchiy, *"Motsart i Sal'yeri," tragediya Pushkina*, 46.

25. Rimskiy-Korsakov, *Letopis'*, 267.

26. Ibid., 268.

27. Ibid.

28. The most advertised of these soak-ups was Rimsky-Korsakov's immersion into fugal writing in the summer of 1875.

29. Rimskiy-Korsakov, *Letopis'*, 268. The composer dedicated *Mozart and Salieri* to Dargomyzhsky, but he could just as well have added Musorgsky's name to the dedication: the soliloquies of his (as well as Pushkin's) Salieri nod more to the monologues of the guilt-ridden Boris than to Don Juan's poetic philosophizing. All the same, Rimsky-Korsakov's dedication was to a great extent a matter of artistic obligation, as 1897 marked the silver jubilee of *The Stone Guest*'s premiere: in 1872, three years after its author's

death, the opera was finished by Cui, orchestrated by Rimsky-Korsakov, and performed at the Mariinsky.

30. Frolova-Walker, "Salieri's Revenge."

31. Rimsky-Korsakov reported on Stasov's reaction to his revision of *Boris* in his letter to Yastrebtsev of 29 June 1896. See N. A. Rimskiy-Korsakov, *Perepiska s V. V. Yastrebtsevïm i V. I. Belskim*, ed. L. G. Barsova (St. Petersburg: Sankt-Peterburgskaya konservatoriya, 2004), 65–68. Although Stasov would soon change his official stance on Rimsky-Korsakov's noble effort to revitalize Musorgsky's opera, he did not retract his critique until he heard *Mozart and Salieri*.

32. Rimsky-Korsakov's engagement with Musorgsky's works was a lifelong affair. In the spring of 1882, while editing the romances and the opera *Khovanshchina* by his recently deceased friend, Rimsky-Korsakov wrote to Semyon Kruglikov: "I think sometimes that my name is Modest Petrovich and not Nikolai Andreyevich." His letter is quoted in Andrey Rimskiy-Korsakov, *N. A. Rimskiy-Korsakov: Zhizn' i tvorchestvo* (Moscow: Muzgiz, 1936), 77.

33. Yastrebtsev reports this saga from Rimsky-Korsakov (who, in his turn, heard it from Director of St. Petersburg Imperial Theaters Vsevolozhsky) in his detailed recollection of his meetings with the composer. See Vasiliy Yastrebtsev, *Rimskiy-Korsakov: Vospominaniya Yastrebtseva*, vol. 1 (Leningrad: GMI, 1953–54), 424.

34. Ibid., 1:434.

35. In addition to his summer of counterpoint in 1875, another bout of self-education happened in the late 1880s, when Rimsky-Korsakov, awed by the Russian premiere of Wagner's *Ring*, immersed himself in the study of Wagner's orchestra.

36. Rimsky-Korsakov describes, in some juicy detail, his potential "La calumnia" in his letter to Yastrebtsev, 29 June 1896, *Perepiska s V. V. Yastrebtsevïm i V. I. Belskim*, 67.

37. Yastrebtsev, *Rimskiy-Korsakov: Vospominaniya*, 1:429. The same day Yastrebtsev sent a letter to Rimsky-Korsakov in which he tried to soothe the composer by, among other things, casting "coldness" as his music's advantageous trait. "Coldness" was, by implication, a running theme of their prior discussions and a core of Rimsky-Korsakov's self-criticism. See *Perepiska s V. V. Yastrebtsevïm i V. I. Belskim*, 87.

38. Rimskiy-Korsakov, *Letopis'*, 268.

39. Few Rimsky-Korsakov scholars have no say on *Mozart and Salieri*; moreover, several studies of this opera have been done by specialists in other musical chronologies or even in other disciplines. Among the academics, Chigaryova is a specialist in eighteenth-century music and Emerson is a literary and cultural scholar. Though most of these scholars give the laurels (directly or indirectly) to Rimsky-Korsakov's Mozart, there are marked exceptions, mostly coming from the hardcore Musorgskians or Stanislavskians. On the Russian-Soviet side, Abram Gozenpud (a theater historian as well as musicologist) elevated Salieri's part as more dramatically persuasive, closer to the Stanislavskian ideal, than Mozart's. See A. Gozenpud, *N. A. Rimskiy-Korsakov: Temï i idei yego opernogo tvorchestva* (Moscow: Muzgiz, 1957). In Anglophone musicology, Richard Taruskin likewise sees Rimsky-Korsakov's Salieri, along with this hero's perhaps most direct musical antecedent, Musorgsky's Boris Godunov, as a far more forceful contender for the listener's ear than Rimsky-Korsakov's Mozart. Expectedly, these verdicts are based by and large on the protagonists' vocal articulations.

40. See A. I. Kandinskiy, "O muzïkal'nïkh kharakteristikakh v tvorchestve Rimskogo-Korsakova 90-kh godov," in *N. A. Rimskiy-Korsakov: Issledovaniya, materialï, pis'ma*, ed. D. B. Kabalevsky et al. (Moscow: Akademiya nauk SSSR, 1954), vol. 1, 79–144, esp. 110–11.

41. Botstein, "Aesthetics and Ideology in the Fin-de-Siècle Mozart Revival," *Current Musicology* 51 (1993): 6.

42. Ibid.

43. Guido Adler, 1906 speech, Guido Adler Archive, University of Georgia, as quoted in ibid., 10.

44. Irina Paperno, Introduction and chap. 1 in *Creating Life: The Aesthetic Utopia of Russian Modernism* (Stanford, CA: Stanford University Press, 1994), 1–23.

45. Ibid. Much inspired by various Christian gnostic traditions, the "aesthetic utopians" often blended the catastrophic and the revelatory aspects of apocalypse, imagining it as both a final disaster and a final salvation.

46. Yastrebtsev, *Rimskiy-Korsakov: Vospominaniya*, 2:314

47. Several scholars have discussed the multiplicity of *Kitezh*'s literary and musical stock, but most comprehensively the many planes and forms of the opera's diversity (historical, symbolist, operatic, religious, folk-spiritual) are explored in Simon Morrison, "Rimsky-Korsakov and Religious Syncretism," in *Russian Opera and the Symbolist Movement* (Berkeley: University of California Press, 2002), 115–83.

48. Richard Taruskin, "The Legend of the Invisible City of Kitezh and the Maiden Fevroniya," *The New Grove Dictionary of Opera*, 2002.

49. N. A. Rimskiy-Korsakov, *Muzïkal'nïye stat'yi i zametki*, ed. Mikhail Gnesin (St. Petersburg: Tipografiya M. Stasyulevicha, 1911), 220.

50. Rimskiy-Korsakov, *Letopis'*, 231.

51. That essay, along with just a few other items tackling matters of musical pedagogy, is all that remained for posterity from Rimsky-Korsakov's aesthetic project. Early in 1894 the composer burned most of what he had by then written, deeming it unworthy of being shown to the wider world. All dates used here are Rimsky-Korsakov's and follow the Julian calendar.

52. Rimskiy-Korsakov, *Muzïkal'nïye stat'yi i zametki*, 77–78.

53. Ibid., 78.

54. Ibid. On Mozart as representative of the "free style" see also Rimsky-Korsakov's aesthetic jottings compiled posthumously under the title "Selected Pages from the Outline of a Treatise on Musical Arts" (218). It is also of note that the freedom in heterogeneity of Mozart's music was a punchline of Alexandre Oulibisheff's monumental *Nouvelle biographie de Mozart* (1843), of which the Russian translation, by Modest Tchaikovsky, came out in 1890. It was Mozart's stylistic variety, Oulibisheff maintained, that made up "Mozart's mission" of harmonious marriage of the contrasting German and Italian musical schools. Although Rimsky-Korsakov nowhere acknowledges his indebtedness to Oulibisheff's work, his formulations of Mozartean freedom (*svoboda*) and diversity (*raznoobraziye*) all but coincide with Oulibisheff's verbiage.

55. Rimskiy-Korsakov, *Muzïkal'nïye stat'yi i zametki*, 80–81.

56. Ibid., 81, 83.

57. Ibid., 85–88, 105. The institutional scope of the Conservatory, at least at the time, did not provide for a career in thinking about music in addition to careers in performance or composition; that is, in what I call "doing music." Hence, it never occurred (and perhaps could not have occurred) to Rimsky-Korsakov that his "theorists" may not have studied music in order only to produce more music.

58. Ibid., 94, 106.

59. Rimsky-Korsakov's list includes more than two sources (mostly just names) that he consulted while working on his aesthetic tract; among others, there were Spinoza, Spencer, and Guyot. Nevertheless, not only does he give more emphasis to Ambros and Lewes in his *Letopis'*, but their works also seem to receive the most resonance (both conceptual and terminological) in his texts. Ambros's 1856 study, which was a multimedia-friendly response to Eduard Hanslick's notorious paean to music's autonomy, *Vom Musikalisch-Schönen* (*On the Musically Beautiful*), which came out in Russian translation in 1889, is mentioned by both Rimsky-Korsakov in his *Letopis'* (231) and more than once by Yastrebtsev. As for G. H. Lewes, a good number of whose works had been translated into Russian and had become bestsellers by the time of Rimsky-Korsakov's aesthetic quest, the only Lewes study mentioned in the *Letopis'* is *The Biographical History of Philosophy*, which

had gone through three Russian editions before 1892. It is more than likely that Rimsky-Korsakov also read Lewes's multi-volume psycho-physiological treatise *Problems of Life and Mind* (1874–79), published in Russian as *Voprosï o zhizni i dukhe* (Questions of Life and Spirit) between 1875 and 1880. Not only does he use the novel, idiosyncratic terminology from that work in his essays, but even his later avowedly pantheistic pronouncements echo Lewes's monist formulations.

60. Ambros, in his own turn, lifted the notion of moods (*Stimmungen*) from A. B. Marx's 1855 treatise *Die Musik des neunzehnten Jahrhunderts und ihre Pflege: Methode der Musik*. But if for Marx "the music of moods" (alternatively translated into English as "the music of the soul") was a historical phase of Western music's development, superseding "the crystalline music" of the Renaissance and early Baroque and preceding "the music of the spirit" of the Romantic era, Ambros took the moods as altogether the primary content of music as a medium.

61. Wilhelm August Ambros, *The Boundaries of Music and Poetry: A Study of Musical Aesthetics*, trans. by J. H. Cornell (New York: Schirmer, 1893), 69, 125.

62. Ibid., 123, 142.

63. Rimskiy-Korsakov, *Muzïkal'nïye stat'yi i zametki*, 148–56. Italics are Rimsky-Korsakov's. Never contesting Wagner's genius and in fact giving much praise to his "marvelous orchestration," Rimsky-Korsakov nevertheless critiqued all other aspects of Wagnerian style, mainly for monotony, or *odnoobraziye*, the qualification that pops up relentlessly on every single page of his Wagner essay.

64. Dzhordzh Genri L'yuis, *Voprosï o zhizni i dukhe* (St. Petersburg: Znanie,1875–76); and *Izucheniye psikhologii, eyo predmet, oblast' i metod (prodolzheniye Voprosov o zhizni i dukhe)* (Moscow: A. Lang, 1880). The prominence of Lewes's *Problems of Life and Mind* in Russia is evidenced by the inclusion of this study in several entries of the Brockhaus and Efron encyclopedia; or the claims by Bekhterev and Stanislavsky of having been inspired by that and other Lewes works. What's more, that book even surfaced as an important read in literary fiction, for instance in *Siberian Tales* by Vladimir Korolenko.

65. While Lewes is careful not to confuse his empiricist notion of mind with the idealist—and so, for him, fallacious—concepts of soul, or spirit, in Russian translation Lewes's mind appears, ironically (yet idiomatically for the time and place), as either soul (*dusha*) or spirit (*dukh*).

66. Lewes, *Problems of Life and Mind*, esp. 153–61.

67. Ibid., 177.

68. Ibid.

69. Ibid., 147. On the broader Victorian contexts of Lewesian empiricism and sense-centeredness, see Vanessa L. Ryan, *Thinking Without Thinking in the Victorian Novel* (New Haven: Yale University Press, 2012); and Benjamin Morton, *The Outward Mind: Materialist Aesthetics in Victorian Science and Literature* (Chicago: Chicago University Press, 2017).

70. Ibid., 161. Although the phrase "common to all" suggests a universalist stance, Lewes, highbrow Victorian that he was, confident of the superiority of his own time, place, and English "race," does hold a cultural-relativist position when discussing "the store of experiences." By "common to all" he meant "common to all within a certain social group."

71. Rimsky-Korsakov, *Muzïkal'nïye stat'yi i zametki*, 119. Italics are Rimsky-Korsakov's. That this was not just a pipe dream of an idealist teacher is evidenced by the implementation in the later 1890s by Rimsky-Korsakov himself (at the St. Petersburg Conservatory) and by his former student Anton Arensky (at the Moscow Conservatory) of the practice of teaching by concrete and varied example, a sort of revival of the eighteenth-century practice of *partimenti*. See Robert O. Gjerdingen, "*Gebrauchs*-Formulas," *Music Theory Spectrum* (Fall 2011): 191–99.

72. Ibid., 108.

73. A good overview of Rimsky-Korsakov's anti-decadent stance, different in conceptual context from this essay yet still supporting its claims, can be found in Rutger

Helmers, "Rimsky-Korsakov, *The Tsar's Bride*, and the Fate of Music in the 20th Century," in *Rimskiy-Korsakov i yego naslediye v istoricheskoy perspektive*, ed. Lydia Ader (St. Petersburg: GMTiMI, 2010), 335–41. Also see chap. 4, "*The Tsar's Bride* and the Dilemma of History" of Helmers's monograph *Not Russian Enough? Nationalism and Cosmopolitanism in Nineteenth-Century Russia* (Rochester, NY: Rochester University Press, 2014).

74. Rimsky-Korsakov's letter from 3 March 1897, *Perepiska s V. V. Yastrebtsevïm i V. I. Belskim*, 244.

75. Ibid., 247, Belsky's letter from 26 May/7 June, 1897. (Since Belsky was writing from Germany, he double dated his letter according to both Julian and Gregorian calendars.) Notably, the performance Belsky attended was the revival of *Don Giovanni*'s 1787 premiere, with the original Mozart orchestra of only "27 chamber musicians" (as Belsky details in his letter) as well as the restored final sextet.

76. Ibid., 250, Rimsky-Korsakov's letter from 29 May. Italics are Rimsky-Korsakov's; the composer also uses an ecclesiastical, high-register form of the noun "mother"— *mati* rather than *mat'*—thus stressing the spiritual as well as material implications of the genitive potential of Mozart's music.

77. Wye Jamison Allanbrook, *The Secular Commedia: Comic Mimesis in Late Eighteenth-Century Music*, ed. Mary Ann Smart and Richard Taruskin (Berkeley: University of California Press, 2013), 60. Although in her book Allanbrook compellingly argues against the biased organicist readings of late eighteenth-century music by the Romanticist scholars, the abstract, autonomous, and self-propelling organism of her adversaries is a far cry from the connected and collaborative Lewesian organism, itself a version of the eighteenth-century Proteus. Lewes's vision even chimes with Allanbrook's in accounting for the dark side, a potential excess of diversity—the unhealthy overflow of "phantoms" of imagination insinuating themselves into the community with the same ease as the "real" sensory facts. Such, for Rimsky-Korsakov, would indeed be the darkest underside of the Wagnerian doxa.

78. On *Don Giovanni* as an exemplary musical fiction of "being as moving," one enlisting the universe of social dance as the measure of its heroes' stations and relations, see esp. "Part III, *Don Giovanni*" in Wye Jamison Allanbrook, *Rhythmic Gesture in Mozart: "Le Nozze di Figaro" and "Don Giovanni"* (Chicago: Chicago University Press, 1983), 197–325.

79. Save for the orchestral prelude, Mozart's "Aha!" is the first full cadence in the first scene. All through the opera, Mozart's part almost always participates in cadential action whereas Salieri's emphasizes instability.

80. On "sensibility" as a newly marked attitude (that is, culture) as well as a circumscribed musical sign (that is, topos) by the middle of the eighteenth century, see particularly Leonard Ratner, *Classic Music: Expression, Form and Style* (New York: Schirmer, 1980); Matthew Head, "Fantasia and Sensibility," in *The Oxford Handbook of Topic Theory*, ed. Danuta Mirka (Oxford: Oxford University Press, 2014), 259–78; and Robert Gjerdingen, *Music in the Galant Style* (Oxford: Oxford University Press, 2007).

81. This phrase comes from yet another of Rimsky-Korsakov's attempts at an aesthetics in 1902, collated with his other aesthetic jottings in Rimskiy-Korsakov, *Muzïkal'nïye stat'yi i zametki*, 220.

82. Ibid., diary entry, 9 March 1904, 222. Italics are Rimsky-Korsakov's. The entry's immediate context was Rimsky-Korsakov's attendance of a performance of Bach's St. John Passion, which he found too antiquated to move the contemporary listener. Mozart's musical modus operandi, on the other hand, he argued, was still effective, and thus constituted the originary source of his own evolutionary line.

83. Yastrebtsev, *Rimskiy-Korsakov: Vospominaniya*, 1:477.

84. Rimskiy-Korsakov, *Letopis'*, 270.

85. Among the sources cited in this study, for instance, Caryl Emerson's incisive discussion of the opera starts as follows: "In August 1898 in his St. Petersburg quarters, Rimsky-Korsakov (1840–1908) held a run-through of his just completed chamber opera

*Mozart and Salieri*. A gifted young bass from the provinces, Fyodor Chaliapin, sang both vocal parts; at the keyboard was Sergei Rachmaninoff." Here three separate events—the opera's completion (August 1897), its first play-through at the Rimsky-Korsakovs' (November 1897), and the legendary Chaliapin-Rachmaninoff home show with no Rimsky-Korsakov present (August 1898)—become one. (See Emerson, "Little Tragedies, Little Operas," 272.) The August 1898 play-through was organized by Savva Mamontov as a preliminary reading of the opera before it was put into production by the Moscow Private Opera and premiered in November that year.

86. Mikhail Lunacharsky (a brother of the future Narkom Anatoly) was a jurist, singer, and one of the founders of the St. Petersburg Society of Musical Meetings (Sankt-Peterburgskoye obshchestvo muzïkal'nïkh sobraniy). Until his Society started staging operas composed or edited by Rimsky-Korsakov (Lunacharsky was the first performer of Tokmakov in the third version of *The Maid of Pskov* and the first performer of Boris in Rimsky-Korsakov's revision of *Boris Godunov*), his repertoire included mainly romances and solo parts from Bach's and Mendelssohn's oratorios. See Yu. Keldïsh, ed., *Muzïkal'naya entsiklopediya*, 6 vols. (Moscow: Sovetskaya entsiklopediya, Sovetskiy kompozitor 1976), 3:339.

87. Nadezhda Zabela (also known as Zabela-Vrubel) became *the* Rimsky-Korsakov singer in the late 1890s; she premiered all major female roles in his fin-de-siècle operas. Her husband, famous painter Mikhail Vrubel, created the sets and costumes for the first production of *Mozart and Salieri*. Her letter is quoted in F. S. Fialkovskiy, ed., *N. A. Rimskiy-Korsakov: Iz semeynoy perepiski* (St. Petersburg: Kompozitor, 2008), 198. For more on Zabela, see Marina Frolova-Walker's introduction to the correspondence published in this volume.

88. Olga Haldey, *Mamontov's Private Opera: In Search of Modernism in Russian Theater* (Bloomington: Indiana University Press, 2009), 160. The section "I Want to Be a Musician: Nadezhda Zabela" details the controversial relationship, as well as the ideational divergence, between Mamontov and Zabela.

89. Ivan Lipaev, "*Mozart and Salieri* in Moscow," *Russkaya muzïkal'naya gazeta* 1 (1899): 12–13. The opera was premiered in a double bill with Gluck's *Orfeo*.

90. Ibid.

91. That this is how Rimsky-Korsakov may have indeed viewed Lipaev's review is evidenced by Yastrebtsev's recollection of himself and Rimsky-Korsakov being so pleased with the review that Yastrebtsev decided to subscribe to *Russkaya muzïkal'naya gazeta*. See Yastrebtsev, *Rimskiy-Korsakov: Vospominaniya*, 1:461.

92. "Operï i kontsertï: 'Motsart i Sal'yeri' v Chastnoy Opere," *Russkaya muzïkal'naya gazeta* 12 (1899): 373–75. The review was unsigned, but even its first readers recognized in its style as well as its manner of partisanship the pen of Evgeny Petrovsky, a co-editor as well as a sponsor of *Russkaya muzïkal'naya gazeta*. A degreed financier and an owner of apartment buildings in St. Petersburg, he was not a musician; however, with some self-schooling in music, he became one of the staunchest Russian Wagner propagandists. See Rosamund Bartlett, *Wagner and Russia* (Cambridge: Cambridge University Press, 1995), esp. chap. 3.

93. Ibid.

94. According to Yastrebtsev, the entire Rimsky-Korsakov circle found Petrovsky's review despicable, and Stasov even sent an angry letter to the journal's editor-in-chief Nikolai Findeisen demanding an apology. See Yastrebtsev, *Rimskiy-Korsakov: Vospominaniya*, 2:72–73. Eventually, Petrovsky and Rimsky-Korsakov made up, and Petrovsky even served as the librettist of Rimsky-Korsakov's 1902 opera *Kashchei the Deathless*.

95. German Larosh, "Po povodu odnogo spektaklya," *Mir iskusstva* 9 (1899): 91–95.

96. Ibid., 95.

97. Richard Taruskin, *Defining Russia Musically: Historical and Hermeneutical Essays* (Princeton: Princeton University Press, 1997), 276; German Larosh, "Vospominaniya o

Chaykovskom," first published in *Novosti* (1893), 323, reprinted in G. A. Larosh, *Sobraniye muzïkal'no-kriticheskikh statey* (Moscow: Gosudarstvennoe muzïkal'noe izdatel'stvo, 1922), vol. 2, part 1, 12.

98. Arkadiy Klimovitskiy, "Motsart Chaikovskogo, fragmentï syuzheta" and "*Pikovaya dama* Chaikovskogo: Kul'turnaya pamyat', kul'turnïye predchuvstviya," in *Pyotr Il'yich Chaykovskiy: Kul'turnaya pamyat', kul'turnïye predchuvstviya, kul'turnïye vzaimodeystviya* (St. Petersburg: Petropolis, 2015), 145–90, 35-102.

99. Ibid., 155, 76.

100. Taruskin develops a corresponding argument, focusing on the mediating role in Tchaikovsky's operas of the conventions of Russian domestic romance, in his "Tchaikovsky and the Ghetto," in *Defining Russia Musically*, 48–60. Klimovitsky sees that early nineteenth-century tradition (what he calls the Russian "sensibility style"), revived in *Eugene Onegin* and elsewhere, as an outgrowth of the domesticated Mozartean stance. See esp. 74–77.

101. German Larosh, "Muzïkal'nïye vpechatleniya i zametki," *Golos* (1878), 254, reprinted in Larosh, *Sobraniye muzïkal'no-kriticheskikh statey*, vol. 2, part 1, 170. To be sure, in his 1899 review of Rimsky-Korsakov's opera, Larosh also discusses differences between Tchaikovsky and Rimsky-Korsakov, the key one, in his opinion, being the contrast of "ever-fermenting" (Tchaikovsky) and "ever-disciplining" (Rimsky-Korsakov) personalities.

102. Rimsky-Korsakov to S. N. Kruglikov, 18 February 1898, as quoted in Andrey Nikolayevich Rimsky-Korsakov, *Nikolay Andreyevich Rimskiy-Korsakov: Zhizn' i tvorchestvo* (Moscow: GMI, 1930), 4:112–13. Italics are Rimsky-Korsakov's.

103. Yastrebtsev, *Rimskiy-Korsakov: Vospominaniya*, 1:203–4.

104. Taruskin, *Defining Russia Musically*, 276.

105. Yastrebtsev, *Rimskiy-Korsakov: Vospominaniya*, 1:331.

106. Ibid., 1:430.

107. Rimskiy-Korsakov, *Letopis'*, 93.

108. Quoted in *N. A. Rimskiy-Korsakov: Issledovaniya, materialï, pis'ma*, 1:295.

109. Emil (Emiliy) Borman, review in *St. Petersburger Zeitung*, 23 April 1899. As quoted in Yastrebtsev, *Rimskiy-Korsakov: Vospominaniya*, 2:79.

110. Ibid.

111. Luba Golburt, *The First Epoch: The Eighteenth Century and the Russian Cultural Imagination* (Madison: University of Wisconsin Press, 2014).

112. Here I borrow the shape of the argument from Richard Taruskin's chapter "Tchaikovsky and the Human," in *Defining Russia Musically*. Taruskin, however, discusses Tchaikovsky's eighteenth-century values of pleasure and merriment in opposition to the privileged musicological perspective of greatness rooted in nineteenth-century German philosophy, the perspective from which the composer had been routinely judged (and pronounced a failure) in the West until Taruskin's groundbreaking book. This essay is concerned with a far more circumscribed (both historically and geographically) aesthetic territory, and by no means do I claim similar differentiation between Tchaikovsky and Rimsky-Korsakov.

113. Yastrebtsev, *Rimskiy-Korsakov: Vospominaniya*, 1:52. The verdict concerns Tchaikovsky's *The Nutcracker*.

114. Simon Morrison, "Chaikovsky and Decadence," in *Russian Opera and the Symbolist Movement*, 69.

115. That play, by Albert Guinon, briefly appeared in Republican France in 1901 but was quickly banned for its blatant xenophobia. See Robert Justin Goldstein, "France," in *The Frightful Stage: Political Censorship in the Theater in Nineteenth-Century Europe*, ed. R. J. Goldstein (New York and Oxford: Berghan Books, 2009), 109. For the description of the program at the Hermitage Theater on 22 February 1902, see "Spektakli v teatre Imperatorskogo Ermitazha" in *Yezhegodnik Imperatorskikh Teatrov* (Yearbook of the Imperial Theaters), ed. L. A. Gelmersen (St. Petersburg: Izdaniye Direktsii Imperatorskikh Teatrov, 1901–1902), 13–14; for the Russian translation of the French play, see supplement (*prilozheniye*) 6.

Orientalism and *The Golden Cockerel*

# Nikolai Rimsky-Korsakov and His Orient

## ADALYAT ISSIYEVA

Rimsky-Korsakov's contributions to both Russian and general European music with oriental subjects are widely acknowledged by researchers and have been emulated by many Russian as well as Western European composers (Glazunov, Stravinsky, Debussy, Ravel).[1] His evaluation of his own music evoking the Orient, however, was far more critical and less enthusiastic. Just a few months before his death, in a conversation with his Armenian student Alexander Spendiarov, witnessed by V. V. Yastrebtsev, Rimsky-Korsakov declared that in comparison with Spendiarov's Orient his own Orient was "somewhat far-fetched and speculative" since the Orient "was not in his blood" and, therefore, he could not produce something "authentic" or "truly valuable" in this area.[2] Why, after composing his world-acclaimed symphonic pieces *Antar* and *Sheherazade*, did Rimsky-Korsakov still doubt his ability to compose oriental music? In the second half of the nineteenth century, the Russian public (and the Kuchka) had high expectations of how music should reflect reality.[3] After Félicien David's *Le désert,* which was inspired by his travel to the French Orient; Mily Balakirev's *Tamara,* inspired by music of peoples living in the Caucasus; and Camille Saint-Saëns's oriental works, the opera *Samson et Dalila* and the "Egyptian" Piano Concerto, motivated by the composer's travels to Algiers and Egypt, it seemed almost indispensable for a respected composer to be immersed in oriental culture before creating a proper (read "authentic") oriental piece of music. Other conditions could also include cultural or genetic inheritance, which, in the case of Russia, was not unusual because of Russia's unique geographical advantage of sharing land with the East and steady assimilation over a few centuries of eastern and southern peoples living on the outskirts of the empire. In the Russian imagination, being born in a city or a village with a high Asian population or having an Eastern lineage (no matter how many centuries it dated back), enhanced a composer's credentials to write in an oriental idiom, never mind being raised in what was thought as a perfectly Western society (like Borodin, Rubinstein, or Spendiarov).

Rimsky-Korsakov met none of these conditions. His Russian lineage could be traced back fourteen generations,[4] and his limited encounters with Middle Eastern, Asian, or other non-Western musicians, which left marks on his works, can be counted on the fingers of one hand. In the early 1860s, during his trip around the world on the clipper *Almaz* as an officer in the tsar's navy, he heard some Native American musicians playing at a New York museum; then, during his travel to Russia's East in 1874, he enjoyed the performance of Gypsy musicians; and late in his life, in the summer of 1889 at the Paris World Exposition, he was impressed by Hungarian and Algerian musicians.[5] However, all of these experiences, along with other scattered overhearings of Russia's Asian or Caucasian musicians in Russian metropoles, were not sufficient to give him confidence to claim that he understood the spirit of eastern music. To be fair, especially in his earlier pieces, Rimsky-Korsakov made multiple attempts to present "authentic" oriental material by employing original Caucasian tunes from Balakirev's sketchbook (discussed below), or introducing a couple of his own transcriptions from friends who had traveled to the East, or incorporating a few Arabic songs from two collections published in the 1860s in French.[6] (Russian musical ethnographies on Eastern peoples started appearing only in the last two decades of the nineteenth century).[7] He also seemed to follow Balakirev's advice to pay particular attention to rhythmical aspects of non-Western music—the feature that Rimsky-Korsakov later claimed to be one of the most important in music in general.[8] Indeed, each time he encountered musicians, he paid attention not to their entire performance but rather to some elements of it: striking rhythmical figures, scales, or ornamentation.[9] Yet because of a vague notion of "artistic truth," which assumed only a partial correspondence to reality, Rimsky-Korsakov was able to produce "all-purpose oriental idioms"[10] and managed to avoid any critique by his contemporaries for not being sufficiently authentic in representing the Orient.[11]

Despite being raised on nineteenth-century Orientalist musical conventions, his view of the East underwent a profound transformation and departed from Orientalism; it developed from simple imitation and reliance on the Orientalist truisms to the critique of these very truisms.[12] Rimsky-Korsakov's last opera, *The Golden Cockerel*, demonstrates that his attitude toward Russia's eastern neighbors drastically changed. After the disastrous confrontation with Japan that brought Russia to the 1905 Revolution, Rimsky-Korsakov, like many other Russian intellectuals, questioned the legitimacy of the war and expressed his disagreement over the autocracy's Eastern diplomacy.[13] His *Golden Cockerel* problematizes Russian officials' vision of Asia as the "Yellow Peril" and prophetically warns that an oversimplification of an unknown and sophisticated East, personified by the Queen of Shemakha and the Astrologer, could bring about the downfall of the empire. The opera's two most fantastic and undeniably eastern characters help to reveal not only the absurdity of Russia's political system but Rimsky-Korsakov's own skepticism vis-à-vis Eurocentric legitimations of colonial conquest.

Before going on to discuss how and why Rimsky-Korsakov came to revise his contemporaries' perception of the Orient as well as his own, let us first consider his early works with oriental subjects and trace the main stages in the development of his musical Orient.

## Early Influences

Rimsky-Korsakov's early impressions of the East were mediated by Mily Balakirev, who, in Rimsky-Korsakov's own words, was his "alpha and omega" at that time.[14] After his second trip to the Caucasus in 1863, Balakirev brought a number of transcriptions of traditional tunes, many elements of which traveled directly from his sketchbook to Rimsky-Korsakov's music.[15] The young naval officer's heavy dependence on Balakirev's Eastern vocabulary is fairly obvious in his early oriental art songs "Yel' i pal'ma" (The Pine and the Palm), "Plenivshis' rozoy solovey" (Enslaved by the Rose, the Nightingale)," and "Kak nebesa tvoy vzor prekrasen" (Thy Glance Is Radiant as the Heavens). Rhythmical figures in the accompaniment (subdividing the second beat with shorter notes), melodic ornamentations, and harmonic progressions (especially sustained bass with changing harmony on the top)—all recall the Balakirev pieces inspired by his Caucasian trip.[16] Even twenty years later, Balakirev's transcriptions of Caucasian tunes reverberated in Rimsky-Korsakov's imagination. In *Sheherazade*, for instance, Rimsky-Korsakov closely followed a melody to which Balakirev was particularly attached, the traditional Georgian song "Akh, Dilav!" (no. 19 in Balakirev's sketchbook).[17] The second phrase of "Akh, Dilav"—with its characteristic rhythm and a descending stepwise motion from the fifth to the third scale degree touching a lower neighbor note—bears a striking resemblance to the main theme (Kalender Prince) of the second movement of Rimsky-Korsakov's symphonic piece (compare Examples 1a and 1b).

Example 1a. "Akh, Dilav" from Balakirev's sketchbook, mm. 4–6.

Example 1b. Rimsky-Korsakov, *Sheherazade*, movement 2, mm. 348–51.

Another example of the remarkable similarity between Balakirev's transcriptions and Rimsky-Korsakov's music is found in the violin solo from the first movement of *Sheherazade*. The triplet arabesque replicates almost exactly a tune from Balakirev's sketchbook that is possibly of Chechen origin (no. 10 in Balakirev's sketchbook). Like Balakirev's transcription, the melody in *Sheherazade* moves down in triplets touching the upper neighbor note; in both examples it is played against a suspended note and then is repeated one step down (compare Examples 2a and 2c). Most probably Rimsky-Korsakov borrowed this whirling motive of triplets from Balakirev's symphonic poem *Tamara*, since, as we can see from Examples 2b and 2c, he almost exactly repeated the contour of his teacher's tune.

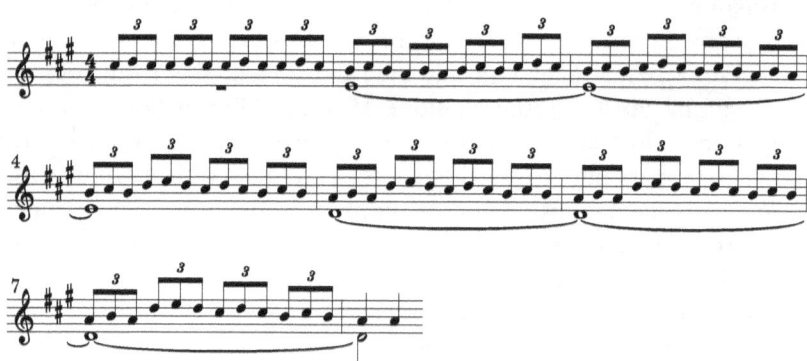

Example 2a. tune no. 10 from Balakirev's sketchbook, mm. 1–8.

Example 2b. Balakirev, *Tamara*, mm. 35–37.

Example 2c. Rimsky-Korsakov, *Sheherazade*, mov. I, mm. 94–101.

Besides Balakirev's musical language, Rimsky-Korsakov was strongly influenced by Dargomyzhsky's oriental idioms. The convergence between the two composers took place exactly as Rimsky-Korsakov started feeling "some signs of coolness" between himself and Balakirev, because of the latter's "cutting paternal despotism."[18] Throughout the winter of 1867 and 1868, Rimsky-Korsakov participated in weekly gatherings at Dargomyzhsky's house, and it was during this time that Musorgsky and Cui suggested to Rimsky-Korsakov that he write music based on Osip Senkovsky's famous "Arabian tale."[19] The Orientalist aspects of Senkovsky's *Antar* are hard to deny; the East is characterized through three main

Example 3. Dargomyzhsky's arrangement of "Algerian Tune."

Orientalist clichés: revenge, power, and love, which a male protagonist, Antar, wants to experience.[20] In the desert of Palmyra he meets and saves a gazelle, who turns out to be the *peri*, or fairy, called Gul Nazar, the Queen of Palmyra. As a reward for his courage, she promises him to fulfill three wishes. None of the wishes, however, brings Antar eternal bliss, so to fulfill his last wish Peri Gul Nazar takes Antar's life with a final embrace. Since Rimsky-Korsakov presented Antar with Western musical vocabulary and Gul Nazar with that of the East, Francis Maes argues that the story's ending suggests that oriental female sensuality does "exert a paralyzing, indeed destructive influence" over a Western man.[21]

Leaving aside the Orientalist message of the story, one must ask, does the music truly portray Peri Gul Nazar as a sensual force who exercises power over the male protagonist? Let's consider the last movement, in which Gul Nazar is characterized by a traditional Algerian tune, which was first published in a book by Alexander Christianowitsch, *Esquisse historique de la musique arabe aux temps anciens*, then arranged by Dargomyzhsky and given to Rimsky-Korsakov as a source for inspiration.[22] According to Rimsky-Korsakov, he kept Dargomyzhsky's harmonization at the beginning

Example 4. Rimsky-Korsakov, *Antar*, mov. IV, mm. 13–28.

of the Andante amoroso.[23] Indeed, both melodies are harmonized similarly and have almost identical voice leading (even the parallel thirds in the accompaniment at the end of the tune). Dargomyzhsky's arrangement does not provide a clear tonal center; the accompaniment oscillates between C-major, E-minor, A-minor, and F-major chords, creating—with its diatonic coloring and preponderance of minor chords—a rather somber mood (see Example 3).[24] Rimsky-Korsakov's harmonization, however, gives a slightly better sense of a tonal center. He moves the melody up a semitone to D-flat major—Balakirev's favorite tonality for the expression of love—and, subtly shifting the harmony toward a major color, he escapes from Dargomyzhsky's somberness (see Example 4). By slightly changing the melody's rhythmical pattern, making it more capricious and less even, Rimsky-Korsakov refines the melody's sensitivity and enhances its tenderness and delicacy. It is hard to claim, however, that there is any trait of overt sexuality or explicit sensuality in the music. Rather, while using the Orientalist story, Rimsky-Korsakov takes a path of more complex representation that does not reduce the oriental female to exclusively seductive characteristics. Peri Gul Nazar, in Rimsky-Korsakov's view, has a charming and complex nature and can reveal various sides of her personality, including melancholy and contemplativeness.

By sticking closely to Dargomyzhsky's harmonization of the "Algerian Tune," Rimsky-Korsakov followed his example in arranging Algerian music as simple, non-Orientalizing, and free of conventional romantic exoticism. The other two elements inspired by Dargomyzhsky and found in Example 4—augmented harmony (measure 15) and a particular rhythmic-melodic figuration (measure 24)—confirm once again Rimsky-Korsakov's allegiance to Dargomyzhsky's oriental vocabulary. In a conversation with Yastrebtsev, Rimsky-Korsakov once noted that augmented harmony was prominent in Dargomyzhsky's music, and appeared for the first time in his *Finnish Fantasy* (1867).[25] Actually, Dargomyzhsky had used an augmented triad for the first time in his "Oriental Song" fifteen years earlier, in 1852, and Rimsky-Korsakov was well familiar with that art song.[26] The augmented harmony in Dargomyzhsky's "Oriental Song" appears quite unconventionally: the opening chords of the piano interlude, instead of giving a clear sense of the key, slowly unfold the augmented triad in a low register, emphasizing the exotic character of the song's protagonist through tonal ambiguity. The same chord is heard at the very beginning of Dargomyzhsky's "Oriental Choir of Hermits" from his unfinished opera *Rogdana* and is also found in his art song evoking Spain, "Ya zdes' Inezil'ya" (I am Here, Inezil'ya), as well as in the above-mentioned *Finnish Fantasy*, and in his opera *The Stone Guest* (in the scene with Don Juan and the statue), suggesting that for Dargomyzhsky an augmented triad signified otherness in general.[27]

Another rhythmic-melodic gesture originating from Dargomyzhsky's art songs is a melodic figure that was often used by members of the Kuchka to represent the Orient. It is a relatively long note (a quarter or a half note) tied to a group of four thirty-second notes, the second of which touches the upper neighbor note, and then the melody moves three steps down before repeating the last note twice (see Example 4, measure 24). Examples of this figure appear in Dargomyzhsky's Eastern aria "O deva-roza, ya v okovakh" (Oh Rose-Maiden, I Am in Shackles, 1858), Balakirev's "Gruzinskaya pesnya" (Georgian Song, 1863), Rimsky-Korsakov's "Plenivshis' rozoy, solovey" (Enslaved by the Rose, the Nightingale, 1866), Musorgsky's "Pesnya Baleartsa" (Song of the Balearic Islander) from his unfinished opera *Salammbô*, César Cui's "Le Turc" (late 1880s), Glazunov's oriental art song "V krovi gorit ogon' zhelan'ya" (The Fire of Desire Burns in My Blood, 1888) and his "Arabskaya melodiya" (Arabian Melody, 1885), and many others. In *The Golden Cockerel*, Rimsky-Korsakov uses this figure to characterize the Queen of Shemakha in her most sensual or emotionally charged moments; she sings it when

Example 5. Rimsky-Korsakov, *The Golden Cockerel*, Act 2.

she describes her sensual dream and when she recalls her home, which brings her to a weeping emotional outburst (see Example 5).

Although Rimsky-Korsakov and the Kuchka generally downplayed or deliberately ignored the influence of Anton Rubinstein on their music, as Marina Frolova-Walker has observed, a number of elements from Rubinstein's music were appropriated by the kuchkists, including Rimsky-Korsakov. Though characterizing Rubinstein's compositions as "hopelessly monotonous," Rimsky-Korsakov excluded some of his works—mainly the ones with oriental subjects—from his list of "colorless" and "unoriginal" music, and drew a wealth of exotic elements from them.[28] For our purposes, Rubinstein's cycle of *Persian Songs* is of interest, first because it is one of the few Rubinstein pieces accepted by the Kuchka as being "significant" or "original"; and second because it provides clear evidence that Rimsky-Korsakov studied Rubinstein's music closely and borrowed a few particular gestures from it. Take for instance song no. 6 "Nas po odnoy doroge sud'ba s toboy vedyot" (Destiny Drives Us on the Same Path) from *Persian Songs*. The second half of the song is based entirely on a long melisma in the vocal line accompanied by sustained chords in the right hand and the imitation of a plucking instrument playing perfect fifths in the left (see Example 6a). In his clarinet solo from *Sheherazade*, Rimsky-Korsakov not only replicates the melodic contour of the vocal melisma, but also uses almost the same harmonic progression to support

Example 6a. Rubinstein, "Nas po odnoy doroge" from the cycle *Persian Songs*, mm. 11–14.

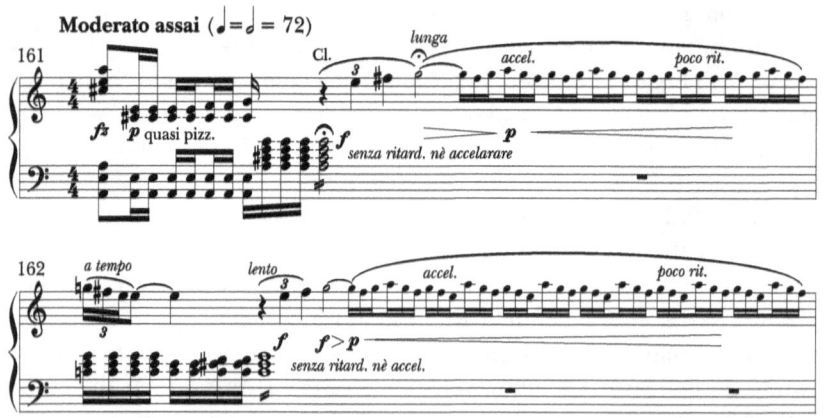

Example 6b. Rimsky-Korsakov, *Sheherazade*, mov. II, mm. 161–62.

it: the dominant seventh chord in Rubinstein's art song is changed by a minor-minor chord on the same scale degree, while Rimsky-Korsakov, instead of using a minor-minor chord, cuts its lowest note, turning the chord to a simple C-major triad (see Example 6b).

## The Last Opera

Throughout his life, Rimsky-Korsakov continued to evoke the East, relying on musical conventions and "artistic truth" established in Russian music literature. Some contemporary critics, however, found Rimsky-Korsakov's oriental pieces shallow, albeit not on the grounds of inauthenticity. It is hard to believe, but the premiere of *Sheherazade*, the most famous of Rimsky-Korsakov's oriental pieces, was almost cancelled because the Imperial Russian Musical Society objected that it "might corrupt the taste of our musical youth."[29] Even after the symphonic suite was accepted, thanks to the intervention of July Ivanovich Johansen, the director of the St. Petersburg Conservatory, Rimsky-Korsakov was paid only fifty rubles, or half the stipulated composer's fee for the performance of a symphonic work, since *Sheherazade* appeared to be "too light and playful to qualify for that fee."[30]

The composer took this lesson seriously, and for nine years after 1888, he wrote almost exclusively opera, creating at the incredible pace of one per year. Rimsky-Korsakov's last opera, *The Golden Cockerel*, cannot be accused of any superficiality or "lightness." The musical language—with its highly sophisticated harmony and intellectually produced symmetry, refined melodic contours, utterly satirical and simultaneously exquisite symbolic vocabulary—reached the pinnacle of musical and aesthetic perfection.

The opera was meant to offend the authorities and the tsar himself, whose absurd actions eventually cost him his life. One year after the disastrous loss in the Russo-Japanese War (1904–1905), which had led Russia to its first large-scale revolution in 1905, and after Rimsky-Korsakov's defamatory dismissal from the St. Petersburg Conservatory, the composer was motivated to highlight all the abominations of autocratic rule as "la bestialité dans toute sa candeur" (as Rimsky-Korsakov put it) with "caustic humor" and even biting sarcasm.[31] Besides being deeply unsatisfied with the ugly political situation and foolish complacency of the authorities, Rimsky-Korsakov, like many other members of liberal society, was frustrated with Russian policies in the East. In a number of letters and exchanges with close friends such as Belsky, Yastrebtsev, and Glazunov, he expressed his deep concern (indeed, distress and grief) over Russia's Eastern affairs.[32]

On 5 August 1904, Rimsky-Korsakov wrote a letter to his former student, friend, and colleague Glazunov:

> And what horrors are now going on in the East. Port Arthur is clearly living out its last days. We will have many more victims in this damned war! . . . "Monkeys, just monkeys![33] We will smother them with our caps, we will drag them by their ears!"— that's what was said here. "After the first battle on dry land, it will be all over for the Japs!" and so forth— and look what actually happened. I have to admit, I can't get the war out of my head.[34]

In light of these remarks, Gerald Abraham's claim that the summer of 1904 passed peacefully for Rimsky-Korsakov, although "the disasters of Japanese War wounded his patriotic pride," and "thousands of Russians were dying round Port Arthur," does not accurately reflect the composer's state of mind.[35] Not only was he concerned about the war and the people dying on both sides, but like many members of Russia's intelligentsia, disagreed with the blatantly racist descriptions of the Japanese.[36] A little over two years after this letter, Rimsky-Korsakov and his librettist Belsky used the monkey image to describe Tsar Dodon, distancing themselves from the official discourse about the East and from Russia's own embarrassing cultural, racist, and colonialist mimicry (often referred to as "aping") of the West.[37] It should not then be a surprise that when Ivan Bilibin (1876–1942) later drew illustrations for *The Golden Cockerel*'s score and designed the stage decoration for its premiere production at Zimin's Private Opera in Moscow in 1909, he portrayed Tsar Dodon with unambiguously Asian features.[38] The propaganda of stereotypes had little or no impact on the Russian intelligentsia. Even during the most difficult wartime moments, Russian artists and literati (Valery Bryusov, Vyacheslav Ivanov, Zinaida Gippius, and others) tended to see the Japanese foe philosophically, often as something inevitable, like a cleansing storm, as Yuliya Mikhailova has stressed.[39] Japanese art and culture was admired by many artists, including Bilibin, who considered it modern.[40] At the height of the Russo-Japanese War, despite mounting fear of a Yellow Peril, Bilibin painted a series of watercolor illustrations for Pushkin's "Tale of Tsar Saltan" that suggested the preponderant influence of Katsushika Hokusai's *Thirty-Six Views of Mount Fuji* (1831).

As Japan's gaze turned to the West in the Meiji period (1868–1912), "seeking knowledge throughout the world so as to strengthen the foundation of imperial rule,"[41] Western artists and intellectuals became increasingly fascinated with the nation's premodern culture and art. The craving for Japanese culture among Russian artists and the general public exploded after the exposition of Sergei Kitaev's collection of Japanese woodblock prints in 1896–97 in St. Petersburg and Moscow.[42] The exposition fueled a boom of Japanese exhibitions, events, and publications—a *japonisme* that introduced Russians to the small country located just beyond the empire's Pacific frontier.[43] In 1897 *Niva*, one of the most popular weeklies, published an essay by Kitaev on his collection and also featured Igor Grabar's manifesto on modern art, in which the young art critic proclaimed Japanese methods of painting a model for the expression of *subjectivity*, and thus the model for modern works of art in general.[44] Other events related to Japanese culture included the 1901 performance of a Japanese drama troupe in St. Petersburg, the 1901–1902 exhibition of Japanese engravings from the collection of Prince Sergei A. Shcherbatov and Vladimir V. von Meck (a grandson of Tchaikovsky's patron Nadezhda von Meck), the 1903 St. Petersburg "modern art" exhibition of Japanese woodcut prints curated by Shcherbatov and Igor Grabar, coupled with the publication of Grabar's *Japanese Color Woodblock Prints*,[45] the 1905 exhibition of Hasegawa's woodblock prints, and the 1906 exposition of Chinese and Japanese works of art and religious artifacts from the collection of N. P. Kalabushkin. The latter two exhibitions took place during and after the Russo-Japanese War. Indeed, as Rosamund Bartlett points out, "No other country in the world had ever found itself in the position of being simultaneously at war with, and culturally in thrall to, Japan: this was a unique situation."[46]

Rimsky-Korsakov and Belsky reworked Pushkin's "Golden Cockerel" to ensure that their contemporaries would not miss the opera's connection to Japan, adding a number of features revealing the Queen of Shemakha's Japanese origin. (In Pushkin's tale, the Queen has but one line of indirect speech). In the opera she introduces herself with an aria addressed to the Sun—the symbol of Japan; when Dodon asks where her home is, she answers that she comes from an "island floating between the earth and sky," and to reach it, one needs to move toward the East.[47] Despite the fact that some Russian writers, including composer and teacher Mikhail Gnesin, interpret the Queen's description of her country as evidence of her "fairy-tale dream-like origin,"[48] this image is not far from Rimsky-Korsakov's own impressions of Japan. The composer's perception of this country was shaped in his childhood by the letters of his elder brother, Captain-Lieutenant Voin Rimsky-Korsakov, who traveled to Japan as a commander of the schooner *Vostok* in 1852, and by the famous writer Ivan Goncharov, who participated in the same journey as secretary of Admiral Putyatin and described this trip in his extremely popular book *Frigate "Pallada."*[49] Although in his letters written home Voin complained that he had no chance to land on Japanese soil and had almost no personal contact with the Japanese people, he saw some Japanese women on boats passing by the Russian ships and described them in flattering terms, at one point even musing about being captivated by one of them.[50]

Undoubtedly familiar with Goncharov's literary travelogue, which contains many pages devoted to Japan, the composer of *The Golden Cockerel* could have been infatuated with the writer's idealized and highly refined vision of Japan, presented rather as an unreal "thrice-tenth tsardom," or a far-off place in Russian fairy tales: "What is this? A stage décor or reality? What a [marvelous] place . . . everything is so harmonious, so little resembling real life, that you begin to have doubts: is this scene an artist's picture, or taken entirely from a fairy-tale ballet?"[51] Rimsky-Korsakov and Belsky may also have borrowed from Goncharov's "Dream of Oblomov" the idea for Tsar Dodon's dream, that described the protagonist's reverie about this most "blessed corner of earth" (an element that was not present in Pushkin's tale). It seems that Rimsky-Korsakov also shared Goncharov's distaste for European imperialism in Asia. After reflecting on how Japan is different linguistically, culturally, and historically from Europe, Goncharov defended the country's choice to stay closed to the West, since the Japanese "did not see any good from the Europeans, but much evil."[52]

Rimsky-Korsakov's understanding of Japan as a highly aestheticized, refined, mysterious, and attractive land seems to be metaphorically connected to the Queen of Shemakha, the oriental beauty; her utterly exotic and bellicose nature resonated with the perception of Japan promoted in the Russian press.[53] One of the earliest critiques of the first performance of *The Golden Cockerel* is worth citing in full, since it perfectly captures Shemakha's sophisticated musical character:

> This character [of the Queen of Shemakha] is something new, something unseen before in our musical literature. It contains the venom of sarcasm, the primordial seductive graces of the fairy-tale Orient, a poignant and almost realistic tragedy of a lonely female soul looking for a worthy conqueror, along with a sort of predatory demonism with claws that are sometimes hidden, sometimes revealed. All

these diverse and seemingly contradictory qualities are melded together by the charms of music into something integral, living, vivid, and mysteriously beautiful. Melodies endlessly flow from the lips of the Queen of Shemakha—almost all breathing an Eastern chromaticism, each one more beautiful than the next, and there is no limit to this sea of song that reflect a thousand shades of passion, dreams, playfulness, and mockery.[54]

It must be stressed that Rimsky-Korsakov resisted the one-sided, negative characterization of the Queen that Belsky had initially envisioned. In a letter to the composer, Belsky urged Rimsky-Korsakov not to "ennoble the immodest pranks of the Queen by casting out from the instrumentation all its sultry sensuousness."[55] "The Queen," he continued, "is the devilish seductiveness of sensual beauty, and turning her into an ideal of pure beauty would first of all eliminate the moral meaning of the plot as well as the contrast between the evil that reigns without limit on the stage vs. the spectators' feeling that, somewhere, good triumphs over all."[56] Rimsky-Korsakov, however, created an extremely complex Shemakha. Unlike many simplistic representations used by contemporary Western composers for oriental female characters, Rimsky's utilized generic and stylistic diversity as well as intricate harmonic language to endow his oriental queen with a complex personality, one that experienced and expressed a wide spectrum of emotions and expressions, from sarcasm to the poetic sublime. Two diametrically opposing musical characteristics of the Queen are presented in her entrance aria "Otvet' mne zorkoye svetilo" (Respond to Me, Vigilant Luminary): one is lyrical, diatonic, and tonally stable; and the other one is instrumental, technically sophisticated, chromatic, tonally unstable, and ornamental—both encapsulate her multifaceted character, which is gradually unveiled throughout the opera (see Example 7a).[57]

Significantly, the composer did not attempt to Japanize Shemakha's musical vocabulary; rather, he used gestures associated in Russian music with a generalized idea of the Orient. The aria's purely diatonic opening phrase resembles Rubinstein's song no. 12 (the text of which also refers to the Sun) from his cycle of *Persian Songs*, and its second half is based on highly chromatic sliding-down figures followed by vocalizations with augmented seconds à la *Prince Igor* or *Sheherazade*—none of which are associated with Far Eastern music (see Example 7a). It seems that Rimsky consciously resisted musical stereotypes connecting pentatonic scales with the Far Eastern world: in his transcription of the "Eastern melody"

Example 7a. Rimsky-Korsakov, aria of the Queen of Shemakha, "Otvet' mne zorkoye svetilo."

Example 7a. continued

(possibly of folk origin) that inspired the opening phrase of Shemakha's aria, the composer changed a clearly pentatonic theme into an undeniably diatonic one (compare Examples 7a and 7b).[58]

Example 7b. "Eastern melody" from Rimsky-Korsakov's sketchbook.

As the Russian musicologist Boris Asafyev has noted, the "elements of the Queen of Shemakha are found in the music of nearly all of her predecessors."[59] Yet for Asafyev it remained a riddle of "how and why they would be imparted with such a sharp bias, why they are gathered together in the final work of the composer as in a conjurer's trick."[60] The reading of Shemakha as a metaphor for Japan clarifies why Rimsky-Korsakov insisted on such a complex and contradictory representation of her character. Like Japanese art, Shemakha is sophisticated, refined, and symbolic, and can conquer the hearts and minds with her beauty; like the Japanese army, the Queen can be dangerously powerful—any attempt to subjugate her may end badly for the assailant; and, like the war with Japan that revealed Russia's military incompetence, the Queen reveals the incompetence of Dodon's rule, bringing down his kingdom.

If the function and symbolic meaning of Shemakha and Tsar Dodon in Belsky and Rimsky-Korsakov's rendition of Pushkin's fairy tale are now more or less clear to the reader, the character of the Astrologer continues to raise many questions. Some researchers have suggested that Rimsky-Korsakov meant to represent himself in the Astrologer (and that he even joked about it), and in the first production Bilibin presented the magician as visually similar to Rimsky-Korsakov.[61] Others compared him to a fragile and chaste child, the murder of whom must be followed with retribution; or as a "stranger from the infinite heavenly domain" who can hear the "music of the spheres" and can "bring to this sinful earth . . . the highest wisdom or the highest justice."[62] Yet others saw in the Astrologer a "sinister figure" characterized with the most "artificial" musical language.[63] At first glance, the Astrologer does not seem to engage in any power struggle with Dodon or the Queen (except for a short squabble with the Tsar for the oriental beauty that ends pitifully for the Astrologer). According to Belsky's Preface to the opera, however, the Astrologer appears to be the mastermind behind the curtain who manipulates both Tsar and Queen, and arranges their fatal encounter. To better understand the message that Rimsky-Korsakov and Belsky meant to send through the Astrologer, one must understand the war Russia was fighting with Japan, and Nicholas II's advisors who stood behind the scenes.

Russia's imperial ambitions in the Russo-Japanese War are unquestionable; equally undeniable, these ambitions were stimulated by competition with Western powers, specifically the Russo-British confrontation over dominion in Central Asia and the Far East, known as "The Great Game." While Kaiser Wilhelm of Germany encouraged Nicholas II to establish Russian power in Korea and China, believing Russia's preoccupation with the East would distract Germany's ostensible political ally from Western affairs (the Balkans), Great Britain was strengthening its economic and political presence in Asia. Both factors bolstered the Russian government's belief that only expansionist policies in the East could prevent a British commercial and military presence in those Central Asian territories "dangerously close" to Russia. But the political state of affairs was not the only reason driving Russian officials to stretch so sweepingly into the Far East. Some contemporary observers and later historians suggested that ideological and religious factors played just as important a role in Russia's Eastern policies. Many members of the upper class, including Prince Ukhtomsky, Minister of Finance Sergei Witte, and Tsar Nicholas II himself, believed in Russia's strong connection to Asia and Buddhism through the Aryan peoples who practiced it.[64] Inspired by the enthusiasm of Russian Asians Pyotr Badmaev, a doctor, and Lama Agvan Lobsang Dorzhiev, the political and spiritual advisor of Dalai Lama XIII, who claimed that the Russian presence in the East was predicted in ancient Buddhist scripts, Ukhtomsky and Witte convinced Tsar Alexander III (and later, to a greater extent, Nicholas II) that Russia, as a direct inheritor of the Mongol Empire, was destined to become the leading power in Asia.

Leaving aside all the period's political intricacies, let us concentrate on Pyotr Badmaev, since it will not only shed light on the most mysterious character of the opera but suggest an intriguing political twist to the operatic story. The son of a wealthy Buryat Mongol cattle farmer,[65] Zhamsaran Badmaev, who claimed to be an offspring of Genghis-Khan, came to St. Petersburg from a remote Irkutsk region southeast of Lake Baikal.[66] Baptized as Pyotr Alexandrovich Badmaev (taking his first name after his role model Peter the Great and his patronymic honoring his godfather, the Grand Duke Alexander Alexandrovich, the future Alexander III), he rose to the highest reaches of Russian society thanks to his talents, both as practitioner of Tibetan medicine and as a diplomat (Figure 1). After studying at the Faculty of Oriental Languages at St. Petersburg University (from which he did not graduate), he entered Imperial service in the Asiatic

Figure 1. Pyotr Badmaev.

Department of the Ministry of Foreign Affairs. In 1893 Badmaev wrote a memorandum to his godfather, in which he proposed the overthrow of the decaying Qing (or Manchu) dynasty and the annexation of China, Mongolia, and Tibet with the help of 400,000 cavalry of the Buddhist army, which was supposedly awaiting the advent of the "White Tsar."[67]

Unlike his own Russian subjects, who often rebelled against the tsar, these Asian peoples would be more loyal to the monarch, since they believed in his divine provenance and the notion of the "White Tsar."[68] For them the Russian autocrat was a reincarnation of White Tara (or Dara-ekhe), a female bodhisattva, who in Mongol tradition protects the Buddhists and

Figure 2. Ivan Bilibin, "Tsar Pea," cover of magazine *Zhupel*, 1906.

reincarnates in the North to soften the character of the northern peoples, or he was an emanation of the king of the Tibetan Buddhist mystical kingdom Shambhala, protecting the world from spiritual decay.[69] Despite the tsar's doubts about achieving this "unusual and fantastic plan,"[70] the enthusiastic endorsement of this proposal by Witte persuaded him to approve a subsidy of two million rubles[71] to set up commercial enterprise in the region—money that would in fact cover the gathering of intelligence about Tibet and Manchuria, their political structure, and relationships with their neighbors. The operation allowed Badmaev to travel across Mongolia to Beijing, open a hotel in Chita and a number of trade houses, start publishing newspapers in Russian and Buryat, and establish a school for young Buryats in order to create a cadre of educated Russian Asians who could eventually strengthen cultural ties with and understanding of Mongolia and Tibet.[72] Badmaev's enterprise did not prove successful, however, and the next time he approached Nicholas II for another subsidy he was turned down. Even so, Badmaev retained his influence over the Russian nobility and political elite. In 1900, he opened a Tibetan medical clinic in a prestigious St. Petersburg suburb, where many prominent officials sought alternative health care. Just two years later, he was awarded the high position of State Councilor, and in late 1910, he helped Lama Dorzhiev and fellow Buddhists to build a temple in the capital. Despite considerable opposition from the Orthodox Church, this temple was consecrated in 1913, the 300th anniversary of the Romanovs' rule.[73]

The spectacular rise of Badmaev can be explained by the Russians' deep fascination with Asian culture, and particularly with their view of Tibet as a mystical place imbued with an ancient wisdom lost or corrupted by modern civilization. The spiritualist movement that swept across European and Russian fin-de-siècle society affected the Russian royal family as well. As Sergei Witte noted in his diary, the young tsarevich was simply obsessed with Asia,[74] and before acceding to the throne, undertook a year-long journey to "the Orient," setting out from Greece and Egypt to visit India, China, and Japan, and returning from Vladivostok via the Kazakh, Bashkir, and Kalmyk steppes—the "interior Orient." Prince Esper Ukhtomsky, who accompanied him on this journey and who later shaped Russia's Eastern policies, also shared Nicholas's passion for oriental mysticism, and was personally acquainted with the Russian and American theosophists Helena Blavatsky and Henry Olcott at the headquarters of the Theosophical Society in Madras.[75]

For Badmaev and Ukhtomsky, spiritual matters were closely (and inevitably) interwoven with politics.[76] Badmaev believed Tibet to be the "key to all Asia," the possession of which equaled "domination in [the] entire Buddhist world."[77] In a letter to the tsar written on the eve of the Russo-Japanese War, he advised Nicholas II to pay closer attention to Tibet rather than Japan, and urged him to send special agents to Tibet before the British could take definite control over it.[78] The tsar, who was usually inattentive to his subjects' recommendations, this time heeded Badmaev, and in just two days sent a special mission to Tibet.[79] However, the war with Japan, which erupted three weeks after the mission began, put an end to Russia's diplomatic or political efforts to control Tibet.

The shadowy figure of Badmaev, forgotten for most of the Soviet period, was well-known to many at the turn of the nineteenth century.[80] Badmaev's exotic appearance, a mysterious entourage at his clinic, and the bizarre names of his Tibetan remedies earned him the reputation of a wizard and thaumaturge (*kudesnik, chudotvorets*). Others called him a "wise and cunning Asiatic," who possessed a "large proportion of charlatanism" and later accused him of a secret alliance with Rasputin.[81] To many contemporaries Badmaev was a symbol of the autocracy's decline and disorder during its final years under Nicholas II. War Minister Aleksei Kuropatkin, for instance, complained about Badmaev's detrimental influence on the tsar:

> I think that one of the most dangerous features of the sovereign is his love of mysterious countries and individuals such as the Buryat Badmaev and Prince Ukhtomsky. They inspire in him fantasies of the greatness of the Russian tsar as master of Asia. The Emperor covets Tibet and similar places. All this is very disquieting and I shiver at the thought of the damage this would cause to Russia.[82]

Given the West's increasing fears of a supposed Yellow Peril, which was rooted in "scientific" racism and colonialist anxiety about a Sino-Japanese alliance, it is little wonder that the negative image of Russia's Eastern subjects got the upper hand regarding the image of the wise and mystical Orient. One of the most unflattering representations of Badmaev—and his dangerous proximity to the tsar—was captured by Ivan Bilibin in his *lubok* (cartoon), which appeared in early 1905 on the cover of the satirical journal *Zhupel*, and was said to be the source of inspiration for Rimsky-Korsakov's *The Golden Cockerel*. Dominant in this *lubok*, among the tsar's advisors who approve (or maybe even incite) the monarch to put forward his silly plan to annex the Moon is the figure of a Mongol-featured nobleman wearing Russian attire, who leans close to the tsar and over his young son, the tsarevich (Figure 2). Although the caption contains no mention of Badmaev, the only Asian-looking person close to the tsar who influenced Russia's Eastern policies was the doctor Badmaev. It seems that Bilibin was quite familiar with Badmaev's case and meant the cartoon to reflect the situation at the court and popular depictions of Badmaev as the "cunning Asiatic."

Probably well aware of his reputation, Badmaev tried to defend himself by explaining his actions in the press and publishing two editions of his book *Russia and China* (in 1900 and 1905). The work included a slightly shorter version of his 1893 memorandum and his multiple letters to the tsar. The preface to the second edition is particularly interesting for two reasons. First, it assesses the tsar's failure to heed the wise advice of people better-informed about the situation in the Far East (that is, Badmaev himself), and the resulting less than coherent Eastern policies. Second, Badmaev's striking description of China as backward in civic consciousness and absolutely corrupted by its dynastic heirs echoes liberally inclined Russian society's views of autocracy with its inefficient and repressive system of administration. Consciously or unconsciously, Badmaev's description of China contributed to the Russian liberals' critique of the tsarist autocracy, corrupted and ossified in its decaying traditions.[83]

Bearing this context in mind, the basic elements of the operatic story of *The Golden Cockerel* fall into place and Belsky's Preface to the opera can be interpreted as follows: "A wizard [Badmaev], still alive today sought by his magic cunning to overcome the daughter of the Aerial Powers [Tibet]. Failing in his project, he tried to win her through the person of Tsar Dodon [Nicholas II]." However, "he is unsuccessful," for two reasons: because of the Russo-Japanese War and because, despite being fascinated by Tibet, Nicholas II was reluctant to advance to this absolutely unknown territory and the case did not go further than some formal diplomatic exchanges with Dalai Lama XIII.[84] Badmaev's plans were never realized, so "to console himself, he presents to the audience, in his magic lantern" (or in his self-defensive books) "the story of heartless royal ingratitude."[85] In the Epilogue, the Astrologer (after having been killed) returns to the stage and claims that the only real people in the opera were the Queen of Shemakha and himself. Rimsky-Korsakov's suggestion—or rather, that of his librettist Vladimir Belsky since this ending was his idea—is that just as the kingdom of Tsar Dodon is unreal, so too is the authority of Russia or of the Russian tsar. Being a puppet manipulated by two oriental powers—the external eastern beauty and the internal "other"—Tsar Dodon is unable to act independently or adequately. Seen this way, his downfall is a logical end of his existence. The Orient, by contrast, while being mystical and alluring, can exercise real power, unmasking the ostentatious but absolutely fictitious world of tsardom. What appears to be real is unreal and what seems to be imagined demonstrates absolutely realistic force.

Rimsky-Korsakov's Orient is imbued with a wide range of images and attitudes, some inspired by the music and art of his time, others originating in his own reflections on the contemporary cultural and political state of affairs. Unfortunately, the overwhelming popularity of *Sheherazade* and Diaghilev's Orientalized ballet version of it (of which Rimsky-Korsakov would never have approved), have overshadowed the composer's efforts to represent the whole complexity of the East. His *Antar*, which musically de-Orientalized the Algerian song from Salvador Daniel's collection, is often mentioned in just a single sentence along with *Sheherazade*, which presents a synthesis of Russian musical vocabulary depicting the Orient. Thus Rimsky-Korsakov's attempt to move beyond Orientalism, his efforts to demystify the oriental world, as well as his disagreement with Russian policies in the East and his liberal social consciousness, show that he resisted the contemporary Orientalist discourse. Although his music might not have reflected the most "authentic" vocabulary, his appreciation of and concern for the Orient was genuine. In the context of a growing and multiethnic empire that brought Russian composers into closer contact with Russia's Asians, Rimsky-Korsakov's Orient emerges as something far more complex and profound than we have yet understood.

# NOTES

I would like to express my gratitude to Anna Berman, Marina Frolova-Walker, Lars Lih, Alyssa Michaud, David Schimmelpenninck van der Oye, Anthony Sheppard, Richard Taruskin, Kym White, and the editors of this volume for their helpful suggestions and thoughtful advice.

1. On Rimsky-Korsakov's oriental style, see Yuly Engel, "'Zolotoy Petushok' (Bolshoy Teatr, 06 Noyabrya)," in *Izbrannïye stat'yi o russkoy muzïke, 1898–1918* (Moscow: Sovetskiy kompozitor, 1971), 265–74; Boris Asafyev, "Kingdom of *Skomorokhi*," in *Symphonic Etudes: Portraits of Russian Operas and Ballets*, ed. and trans. David Haas (Lanham, MD, Toronto, Plymouth, UK: Scarecrow Press, 2008), 139–44; Gerald Abraham, *Studies in Russian Music: Critical Essays* (1936; New York: Books for Libraries Press, 1968), 299–310; Evgeniya Gordeyeva, "Fol'klornye istochniki 'Antara' i 'Ispanskogo kaprichchio,'" *Sovetskaya muzïka* 6 (1958): 33–41; V. Berkov and V. Protopopov, "Zolotoy Petushok," in *Operï Rimskogo-Korsakova: Putevoditel'*, ed. I. Uvarova (Moscow: Muzïka, 1976), 449–53; A. I. Kandinskiy, *Istoriya russkoy muzïki*, vol. 2 (Moscow: Muzïka, 1979), 85–86, 169–88, 231–34, 245–48; A. A. Solovtsov, *Nikolay Andreyevich Rimskiy-Korsakov: Ocherk zhizni i tvorchestva* (Moscow: Muzïka, 1984), 40–48, 136–58, 332–50; Steven Griffiths, *A Critical Study of the Music of Rimsky-Korsakov, 1844–1890* (New York and London: Garland Publishing, 1989), 13–14, 24–34, 93–100, 280–85; Richard Taruskin, "'Entoiling the Falconer': Russian Musical Orientalism in Context," *Cambridge Opera Journal* 4/3 (1992): 253–80; Taruskin, *Stravinsky and the Russian Traditions: A Biography of the Works Through "Mavra"* (Berkeley: University of California Press, 1996), 468–71, 740–48; Taruskin, "Yevreyi i Zhidy: A Memoir, a Survey, and a Plea," in *On Russian Music* (Berkeley: University of California Press, 2008), 197; Simon Morrison, "The Semiotics of Symmetry, or Rimsky-Korsakov's Operatic History Lesson," *Cambridge Opera Journal* 13/3 (2001): 261–93; Francis Maes, *A History of Russian Music: From "Kamarinskaya" to "Babi Yar"*, trans. Arnold and Erica Pomerans (Berkeley, Los Angeles, London: University of California Press, 2002), 80–82; Marina Frolova-Walker, *Russian Music and Nationalism from Glinka to Stalin* (New Haven and London: Yale University Press, 2007), 149–55, 219–20; Nasser Al-Taee, "Under the Spell of Magic: The Oriental Tale in Rimsky-Korsakov's *Scheherazade*," in *Representations of the Orient in Western Music: Violence and Sensuality* (Farnham and Burlington: Ashgate, 2010), 225–52; Inna Naroditskaya, *Bewitching Russian Opera* (Oxford and New York: Oxford University Press, 2012), 221–23, 250–54; Margarita Chizhmak, "Nikolai Rimsky-Korsakov's Opera 'The Golden Cockerel,'" *Current Exhibitions* 34 (2012): 54–65.

2. See V. V. Yastrebtsev, *N. A. Rimskiy-Korsakov: Vospominaniya Yastrebtseva*, vol. 2 (Leningrad: Muzgiz, 1960), 468. In earlier exchanges with Belsky and Yastrebtsev, Rimsky-Korsakov had declined to write operas or symphonic pieces with oriental subjects, claiming that the only path he was able to take was the path of Russo-Slavic music. See N. A. Rimskiy-Korsakov, *Perepiska s V. V. Yastrebtsevïm i V. I. Belskim* (St. Petersburg: Russkaya kul'tura, 2004), 244; and Yastrebtsev, *Rimskiy-Korsakov: Vospominaniya*, 2:428.

3. Some Kuchka members seemed to be deeply preoccupied with accuracy in representation. This explains why Musorgsky dropped his project of composing the opera *Salammbô*. As Nikolai Kompaneysky recalled, he thought it "would have been futile" to represent the Orient musically, "without having seen it or knowing its melodies." See Iuriy Keldïsh and Vasiliy Yakovlev, eds., *M. P. Musorgskiy, k pyatidesyatiletiyu so dnya smerti, 1881–1931: Stat'yi i materialï* (Moscow: Gosudarstvennoye muzïkal'noye izdatel'stvo, 1932), 110.

4. See A. N. Rimskiy-Korsakov, *Nikolay Andreyevich Rimskiy-Korsakov: Zhizn' i tvorchestvo*, vol. 1 (Moscow: Muzgiz, 1933), 5–7; Tat'yana Rimskaya-Korsakova, "Rodoslovnaya," *Muzïkal'naya akademiya* 2 (1994): 9–23.

5. See Rimskiy-Korsakov, *Polnoye sobraniye sochineniy: Literaturnïye proizvedeniya i perepiska*, vol. 5 (Moscow: Muzïka, 1965), 75; and Rimsky-Korsakov, *My Musical Life* (New York: Tudor Publishing, 1935), 60, 128, 256–57.

6. In his opera *Mlada*, Rimsky-Korsakov used his own transcription of an "Indian" tune from the famous Russian artist and traveler Vasili Vereshchagin. See V. A. Obram, "Rimskiy-Korsakov i narodnaya pesnya," in *Rimskiy-Korsakov. Issledovaniya, materialï, pis'ma v dvukh tomakh*, ed. Mark Yankovskiy et al., vol. 1 (Moscow: AN SSSR, 1953–54), 274–75. The two French sources were used to create an oriental flavor in Rimsky's symphonic suite *Antar*. From Salvador Daniel's *Album de douze chansons arabes, mauresques et kabyles* he used "Ma Gazelle" as a leitmotif for Peri Gul-Nazar, "Yamina" (in the first movement), and "Chebbu-Chebban" as the second subject of the third movement; and from Alexandre Christianowitsch's *Esquisse historique de la musique arabe* (1863) he incorporated a melody from Nouba Raml.

7. See chapter 2, "Building Images of the 'Other': Russian Musical Ethnographies of Intra-Imperial Orientals" in my dissertation "Russian Orientalism: From Ethnography to Art Song in Nineteenth Century Music" (PhD diss., McGill University, 2013), 75–147.

8. See Balakirev to Rimsky-Korsakov, 14 December 1863, in Rimskiy-Korsakov, *Polnoye sobraniye sochineniy: Literaturnïye proizvedeniya i perepiska*, 5:75. In a conversation with Yastrebtsev, Rimsky-Korsakov once stated categorically: "I repeat, the main thing in music is not melody nor even harmony, but rhythm and only rhythm." See V. V. Yastrebtsev, *Reminiscences of Rimsky-Korsakov*, ed. and trans. Florence Jonas (New York: Columbia University Press, 1985), 80. Rimsky-Korsakov's other statements on rhythm are found in his correspondence with Glazunov and Belsky. See Rimskiy-Korsakov, *Literaturnïye proizvedeniya i perepiska*, 6:83; Rimskiy-Korsakov, *Perepiska s V. V. Yastrebtsevïm i V. I. Belskim*, 265.

9. See Rimsky-Korsakov, *My Musical Life*, 128, 257.

10. Taruskin, "Yevreyi i Zhidy," 197.

11. On "artistic truth" in Russian music, see Taruskin, "'Entoiling the Falconet,'" 258–59; Taruskin, *On Russian Music*, 360; Olga Haldey, *Mamontov's Private Opera: The Search for Modernism in Russian Theater* (Bloomington: Indiana University Press, 2010), 57–59; Adalyat Issiyeva, "Dialogue of Cultures: French Musical Orientalism in Russia, 'Artistic Truth,' and Russian Musical Identity," *La Revue musicale OICRM* 3/1 (2016): 71–92.

12. See Edward Said's study of the colonization and representation of the Orient in Western European literature and art, in which he defines "Orientalism" as a Western construction, a system of knowledge used by colonial powers to "dominate, restructure, and have authority over the Orient." Said, *Orientalism* (New York: Pantheon, 1978), 3.

13. Some historians argue that Japanese intelligence played a significant role in inflaming the internal political situation to create a war on two fronts. See Dmitrii Pavlov, "Japanese Money and the Russian Revolution, 1904–05," in *Acta Slavica Iaponica* 11 (1993): 79–87.

14. Rimsky-Korsakov, *My Musical Life*, 56.

15. In chapter 4 of my dissertation I discuss how some ethnographic material that Balakirev brought from his trips to the Caucasus traveled to the music scores of his circle's members. See A. Issiyeva, "Russian Orientalism," 229–43, 294–307. Balakirev's transcriptions of Caucasian tunes are published in B. M. Dobrovol'skiy, "M. A. Balakirev: Zapisi kavkazskoy narodnoy muzïki," in *Miliy Alekseyevich Balakirev: Vospominaniya i pis'ma*, ed. Yu. A. Kremlev, A. S. Lyapunova and E. L. Frid (Leningrad: Gosudarstvennoye muzïkal'noye izdatel'stvo, 1962), 432–53.

16. Rimsky-Korsakov himself acknowledged this fact on several occasions. See Rimsky-Korsakov, *My Musical Life*, 58–60; Yastrebtsev, *Reminiscences of Rimsky-Korsakov*, 48, 182–85.

17. Balakirev sent this tune (along with other Caucasian transcriptions) to his French colleague, ethnographer Louis-Albert Bourgault-Ducoudray, who in the 1880s was

writing his opera *Tamara*. See Dobrovol'skiy, "M. A. Balakirev: Zapisi kavkazskoy narodnoy muzïki," 434, 452.

18. Rimsky-Korsakov, *My Musical Life*, 81.
19. Ibid., 78.
20. On this subject, see Maes, *A History of Russian Music*, 80–82.
21. Ibid., 82.
22. See A. Christianowitsch, *Esquisse historique de la musique arabe aux temps anciens avec dessins d'instruments et quarante mélodies notées et harmonisées* (Cologne, 1863). Pekelis points out that Dargomyzhsky knew Christianowitsch, probably before the publication of his *Esquisse historique*, and met with him on several occasions in St. Petersburg as well as in Leipzig in 1864. See M. Pekelis, *Aleksandr Sergeyevich Dargomïzhskiy i yego okruzheniye, Tom 3 (1858–1869)* (Moscow: Muzïka, 1983), 31.
23. Ibid., 81.
24. According to the key signature, it is C major, as in Christianowitsch's arrangement, but in Dargomyzhsky's harmonization the C-major chord appears only twice in the first inversion and in a context that weakens its function. See Christianowitsch, "Nouba Raml: Derdj harmonisé," in *Esquisse historique de la musique arabe*, xiii.
25. See Yastrebtsev, *Reminiscences of Rimsky-Korsakov*, 451.
26. Rimsky-Korsakov, *My Musical Life*, 19.
27. Rimsky-Korsakov similarly used the augmented triad to represent the Otherness in his early art songs "Enslaved" and "Hebrew Song," and in the melodies sung by the Astrologer and the Queen of Shemakha in *The Golden Cockerel*. As Marina Frolova-Walker points out in *Russian Music and Nationalism*, in Russian tradition augmented triads are linked to the whole-tone scale that is associated with the musical character of Chernomor, the evil magician from Glinka's opera *Ruslan and Lyudmila* (184–86).
28. As Yastrebtsev recalled, this list included "the choruses from *The Tower of Babel*, the dances from *The Demon* and *Feramors*, some of *The Maccabees*, *Azra*, the *Persian Songs*, etc." Yastrebtsev, *Reminiscences of Rimsky-Korsakov*, 100. On Rubinstein's identity in the eyes of Russian composers, see Frolova-Walker, "The Disowning of Anton Rubinstein," in *"Samuel" Goldenberg and "Schmuyle,"* Studia Slavica Musicologica 27 (Berlin: Verlag Ernst Kuhn, 2003), 19–60.
29. Yastrebtsev, *Reminiscences of Rimsky-Korsakov*, 45.
30. Ibid.
31. Ibid., 399.
32. On 31 March 1904, the day of the destruction of the battleship *Petropavlovsk*, Yastrebtsev confesses that their "conversation was limited almost entirely" to this "terrible" event and the "deaths of Admiral Makarov, the artist Vereshchagin, and the Rimsky-Korsakov relative Mikhail Pavlovich Molas, Chief of Staff of the Pacific Squadron." See Yastrebtsev, *Reminiscences of Rimsky-Korsakov*, 340. Later that year, in June 1904, Belsky sent Rimsky-Korsakov a picture of Alfred Kubin, *Das Grausen* (The Horror), which he hoped would inspire Rimsky-Korsakov to compose a symphonic poem. According to Belsky, the painting was an ominous prediction of a Russian ship blown up by a mine. See N. Rimskiy-Korsakov, *Perepiska s V. V. Yastrebtsevïm i V. I. Belskim*, 331.
33. This language was used by Nicholas II who perceived and called Japan's army no more than a band of "little brown monkeys (macaques)." See Schimmelpenninck, "Russian Military Intelligence on the Manchurian Front," *Intelligence and National Security* 11 (1996): 29.
34. Rimskiy-Korsakov, *Polnoye sobraniye sochineniy: Literaturnïye proizvedeniya i perepiska*, 6:146.
35. Gerald Abraham, *Rimsky-Korsakov: A Short Biography* (New York: AMS Press, 1975), 115.
36. In the popular press and in Russia's distinctive folk art prints, the *lubki* (plural of *lubok*), the Japanese on the eve of the war were described and portrayed in belittling

terms—as animals (apes, dogs, insects), or as women, little children, and semi-humans. Susanna Soojung Lim, *China and Japan in the Russian Imagination, 1685–1922* (London and New York: Routledge, 2013), 135–45.

37. In the second act of *The Golden Cockerel*, the slaves of the Queen describe Dodon as "Dull of brain, to think unable; Faults in every gesture bearing, Monkey, human garments wearing."

38. Bilibin's attitude toward the East requires more detailed research. It could be argued that, by portraying Dodon as an Asian, the Russian artist either distanced himself from the racist perspective on the Japanese or, since Dodon presented the most foolish character of the opera, was suggesting that Asiatic stupidity was adopted by the Russian ruler.

39. Yuliya Mikhailova, "Images of Enemy and Self: Russian 'Popular Prints' of the Russo-Japanese War," *Acta Slavica Iaponica* 16 (1988): 31, 45.

40. See E. E. Kuzina, "Patriotizm, voploshchenïy v krasote: Zhizn' i tvorchestvo I.Ya. Bilibina," *Kul'tura i vremya* 43/1 (2012): 78–80; Lim, *China and Japan in the Russian Imagination*, 135–37.

41. Cited in *Sources of Japanese Tradition*, vol. 2: *1600 to 2000*, ed. Willian De Bary et al. (New York: Columbia University Press, 2005), 672.

42. On *japonisme* in Russian culture, see Yelena D'yakonova, "Yaponizm v graficheskom iskusstve serebryanogo veka," *Yaponiya: Put' kisti i mecha* 2 (2002): 6–11; Diakonova, "*Japonisme* in Russia in the Late Nineteenth and Early Twentieth Centuries," in *Japan and Russia: Three Centuries of Mutual Images*, ed. Yulia Mikhailova and M. William Steele (Folkestone, UK : Global Oriental, 2008), 32–46; Bartlett, "Japonisme and Japanophobia: The Russo-Japanese War in Russian Cultural Consciousness," *Russian Review* 67 (January 2008): 8–33; Susanna Lim, *China and Japan in the Russian Imagination*, 133–46.

43. The term *japonisme* originally referred to the Japanese influence on avant-garde painters in the late nineteenth century, but it is now understood in broader terms as the embrace of a wide range of Japanese art forms and styles, not only by the artistic elite but also by consumers in general. See Bartlett, "Japonisme and Japanophobia."

44. I. Grabar, "Upadok i vozrozhdeniye," in *Niva, literaturnoye prilozheniye* (1897): 55.

45. I. Grabar, *Yaponskaya tsvetnaya gravyura na dereve* (Japanese Colour Woodblock Prints) ([St. Petersburg]: Izd. Kn. S. A. Shcherbatova i V. V. f[on] Mekk, 1903).

46. Bartlett, "Japonisme and Japanophobia," 9.

47. "Da, doyedesh' do vostoka, tut i est' moya strana, / Pestrïm marevom vidna. / Mezhdu morem i nebom visit ostrovok. / Chto ni chas ochertan'ya menyaya" (Yes, ride to the orient; my country is there. It spreads out like a glittering mirage. Between the sea and the sky there floats an island. It constantly changes shape). For the full translation of the libretto, see *Le coq d'or. The Golden Cock: An Opera in Three Acts; Music by N. Rimsky-Korsakov* (New York: Fred. Rullman Inc., [1918]); *Libretti of Russian Operas: With International Phonetic Alphabet Transcriptions and Word-For-Word Translations, Including a Guide to the IPA and Russian Lyric Diction*, vol. 1 (Geneseo, N.Y.: Leyerle, 2004), 419–86.

48. Mikhail Gnesin, *Mïsli i vospominaniya o N. A. Rimskom-Korsakove* (Moscow: Gosudarstvennoye muzïka'noye izdatel'stvo, 1956), 178.

49. On Voin Rimsky-Korsakov's letters from Japan to his family, see William. W. McOmie, "Bakumatsu Japan Through Russian Eyes: the Letters of Kapitan-Leitenant Voin Andreevich Rimsky-Korsakov," *NAOSITE* (March 1994): 35–51; I. A. Goncharov, "Fregat 'Pallada': Ocherki puteshestviya v dvukh tomakh," in *Sobraniye sochineniy*, vol. 3 (Moscow: Gosudarstvennoe izdatel'stvo khudozhestvennoi literaturï, 1959).

50. Voin noted that Japanese women dressed simply, in gray or blue, and that they had fashionable hairstyles, and that "even fashionable European ladies, especially brunettes, would not be averse to having their hair done à la Japonaise." See McOmie, "Bakumatsu Japan Through Russian Eyes," 48.

51. Goncharov, *Sobraniye sochineniy*, 3:13.
52. Ibid., 47.
53. Rotem Kowner, "Nicholas II and the Japanese Body: Images and Decision-Making on the Eve of the Russo-Japanese War," *Psychohistory Review* 26/3 (1998): 225–27; David Wells, "Introduction," in *Russian Views of Japan 1792–1913: An Anthology of Russian Travel Writing*, ed. and trans. D. Wells (London and New York: Routledge, 2004), 25; Stephen Norris, *A War of Images: Russian Popular Prints, Wartime Culture, and National Identity, 1812–1945* (DeKalb: Northern Illinois University Press, 2006); Lim, *China and Japan in the Russian Imagination*, 135–46.
54. Yuly Engel, "'Zolotoy Petushok' (Bolshoy Teatr, 06 Noyabrya)," in Iosif Filippovich Kunin, ed., *Izbrannïye stat'yi o russkoy muzïke, 1898–1918* (Moscow: Sovetskiy kompozitor, 1971), 271.
55. Rimskiy-Korsakov, *Perepiska s V. V. Yastrebtsevïm i V. I. Belskim*, 380.
56. Ibid.
57. "Respond to me, vigilant luminary! / You come to us from the east; / Have you visited my native land, / The country of fairy dreams? /Are the roses still glowing there / And the bushes of burning lilies? / Do the turquoise dragon-flies / Still kiss the gorgeous leaves?" The first part of the aria Rimsky-Korsakov recycled from his unfinished opera *The Barber of Baghdad* based on *One Thousand and One Nights*; the diatonic theme was meant to characterize the opera's female character, a daughter of a qadi, a Muslim judge. See A. Gozenpud, "Neosushchestvlennïy opernïy zamïsel," in *Rimskiy-Korsakov. Issledovaniya, materialï, pis'ma*, 2:253–60.
58. Rimsky-Korsakov's sketch of the "Eastern melody" is cited in Kandinskiy, *Istoriya russkoy muzïki*, 2:180.
59. Asafyev, *Symphonic Etudes*, 142.
60. Ibid.
61. According to the Russian music critic Yuly Engel, Rimsky-Korsakov once said, "Actually, the Astrologer should be made up to look like me." Engel, "'Zolotoy Petushok' (Bolshoy Teatr, 06 Noyabrya)," 278.
62. Kandinskiy, *Istoriya russkoy muzïki*, 2:182–83.
63. Abraham, *Studies in Russian Music*, 297, 303.
64. In the late nineteenth century, theories connecting Russian people to the Aryan race were much prized by higher-class society and the intelligentsia. They believed that Russians were closely related to Aryans through Scythian tribes that in ancient times moved from Asia to Eastern Europe and mixed with the local population.
65. The Buryats are the largest indigenous group living in Buryat Republic (south and east of the Lake Baikal, Siberia). They are the northernmost of the Mongol peoples and share language and many customs with other Mongols.
66. On the life of Badmaev, see V. P. Semennikov, "Tibetskiy vrach i russkaya monarkhiya," in *Za kulisami tsarizma: Arkhiv tibetskogo vracha Badmayeva*, ed. Semennikov (Leningrad: Gosudarstvennoye izdatel'stvo, 1925), iii–xxxiv; David McDonald, "Petr Badmaev," in *Russia's People of Empire: Life Stories from Eurasia, 1500 to the Present*, ed. Stephen M. Norris and Willard Sunderland (Bloomington: Indiana University Press, 2012), 199–209; Boris Gusev, "Moy ded Zhamsaran Badmayev: Iz semeynoy khroniki," *Novïy mir* 11 (1989): 199–226; Gusev, *Pyotr Badmyayev: Krestnik imperatora, tselitel', diplomat* (Moscow: Olma-Press, 2000); I. V. Lukoyanov, "Vostochnaya politika Rossii i P. A. Badmayev," *Voprosï istorii* 4 (2001): 111–26.
67. Badmayev, "Zapiska Badmayeva Aleksandru III o zadachakh russkoy politiki na aziatskom vostoke," in Semennikov, *Za kulisami tsarizma*, 72.
68. On the idea of the "White Tsar," see V. V. Trepalov, *"Belïy tsar": Obraz monarkha i predstavleniya o poddanstve u narodov Rossii* (Moscow: Institut russkoy istorii, 2007).

69. Badmayev, "Legenda o belom tsare," in Semennikov, *Za kulisami tsarizma*, 57–59; Alexander Andreev, "Agwan Dorjiev and the Buddhist Temple in Petrograd," in *Cho Yang: The Voice of Tibetan Religion and Culture* (Dharamsala: Gangchen Kyishong, 1991), 216.

70. Alexander III wrote these words on the document responding to Badmaev's memo. See Semennikov, *Za kulisami tsarizma*, 81.

71. To compare, in 1867 Alaska was sold to the United Stated for the price of less than eleven and a half million rubles.

72. McDonald, "Petr Badmaev," 203.

73. Prominent Russian Orientologists or specialists in Oriental Studies, such as Vasily Radlov and Sergei Oldenburg, and artists, such as Nicholas Roerich and Maximilian Voloshin, participated in this event.

74. See S. Iu. Witte, *The Memoirs of Count Witte* (New York: Sharpe, 1990), 127.

75. K. Paul Johnson, *Initiates of Theosophical Masters* (Albany: State University of New York Press, 1995), 126–33. Before the "Grand Tour" Ukhtomsky also traveled to Siberia and China, where he developed connections with Russia's Buddhist minorities. The objects of Asian art he acquired, from all regions, became the largest such collection in Russia.

76. See Marlène Laruelle, "'The White Tsar': Romantic Imperialism in Russia's Legitimizing of Conquering the Far East," *Acta Slavica Iaponica* 25 (2008): 113–34.

77. Badmayev, "Pamyatnaya zapiska Badmayeva o protivodeystvii anglichanam v Tibete," in Semennikov, *Za kulisami tsarizma*, 110.

78. Ibid.

79. *Dnevnik Imperatora Nikolaya II, 1890–1906 g.* (Moscow: Polistar, 1991), 135; N. A. Yermakov, "Pod'yesaul Ulanov i lama Ul'yanov," in *Ocherki istorii Rossiyskoy vneshney razvedki v 6 tomakh*, vol. 1 (Moscow: Mezhdunarodnïye otnosheniya, 1996), 183–91.

80. In one of the letters to Nicholas II, Badmaev claimed that in his clinic he treated 17,000 to 20,000 people per year.

81. For these references, see David Schimmelpenninck van der Oye, "Tournament of Shadows: Russia's Great Game in Tibet," in *The History of Tibet*, vol. 3: *The Modern Period: 1895–1959, The Encounter with Modernity*, ed. Alex MacKay (London: Routledge, 1993), 49; S. Yu. Vitte and B. V. Anan'yich, *Iz arkhiva S. Yu. Vitte: Vospominaniya, Tòm 1: Rasskazï v stenograficheskoy zapisi* (St. Petersburg: Dmitriy Bulanin, 2003), 433; V. V. Shul'gin, *Godï. Dni. 1920 god* (Moscow: Novosti, 1990), 311, 312; Semennikov, *Za kulisami tsarizma*, xx; and Victor Alexandrov, *The End of the Romanovs* (Boston: Little, Brown, 1966), 118.

82. A. N. Kuropatkin, *Dnevnik*, 22 September 1899, quoted in K. Meyer, S. B. Brisac, *Tournament of Shadows: The Great Game and the Race for Empire in Central Asia* (Washington, DC: Counterpoint, 1999), 281.

83. In Russian literature the word *kitayshchina*, meaning Sinoism, had a negative connotation, referring to the Asiatic features of tsarism—its oriental despotism, backwardness, and political stagnation.

84. See Schimmelpenninck van der Oye, "Russia's Great Game in Tibet," *Toronto Studies in Central and Inner Asia* 5 (2002): 35–52.

85. See W. Bjelskij, "Preface," in N. Rimski-Korssakow, *Der goldene Hahn: Oper in drei Akten* (Frankfurt, London, New York: C. F. Peters, n.d.), 3.

# The Golden Cockerel, Censored and Uncensored

## SIMON MORRISON

The princess will remain captive to the astrologer; and the astrologer, bound up in major slumber by the princess, until the last day, unless the mystic hand shall grasp the fated key, and dispel the whole charm of this enchanted mountain.

—Washington Irving,
"Legend of the Arabian Astrologer," 1832

The journey of Rimsky-Korsakov's *The Golden Cockerel* (*Zolotoy petushok* or *Le coq d'or*) from premiere to the present can be summarized in a single convoluted sentence: An 1832 short story by American author Washington Irving became an 1834 fairy tale in verse by Alexander Pushkin, which in turn became a three-act opera by Rimsky-Korsakov composed in 1907 (with a libretto by Vladimir Belsky) that premiered in 1909 before becoming first a three-act opera-ballet in 1914 (choreographed by Michel Fokine, though Rimsky-Korsakov's widow mobilized to have it prohibited owing to cuts to the music), then a three-act opera-ballet in 1918, then a one-act ballet in 1937, and finally a two-act ballet in 2012. Even Rimsky-Korsakov's original was subject to extensive revision. The two years between the creation of the opera and its premiere entailed a process of review and adjustment—or rather, of censorship—by government officials attuned to the political implications of the work.

Indeed, in any guise and every era, *The Golden Cockerel* has been interpreted as explicitly political, with the history of its censorship being attached to the opera and ballet as a kind of invisible remnant of revision. Yet there is also an aesthetic argument to be made about *The Golden Cockerel*, centering on magic, charm, and enchantment. In a tale about a magician, Rimsky-Korsakov is of course the true magician, the real "Oriental Wizard."[1] Just like the source text, derived by Pushkin from Irving,[2] the opera is a spectacular conjuration, a comprehensive collection of references to other works in which Russian anti-Enlightenment masquerades as Islamic anti-Enlightenment. Everything seems to be a quotation. *The Golden Cockerel* becomes a caricature of a caricature, a mock juxtaposition of the Russian national style (the sound of the kuchka, or Russian nationalist music) with magical and oriental modes that make enchantment not the means, but the ends.

Pushkin's fairy tale (*skazka*) and Belsky's libretto both tell of Tsar Dodon, ruler of a fairy-tale realm. He bears no plausible likeness to an actual historical figure, but he is the butt of jokes that, at times, point to something beyond the make-believe. Dodon convinces himself that he is about to be attacked by the Queen of Shemakha, an individual so exotically-erotically beautiful that he cannot help but fall in love with her. In planning for battle, he seeks the counsel of the Astrologer, who gives him an unusual kind of air-raid siren: a cockerel that will sound the alarm if invasion is imminent.[3] But the golden bird, "a mechanical marionette amid real marionettes," according to Boris Asafyev, proves unreliable.[4] On its random cue, Dodon sends his two sons into battle. They end up slaying each other, forcing Dodon to lead the charge against the Queen himself. He carries a rusty shield, a reference to Cervantes's *Don Quixote*, and/or to the Imperial Russian Army's obsolete weapons. Again in response to the cockerel's cry, Dodon encounters the Queen, who seduces him by singing a nostalgic hymn to the sun. Even by Orientalist standards, the Queen is an outrageous character, and her morphology is especially complex; extend Shemakha to Shemakhanskaya, as the musicologist Olga Skrinnikova has suggested, and the Sanskrit words *ahan* (day + night) and *ahana* (morning + evening light) can be detected.[5] In the middle of the middle act of the opera, the action pauses as the Queen sings again of veils and feasts, maidens, turquoise dragonflies, and passionate dreams of forbidden love. Smitten, Dodon instantly proposes marriage, and she accepts—thus taking control of his kingdom. Following a resplendent wedding procession, Dodon meets the Astrologer, who selects the Queen as a reward for his assistance. Dodon refuses and flies into a rage, then is pecked through the jugular by the cockerel. In the epilogue, as in the prologue, the Astrologer makes plain that the tale is of his own contrivance. He and the Queen are real, but no one else.

The text had a context, which became pretext for a subtext. The story might be interpreted as referring to the intrigue unfolding between Alix of Hesse (Alexandra Fyodorovna), spouse of Tsar Nicholas II, and a Siberian mystic faith healer named Grigori Rasputin. Tongues wagged in the court and on the streets about their relationship, and about Rasputin's nefarious influence over the tsar and affairs of state in the twilight of the imperial era. But there is another, easier point of comparison: The draft of the opera seems also to allude to the disastrous Russo-Japanese War of 1904–1905, a humiliation for Russia that grievously threatened the reign of Nicholas II. Reports of naval defeats on the shores of the Pacific spurred demands for social reform and representative government, which precipitated the Bloody Sunday massacre, when Imperial Guard police opened fire on unarmed petitioners heading to the Winter Palace.

Led by a priest, Georgi Gapon, the petitioners bore with them a list of seventeen demands for individual freedoms, improved working conditions, and representation. By the end of that day, 9 January 1905, several hundred people had been killed and wounded (according to unofficial accounts, up to four thousand). The revolts, strikes, and mutinies persisted until the publication of the October Manifesto, which pledged reform.

Rimsky-Korsakov joined the fray in the middle of March of 1905, endorsing a newspaper petition and publicly refusing to teach his composition and orchestration classes at the St. Petersburg Conservatory. He sided with striking students against the administration of the Conservatory, arguing that lessons should be halted for the rest of the academic year. For this, his lone act of political activism, he temporarily lost his post; a performance of one of his operas, *Kashchei the Deathless*, served as pretext for a massive political protest.[6] Ultimately, the tumult—the letters of support from strangers, the drama of his rehiring in March and December of 1905, the teasing he endured for supporting his students—made him uncomfortable. As Marina Frolova-Walker writes: "He was rather embarrassed by his newly acquired fame as a revolutionary, and had no desire to exploit the dramatic potential of his predicament further."[7] There would be no grand historical operas in his future, and nothing particularly personal. Nor would he join other members of the artistic elite in lamenting what might have been.[8]

Instead, Rimsky-Korsakov responded to the events of 1905 with a fairy-tale opera of funny rhymes. He was inspired by an image published at the end of that year in the second issue of the savagely satirical magazine *Zhupel* (Bugbear). *Zhupel* lasted just three issues of tiny print runs before being shut down by the police, but the publication left its mark. The cover image of the second issue, by Ivan Bilibin, depicts "Tsar Pea" beside his warrior-prince son, shown picking his nose, and three boyars with their heads bent down. Tsar Pea (also known as Old King Cole, akin to Dodon, likened to Nicholas II) gazes at the full moon, imagining its absorption into the Russian Empire.[9] Bilibin, who briefly went to prison for his subversive graphic designs, provided the visuals for the premiere production of *The Golden Cockerel* in 1909.

Rimsky-Korsakov announced his commitment to the opera on 19 October 1906, ten months after his return to the faculty of the Conservatory: "It's not a joke, I want to compose *The Golden Cockerel*. A hee hee hee and a hah hah hah."[10] He and Belsky were in touch throughout the compositional process—in person when they were both in St. Petersburg, otherwise through correspondence sent from the manor house the composer had rented in Lyubensk, south of St. Petersburg close to Pskov.[11] Work began in earnest with the composer considering and reconsidering the tonal color of the overture and, because the erudite Belsky did not seem to be churning them out fast enough, proposing verses of his own to describe the golden cockerel. These are revealing: Rimsky-Korsakov imagined a sultry landscape, the cockerel glittering on its spoke in the baking sun, but also the endless, carefree days at Dodon's court interrupted when "a black cloud arises from the east—is this not a bad portent?"[12] Dodon's minions live their dull lives, until, the composer suggests, the Russo-Japanese War.

He and Belsky tussled over the conception of the Queen of Shemakha, and whether or not referencing the powerful troops under her command masked the fact that her triumph over Dodon is purely amorous, that the defeat is "with beauty alone."[13] The Orientalism of the episode had its origins in Mikhail Glinka's *Ruslan and Lyudmila* (1842). Rimsky-Korsakov relied on Glinka's "Eastern mode," but chafed when Belsky pointed out the adoption. "I have the right, since I did something original with it," the composer protested.[14] Rimsky-Korsakov had a tic of blatantly quoting other composers—especially Wagner—then acting surprised when colleagues noticed what he obviously meant for them to hear and then schooling them on his clever semantic and syntactic reworking of the borrowed material. Glinka is here, likewise Alexander Serov, and Mily Balakirev, Alexander Borodin, Modest Musorgsky, Rimsky-Korsakov himself, as well as Rimsky-Korsakov's cleaned-up, stylized, anthologized folksong arrangements. If an opera could be like a dictionary, this is it, and to look up the source of one of Rimsky-Korsakov's paraphrases is to encounter additional paraphrases.

Rimsky-Korsakov certainly outdid Glinka in representing the Queen of Shemakha with not one but two Eastern modes. The first adds a raised fourth to A minor; the second raises the second and fifth scale degrees of E major from F$\sharp$ to F$\times$ and B to B$\sharp$ respectively. The pitches rise and fall in orgiastic outbursts that usually follow a fermata, as though the semitone alterations and augmented seconds had been bottled up, awaiting release as soon as the

Figure 1. Ivan Bilibin, "Tsar Pea," cover of magazine *Zhupel*, 1906.

glittering, turban-wearing heroine—accompanied by four slave girls playing respectively a zither, rebec, reed, and drum—turns to face the sun.

Praising Belsky's work on the libretto, the composer offered some detailed suggestions and even noted that the censors too would have their say. "Let's do it like this," Rimsky-Korsakov said of the epilogue:

> Following the final chorus and the words "What shall the new dawn bring?" the entr'acte curtain quickly descends and the astrologer comes out; addressing the public, he says that he

had put on a Shrovetide show and that the public could go to sleep "until the dawn" and "the rooster." The astrologer falls through a trap door in the stage floor; we hear the loud cockerel motive in the trumpets at the same pitch as the start but harmonized at the final *ff* with an A♭ chord or an augmented F♭–C–A♭. The astrologer needs to be given 4, 6, or at the most 8 lines.

Do it, my dear. You'll make it as excellent as always, and what a wonderful frame our fable will have! The music comes full circle and the idea is good; so let them [the censors] cut it, or permit the end—what do we care? No, for sure they won't prohibit it: since all that we are saying is "sleep 'til dawn" or "'til the rooster crows," we are "completely trustworthy," because those expressions are so vague that no one can tell when exactly the "dawn" we are talking about will come.[15]

Upon completion, the libretto went to Rimsky-Korsakov's publisher (Jurgenson), who sent it to the Office (Kontora) of the Imperial Theaters and the Censorship Bureau. The galley included a foreword, by Belsky, meant to reduce suspicion of subversive intent. "The common human character of Pushkin's tale of the golden cockerel—a tragicomedy teaching the fatal consequences of human passions and weaknesses—permits us to present the plot in any time and place," Belsky begins. He mentions the nonsense rhymes and jingles (*pribautki*) found elsewhere in Russian literature, the oriental influence on *The Golden Cockerel*, and the moral lessons carved into Russian folk woodcuts, from which Pushkin derived his tale. Belsky's libretto bears a simple message, but also leaves questions unanswered, as he admits. Did, for example, the Astrologer and the Queen of Shemakha conspire against Dodon? Long, long ago, "a magician who is still alive tried to use his magical cunning to overcome the daughter of the air [Aerial]. Lacking the strength to succeed, he tried to take her from Dodon's hands, but suffered, as is well known, a defeat," Belsky explains. "The story of Dodon's odious ingratitude" offers the magician some "comfort."[16]

If there is a political message in the preface to the libretto, it is directed against those in Belsky's circle, including the Russian "mystic" Symbolists, who, at a decadent remove, interpreted the events of 1905 as theatrical spectacle. Or perhaps the preamble to one: the real revolution would be musical, hallucinogenic, and orgiastic. The Symbolists loved masquerades, the occult, esoteric religions, mind-altering substances, and phantasmagoria; these things allowed them to allegorize the porousness of the phenomenal world. Belsky was more attracted to the Symbolists than Rimsky-Korsakov and so offered them a magic lantern show and masked two-dimensional figures in *The Golden Cockerel*. But he left it unclear whether anything existed behind the play of surfaces. There might be a higher, ultimate realm; there might also be nothing. Perhaps opera was as close to magic as it comes.

Despite Belsky's efforts, the libretto ran afoul of the censors. The struggle to gain approval is described by Vasili Yastrebtsev, who identifies the central players in the fracas, including Aleksey Belgard, director of publications in the Censorship Bureau. Yastrebstev also ascribes blame to the intendant of the Imperial Theaters in St. Petersburg, Vladimir Telyakovsky, who had less of an interest in bringing Pushkin to the opera and ballet stage than did his predecessor Ivan Vsevolozhsky. Telyakovsky's sidekick in Moscow, Konstantin Gershelman, was also involved; a former officer with the Finnish regiment of the Russian Imperial Army, Gershelman settled into theatrical administration after retiring his military commission. This Gershelman tends to get confused with another one, Sergei, the governor general of Moscow, and for good reason. He too entered the debate about staging *The Golden Cockerel*.

Yastrebtsev summarized the deliberations on 27 February 1908: "At around five-thirty Nikolai Andreyevich phoned to tell me that the drama censor had scribbled all over his *Golden Cockerel*. First the libretto was returned 'clean,' but then, the very next day (probably because of some adverse criticism), the censor requested it again, and this was the result: the Prologue, Epilogue, and many of Pushkin's words were crossed out. . . . At the same time, much crueler things were left in. 'What fools!' exclaimed Rimsky-Korsakov. 'I'm certain they really don't know Pushkin's tale at all.'"[17]

Indeed Rimsky-Korsakov greeted the news with sarcasm. "I've just received notice from the Office of the Imperial Theaters that the dramatic censor grants permission (!) for the opera to be performed," he told Belsky, "so long as several parts of the text are excluded (all of the introduction, conclusion, and 45 other lines). In sum, *The Golden Cockerel* might only be seen in Paris."[18] Belsky was partly to blame, since he had inserted lines of his own to sharpen the satire, including, at the end of the opera, "Kak zhe budem bez tsarya?" (How can we live without the tsar?).

Two days later Yastrebtsev updated the situation: "Nikolay Andreyevich told me that he and Belsky had gone to see Telyakovsky about *The Golden Cockerel*. This whole stupid incident with the censor was entirely Telyakovsky's fault, since it was he who wanted Belgard to take a closer look at the text. Otherwise, he said, Gershelman (in Moscow) might forbid it. This time the censor 'overdid' it; finding nothing to 'censor' on the first reading, on the second—he crossed out many lines, mostly Pushkin's!"[19] Thus the bureaucratic buffoonery in the opera mirrored the bureaucratic bumbling about the text.

Yet the situation was not as grave as it seemed. The director of the Imperial Theaters summoned Belsky for a chat, and then Belsky spoke with the censor, Belgard. The libretto, which Jurgenson had already typeset, was tweaked, and Belsky signed off on the changes that had to be made. At least some of the cuts were restored.

Rimsky-Korsakov's thoughts turned to a production in Moscow, to be followed by one in St. Petersburg, but then he died. He heard the opera sung and played in his salon, but did not live to see it staged. Nor, of course, did he last long enough to experience another battle with the censors, though he received word, on the eve of his death, of disquiet in Moscow. The governor-general, Sergei Gershelman, decided to censor (or censure) the censor, Belgard. Gershelman demanded—for the sake of the actual, divine sovereign and his court—that the opera be shelved, perhaps for good. Despite Belsky's and Rimsky-Korsakov's conception of the opera as an amusing fable, a fairground amusement, Gershelman found nothing funny:

> Despite softening certain expressions in the censored version (replacing, for example, the oft-repeated words of the cockerel, "kriki-kiri-ku-ku, tsarstvuy lezha na boku" [cockadoodle-doo; rule, lying on your side] with "Spi bespechno na boku" [Sleep lightly on one side], the intent of the libretto, which includes only 100 lines from Pushkin's tale, remains exactly the same: to insult and ridicule the dignity of the tsar.
>
> In the first act description of the parliament, the tsar is shown agreeing with the most ridiculous opinions. On p. 15 the astrologer, refusing to believe the tsar's solemnly given promises, asks for a "legal" guarantee. The tsar thinks only of sleep and food. The housekeeper, Amelfa, uses the word "tsar" in the most inappropriate ways, for example on p. 16, "Il' otvetyat tsarskim dumam nachinennïye izyumom chernoslivinki v vine" [Or small plums stuffed with raisins will answer the tsar's thoughts]." On p. 20, "The tsar sits in a steam bath covered in soap suds." The housekeeper sleeps in the same bed as he does (p. 17). In the second act, the Queen of Shemakha insists on the tsar dancing with a granny's kerchief tied 'round his head (pp. 36, 37, and 38). Slaves

mock the tsar (p. 39). In Act 3 the people sing a song where humility is feebly mocked (p. 42).[20]

Gershelman refused to permit a performance at the Moscow Imperial Bolshoi Theater, and the theater had no choice but to comply. Meanwhile, Belsky ended up having to again rework a libretto that in St. Petersburg had already been both rejected and approved by Belgard. Understandably, the assignment baffled him, since changing the words implied changing the music to which those words were attached, something Rimsky-Korsakov could not do from the grave. Belgard came gingerly to Belsky's defense, timorously informing the governor-general that owing "to the impossibility of making corresponding changes in the music, the author of the libretto has provided a new version, in which he refrains entirely from referring to Dodon as a tsar, calling him instead "a *voyevoda* [provincial governor] under the almighty tsar."[21] Perhaps, Gershelman replied, but he nevertheless demanded additional changes: the "throne" in the opera needed to become a "chair," for example.[22] No one was fooled, of course, and underground publications featuring Nicholas II as Dodon (and Tsar Pea) continued to circulate in St. Petersburg and Moscow near the time of the premiere.

In response to the cancellation of the production by the Bolshoi Theater, Rimsky-Korsakov's widow, Nadezhda, granted Sergei Zimin license to stage the opera at his private opera company in Moscow for the opening of the 1909–10 season. Zimin's artistic director, Pyotr Olenin, begged for Gershelman's permission, arguing that hopes for the entire season rested with *The Golden Cockerel*, and that plans for the staging had advanced to the point that it could not be replaced with another opera. His motives were less artistic than financial, and Olenin, a famed opera singer, rather brashly tried to shame Gershelman into doing the right thing: "Such needless impediments to the fulfillment of our theater's mission, such hindrances in its activities, can sap the energy of an entrepreneur [he means Zimin] with the sad consequence of us having one less theater—and we have so few of them—and might end up depriving 200–300 people, our theater's employees, of good salaries."[23] Gershelman backed down, and thanks to the intervention of Olenin, Zimin reaped the profits that would otherwise have gone to the Bolshoi. Zimin congratulated himself on the success of the premiere production of *The Golden Cockerel* in his diaries, including a cartoon of a cockerel perched atop his theater, dropping golden eggs into the box office (Figure 2).

Zimin's summation of the events leading to the performance is humorous; he had published, he noted, an illustrated edition of Pushkin's tale

Figure 2. Sergei Zimin's cockerel doodle.

that included prints of Bilibin's multi-hued folklore-inspired costumes and decorations for the opera. It differed from the libretto that was put on sale, which differed from the words sung by the singers. "Clearly, our idle wise men [Gershelman, Belgard] changed their minds [about *The Golden Cockerel*], thinking it had political subtexts. Such could not, of course, be tolerated."[24] The Bolshoi Theater staged the opera two months later. Zimin's production received the stronger reviews.

In 1918, Adolph Bolm brought *The Golden Cockerel* to the Metropolitan Opera, prompting a sumptuously illustrated article in the *New York Times*. The reporter described the logistical nightmare of getting the opera to the United States from Russia before noting the opera's "bitter irony toward a paternal government, savage satire as regards the Russian people."[25] The production was interpreted as a portrait of the decline of Imperial Russia in the run-up to the Revolution, specifically the 1905 uprising against the abuses of the last tsar, Nicholas II, and the entire clueless, snoozing aristocratic establishment. Obviously the Russian censors had hoped to prevent just that interpretation, but Rimsky-Korsakov's publisher, P. Jurgenson, printed the music and libretto without the changes entered, allowing the uncensored version to be performed in subsequent years.

Yet what else might the work, in any form, be about? Is there space for interpretation beyond the politics of 1905? Three spheres emerge in the opera as in the ballet versions of *The Golden Cockerel*: the human, represented by Dodon (his name deriving, according to Belsky, from the Italian Dido, *Didone*,[26] but perhaps also from the French words *fais dodo*, meaning "Go to sleep") and his court; the fantastic, where the Astrologer dwells; and the erotic exotic, home to the Astrologer's forever beloved Queen. The opera inverts Russian convention: the real Russian characters lose; the fake ones, the non-Russian characters from who knows where, win (or at least have the last word). The spheres overlap, but the composer seems most invested in the Queen and her domain. Rimsky-Korsakov began composing there, and the music of the middle act spreads outward, as if spun in a centrifuge, reaching both forward and back. The music does not progress in narrative form; rather it radiates, inward and outward. The music Dodon sings, and pantomimes, interacts with the whole-tone and octatonic music of the Astrologer (when Dodon realizes, at rehearsal number 98 of Act 2, that his dreams of the queen might be coming true), which interacts in turn with the semitone-and-augmented-second-laden music of the Queen. She reigns supreme, exerting power over the Astrologer, who exerts power over Dodon.

Richard Taruskin, a strong advocate for and defender of Rimsky-Korsakov's fifteen operas, has called *The Golden Cockerel* a "trifling parody" compared to the others.[27] Marina Frolova-Walker, however, describes the score as a kind of swan song to all that had defined Russianness in music as prescribed by the Kuchka—especially considering that if Rimsky-Korsakov had been interested in setting authentic urban and rural (popular) songs, as opposed to lampooning them, he could have consulted the recordings made by the ethnomusicologist Yevgeniya Linyova.[28] Both Taruskin and Frolova-Walker point out that Rimsky-Korsakov knew these phonographs, but obviously did not find them useful. Instead, the composer clearly enjoyed abusing the Russian nationalist music of his own past, presenting folk fare in *The Golden Cockerel* in caustic travesty. In Frolova-Walker's telling: "The goal of unifying the nation through music was now gone: there would be no more *Ruslan*s or *Prince Igor*s."[29] The impresario Sergei Diaghilev staged *The Golden Cockerel* in Paris. In doing so, he said goodbye to nationalism and welcomed, within the repertoire of his company the Ballets Russes, an updated aesthetic: neo-nationalism.

At the end, the Astrologer points out that he and the queen are more real than the tsar and his court. This brings to mind a favorite Russian Symbolist neo-platonic conceit: the notion that the spirit world lays claim to essences, whereas our material sphere is a black-and-white, two-dimensional representational desert. Yet here the real does not counter the unreal to make a grand point about the fictive nature of the world as constructed by language, social codes, or political systems; rather, as Belsky's libretto makes clear, nothing is real—except perhaps as children might see things, improving upon their surroundings by adding brighter colors, unreflectively, enchantingly. "The result," the American cultural critic Carl Van Vechten wrote of Bolm's production at the Metropolitan Opera, "astonished and entertained nearly everybody, except a few old fogies who seemed to feel that entertainment in an opera house was sacrilege."[30]

What is the nature of that entertainment? What is its "fated key," to quote Washington Irving? Why the resplendent emptiness of the popular wedding processional, which dazzled the *enfant terrible* composer Sergei Prokofiev despite the insipid melodic material?[31] And why, amid the silliness, the inclusion of a meltingly beautiful lullaby, which spools out from the words "rule, lying on your side"? Rimsky-Korsakov's colleague and former student Anatoli Lyadov extolled the episode as "so peaceful, so quiet in the scene where Dodon is lulled to sleep . . . that it seems you can hear a fly flying and beating its wings against the glass."[32] The syntax is progressive, experimental even, but the composer confessed that he was working with "bizarre harmony" in the "newest style" simply to demonstrate to his younger, brasher colleagues that "he could do it, too."[33]

Yet even in the densest chromatic passages, which are deployed forward and backward in the score, Rimsky-Korsakov wanted the listener to perceive a sense of strict order. The magic is of a hyper-rational sort: controlled, disciplined, and inorganic, relying on recurring splashes of orchestral color that emerge as discrete *leit*-timbres. The music supposedly meant to capture desire, sensual delight, is subject to sequential transposition, whereas one might expect the opposite. Given that desire runs counter to reason, wouldn't musical destabilization and non-repetition seem more fitting? Rimsky-Korsakov delighted in the polyvalence of his dissonant sonorities, their potential resolution in two or more keys. Still, he wanted to avoid planting noise in the ear or straying into the dreaded decadence of the Russian Symbolist composer Alexander Scriabin, his aesthetic and technical antipode. Thus careful attention is paid to voice leading and the convincing, satisfying tonal resolution of non-tonal chords. "A composer must be in full command of his tonal forces," he explained, "otherwise they will master him. Bear in mind that like a composer without knowledge, so music—especially daring harmonies—is not good at all without clear part writing, since when harmonies are complicated and tricky, part writing is everything."[34]

The musicologist Marina Rakhmanova has puzzled over these musical paradoxes and contradictions, wisely choosing to leave them unresolved. She has also considered the matter of good versus evil in the opera and the ambiguous conduct of the central characters, but ultimately defaults to quoting from reviews of the original Zimin Opera production. She references in particular Yuliy Engel, who considered *The Golden Cockerel* "forceful, profound, serious, and in spite of its allusiveness—or perhaps precisely because of it—replete with irresistible charm."[35] Here, then, is the key: charm. Allusions cannot be deciphered, try as the earnest semiotician might; the piling on of signs leads to no one certain signified. (The Imperial censors aided the composer's cause by reducing the text to doggerel, a string of impish one-liners in place of dialogue.) The musical quotes from Borodin and Musorgsky, along with Rimsky-Korsakov himself, point only to their own superfluousness, which is ultimately how they come to speak of something else. And that something else is the power of enchantment—a power heard, in a very different context, by the philosopher Vladimir Jankélévitch. In her introduction to Jankélévitch's meditation on "music and the ineffable," musicologist Carolyn Abbate defines enchantment as an alternative to Romantic subjective expression in sound. Whereas tonal progressions, organic growth, and motivic elaboration in nineteenth-century music generally attempt to engage the intellect through modes of narrative development, Rimsky-Korsakov's colorful orchestral tapestries charm through elaborations of timbre that become more and more affective through sheer repetition and excess. Like the French modernists that followed him, Rimsky-Korsakov relies in *The Golden Cockerel* on "objective impression, impressiveness, and automaticism."[36]

The sounding surface of the score is meant to dazzle rather than depict, and the music avoids structured argument in favor of easy repetition, kaleidoscopic patterns, and energetic colors. Herein lies its charm, which is also obviously embodied in the Astrologer. His singing, in the uncanny quasi-castrato range of *tenore altino*, grows ever more compelling, enchanting. Forget the cardboard-cutout characters, the musical borrowings, and four-square phrasing: listen to the grain of his voice. Rimsky-Korsakov contrasts the Astrologer's keening exhortations with the opera buffa outbursts of the tsar, the courtiers, the merchants, and the people on the street. Ultimately the Astrologer captivates us all with his insight, his seemingly magical capacity to find meaning and divine the intentions of the world.

These ideas are present in the version of *The Golden Cockerel* choreographed by Alexei Ratmansky in 2012 for the Royal Danish Ballet and performed by American Ballet Theater in the spring of 2016. Ratmansky's interpretation trades politics for aesthetics, and music for dance. Ratmansky set a radically revised score; on his instruction, the composer and musicologist Yannis Samprovalakis excised the vocal parts and reduced the length by about a third. It is obvious that Rimsky-Korsakov's extremely litigious heirs would not have been pleased by this particular transposition, given their appalled reaction to the Diaghilev Paris production of 1914, a "ballet-cantata" modeled on Russian folk woodcuts that, in the opinion of Rimsky-Korsakov's widow, "distorted the fundamental features of the work as an operatic composition."[37]

Reaction to Ratmansky's effort was mixed. Critics Alastair Macaulay and Apollinaire Scherr both questioned the musical bowdlerization as well as Ratmansky's choreographic conception, especially as compared to what is known of Fokine's.[38] Reviewers were united, however, in praising the mechanical movements and surprising contortions of Skylar Brandt, the ballerina (for the first cast) in the all-important role of the cockerel. "She slides on her pointes and bends 90 degrees at the waist," the dance critic Marina Harss writes enthusiastically, "and then she folds about eight ways to land on her knees on the floor."[39]

Other characters seemed to have sprung to life from folkloric woodcuts and socialist realist canvases; likewise the music, as Jankélévitch sensed, possesses "a character that is more graphic and visual than auditory."[40] Designer Richard Hudson's vibrantly colored sets and intricately stitched costumes pay homage to painter Natalia Goncharova, who, in her work for the Ballets Russes, represented the people and places of Russia with a dazzle of energetic reds, yellows, and greens derived from folk handicrafts, paintings, and prints. (According to an article in *Vogue*,

Figure 3. Skylar Brandt and Duncan Lyle in
*The Golden Cockerel,* American Ballet Theater, 2016.

Hudson's "palette of brights" also reflects "the ongoing fad for '70s bohemia." His costumes "were dyed, painted, appliquéd, and embroidered" by hand, but also by computer.)[41] Ratmansky, too, draws on the past. His choreography quotes Fokine's 1937 revival of the 1914 Ballets Russes production as captured on eighteen minutes of silent film.[42] Ratmansky resets, intact, the scene at the end of Act 1, in which the plump Dodon mounts a giant wooden stallion and heads off to battle. Thus the golden boy of ballet today salutes Fokine, the cock of the walk a century ago.

In the dance, charm is harder to locate—except when it comes to the sheer strangeness of the title character. The golden cockerel's staccato steps, her spins, and her ports de bras are extremely precise; this is magic of a hyper-rational sort. And Ratmansky chooses to privilege what Rimsky-Korsakov actually dismissed. The Astrologer might have been the composer's soothsayer, but Ratmansky does not do much with him. He is a stock character, akin to the sorcerer in Fokine's and Stravinsky's 1911 ballet *Petrushka*. The Queen, too, is trapped in the ballet equivalent of opera buffa clichés, more a hoochie-coochie entertainer than a source of genuine passion. The music of the "Hymn to the Sun" recalls an earlier example of Rimsky-Korsakov's Orientalism, "The Song of the Hindu Trader" in *Sadko*, but Ratmansky opts to drain it of true heat and make it sexy in American sitcom fashion, with the Tsar's scepter suggesting, in the tackiest moment of the staging, a phallus. The Queen's upper-body glamor grows monotonous, and her pointe shoes clunkier, in Dodon's presence.

Most important, the workaday peasants are much more than the genuflecting dupes represented in Rimsky-Korsakov's music and Belsky's libretto. Ratmansky could not—would not—mock the people; instead, he shows true tenderness. If his production has a politics, it lies in his desire to enrich the movements of incidental characters, the bit players in this "odd fantasia on kings at war."[43] Ratmansky assigns his most poignant steps and gestures to the humble folk; his movements capture their torments and anguish, humor and humanity. Sometimes the emotion comes through in a slight tremble in the torso and shifting of the weight in the feet. At other times, their anticipation has them almost jumping out of their skin in their patterned, individuated costumes. Ratmansky shows his corps de ballet true love, the ultimate enchantment. They are innocent. They are beautiful. They are just.

# NOTES

1. Edgar Istel and Theodore Baker, "Rimsky-Korsakov, the Oriental Wizard," *The Musical Quarterly* 15/3 (1929): 388–414.

2. It tends to be written that "two chapters" of Washington's *Tales of the Alhambra* informed Pushkin's fairy tale, but the first of these, "The House of the Weathercock," is merely a two-page preface to the second, the "Legend of the Arabian Astrologer." For a useful comparison of Irving's and Pushkin's texts, see Gerald Abraham, "Satire and Symbolism in *The Golden Cockerel*," *Music & Letters* 52/1 (1971): 46–54.

3. The Astrologer is reminiscent of the astrologer king of Francesco Cavalli's 1652 opera *Veremonda*, which draws from the same epic historical literature as Irving's *Tales of the Alhambra*. Cavalli's opera is set in Alhambra, a Spanish Muslim fortress located in Granada, Andalusia, Spain. The astrologer king in Cavalli's work is reluctant to head into battle, preferring to spend his time following the stars. In Rimsky-Korsakov's opera something of the opposite occurs: the king (tsar) is prompted to take up arms by an astrologer.

4. B. Asaf'yev, "Skomorosh'ye tsarstvo," in *Simfonicheskiye etyudï* (1922; repr. Moscow: Kompozitor, 2008), 138.

5. Ol'ga Skrïnnikova, "'Zolotoy petushok'—zagadki mifa," *Muzïkal'naya akademiya* 1 (2008): 135. Skrïnnikova argues that Shemakha's singing recalls, in its half-step scalar alterations, augmented seconds, and mixed rhythmic values, Rimsky-Korsakov's Kashcheyeva (from his opera *Kashchei the Deathless*, 1902), as well as his Swan Princess (*The Tale of Tsar Saltan*, 1900). She is also Cleopatra in this interpretation, and the Roman goddess Venus.

6. See, on these events, Lynn Sargeant, "*Kashchei the Immortal*: Liberal Politics, Cultural Memory, and the Rimsky-Korsakov Scandal of 1905," *Russian Review* 64/1 (2005): 22–43.

7. Mark Humphreys et al., "Rimsky-Korsakov," *Grove Music Online*, http://www.oxfordmusiconline.com/subscriber/article/grove/music/52074pg1.

8. Avril Pyman translates a bitterly sarcastic poem by Valeriy Bryusov, composed in response to the October Manifesto, in which the fifth line reads: "Half measures, though, are detestable." Pyman, *A History of Russian Symbolism* (Cambridge: Cambridge University Press, 2006), 252.

9. Abraham, "Satire and Symbolism in *The Golden Cockerel*," 51, relies on a Soviet source, a 1953 article by Abram Gozenpud, for inaccurate information about the date and content of this image.

10. Rossiyskiy institut istorii iskusstv (Russian Institute for Art History, hereafter RIII), f. 7, r. XI, d. 8, l. 38 ob.

11. Belsky (1866–1946) studied law and economics before turning to literature. He assembled the libretti for the last four of Rimsky-Korsakov's operas, pushing him in unusual, non-kuchkist directions. *The Legend of the Invisible City of Kitezh and the Maiden Fevroniya* (1904) would not have come into being were it not for Belsky's interest in pantheism and the religious-philosophical pursuits of the Symbolists.

12. RIII, f. 7, r. XI, d. 8, l. 42 ob., 13 June 1907.

13. Ibid., l. 43, 15 July 1907.

14. Ibid., l. 45 ob., 13 August 1907.

15. Ibid., ll. 44–45, 4 August 1907. These and other letters concerning the genesis of the opera are quoted in an article by Nelli Bikbayeva for a 2011 production of *The Golden Cockerel* at the Bolshoi Theater, "Poymat' 'Zolotogo petushka.' Khronika sozdaniya operï," http://www.rimskykorsakov.ru/110821.html. See also A. N. Rimskiy-Korsakov, *N. A. Rimskiy-Korsakov: Zhizn' i tvorchestvo*, *Vïpusk V* (Moscow and Leningrad: Gosudarstvennoye muzïkal'noye izdatel'stvo, 1946), 128–60.

16. A. N. Rimskiy-Korsakov, *N. A. Rimskiy-Korsakov*, 129–30; V. Biélsky, "Préface" (Predisloviye), in N. Rimsky-Korsakow, *Le coq d'or, conte-fable: Opéra en 3 actes* (Leipzig: P. Jurgenson/Rob. Forberg, 1907), n.p.

17. V. V. Yastrebtsev, *Reminiscences of Rimsky-Korsakov*, ed. and trans. Florence Jonas (New York: Columbia University Press, 1985), 442–4[3].

18. RIII, f. 7, r. XI, d. 8, l. 49, 25 February 1908.

19. Yastrebtsev, *Reminiscences of Rimsky-Korsakov*, 444.

20. Rossiyskiy gosudarstvennïy istoricheskiy arkhiv (Russian State Historical Archive), f. 776, op. 25, d. 937, l. 8, 24 April 1908.

21. Ibid., l. 39, n.d.

22. Ibid., l. 40, 21 January 1909.

23. Ibid., l. 42, n.d.

24. See Sergey Ivanovich Zimin, *Zapiski opernogo antreprenera*, ed. V. Pronin (Moscow: MF "Pokoleniya," 2013), 186–87, 195.

25. "The music was in Moscow, and thither young Gest [a Russian soldier] started on leave from his regiment in Petrograd. A vast empire was in the first days of revolution. The soldier went unchallenged, but not so the train. Sixty-five miles from the older city it came to a halt, and the Metropolitan's messenger had no choice but to finish on foot. When he retraced that march some days later with the coveted music he had to buy a peasant's horse, hitch two long poles to the saddle, and on this rude 'drag' or 'trailer' fasten the dozens of packages which he presently forwarded oversea, week by week, for months afterward." "'Coq d'Or' and Its Grim Satire on Russia Today—Music Delayed a Year by Revolution, a Lifetime by Censor," *New York Times*, 3 March 1918.

26. Belsky was perhaps referring to the oft-set Pietro Metastasio libretto *Didone abbandonata*, telling of Aeneas's forsaking of Dido, Queen of Carthage. In *The Golden Cockerel*, the genders are reversed. Instead of an exotic woman being abandoned by an epic hero on a quest, the exotic woman, the Queen of Shemakha, does the abandoning.

27. Richard Taruskin, "Rimsky-Korsakov, Nikolay Andreyevich," *Oxford Music Online*, http://oxfordmusiconline.com/subscriber/article/grove/music/O002126.

28. Marina Frolova-Walker, *Russian Music and Nationalism from Glinka to Stalin* (New Haven: Yale University Press, 2007), 218–25.

29. Ibid., 225. Frolova-Walker goes on: "The high tragedy of the nation's suffering that ennobled *Boris Godunov* was gone, too. The romantic conception of beauty which animates the best pages of *The Snowmaiden* or *Kitezh* had also disappeared. Folk material was now used to present the vulgar everyday present (as in *Petrushka*), or the archaic past to which our human link was broken (as in *Les Noces*). There was no longer a noble folk heritage to be polished up and presented to best advantage within operas and symphonies, but only a repository of material affording opportunities to amuse or even repel, as in *The Rite of Spring*."

30. Carl Van Vechten, *In the Garret* (New York: Knopf, 1920), 230.

31. Sergey Prokofiev, *Diaries 1907–1914: Prodigious Youth*, trans. Anthony Phillips (Ithaca, NY: Cornell University Press, 2006), 58; entry of 3 August 1908.

32. Yastrebtsev, *Reminiscences of Rimsky-Korsakov*, 454.

33. Ibid., 413.

34. Ibid.

35. M. P. Rakhmanova, *Nikolay Andreyevich Rimskiy-Korsakov* (Moscow: Rossiyskaya akademiya muzïki im. Gnesinïkh/Gosudarstvennïy institut iskusstvoznaniya, 1995), 212–15, esp. 214.

36. Carolyn Abbate, "Jankélévitch's Singularity," in Vladimir Jankélévitch, *Music and the Ineffable*, trans. Carolyn Abbate (Princeton: Princeton University Press), xvii.

37. Quoted in Richard Taruskin, *Stravinsky and the Russian Traditions: A Biography of the Works Through "Mavra"* (Berkeley and Los Angeles: University of California Press, 1996), 2:1074.

38. Alastair Macaulay, "Review: 'The Golden Cockerel' at American Ballet Theater Honors Its Origins," *New York Times*, 8 June 2016; http://www.nytimes.com/2016/06/08/arts/dance/review-the-golden-cockerel-at-american-ballet-theater-honors-its-origins.html; Apollinaire Scherr, "The Golden Cockerel, American Ballet Theatre, New York," review, *Financial Times*, 7 June 2016; http://www.ft.com/intl/cms/s/0/b80d3142-2c12-11e6-bf8d-26294ad519fc.html#axzz4BU3a19Vt.

39. Marina Harss, "American Ballet Theatre—The Golden Cockerel—New York," *Dancetabs.com*, 7 June 2016; http://dancetabs.com/2016/06/american-ballet-theatre-the-golden-cockerel-new-york/.

40. Jankélévitch, *Music and the Ineffable*, 20.

41. Laird Borrelli-Persson, "Richard Hudson's Costumes for ABT's *The Golden Cockerel* Are on Point (and Pointe) With the Folklore Trend in Fashion," *Vogue*, 8 June 2016, http://www.vogue.com/13444131/ballet-trends-richard-hudson-costume-design/.

42. New York Public Library, Jerome Robbins Dance Division, MGZIA 4-7264. The film was made during the 1940–41 season of the Ballet Russe de Monte Carlo at the 51st Street Theater in New York.

43. As Fokine's version was dubbed by a writer for the *New York Times* before its American premiere. "Ballet Has Its Day in 'Coq d'Or,'" *New York Times*, 24 February 1918.

# Staging Defeat: *The Golden Cockerel* and the Russo-Japanese War

## MARINA FROLOVA-WALKER

Rimsky-Korsakov's *Golden Cockerel* is an outlier, a bitter satire after a stream of fairy-tale and historical operas. This bitter note is all the more disconcerting for its contrast with the uniformly benign and positive character of the composer's previous music. Even when his chosen scenario required him to present fearful scenes, like the enemy invasion in *Kitezh*, his highly polished craftsmanship always sweetened the pill.[1] But the *Cockerel* is another matter: it negates and mocks all that Rimsky-Korsakov had previously exalted in his operas. Gone is the glory of the Russian nation, its rulers and people. Gone, even, are the musical idioms of the "Russian style" that Rimsky-Korsakov and his colleagues had lovingly nurtured. All these were subjected to ridicule. *The Golden Cockerel* was not merely another Russian opera, but a negation of Russian opera.

What prompted this hostile outburst? In this essay I will focus on the principal reason, which is often cited as a fact,[2] but rarely receives any explanation, namely the Russo-Japanese War of 1904–1905. It ended in catastrophic defeat for Russia, followed by a revolution. I hope to demonstrate that Rimsky-Korsakov and his librettist saturated the libretto with direct and recognizable references to the recent war, turning the opera into a kind of topical political theater. I will then recount more briefly the musical aspects of Rimsky-Korsakov's satire (which I have tackled elsewhere),[3] assessing whether the musical and political satires mutually reinforce each other.

The main literary source for the *Cockerel*'s libretto is Pushkin's brief fairy tale in verse, which is in turn based loosely on a Washington Irving novella.[4] Pushkin's tale is striking for its wit and element of mystery, but the state censors detected two lines in particular that might be construed in a subversive way. The cockerel's call when there was no impending danger was "The Tsar may recline," by which Pushkin referred sarcastically to the laziness of Tsar Dadon, "Dodon" in the opera; this line was removed by the censors. They also removed the closing motto, a potential call to arms: "This tale is a lie but it contains a hint, a lesson for the young."[5] The transformation of Pushkin's mere 250 lines into an opera-length satire required many additional lines, which were expertly created in the style of Pushkin by Rimsky-Korsakov's longtime librettist Vladimir Belsky, who collaborated closely with the composer. We have very little information on the genesis of the libretto, so I will have to infer the relationship between the finished text and the events of 1904–5.[6]

But first let us recount the causes and main events of the Russo-Japanese War. Russia's Trans-Siberian Railway was designed to unite the economies of the eastern and western parts of the country. As construction extended toward the cold-water Pacific port of Vladivostok, a deal was struck with China for a joint project to take the railway by the most direct route to the port, through Manchuria (the only internal Russian route required a lengthy detour far to the north). Russian interests in Manchuria expanded with the acquisition of Port Arthur, a warm-water Pacific harbor on Chinese territory adjacent to Korea. The opportunity to utilize the port arose after Japan was forced by France, Germany, and Russia to withdraw from Korea, in favor of the Korean court and Chinese interests. Russia advanced into Port Arthur and eventually persuaded the Chinese court to recognize the fait accompli and rent out the port. Russia was also seen by the Korean court as a protector against Japan, and succeeded in making substantial commercial deals in Korea. Britain had its own interests in developing Pacific trade, and sought to minimize the scale of any Russian rivalry, leading it into an obvious alliance with a frustrated Japan.

By 1903, the Japanese were no longer prepared to tolerate further Russian consolidation in the region, but looked first to a diplomatic solution, whose major points were acceptance of Russian influence in Manchuria in exchange for Russia allowing Japan to advance its interests in Korea as it saw fit. The Japanese and Russian positions were close, and an agreement could have been reached, but the Russian court was playing for time, and the Japanese eventually broke off negotiations, convinced that the Russians were merely strengthening their positions in preparation for war. The German Kaiser had played a role in the delaying tactics, causing Tsar Nicholas to believe that he could count on German assistance if war broke out with Japan; the Kaiser had no such intentions, and his interests lay in breaking up Russia's alliance with France, which was unhappy with Russian expansion in East Asia. Nicholas also expected that Japan would simply back down rather than risk war against a major European military power. Parts of the Russian press contributed to mounting national hubris, presenting the impending conflict as a chance

Figure 1. *We'll Just Sit Looking Out to Sea and Wait for the Weather*, a Russian poster from 1904, portraying a Cossack defending Manchuria and Port Arthur, opposed by three characters: Uncle Sam and John Bull (USA and Great Britain) are pushing a tiny figure representing Japan, while an even smaller Chinese character is looking on. The slogan is a paraphrase of a Russian saying that is literally about waiting to see if the weather is suitable for sailing, and figuratively about a wait of uncertain duration, or a hope that may not materialize. In the present context, it suggests that the Russians are so confident that they can afford to wait in harbor rather than launching an attack; only if the weather (Japan) turns, will they set sail.

to demonstrate white mastery over a yellow race. The Kaiser, in his personal letters, had told Nicholas to stand up for the white race.[7]

The Japanese broke off diplomatic relations on 6 February 1904, and declared war two days later, initiating hostilities the same day, before Russia had received the declaration. A torpedo attack on the Russian Pacific Fleet in Port Arthur resulted in serious damage to several of its largest ships. Russian newspapers presented both events as evidence of Japan's barbarism and failure to play the games of diplomacy and war by civilized rules:

> Asians do not recognize the European laws that govern foreign relations. After their brutish rupture in relations with a peace-loving Russia, they were quick to mount a still more brutish assault on Holy Russia. Let the Christian nations discover for

themselves, let them see how they have welcomed a barbarian into the family of enlightened states; let them see how they have nurtured a vicious serpent at their breast.[8]

How a port rented from China had become part of "Holy Russia" is anyone's guess. The fighting over Port Arthur developed into a protracted standoff, but it punctured Russian confidence. The next major shock came two months later, when the battleship *Petropavlovsk* tried to break out of Port Arthur harbor, only to be sunk by a Japanese mine. This incident caught the imagination of the Russian public because of some prominent casualties. Among the dead was Admiral Stepan Makarov, who was a naval commander of international renown, together with other senior naval figures, and also the distinguished painter Vasili Vereshchagin, who was fulfilling his state commission as a war artist—a remarkable choice, given his unflinching and controversial depictions of the horrors of war.

This was when the war truly came home to Rimsky-Korsakov. In the diary of his close friend and chronicler Vasili Yastrebtsev, the evening of 31 March 1904 is described thus:

> Our conversation was limited almost entirely to the horrifying destruction of the battleship *Petropavlovsk*, and some of the fatalities: Admiral Makarov, the artist Vereshchagin, and Mikhail Pavlovich Molas, who was Chief of Staff of the Pacific Squadron, and related to the Rimsky-Korsakovs. We wondered who would be called to replace Makarov—Rozhestvensky or Skrydlov?[9]

Clearly Rimsky-Korsakov was shocked at the news, although we cannot yet tell from this what his thoughts were on the wisdom of the campaign. We should recall at this point that Rimsky-Korsakov himself had served as a naval officer during his early years as a part-time composer. Even when he became a Conservatory professor, he remained on the Navy's lists for many years as an inspector of naval bands. He came from a family of naval officers and his family tended to marry members of other naval families: Mikhail Molas, who featured in the conversation above, was the brother-in-law of Alexandra Molas (née Purgold), who was in turn the sister of Rimsky-Korsakov's wife, Nadezhda. Alexandra was a talented singer and a lively member of the Kuchka's extended circle of friends.[10] Rimsky-Korsakov's nephew Fyodor was the captain of the destroyer *Besposhchadnïy* (The Merciless), and the composer was relieved to hear that Fyodor's ship was not sent to the Far East, but left in German docks.[11]

Most of the war's battles were at sea, and so even without documentation of Rimsky-Korsakov's personal reactions, we can easily imagine that he would have keenly followed the events, both from the newspapers and in conversation with better-informed naval colleagues. He would have been capable of following technical details, and we already know how much he felt the losses.

While the sinking of the *Petropavlovsk* was a tragic accident, rather than a sign of bad tactics, the general unfolding of the war revealed how badly the Russians had underestimated the strength of the Japanese. Realizing to the full their previously thwarted ambitions, the Japanese invaded Korea, and soon won control of the country. This also gave them a useful platform from which they could advance by land to Port Arthur, which they cut off in April and subjected to a prolonged siege. The Russian public awaited the fall of the town. When it finally came, on 2 January 1905, the newspapers reported the disaster in bitter and disillusioned terms:

> Port Arthur has fallen. Billions of rubles have been taken from our half-impoverished people and soaked in the blood of tens of thousands of young lives. Such is our colonial policy in the Far East, and exhausted by unequal battle, it has reached its endpoint, laying down our banners at the feet of the victors. Doubt and dread have now taken hold of our souls.[12]

Looking beyond the war, the loss of Port Arthur was a major blow to Russia's long-term plans for projecting itself as a major player in Pacific commerce. The other main plank of Russia's Eastern policy was the railway through Manchuria, and with the fall of the Port, the Japanese were now free to advance westward. The decisive battle of the ensuing land war took place in late February and early March 1905 outside Mukden (now Shenyang), the provincial capital of Manchuria. Although the Japanese were outnumbered and lost a higher proportion of their men, they won on tactics and forced the Russians to flee from their trenches. The Russians also lost all local sympathy from the local population because of their brutal unconcern for civilians, no doubt fueled by the "Yellow Peril" rhetoric of the Russian press, which did not encourage fine distinctions between Japanese, Koreans, or Chinese. The Manchurians began open collaboration with Japanese forces and even formed partisan bands against the Russians. With the Russian retreat to the north of the province after the Battle of Mukden, the Japanese had won their second great prize of the war: control of the railway. Russia's Eastern policy now lay in ruins.

Construction of the railway resumed inside Russia's borders, and was only completed a few months before the fall of the tsar.

With the loss of its warm-water port and the railway by mid-March of 1905, Russia's strategic defeat was complete. Still to come, however, was a strange and tragic appendix to the war. This is the story of the Russian Baltic Fleet, renamed the Second Pacific Squadron and ordered to sail around the world. Their original mission had been to end the Japanese naval blockade outside Port Arthur, after which the combined fleet was to take on the Japanese and defeat them, or at least forestall any Japanese advance on Manchuria. But the seeds of the Second Squadron's demise were already sown in its long journey. In the North Sea, worries over the possibility of attacks from Japanese torpedo boats led to an order from the fleet commander, Admiral Rozhestvensky, that no vessel could be allowed to pass within the limits of the fleet without prior identification (Britain, after all, although a non-combatant, was in alliance with Japan). When they were passing through the relatively shallow Dogger Bank region of the North Sea at night, in foggy conditions, a group of stationary boats was spotted. Taking these to be Japanese vessels lying in wait, the Russians opened fire to preempt any planned torpedo attack. Unfortunately for all, the boats were fishing trawlers from the English port of Hull, and they had only remained stationary because their nets were lowered (known as the Dogger Bank Incident, 21–22 October 1904). In the confusion, even Russian's own cruiser *Aurora* was damaged by friendly fire, which killed an Orthodox priest on board. The U.S. Navy, a few years earlier, had several such incidents for fear of encounters with Spanish torpedo boats; the technology was still quite new—the first sinking by motorized torpedo was in the early 1890s—and was causing general alarm. The Russian fleet's mistake brought threats of British Navy reprisals, but French mediation lowered the tension, and investigation by an international commission was proposed. The Russians had to assume responsibility, and paid compensation for the three fishermen who had been killed. The immediate strategic consequence was the denial of navigation rights through the Suez Canal, which forced the Russians to take the much longer route around Africa. During the period when the fleet was docked in Tangiers, stories of drinking, fighting, and debauchery began seeping into the press—if true, signs of demoralization were perhaps setting in already. At any rate, the incident played badly in Russia, and it was not until four months after the incident that the commission delivered its verdict, exonerating the Russians of any deliberate or reckless endangering of innocent lives.

Even within the senior ranks of the Russian Navy, there was a lack of consensus over the wisdom of the campaign. The Naval Academy professor Nikolai Klado published no less than eight hostile articles in the press. The first of these were published in the aftermath of the Dogger Bank Incident in the middle of November, appearing in the newspaper *Novoye vremya* (New Era) under the name "Priboy" (Tide). Klado, confident of his position, made no special efforts to conceal his identity beyond the formality of his pen name, and he was arrested before the month was out. But he had assessed the situation correctly, and the immediate outcry from his colleagues ensured his swift release. He wrote further critical articles between January and April of the following year, and one in particular, "Could the Results of the War in the Far East Have Been Predicted?" (4 March), was sufficiently incendiary to elicit an official warning. Some saw Klado as a mere traitor, others as a courageous whistleblower who was usefully revealing serious problems in Russia's armaments industry and in the education of its officers. Leo Tolstoy, in a private conversation said, "True, they delight in war, but Klado has told us that the root of Russia's defeat lies in its indifference to military education."[13] Klado's celebrity extended even to the thirteen-year-old Sergei Prokofiev, who was fascinated by the professor's scientific approach to naval combat, and even made an unsuccessful attempt to meet him.[14]

Klado's next piece, "After the Departure of the Second Pacific Squadron," led his seniors in the Navy Ministry to call for him to be put on trial, but Nicholas II, who knew him personally, decided that dismissal would suffice in the circumstances.[15] Eventually even Admiral Rozhestvensky, commander of the Second Squadron, looked back on the failed mission with words of contrition: "If only I had possessed just a spark of civil courage, I would have proclaimed to the world: Take good care of these, the fleet's last resources! Don't send them off to perish! But that much-needed spark was lacking in me."[16]

As Adalyat Issiyeva points out in this volume, the librettist Belsky proposed in June that Rimsky-Korsakov should consider a symphonic piece inspired by a nightmarish Alfred Kubin drawing, *Das Grausen* (The Horror).[17] This Goyaesque image must have seemed to Belsky like the perfect symbol for the *Petropavlovsk* hitting a mine outside Port Arthur. The proposal came more than two years before work began on the *Cockerel*, so there were already signs that Rimsky-Korsakov's next major work was likely to reflect these terrible events. Rimsky-Korsakov himself reflected on the war in a letter to Glazunov, in August:

> Fyodor Rimsky-Korsakov [a nephew] is in command of the destroyer *Merciless*, and judging from the telegram, it's currently in a German port along with another destroyer, the

*Tsesarevich*. The ships will be decommissioned, and I'm very happy for Fyodor that they won't be sending him into battle now. What dreadful things are going on in the East! Port Arthur is obviously living through its last days. And according to today's papers, the *Rurik* has been sunk. This damned war hasn't claimed its last victims yet, and it's not going to stop any time soon. "They're nothing but a pack of monkeys! We'll teach them a lesson they won't forget, by jingo!"—that's what our lot used to say. "Come the first land battle, the Japs will be done for" etc.—and this is how it's turned out. I must admit that I just can't get this war out of my head.[18]

What, then, of the Second Pacific Squadron when it eventually arrived in the Pacific? The circumnavigation of Africa extended the journey by months. Having rounded the Cape, France allowed the fleet to dock in Madagascar at the end of 1904. While they were still docked, they heard the news of the fall of Port Arthur, which also eliminated the purpose of their mission. They then crossed the Indian Ocean, refueling at sea with German assistance since international law prevented them from refueling in neutral ports (the Germans never entered the war, of course, contrary to the Russian court's expectations). Their next destination was French Indochina (Vietnam), where they stopped during April and early May 1905. For what it is worth, the journey was an unprecedented achievement for any fleet in the days of coal power. The only mission remaining at this stage was to arrive safely in Vladivostok. Rather than risk taking to the high seas, they chose the shortest route, which would take them through the Tsushima Strait between Japanese-controlled Korea and Japan itself. The hope was that they could pass unnoticed under cover of darkness and fog, but a vigilant Japanese merchant crew spotted them, and the remains of the Japanese fleet gathered to intercept them. The battle raged through 27 and 28 May. The Russian fleet was completely destroyed, with only three small vessels managing to escape to Vladivostok. "Tsushima" entered the Russian language with the same resonance that "Waterloo" carried for the French.

How, then, were these terrible events reflected in the opera? Belsky's satirical portrayal of Dodon's call to arms in Act 1 of the *Cockerel* makes references to the preparation of the public for the actual war. Pushkin's Dodon complains about the suddenness of enemy attacks in the past, and this prompts his interest in the "cockerel" device, which is a kind of fairy-tale radar that would scan the surroundings to give advance warning of any hostile troop movements. Belsky makes much of this trope of "suddenness" to remind his audience of the press portrayals of the initial

Figure 2. Alfred Kubin (1877–1959), *Das Grausen* (The Horror), drawing from 1902.

Japanese attack on the ships in Port Arthur harbor. Rumors circulated that the wife of the Russian commander, Admiral Stark, hosted a party that night, and that many of the officers were away from their posts. Although the veracity of this story was disputed, it was too attractive as a metaphor for the unpreparedness of the Russian forces, and featured in expanded or dramatized accounts of the war.[19] Whatever actually took place on the night of 7–8 February 1904, Admiral Stark was held responsible, and he was quickly dismissed from his post.[20] Dodon's fear of sudden attack would have alerted contemporary Russian audiences to the opera's topicality and its satirical target, preparing them to view subsequent events in the same light.

Belsky added a state council for war to Pushkin's story, and his additions all pointed back to notorious incidents in the Russo-Japanese War.

He introduced three new characters: Dodon's two idiot sons, Guidon and Afron, and the military commander Polkan. In response to Dodon's complaints, Guidon makes a suggestion: let us withdraw our troops from the frontier and place them around the capital city, while stocking up well on beer and wine. "That's the kind of war we'd like!" the chorus of boyars replies. While the enemy is busy pillaging the rest of the country without restraint, our troops will have time to build up their strength. The commander Polkan mocks Guidon, saying that the court itself might come under bombardment in that case. Guidon has proposed a ludicrous strategy that is bound to result in a siege of the city, and this, of course, will prompt the audience to recall the complacency that led to the siege of Port Arthur. After the war, a public inquiry into the behavior of Commandant Stoessel during the siege led to bitter recriminations between pro- and anti-Stoessel factions within the military. One of the accusations against Stoessel was his responsibility for the food shortage: he should have, for example, arranged for the growing of vegetables within the city.[21] These postwar squabbles would have been evoked by this scene in the *Cockerel*.

Dodon's second son, Afron, then proposes another solution: the army should advance toward the enemy a good month in advance of the expected battle, in order to meet the enemy in a greater state of readiness. But Polkan shoots this down, too: to work, the enemy would have to conform to the timing laid out in the scenario, though in reality their actions would be unpredictable. This situation again matches part of the Russian campaign in the war, namely the dispatch of the Second Pacific Squadron. The original mission to break the navy blockade around Port Arthur had to assume that the situation would remain unchanged after the squadron's journey of several months from the Baltic to the Sea of Japan. Although the projected journey via the Suez Canal was considerably shorter than the eventual journey around Africa, it was not inconceivable that Japan's ally Britain would find a pretext for closing off that route.

The only voice of reason in Dodon's council of war is Polkan, the military commander. He shares his name with a literary creature that is half-human, half-dog, known for his loyalty and fearlessness in battle, and this gives rise to the barking music Rimsky-Korsakov provides for him.[22] Polkan's contemptuous retorts are received with great hostility by the tsar and the boyars, and he even comes under suspicion of treason. For contemporary audiences, this would have evoked Nikolai Klado's criticisms of the war's conduct, and his hostile treatment by the authorities.

In Act 2, Dodon rides out to join his sons in battle, only to encounter a field already strewn with corpses. This undoubtedly refers to a similar scene in Glinka's *Ruslan and Lyudmila*, but it also would have had clear real-world associations for the audience. The trench warfare at the long Battle of Mukden anticipated the warfare of the First World War, and one newspaper reported that the Japanese were even forced to take up different positions because of the risk of disease spreading from the many corpses on the battlefield. The two sides eventually had to call regular ceasefires in order to bury their dead.[23] On the operatic battlefield, Dodon finds his two sons dead, and discovers that they had managed to kill each other in the confusion of battle. Although this particular episode was already present in Pushkin's original tale, the reference to mistaken identity on the battlefield would have reminded the audience of the Dogger Bank Incident and the friendly fire that killed the Orthodox priest onboard the *Aurora*.

Beyond these concrete references to the events of the war are a group of more general characterizations of Russia's oriental enemy, both in the opera and in real life. Pushkin's (Middle Eastern) Queen of Shemakha was retained in the opera—her elimination might have seemed a step too far from the original, which was undoubtedly familiar to the audience. This creates a minor obstacle if the opera's enemy is to symbolize the Japanese, since images of seductive femininity were remote from any of the actual imagery used in the press or other Russian culture of the period. Nevertheless, when Dodon asks the Queen where her homeland lies, she answers: "As soon as you get to the East, you will see my country there, in a colorful haze," and she describes it as an island (this was not in the Pushkin source). This fits the plain meaning of the story well enough, as part of the Queen's attempt to charm Dodon, but within the political allegory, it helps the audience identify Shemakha with Japan. Belsky's main focus, however, was on matching opera and reality through his representation of *changes* in attitude to the enemy. The Japanese enemy was initially a complete unknown. St. Petersburg was not filled with military and businessmen from the Russian Far East, so the public had only a hazy knowledge of Chinese and Koreans, let alone the still more remote Japanese. A war requires speakers of the enemy's language, whether for negotiation, spying, or interception of messages, but neither St. Petersburg nor Moscow could provide anyone with sufficient expertise in the Japanese language.

The initial representations of the Japanese in the Russian press focused on their supposed weakness. A fictitious piece of wishful thinking published by *Rus'* is set in a Japanese tea shop in Russia: an army reservist, picking up one tea seller after another, gives each a vigorous shaking. "I'm a reservist," he says, "and perhaps I'll have to go to war. But I've never seen any Japanese in my life before. So, I've come here to try them out. They're not up to much—a Jap is just too weak by our standards.

I'd need six or seven of them just to exercise my left arm."[24] Japanese paganism and skin color were also presented as signs of their inferiority.

After the war began, and the Japanese immediately gained the advantage, the Russian press was forced to change tack, and the Japanese were now portrayed as fierce but emotionless warriors armed with the latest in technology.[25] In Belsky's libretto, the Russians initially feel superior to the Queen of Shemakha, and Polkan mocks her; for example, when the Queen sings about her longing for caresses and kisses, Polkan responds: "You'll get them, you'll get them, don't you worry." But the opera then reverses perceptions, portraying the Queen and her country as much more sophisticated: her music is highly refined (if rather decadent) in the musical competition with the Russian court, while the Russians are given much more primitive and rough-hewn music. The Queen's vocal virtuosity together with the harmonic complexity of her music are heard alongside the crude "Siskin-piskin" nursery-rhyme tune. Never before in Russian opera had the oriental world been presented as superior to the Russian world—unsurprisingly, since until 1904, Russia had prevailed in battle as it expanded eastward.[26] Later, when the Queen makes Dodon dance, he is thoroughly humiliated as she urges him on, comparing him at different moments to a turkey, a crab, or a camel. Here we have a clear element of self-parody from Rimsky-Korsakov: in his opera *Sadko*, from a decade earlier, the scene in the Underwater Kingdom presents the Russian Sadko forcing the rulers of the Kingdom to dance uncontrollably (a plot device reused by Stravinsky in *The Firebird*).

One further possible contemporary reference comes to mind when we witness the exotic procession of Act 3 in the *Cockerel*, featuring a group of monsters in addition to black and oriental slaves. This would have reminded the audience of Japanese prisoners of war, when they were paraded before onlookers in Moscow and other Russian cities.[27]

Finally, we must consider the most politically provocative references: the implied comparison between Dodon and Nicholas II. Now, Nicholas was known as an outdoor type, a keen horseman, whereas Dodon tends to stay in bed. Even so, Nicholas, rightly or wrongly, had a reputation for throwing his energies into his domestic and social life, and his apparent lack of concern for the affairs of state have a parallel in Dodon. During the war, the tsar came under criticism for mounting lavish celebrations at the birth of his son and heir Aleksei during the summer of 1904, which seemed of greater interest to him than extricating Russian forces from impending defeat in the Far East. Rimsky-Korsakov described the opera's "sleep" sequence as an illustration of "state Oblomovism," referring to the literary character from Goncharov who symbolized Russian inaction and procrastination.[28] From the diaries Nicholas left, we do in fact know

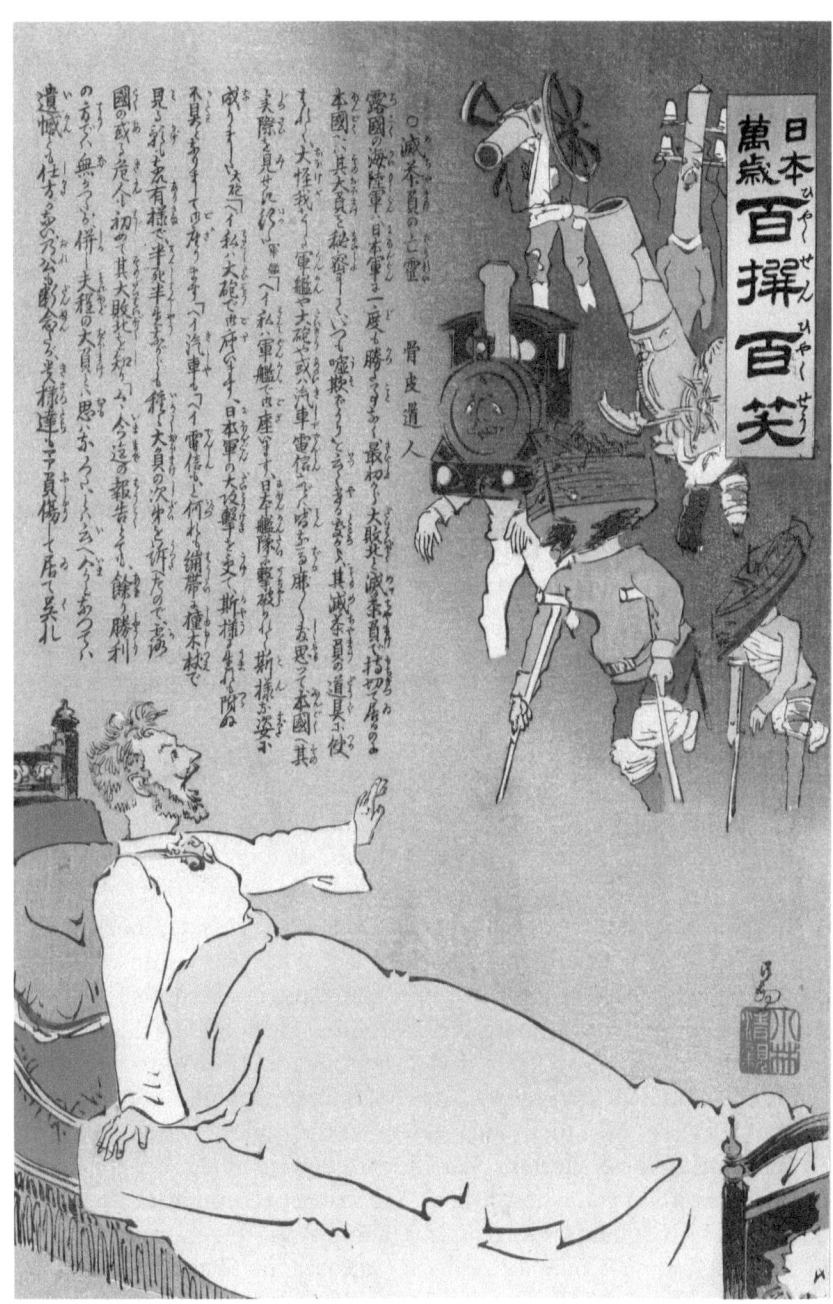

Figure 3. Japanese wartime woodblock print (1904 or 1905) by
Kobayashi Kiyochika (1847–1915), showing Nicholas II in bed confronted by a
nightmarish parade of symbols representing his losses in the war.

that he worried about the war,[29] but the memoirs of the generals close to him tell us that he never displayed any emotion over the war when he was in their company.[30]

Perhaps the most striking of all the parallels actually comes, by coincidence, from the original Pushkin tale. Unlike most Russians, Nicholas did know Japan, but his experiences there can hardly have left him well disposed toward the country. On an 1891 state visit to Japan, three years before he succeeded to the throne, Nicholas was attacked in the city of Otsu by a deranged sword-wielding member of the Japanese security contingent, who inflicted four wounds before he could be stopped. The worst of these was to the forehead, leaving fragments of bone that had to be removed in a subsequent operation. The damage left Nicholas with a scar and a lifetime of headaches. At the end of the opera, the Cockerel pecks Dodon on the forehead, killing him instantly. We know that the "Otsu Incident" had not been forgotten during the war, since the following scurrilous lyric was sung to the melody of the Russian national anthem:

| | |
|---|---|
| *Bozhe, tsarya khrani* | God save our gracious tsar! although |
| *Nam on ne nuzhen* | We can't say that we need you, sir, |
| *V lob on kontuzhen* | Now that the Japanese, our foe, |
| *Yapontsami.*[31] | Have rapped you on the head, sir. |

In the opera, after the Cockerel kills Dodon, the people, shocked and baffled, ask "What will the new dawn bring? What will we do without a tsar?" The image of a cockerel on a spire could also invite comparison with the famous double-headed eagles on the spires or domes of the Kremlin towers (the first of these appeared as early as the middle of the seventeenth century). A later cartoon portrays Nicholas after his abdication, with the caption "Let's see how they manage without the eagle . . ." (see Figure 4).

In listing all these allusions, I am not attempting to legislate for future productions: the production history and critical reception of the opera point to its rich potential for reinterpretation. What this exercise allows us to do, rather, is to discover the political radicalization of its creators. At the beginning of the 1905 Revolution, Rimsky-Korsakov described himself as "bright red,"[32] and became a figurehead in the revolutionary movement. The leadership of the Conservatory did not wish its students to continue their involvement in the capital's increasingly heated demonstrations. Rimsky-

Figure 4. "Let's see how they manage without the eagle . . ." Russian postcard from 1917.

Korsakov was appointed as a mediator, but took the students' side and called for the resignation of the Conservatory's director. The result was the expulsion of the leaders of the politicized students, and Rimsky-Korsakov's dismissal from his professorial post. He then became a celebrity of sorts, his name cited in all the papers. Letters of protest came from intellectuals and artistic figures around the country, and, to his acute embarrassment, groups of concerned peasants sent him donations, worrying, perhaps, that he might become destitute. Several of his colleagues resigned in sympathy, and there was a student walkout involving many more than the students who had sparked the controversy. Glazunov, who was among those who had resigned in sympathy, was appointed the new director, and he reinstated Rimsky-Korsakov immediately. He was about to retire in any case, but he could now do so with honor and with pension rights. Soviet music historians later boosted Rimsky-Korsakov's posthumous prestige by highlighting his 1905 actions.

So far, we have dealt more with Belsky's role in transforming Pushkin's tale into a (tacit) commentary on the war and the current state of Russia. Rimsky-Korsakov had the more difficult task of working out the musical implications of his new political stance in the *Cockerel*. He had spent the previous four decades—his entire career as a composer—cultivating the "Russian style" alongside his Kuchka colleagues. He had made recent detours into more Italianate and Wagnerian writing, but the *Cockerel* required him to address the Russian style. What should be done with the familiar musical idioms when their ideological underpinnings are twisted or negated? In a world where Russians lose and orientals win, the standard narrative of Russian opera was reversed: how does this affect the meaning of these idioms? The *Cockerel* also presents the traditionally fantastic characters, the Astrologer and the Queen, as "real," while those who were traditionally real (the Russian side) are presented unrealistically, as absurd fantasy figures in a "dream." But the old (Russian) reality had been represented through stable diatonic harmony, while the fantastic characters were given music that used chromatic schemes such as the octatonic scale—known in Russia as the "Rimsky-Korsakov scale." What was now to become of this musical and dramatic opposition?

These questions are not easy to answer, and Rimsky-Korsakov's own pronouncements do not necessarily cast much light on the matter:

> I myself am writing in the same way as before, which isn't good. The *Cockerel* could have appeared as early as the 1880s, and then it would have fitted its time better.[33]

This statement appeared within a discussion on the subject of originality, and Rimsky-Korsakov seems to be unhappy that he did not manage to sustain his stylistic departures from the norms of the Kuchka's Russian style, departures found in *The Tsar's Bride* or *Servilia*. This issue was also raised by Belsky, who noticed a particular scale in Glinka, and challenged Rimsky-Korsakov over his use of the same scale six decades later. Rimsky-Korsakov had to defend himself, explaining how he had extended and modified Glinka's ideas, and illustrating his points with music examples—he could not easily brush aside a style that had taken him many years of painstaking work to develop.[34]

But the *Cockerel*, of course, could not have appeared in the 1880s, when Rimsky-Korsakov was using his new mature operatic style in earnest, as in *The Snow Maiden*. In order to be usable for political satire, that style had to become overfamiliar, clichéd, even cartoonish. As it happens, his opera *The Tale of Tsar Saltan* (1900) served as an excellent preparation for this step: the plot was sufficiently dehumanized and the musical idiom consciously stylized—*stilizatsiya* was the Russian term, suggesting exaggeration. Rimsky-Korsakov was already parodying himself, rather than just repeating himself. Perceptive listeners noticed the subtle change of perspective, and connected it with wider fin-de-siècle preoccupations in the arts. Rimsky-Korsakov preferred to deny that his music had any kinship with decadent art, where style became everything, but it hardly seems unfair to conclude that this was a pose. There is just one step between *stilizatsiya* and outright cartoon satire, a step that the artist Ivan Bilibin had taken during the 1905 Revolution. Rimsky-Korsakov followed him in the *Cockerel*, and now the dehumanization of the Russian style, already evident in *Saltan*, was completed.

At the beginning of the war, Rimsky-Korsakov was asked to participate in a "patriotic" charity concert for wounded soldiers. It is not clear who chose the piece for him to perform, but it is clear that he would not have chosen it himself:

> I had to conduct the march from *Tsar Saltan* as a patriotic piece(!) . . . I was annoyed with myself, annoyed that I had been so stupid as to agree to conduct this fragment, which was to disown the true significance and meaning of my work.[35]

The stylized Russianness of a fairy-tale kingdom's march was now to serve as a morale-booster for real soldiers of a real Russia that was at war with a colonial rival. As the war continued, and Rimsky-Korsakov became more hostile to it, the embarrassing memory of the *Saltan* march may have lent an edge to his reconsideration of the "Russian style"—could he now rework the style in such a way that it could not be assimilated to future state occasions?

The *Cockerel* thus became a distorting mirror in which the previous seventy years of Russian opera and its nationalist preoccupations found an unflattering reflection. At the beginning of Act 1, the conventionally regal music is implausibly overblown and repetitive for a composer of Rimsky-Korsakov's skills, and the musical gestures associated with Dodon are deliberately clumsy and inane. In his first speech, the tsar complains to the boyar council about the weight of his crown, which harks back to Boris Godunov's dark premonitions at his coronation in Musorgsky's opera. Where Boris was powerful and dignified, Dodon can only whine, and the orchestra reflects this in a mixture of trite folk motives and pedantic contrapuntal passages. This is *musical* satire that required Rimsky-Korsakov, an aesthete and impeccable craftsman, to write in a knowingly flawed manner, and trust that the bulk of his audience would follow the hints.

Dodon's sons, Guidon and Afron, sing music of the "courageous young warrior" type that surfaced in Glinka's *A Life for the Tsar* in Sobinin's role. Though the music remains plausibly heroic, Guidon and Afron sing words that fall dismally short of that heroism. These two young men are as idle and cowardly as their father. There is another Glinka reference at the beginning of Act 2, where the "field of the dead" evokes a similar scene in *Ruslan and Lyudmila* (as mentioned above). Where Glinka's original was haunting, Rimsky-Korsakov's is grimly mocking. Dodon's wailing over the bodies of his sons recalls the famous chorus of the people howling in *Boris Godunov*, a landmark passage in Russian music. But Dodon decides to improve on the original howling figures, taking their descending phrases, and redirecting some of them upward, to ridiculous effect.

Rimsky-Korsakov's mockery extends to that collective character, the Russian People, so often the cherished focus of Russian opera composers, whose powerful choral writing brought the People out of the background and endowed them with agency. Musorgsky, once again, stands out here, and Rimsky-Korsakov refers back to the choral recitatives of *Boris Godunov*'s opening scene at the beginning of his own Act 3: "It's scary, brothers!— Why?— I don't really know myself.— Knock it off!" Further on in Act 3, when the People greet the returning tsar and his bride, their self-abasement is taken to grotesque lengths: "We can bark like dogs and crawl on our knees—whatever will keep you happy." The music of this chorus is laid out in a most peculiar way: the tenors double the soprano part, and the basses do the same with the altos, so that what looks like a four-part score is essentially only two-part writing. Even then, the pairs sometimes cross over, and at other times collapse into unisons within those pairs. Helped little by the minimal accompaniment from the orchestra, the singing sounds weak, creating a kind of acoustic hole in the score. This, of course, is Rimsky-Korsakov's take on the folk-like heterophony that he and his Kuchka colleagues cultivated (Musorgsky above all). A few years earlier, while working on his edition of *Boris Godunov*, Rimsky-Korsakov had amplified and developed Musorgsky's choral textures; but now, on the contrary, he opted for the "impoverished" sound. By this stage, he had access to new publications of Russian folksongs as transcribed from the pioneering phonograph recordings of Yevgeniya Linyova, and these may have been a direct influence on the chorus.[36] Rimsky-Korsakov, in keeping with his preference for sophisticated musical craftsmanship over any folk authenticism, had rejected quasi-heterophonic textures, and simply followed his musical imagination to create beautiful harmonies. We can have no doubt, then, that the clumsy chorus was intended as satire rather than a sincere striving for authenticity.

Rimsky-Korsakov had been complaining about the Kuchka's ideals for a long time, and Musorgsky was his particular bugbear. Although he had been drifting away from the Kuchka for some years, the defining moment of his break was Stasov's reaction to Rimsky-Korsakov's revision of *Boris*. Rimsky-Korsakov had produced a more polished score to ensure that the opera would have a firm place in the repertory (and time vindicated him). Stasov, in many ways the thinker behind the Kuchka's program, was concerned instead to uphold doctrinal purity, and criticized

Rimsky-Korsakov for what he saw as a misunderstanding of Musorgsky's recitatives, which were regarded as a touchstone for the Kuchka's operatic naturalism; they had been pioneered by Dargomyzhsky, and Musorgsky had developed the idea further. Stasov's criticisms prompted Rimsky-Korsakov to write *Mozart and Salieri*, which reinstates Dargomyzhskian/Musorgskian recitative alongside more traditional musical structures that mixed a Mozartized Rimsky-Korsakov with some direct quotations from Mozart. Stasov approved of the result, although he failed to notice that even the recitatives were artfully shaped in their harmonies, creating something akin to sonata structures, and were unlike their models in Dargomyzhsky and Musorgsky. "Can arioso recitative in the manner of [Dargomyzhsky's] *The Stone Guest* be more desirable than music that is true, good and free?" Rimsky-Korsakov asked Belsky, warning his librettist that he should not take the recitatives of *Mozart* as a true endorsement from the composer.[37] Having made his point by musical means, his next opera, *The Tsar's Bride*, took a resolute step toward a "true, good, and free music" that broke several of the Kuchka taboos. He took up various "outdated" Russian idioms that predated Glinka, created discrete arias instead of giving priority to continuity, and also included a range of "un-naturalistic" vocal ensembles, from duets up to a sextet. The issue of Musorgskian recitative reappeared in a discussion between the librettist and composer in the preparatory stages of work on *Saltan*. Belsky proposed that Guidon's vocal lines should be "childish" in character. Rimsky-Korsakov retorted vehemently that "what you write about the character of the Tsesarevich's voice I cannot accept; I want to write music—I don't want to rehash Musorgsky's *Nursery*." (In the context, it was not unfair of Rimsky-Korsakov to assume Belsky had *The Nursery* song cycle in mind.)[38]

Against this background, we have every reason to take the abundance of Musorgskian passages in *Cockerel* as satire, albeit more personal and obscure than the broader satire elsewhere. But Rimsky-Korsakov's remit ultimately takes in the whole of Russian nationalist opera, from Glinka to himself. Even the name "Guidon" is self-mockery: this was the name of the heroic protagonist of *Saltan*, given now to a cowardly fool in the *Cockerel* (the choice of name was free, since this character did not appear in Pushkin). Scholars have also noticed that the musical characterization of Dodon shares much with the characterization of Saltan, turned grotesque, of course.

Let us now look in more detail at the history behind the main conflict of the *Cockerel*, pitting Russians against orientals. In Glinka's *Ruslan*, the substantial passages of oriental music were exciting or beautiful, but the oriental characters, male and female, were overpowered in the end, whether they posed a military threat or a sexual temptation. In Borodin's *Prince Igor*, the most celebrated treasury of exquisite Orientalist melodies, the Russians and the Polovtsians are more evenly matched and neither wins; the very fact that Borodin left the opera unfinished is telling, since it was difficult to see, both dramatically and musically, how a Russian triumph could emerge in an organic way. In Rimsky-Korsakov's own *Kitezh*, the oriental enemy (this time the Tatars) wins in the temporal world, but the defeated Russians have the moral victory, receiving their eternal reward. In the *Cockerel*, the orientals win, but that is not the end of the story. Belsky warned the composer against giving the Queen music that suggested she was purely right and good:

> The Queen symbolizes the seductions of sensual beauty, seductions that are of the devil, so turning her into an ideal of pure beauty would destroy the moral sense of the plot, and also the opposition between a limitless evil ruling everything on stage and a good that the spectator will locate in a higher realm.[39]

In the *Cockerel*, then, both sides are evil, just as in the real world, Russian opposition to their own side in the war did not imply support for the Japanese, who were even more blatantly engaged in the conquest of weaker countries. The oriental side had been dangerous if alluring in Glinka and Borodin, then became pure evil in *Kitezh*, at the price of losing its allure. As Rimsky-Korsakov commented, the Tatars of *Kitezh* are presented "through Russian eyes," and he even gives them a Russian tune that he distorts by stretching one of its intervals into an "oriental" augmented second. In the *Cockerel*, evil is again portrayed through luxurious music, but stylized, this time through excessive sequential repetitions, spinning a chromatic web. But a much more radical change takes place on the Russian side: the diatonic simplicity that had formerly stood for purity and humanity in the face of chromatic seductions (oriental or supernatural) now becomes primitive to the point of ugliness.

The librettist and the composer disagreed over the ending, and therefore had different ideas on how the distorting mirrors and reversals should affect the audience. As Belsky wrote to Rimsky-Korsakov:

> I had counted on the last scene and chorus leaving a serious impression (probably even oppressive), and I was worried that anything addressed directly to the public at the end would destroy the reality of the events just witnessed, and reduce them to a joke. Well, that would be a bad joke indeed.

> But it would seem that this conception doesn't really fit your nature: you can grasp the darkest things very deeply, and yet you would sooner have brightness: you clearly have a desire to mitigate the gloomy impression here, and end the opera on a humorous note.[40]

But Rimsky-Korsakov insisted that he needed a frame for the opera; the Astrologer had set the story in motion, and now he had to return to close it. According to the composer's conception, the Astrologer should tell the audience that they should see the characters as people running around in "funny masks," and he would advise them that they could happily fall asleep now until the dawn—and the cry of the cockerel.[41] Belsky protested that the words "dawn" and "cockerel" had already been used in the previous scene but with different associations, and their reuse would be an unfortunate inconsistency. In the end, he supplied words that met Rimsky-Korsakov halfway, and the Astrologer would tell the audience that the story was only a fable. Perhaps Belsky, in arguing for his own conception, failed to appreciate the virtues of Rimsky-Korsakov's. Beyond the basic aesthetic satisfaction of symmetry, the framing device allowed the opera to remain within the genre of cartoonish satire, so that the killing of Tsar Dodon could not be taken seriously. Although Belsky's final version does not back up Rimsky-Korsakov's conception fully, it seems that the composer's purpose in addressing the audience at the end was to offer a moral choice. They could simply ignore all the hints at a gruesome reality and return to their slumbers until the inevitable and probably shocking awakening. Or they could listen more critically to the Astrologer's falsetto, reject his comforting words, and take the opera as a call to wake up. This makes good sense: born of rage, the opera was itself a cockerel's cry.

# NOTES

1. It may be significant that these scenes of enemy invasion in *Kitezh* were written in 1904, during the Russo-Japanese War.

2. For example, in S. A. Gladkikh, "Vliyaniye russko-yaponskoy voynï 1904–1905 godov na russkuyu kul'turu," *Russkaya kul'tura novogo stoletiya: Problemï izucheniya, sokhraneniya i ispol'zovaniya istoriko-kul'turnogo naslediya*, ed. G. V. Sudakov and S. A. Tikhomirov (Vologda: Knizhnoye naslediye, 2007), 630–45.

3. Marina Frolova-Walker, *Russian Music and Nationalism from Glinka to Stalin* (New Haven: Yale University Press, 2007), 218–25.

4. In 1834, Pushkin reworked Irving's *Legend of the Arabian Astrologer* from the *Tales of the Alhambra*, which had been published in 1832 and translated into French in the same year. Pushkin owned the French edition.

5. Pushkin mentions this in his diary for 1835, see A. S. Pushkin, *Dnevniki. Zapiski*, ed. by Ya. L. Levkovich (St. Petersburg: Nauka, 1995), 47.

6. For the direct information that has been preserved, see Rimsky-Korsakov's correspondence with Belsky, in N. A. Rimskiy-Korsakov, *Perepiska s V. V. Yastrebtsevïm i V. I. Belskim* (St. Petersburg: Sankt-Peterburgskaya konserevatoriya im. N. A. Rimskogo-Korsakova, 2004), letters 149–87.

7. John C. G. Röhl, *Kaiser Wilhelm II: A Concise Life*, transl. by Sheila de Bellaigue (Cambridge: Cambridge University Press, 2014), 84.

8. *Moskovskiy listok*, 28 January 1904, *Gazetnïye starosti*, http://starosti.ru/.

9. Yastrebtsev diary entry, 31 March 1904 (13 April 1904 new style), in, *Nikolay Andreyevich Rimskiy-Korsakov: Vospominaniya V. V. Yastrebtseva*, ed. A. V. Ossovskiy, vol. 2 (Leningrad: Gosudarstvennoye muzïkal'noye izdate'stvo, 1960), 304.

10. Alexandra Molas (1845–1929), née Purgold, took music lessons from Alexander Dargomyzhsky together with her sister, Nadezhda (who became Rimsky-Korsakov's wife). Alexandra was particularly famed for her performances of Musorgsky's songs in domestic setting, and some of them were written with her in mind. After marrying Molas, she held musical soirées at her own home and taught singing. Her most distinguished student was Maria Olenina-d'Alheim, who took the tradition of promoting Musorgsky songs into the next generation through her own performances and her own distinguished soirées.

11. Rimskiy-Korsakov to Glazunov, 5 August 1904, N. A. Rimskiy-Korsakov, *Polnoye sobraniye sochineniy: Literaturnïye proizvedeniya i perepiska*, vol. 6 (Moscow: Muzïka, 1965), 146.

12. *Novosti dnya*, 4 January 1905/22 December 1904, quoting from *Nashi dni*, *Gazetnïye starosti*, http://starosti.ru/.

13. As recounted by Tolstoy's family doctor, Dushan Makovitsky, in his diary entry for 6 March 1905, D. P. Makovitskiy, *U Tolstogo, 1904–10: Yasnopolyanskiye zapiski (dnevnik)*, http://tolstoy-lit.ru/tolstoy/bio/makovickij-yasnopolyanskie-zapiski/index.htm.

14. S. S. Prokof'yev, *Avtobiografiya* (Moscow: Sovetskiy kompozitor, 1982), 171 and 202.

15. Dilbar Klado, "Grazhdanin morya," *Vestnik Yevropï* 11 (2004), see http://magazines.russ.ru/vestnik/2004/11/klad34.html.

16. Cited in A. V. Shishov, *Rossiya i Yaponiya: Istoriya voyennïkh konfliktov* (Moscow: Veche, 2001), 315.

17. Belsky to Rimsky-Korsakov, 13 June 1904, N. A. Rimskiy-Korsakov, *Perepiska s V. V. Yastrebtsevïm i V. I. Belskim*, 331.

18. This quotation is used by Adalyat Issiyeva in the present volume in a different translation, see p. 156.

19. J. N. Westwood, *Russia Against Japan, 1904–05: A New Look at the Russo-Japanese War* (London: Macmillan, 1986), 40.

20. Ibid., 41.

21. Ibid., 110.

22. The name comes from the character Pulicane in Andrea da Barberino's fifteenth-century semi-mythological prose chronicle *I Reali di Francia* (much of it translated from French sources). After Barberino's work was translated into Russian, the character found its way into Russian folktales as "Polkan."

23. *Russkoye slovo*, 16/3 September and 4 December/21 November 1904, *Gazetnïye starosti*, http://starosti.ru/.

24. "Yapontsa probuyut," *Rus'*, 8 February/26 January 1904, *Gazetnïye starosti*, http://starosti.ru/.

25. For example, on the use of the wireless by the Japanese, see *Moskovskiy listok*, 17 March 1904, *Gazetnïye starosti*, http://starosti.ru/.

26. I owe this observation to Tatyana Cherednichenko, who gave a paper on Russian Orientalism in the early 1990s, which was later published as Tat'yana Cherednichenko, "Russkaya muzïka i geopolitika," *Novïy mir* 6 (1995), http://magazines.russ.ru/novyi_mi/1995/6/cheredn.html.

27. *Novosti dnya*, 11 September 1904, *Gazetnïye starosti*, http://starosti.ru/.

28. Yastrebtsev diary entry, 18 April 1907, in *N. A. Rimskiy-Korsakov: Vospominaniya Yastrebtseva*, 2:422.

29. For example, on 1 February 1904, after receiving news of another sinking of a Russian ship, Nicholas wrote in his diary: "Yesterday's sad impressions remained uppermost in my mind all morning: I was frustrated and pained at the thought of what opinions might be formed on the Navy across Russia." Nikolay II Aleksandrovich, *Dnevniki*, http://militera.lib.ru/db/nikolay-2/1904.html

30. General Mosolov, head of the royal Chancellery Office wrote in his memoirs three decades after the Tsushima defeat, "the whole of the Tsar's retinue was astonished at the Emperor's lack of sympathy on hearing of this disaster." A. A. Mosolov, *Pri dvore imperatora* (Riga: Filin, 1938), 125

31. Slightly differing versions of this couplet appear in various popular volumes, such as N. A. Sindalovskiy, *Ocherki Peterburgskoy mifologii, ili Mï i gorodskoy fol'klor* (St. Petersburg: Tsentrpoligraf, 2012), 31.

32. Yastrebtsev diary entry, 19 January 1905, in *Rimskiy-Korsakov: Vospominaniya*, vol. 2: 324.

33. *Stranitsï zhizni N. A. Rimskogo-Korsakova: Letopis' zhizni i tvorchestva*, ed. A. A. Orlova, vol. 4 (Leningrad: Muzïka, 1973), 135.

34. Rimsky-Korsakov to Belsky, 13 August 1907, in *Perepiska s V. V. Yastrebtsevïm i V. I. Belskim*, 391.

35. *Stranitsï zhizni N. A. Rimskogo-Korsakova*, vol. 3, 330.

36. *Velikorusskiya pesni v narodnoy garmonizatsii*, ed. Yevgeniya Linyova (St. Petersburg: Izdaniye Imperatorskoy Akademii Nauk, 1904), vol. 1.

37. Rimsky-Korsakov to Belsky, 18 August 1897, *Perepiska s V. V. Yastrebtsevïm i V. I. Belskim*, 255.

38. Rimsky-Korsakov to Belsky, 25 June 1899, ibid., 279.

39. Belsky to Rimsky-Korsakov, 10 July 1907, ibid., 380.

40. Belsky to Rimsky-Korsakov, 9 August 1907, ibid., 389.

41. Rimsky-Korsakov to Belsky, 4 August 1907, ibid., 387.

Colleagues and Disciples

# St. Petersburg Conservatory and the Beginnings of Russian Musicology

## OLGA PANTELEEVA

The St. Petersburg Conservatory bears Nikolai Rimsky-Korsakov's name not only on account of the composer's contribution to the Russian classical music canon, but because he is perceived as a progenitor of the institutionalized study of music in Russia—both practical and theoretical. His influential textbook, *Principles of Orchestration*, still serves as a reference point in Conservatory curricula. In fact, his longtime position as a reputable Conservatory professor and the reputation of his art as "learned" have tended to undercut his standing as artist, especially "compared to the mythic, tortured figure of the uncouth [and] untutored . . . Musorgsky."[1] It is true that Rimsky-Korsakov played a leading role in shaping the first syllabi of music-theoretical courses at the St. Petersburg Conservatory.[2] However, the lineage that connects these courses to the present-day curricula is by no means as direct as it is sometimes painted.

The first specifically musicological research institution in Russia did not open until September 1921, when the Institute of Art History in St. Petersburg, originally founded by Count Valentin Zubov in 1912 as an institution of higher education, was reorganized into a research institute, within which was a musicology department led by Boris Asafyev.[3] A similar department was soon established in Moscow as well, at the newly opened Russian Academy of Artistic Sciences. Several months prior to the reorganization, in May 1921, Asafyev was arguing for the necessity of such reorganization. An important part of his rationale for establishing a separate academic institution for music scholarship was his trenchant criticism of the conservatories. In a memo he presented to his colleagues on 19 May 1921, Asafyev wrote:

> The issue of establishing an institution of higher music education has been repeatedly raised by interested people in the artistic community but could never be solved in a satisfactory

way, because such an institution has always been conceived of merely as a music school of the conservatory type, i.e., a professional educational institution, which is intrinsically alien to the activities of purely scientific character. . . . Until very recently, chairs of music history and aesthetics [at the conservatories] have been occupied by people who did not possess any specialized training, whereas in the field of music theory the conservatories confined themselves to the type of teaching that had been established once and for all, remaining completely alien to all new developments regarding this issue, as well as to considering the problems of musical composition historically.[4]

Almost five years later, the five-year report of the Institute's Music Department, written by Asafyev's pupil Aleksei Finagin, echoed this sentiment. Until the department was founded, according to Finagin, music scholarship in Russian conservatories was largely equated with practical training needed to impart technical skills to composers. He also pointed out that the musical world had realized only recently that scholarship required a different kind of intellectual engagement than that required for creative work such as performing or composing.[5] Indeed, at least until the mid-1920s the debates on how to study music happened mostly outside the conservatories.

In this essay I elaborate on the reasons why the first Soviet musicologists firmly opposed the type of music-theoretical education represented by the conservatories. I focus on the aspect of the Conservatory curriculum closest to Asafyev's 1920s vision for Soviet musicology—the broad, humanistic approach to studying music introduced at the St. Petersburg Conservatory by Liveri (Liberio) Antonovich Sacchetti (1852–1916), a professor of music history and aesthetics there. I examine the context of Sacchetti's work inside the walls of the Conservatory and the perception of his professorial status outside of it. The desire to reshape in a nationalistic vein the German-forged discipline of musicology—one of the main themes in Russian debates on music scholarship at the turn of the twentieth century—is particularly important for understanding the criticism leveled against Sacchetti's methods. My main sources are the official Conservatory records kept at the Central State Historical Archive of St. Petersburg, Sacchetti's archive at the manuscript department of the National Library of Russia, and the private diaries of Nikolai Fyodorovich Findeisen (1868–1928), an independent scholar whose idea of academic methods and standards differed greatly from Sacchetti's.

Guido Adler's seminal manifesto "The Scope, Method, and Goal of Musicology," published in 1885, is widely considered to have marked the birth of Western European musicology as a scholarly discipline. In Russia, it was an important year for music scholarship as well. St. Petersburg Conservatory, the first institution of higher music education in Russia, introduced its first specialized two-year course in music history. The course was developed and taught by Liveri Sacchetti. The following year Sacchetti was promoted from the rank of senior lecturer to an "ordinary" (regular) professor, becoming the first professor of music history and aesthetics at a Russian institution.[6]

Though there are parallels between Sacchetti's position and that received by Adler in 1898 at the University of Vienna upon commencing his duties there, the two appointments cannot be considered comparable. Adler founded the Musikwissenschaftliches Institut, an achievement that crowned a decades-long quest for the institutionalization of musicology in Austria. Sacchetti's post, on the other hand, is more comparable to the professorship that Eduard Hanslick, Adler's predecessor, had secured back in 1861 upon the publication of his treatise *On the Musically Beautiful* (1854), at a time when musicology as a discipline did not yet exist. Thirty-seven years had to pass between the establishment of this first ever university professorship in music history and the foundation of a musicological institute in Vienna. In St. Petersburg as well, it took some thirty-five years between Sacchetti's appointment and the foundation of the music department of the Russian Institute of Art History.

Over the course of the nineteenth century, musicians and critics all over Europe expressed their discontent at the predominance of foreign musicians, who often had a higher status and higher-paying salaries.[7] Professionalization of musical life in Russia was not an exception. However, in the last quarter of the nineteenth century the national composition of the profession was already changing. It was a time when the predominantly European professors who were invited to teach at the newly established Russian conservatories started accepting into their ranks their first students—home-trained Russian musicians such as Pyotr Tchaikovsky, the first graduate of the composition class.

A parallel can be made here with Russian scientific institutions, to which critics advocated the admission of more Russian scientists. Take, for instance, the "Mendeleyev Affair" at the St. Petersburg Academy of Sciences, Russia's oldest and most prestigious scientific institution, which historically had been dominated by foreign specialists. In 1880, Russian scientists were outraged when Dmitri Mendeleyev, the Russian luminary who formulated the periodic table, was nominated for a chair in chemistry and failed to be elected.⁸ The careers of Sacchetti and Findeisen, both second-generation European immigrants, were typical for this period of change, when the barely existing field of music scholarship was growing indigenous roots, along with, more generally, the professions of musician and scientist. Transitional factors marked both their professional and personal lives, making their interaction a fitting case study, at a time when critics and academics alike were trying to figure out what it meant to be a student of music in Russia.

## Between Europe and Russia

Liveri Antonovich Sacchetti was born on 18 August 1852 in the village Ust-Kenzar in Tambov province. His mother was a Russian noblewoman, his father an Italian flute player and music teacher who had settled in Russia and taken Russian citizenship.⁹ By the time Liveri was born, Antonio Sacchetti has already ended his stint as the solo flautist at the Italian opera in Odessa and was employed as a music teacher at the Tambov Institute.¹⁰ His son demonstrated an aptitude for music very early. Antonio became his first music teacher, and sent him, aged fourteen, to the Conservatory.

Sacchetti graduated from the Conservatory twice: as a cellist under the famous Karl Yulievich Davidov in 1874, and in 1878 as a composer.¹¹ In the second instance he studied under Rimsky-Korsakov and Yuli Ivanovich Iogansen, graduating with a small silver medal. (He also studied music history under Hermann Laroche.) After graduation in 1878 he was appointed teacher of harmony at the Conservatory and, after several promotions, reached the highest rank of Ordinary Professor of the First Degree in 1901.¹² Sacchetti also lectured on aesthetics at the Academy of Arts from 1885 to 1894, and worked with Vladimir Stasov as a librarian at the Imperial Public Library (now the National Library of Russia) starting in 1895. Despite his Italian heritage, Liveri Sacchetti's mother tongue was Russian, and he belonged to the Russian Orthodox faith, as did his wife Alexandra Kanevskaya (also a graduate of the St. Petersburg Conservatory), his daughter Catherine, and his son Alexander, who later studied under sociologist Maksim Kovalevsky and became well known in that field.¹³

In addition to his classes at the Conservatory, Sacchetti sometimes gave public lectures on topics of general interest, such as "Relationship of Music and Text," which he read at the St. Petersburg Conservatory on 18 February 1893.¹⁴ Consider this scathing assessment given to the lecture by the music critic Vladimir Frolov:

Figure 1. Liveri (Liberio) Antonovich Sacchetti.

> Instead of a strictly scientific, substantiated view of the subject, which we, mere mortals, had a right to expect from a "professor" of music history . . . Mr. Sacchetti presented us with some historical hodgepodge of vocal pieces. . . . For a specialist-professor, who preaches to both the musicians and the public from the height of the pulpit, such a purely dilettantish approach is quite unexpected, and deplorable.[15]

Frolov complained about the avalanche of "uncritical"[16] references to ancient and contemporary European authors, which, to his mind, did not contribute much to a real explanation of the relationship between music and text.[17] He had hoped for something more:

> We expected that the professor would clarify in his special lecture the most important issue: the basic laws of the "relationship between text and music," namely: 1) of preserving the prosody and rhythm of the poem, 2) of declamation, 3) of preserving the poetical form of the text and, finally, 4) of the appropriate mood. Unfortunately, the lecturer left us in bewilderment regarding the objective of his lecture.[18]

Vladimir Konstantinovich Frolov (1850–1915) was a music critic for *Petrogradskiy listok* (Petrograd Leaflet), as well as an official at the State Bank and a graduate of the St. Petersburg College of Commerce.[19] Although a complete outsider to the Conservatory and its curriculum, he had in mind a standard to which he felt a Conservatory professor should conform. Failure to explain "the basic laws" was inexcusable for a professor, Frolov implied. Apparently showcasing erudition in the Western intellectual tradition was not enough; for Frolov, academic rigor involved finding out the universal laws that govern the development of art. By 1893 this idea had already become widely accepted in Russian cultural journalism.

Indeed, Sacchetti's talk was not much more than a historical overview of vocal music, in which he referred to no fewer than thirty-two studies in music history—Ambros, Kiesewetter, Spitta, Coussemaker, and others. Nevertheless, he also provided some generalizations. For example, he maintained that monophonic music enhanced the meaning of the words, polyphonic music obscured them and sometimes contradicted their dramatic objective, and homophonic music illustrated the text and enhanced its dramatic effect but sometimes prioritized formal symmetry to the detriment of meaning.[20] Indeed, Sacchetti's conclusions were not so far from the kind of "laws" that Frolov was demanding. The critic apparently did not perceive them amid all the citations from European literature.

A more sympathetic review, voicing similar concerns, had as its object Sacchetti's book *From the Realm of Aesthetics and Music*. The reviewer was well-known music critic Mikhail Mikhailovich Ivanov, no stranger to the aesthetics of music, having published the first Russian translation of Hanslick's *On the Musically Beautiful*. Although wholeheartedly praising Sacchetti's study, Ivanov was less enthusiastic about the author's tendency to include "too many references to others' opinions."[21] Appeals to various authorities lent Sacchetti's analyses the ponderousness characteristic of German aesthetic thought, Ivanov believed.[22]

Sacchetti's knowledge of current developments in European musicology was indeed encyclopedic. Judging by the long lists of books he checked out from the Conservatory library,[23] when he did research for his widely used *Short Historical Anthology of Music from Ancient Times Up to and Including the Seventeenth Century*, he read German, French, Italian, and English fluently.[24] The syllabi of his music history courses at the Conservatory make clear that he had internalized the German master narrative of music history found in such works as the five-volume, comprehensive music history started by August Wilhelm Ambros and continued by Wilhelm Langhans.[25] He was also well versed in the ongoing European aesthetic debate about art and the definition of the beautiful. In his publications Sacchetti often referred to the two works that defined much of this debate: Hanslick's *On the Musically Beautiful* and Ambros's *The Boundaries of Music and Poetry*. In 1890s Russia this centuries-old debate was alive and well.[26] Sacchetti's take can be found in his article "Poetry and the Visual Arts," which opens *From the Realm of Aesthetics and Music*, although he relies heavily on Winckelmann and Lessing.[27] Furthermore, Sacchetti did not remain indifferent to the positivist trend then sweeping the Russian humanities. His article "Foundations of Music Criticism" showed that he, too, was searching for the historical laws and objective criteria governing aesthetic judgment.

As the only Russian to hold a professorship in music history, Sacchetti became spokesperson for the discipline of Russian musicology abroad; the Russian Musical Society repeatedly covered his travel expenses to European events. In 1888 he represented the Conservatory at the International Music Exhibition in Bologna, where he was elected an honorary member of the Accademia Filarmonica.[28] In 1900 the Russian Musical Society sponsored his trip to the International Congress of Music History in Paris to give a talk on the history of Russian Orthodox church music, underwriting the trip with the sizable sum of 750 rubles.[29] In May

1909 he received 500 rubles, his former yearly salary at the Academy of Arts, to participate in the Third Congress of the International Music Society organized by Guido Adler and held in Vienna at the same time as the Haydn Centennial Festival.[30] Following his trip to Vienna, Adler and Sacchetti exchanged letters about Sacchetti's contribution to Adler's edition of the *Corpus scriptorum de musica*.[31]

Sacchetti's Western European colleagues essentialized him as Russian despite his Italian name and linguistic prowess. Whenever he presented his work at international meetings, he spoke on Russian music, although he was hardly a specialist on the subject. In Sacchetti's correspondence with Adler it is evident that Adler expected Sacchetti to work on Russian materials for the *Corpus*. In Russia, however, he was seen, and rightly so, as the poster child of imported (primarily German) humanistic scholarship.[32]

To sum up, Sacchetti's deep knowledge of European scholarship made him a logical candidate for teaching at the St. Petersburg Conservatory, which was from the start a European-oriented institution. However, this quality proved unhelpful in the Russian nationalist climate of the last quarter of the nineteenth century.

## Findeisen's Criticism

Nikolai Fyodorovich Findeisen is best known as the founder and editor of the seminal pre-revolutionary music periodical *Russian Musical Gazette* (RMG). He was one of Sacchetti's most persistent critics, although he never disparaged the professor publicly. He kept his disdain for Sacchetti's work to his diaries, in which we can find more reasons why Sacchetti's scholarship was seen as irrelevant.[33] Born sixteen years after Sacchetti, Findeisen belonged to the next generation of Russian music writers who began to formulate a professional identity and standards for musicological research, despite the absence of institutional career opportunities. This group included Yuli Engel (1868–1927), Alexander Ossovsky (1871–1957), and the slightly younger Boleslav Yavorsky (1877–1942).

Findeisen's family background was not unlike Sacchetti's. His father was Fyodor (Friedrich) Davidovich Findeisen, a German merchant who hailed from Altenberg, Saxony, but grew up in what is now Estonia. His mother, Fyodor's second wife, Nadezhda Osipovna Kubli, had a Swiss father.[34] Although Fyodor Findeisen considered himself Russian, he spoke German as his first language and was a Lutheran, as were his seven children from the first marriage.[35] Nikolai Findeisen, on the other hand, was Orthodox, like his mother, and grew up speaking Russian.

Figure 2. Nikolai Fyodorovich Findeisen.

Unlike Sacchetti, Findeisen never attended the Conservatory and for most of his career was not affiliated with a major music institution. Findeisen was largely an autodidact, gaining academic skills by reading such standard German textbooks as Adolf Bernhard Marx's *Allgemeine Musiklehre* and translating Emil Naumann's *Illustrierte Musikgeschichte* into Russian.[36] He studied music theory privately with the composer Nikolai Aleksandrovich Sokolov, the future professor at the Conservatory who had himself studied under Sacchetti's teachers Rimsky-Korsakov and Iogansen.[37]

Findeisen's real mentor was the cultural critic and fierce proponent of Russian music nationalism, Vladimir Vasilyevich Stasov. He became a role model for Findeisen when he was a nineteen-year-old student ardently interested in the history of Russian music. Over the course of his career Findeisen wrote monographs on Glinka, Serov, Dargomyzhsky, Rimsky-Korsakov, and Rubinstein, as well as on such subjects as art song, early operas, and music criticism in Russia. His magnum opus was the seminal *Studies of the History of Music in Russia from Ancient Times to the End of the Eighteenth Century* (1928–1929).[38] Findeisen's studies on Russian music, based on a hitherto unprecedented number of primary sources, set a new standard for scholarly rigor in music-historical work. He pioneered music source studies in Russia by publishing countless letters of Russian composers in RMG and founded *Muzïkal'naya starina* (Musical Antiquity), an almanac that published primary materials on Russian music history.

Findeisen inherited much from his relationship with Vladimir Stasov, including his contempt for Liveri Sacchetti. Ever the ardent proponent of the New Russian School, and the main ideologue of its war with the westernized Conservatory, Stasov abhorred the idea that Russian talent could benefit from European schooling. That Vladimir Stasov should detest Sacchetti's work was inevitable. In 1896, a year after Sacchetti started working with Stasov at the Imperial Public Library, Findeisen made an entry in his diary:

> Stasov berated Sacchetti—called him stupid and a fool and complained about his assistance (although he is a sweet and kind person, but a fool) . . . Sacchetti is without talent, etc. When Sacchetti was still a Conservatory student, Rimsky-Korsakov, called him a mediocrity. What a professor, historian, scholar, librarian?![39]

Findeisen became known in Europe as a specialist in Russian music, with a solid international reputation, despite being unaffiliated and never having earned a diploma from a university or a conservatory. Oskar Fleischer invited him to become a corresponding member of the International Music Society (IMS); he published in the journal of the Society, as well as in periodicals such as *Die Musik, Neue Zeitschrift für Musik*, and others.[40] When Hugo Riemann needed advice on Russian musical culture, he turned to Findeisen.⁴¹ He also developed a project to found a St. Petersburg branch of the IMS.⁴² Findeisen's amateur status speaks to the openness of the Russian music scholar community at the turn of the century. Neither conservatories nor universities functioned as gatekeepers of the emerging academic music knowledge; instead, researchers and critics built their résumés independently, through publications. From a practical point of view, affiliating with the Conservatory provided neither an intellectual community nor the financial support necessary to carry out research. Nevertheless, by the last decade of the nineteenth century, when Findeisen came of age as a scholar, the status of a Conservatory professor carried prestige and invited certain expectations, at least from outsiders such as Findeisen.

Besides Russian music, Findeisen also possessed a thorough knowledge of Western European music history. His appreciation extended to most of the musical canon, and even included a brief tribute to the Wagner craze of the time. This catholicity precipitated Findeisen's disagreements with his mentor Stasov, whose nationalist convictions became increasingly hard line toward the end of his life. In 1898, for example, Findeisen protested against his teacher's narrow-mindedness in a diary entry:

> [Stasov] sent the stupidest note—he definitely values only his own, and in the work of others (which also goes completely over his head) he sees and gloats only over . . . typos! What a crackpot!⁴³

Even after Findeisen fell out with his mentor, however, his negative attitude toward Sacchetti persisted.⁴⁴ It seems that Sacchetti had no idea about Findeisen's grudge, and his correspondence with Findeisen was unfailingly courteous. In turn, the editor of RMG ran favorable reviews of Sacchetti's books and even an overview of his career.⁴⁵ In his diaries, however, he derided Sacchetti for failing to do enough research to have a thorough knowledge of Russian music. The following diary entry from 1909 sums up Findeisen's grievances:

> Yesterday I was taken aback by the well-meaning stupidity of the silver-haired "scholar" Sacchetti, who came to ask for a recommendation letter to Adler before his trip to Vienna as a delegate. He is going to give a talk on early secular music, before Glinka, focusing on Haydn and the Philharmonic Society; but when I asked him if he was aware of the existence of symphonic concerts and symphonies here in the

eighteenth century, and performances of Haydn's works and oratorios before the foundation of the Philharmonic Society, his agreeable countenance assumed an increasingly surprised expression. "Is it possible? Where did you find all this? I suppose in the Rumyantsev Library, etc., because we sure don't have anything in the Public Library!" Well done, old professor, who in all of his fifty-year-long career did not think to take a peek at the catalogues (of the manuscript department) and accounts let alone to look through old editions of said Public Library, in which he served for many years. . . . Enraptured, he asked me to give him appropriate materials for his upcoming talk in Vienna, and for a subsequent reworking of his *History*. His own materials do not go further than Albrecht's old essays on the Philharmonic Society, and the like. But of course he'd never think of working with *authentic* sources—despite all his certified learning and his professor's title.[46]

In other diary entries Findeisen repeatedly used irony quotes around "scholar" or "historian" in relation to Sacchetti: "Correspondence with Siloti, Pyotr, Sacchetti (asked for materials . . . a 'historian'!)."[47] This suggests that Findeisen's annoyance with Sacchetti was to a great extent fueled by the latter's institutional affiliation and official title. He deplored Sacchetti for tarnishing the professional identity of music historian, an identity that Findeisen was willing to claim for himself. Findeisen's repeated diatribes clearly outline the dual skills a professor of music history worthy of such status should possess: an expertise on Russian music and prowess in working with primary sources. Evidently, Sacchetti was lacking in both. To his credit, Findeisen measured other music writers by the same yardstick. When Alexei Fyodorovich Kal, who with the rank of *Privatdozent* taught music history at St. Petersburg University, picked up materials and scores on his lectures on Musorgsky from Findeisen, the latter ranted:

He admitted that he knew about Musorgsky only . . . from Kompaneysky's article! It is even more amusing that only now, lecturing *at the university*, he studies (?) and learns about the history of music in Russia! A fine historian, a fine Privatdozent![48]

In fact, Findeisen idealized the title of professor and its institutional affiliation, holding it to an impossibly high standard. Since he never experienced firsthand the Conservatory, he could not know that a professorship was in fact of little help when it came to scholarly research. And he was critical not only of "professional" historians, but of professional musicians in general. At Russian Musical Society meetings he observed the bureaucratese, the lack of initiative, and helpless mumbling "as if it were not the main musical institution in Russia, but a circle of incompetent and apathetic provincial dilettantes."[49] The sense of being an outsider permeated Findeisen's diaries. After attending another meeting at the Society he commented bitterly: "The esteemed professors (Sacchetti, Lavrov, Sokolov) must have been surprised at my attendance. Sacchetti is unbearably mealy-mouthed and is such a windbag."[50]

For Findeisen, to be a scholar meant to produce original thought, understood in a nationalist vein. A truly Russian music historian would best the imported European knowledge, not merely perpetuate it. The truth of the matter, however, is that the European-oriented style of Sacchetti's scholarship was only one reason for his failure to nurture a following among scholars outside the Conservatory. Another important reason was rooted in the institution of the Conservatory itself.

## The First Conservatory Courses in Music History and Aesthetics

The first suggestion that the study of music history at the St. Petersburg Conservatory should be deepened came in 1878, in a memo dated 27 July and addressed to the Conservatory Council by Osip Karlovich Gunke, the Conservatory librarian, a composer and the author of a harmony textbook. Gunke was dissatisfied with how music history was taught: students were made to memorize names and dates without being given an overarching concept of the historical evolution of music. Such a perfunctory course might be sufficient for performers, he admitted, but students of composition should have a solid idea of "what kind of music different peoples had, at different stages of its development, and how each composer influenced the subsequent development of the art of music."[51] Toward this end he suggested establishing a professorship in music history, as well as introducing mandatory graduation essays in music history on topics such as "explanation of the origins of various musical forms (oratorio, opera, symphony, overture, etc.), of harmony, melody, and rhythm of different eras (the state of vocal or instrumental music in different centuries), etc."[52] This new undertaking, he claimed, would result not only in the "higher significance of the Conservatory as an institution of higher music education, but also would have, as its direct consequence, the development of the science of music history itself, which is still not at all advanced in Russia."[53]

On 30 September 1878 the Council deemed such an innovation "desirable," and soon invited the renowned music critic Hermann Laroche to rejoin the Conservatory to teach music history to composition students.[54] A comprehensive two-year course was not developed until 1885, however, when the Council approved Liveri Sacchetti's proposition to open a two-year specialized music history course for composers.

Three syllabi from Sacchetti's Conservatory courses have survived: a general music history course, a specialized music history course, and a course in music aesthetics.[55] The specialized history course was a comprehensive survey of music history from "prehistoric" music up to the late nineteenth century and included several sections at the end on Russian music. Its structure and conceptual framework shows that Sacchetti relied on German music histories. The opening sections offered an examination of "prehistoric" music based on the information about music of "currently living savages,"[56] including, in Sacchetti's classification, the Inuit and the indigenous peoples of America, Australia, and Africa.[57] These sections were followed by ones about music of the "oriental people"—Chinese, Hindus, Arabs, Egyptians, Assyrians, Babylonians, Phoenicians, and Jews. This list suggests that the opening sections of Sacchetti's course might have been lifted in their entirety from the opening of the second book of Ambros's *Die Musik des griechischen Altertums und des Orients*.[58] However, in Ambros's history the section on the Orient followed the discussion of Greek music, whereas in Emil Naumann's history and in Sacchetti's course, sections on the Orient preceded the Greek. Sacchetti thus favored study that relied on the Eurocentric evolutionary idea that all peoples progressed along a similar developmental course and the racist assumption that peoples of the East represented lower stages of this development.[59] Apparently Sacchetti did not blindly adopt content from German textbooks, but provided a synthesis favoring some sources above others.

Sacchetti's course further diverged from Ambros's or Naumann's histories in that it started not with the earliest music examples, but with an overview of the discipline of music history as an academic endeavor—its goals, problems, and important landmarks:

> 1. The significance of music history as a discipline, complementing the general history of civilization (for a scholar in general).
> 2. The specifically musical significance of music history: a) as a foundation for music criticism, b) as a guide for musicians' work, c) as an indication of the social significance and status

of music and musicians in different nations and in different historical eras.
3. The contemporary state of music history. Difficulties accompanying its study. Sources.
4. A list and appraisal of the main works on music history (Virdung, Praetorius, Martini, Forkel, Fétis, Kiesewetter, Coussemaker, Ambros, etc.).[60]

. . .

Physiological explanations of the origins of music (Taine and Spencer).[61]

Thus, whatever Findeisen's criticism of his results, from the very beginning Sacchetti tried to frame music history as a scholarly discipline, relying on Hippolyte Taine and Herbert Spencer as the foremost authorities for Russian scholars of the humanities in the second half of the nineteenth century. Such a beginning placed this course firmly in line with a broader, university-based kind of humanistic scholarship.

Meanwhile, more than two years earlier, on 12 February 1883, the Artistic Council of the Conservatory decided it was necessary to introduce a class in aesthetics, but postponed the appointment of a specific lecturer for this class. Eventually they appointed Sacchetti to this position and he produced a syllabus.[62] It did not focus on music per se, but placed music in the context of issues that had been occupying European writers on aesthetics for at least two centuries: distinctions between the beautiful and the useful, the beautiful and the sublime; classification of arts as representational and non-representational, spatial and temporal, etc.; and the application of the scientific method to aesthetics. Evidently influenced by Hippolyte Taine, Sacchetti's idea of the scientific method included four analytical criteria:

a) comparing works of a single author and their relationship to the author's personality;
b) comparing works of artists of the same historical era and their relationship to their time and its character;
c) comparing artistic works of a specific people and elucidating the national element in art;
d) the universal element in art.[63]

Sacchetti's broad scope positioned music as a part of general humanistic inquiry into the arts, transcending the narrow practical focus of music history as previously taught at the Conservatory. These specialized courses were different from existing Conservatory curriculum not only in degree but in kind. Although Sacchetti's promotion to the rank of professor of music history and aesthetics in 1886 was, at first glance, a routine promotion that Conservatory lecturers received after several years of satisfactory work, it was nevertheless unprecedented. Sacchetti's comprehensive expertise, his experience in teaching, and his prestigious institutional affiliation equipped him to become the founder of Russian musicology as a coherent discipline. His elevation had the potential to become a watershed in the process of institutionalizing musicology in Russia. It did not have such far-reaching consequences, however—and not merely because it ran afoul of cultural nationalists such as Stasov and Findeisen.

## History and Theory: A Means for Legitimizing Music as a Profession

One of the main concerns of Conservatory officials in the nineteenth and early twentieth centuries was the necessity to legitimize the making of music as a profession. Lynn Sargeant has described the path to upward social mobility that a Conservatory diploma opened to people from the lower social estates.[64] Upon completing the Conservatory course, worthy graduates were awarded the title of Free Artist. Before the Conservatory was established, this title was granted by the Academy of Art and was associated with certain social privileges. Most important, it allowed the graduates to become "honored citizens" if they did not already belong to this or a higher estate. "Honored citizens" functioned as a buffer between the nobility and the lower estates. Though not formally nobility, honored citizens were similarly exempt from the poll tax, military draft, and corporal punishment, and received an opportunity to apply for inclusion into hereditary nobility as a reward for excellent service.[65] For Jews, the title of honorary citizen provided the right to reside outside the Pale of Settlement.

Whether they would be granted these privileges was a burning question for most conservatory students. Sargeant cites the enrollment data for another conservatory under the jurisdiction of the Russian Musical Society, the Kiev Conservatory. In the years 1915–16 students from noble estates made up slightly more than a quarter of the total student body, and almost exactly half of the students were Jewish.[66] In Moscow and St. Petersburg the conservatories were similarly open to women, non-nobles, and Jews, who were a significant portion of the student population. Sargeant has shown how the path to acquiring a legal right to move to a higher social estate was long and thorny. Whether the title of Free Artist also brought the opportunity for upward mobility was a matter of paramount importance to holders of a Conservatory diploma, and the St. Petersburg Conservatory struggled to secure the legal rights of its graduates as spelled out in its first statute in 1861. The Conservatory's efforts met with opposition from the government, which sought to limit access to the aristocracy. This official pushback had a direct bearing on the status of music history and theory. When the Committee of Ministers approved the official conservatory statute, it demanded that in order to qualify for the title of Free Artist, students must excel in music theory. This provision guaranteed that music theory subjects would enjoy special status at the Conservatory. It also agreed with Anton Rubinstein's own ideal of a well-schooled musician:

> According to this ideal, greater aesthetic and theoretical knowledge distinguished true professionals from amateurs or artisans.... At the same time, the theoretical and aesthetic education of Conservatory musicians provided a rationale to insist on their inclusion in respectable, educated society alongside their less musically skilled but better educated amateur counterparts.[67]

Theoretical knowledge, perceived as proof of one's intellectual prowess and well-rounded education, was thus a defining trait of a professional musician worthy of the title of Free Artist and therefore was indispensable for the prestige of the profession. Furthermore, it was an indispensable skill for professional composers, who held the most prestigious rank within the music profession. In his 1901 project to revise the composition curriculum Rimsky-Korsakov bluntly asserted that "musical creativity is the highest sphere of manifestation of musical talent and the highest branch of activity in the art of music. I believe that all musician-performers will agree with this as well, since such a statement in no way diminishes their significance."[68] Instruction in music theory and history at the Conservatory was thus considered an essentially practical element, providing the professional skills necessary to produce qualified and socially apt composers and performers. The advancement of musicological knowledge was not the rationale for the existence of these subjects. By contrast, theoretical instruction for students of other faculties was different in level, but not in kind.

Instruction in music theory was very hands-on. Records of the meetings of the Conservatory Council and the Artistic Council reveal that changes in music theory curriculum were given much thought and implemented yearly. New classes were introduced, the duration of courses was adjusted, entrance and graduation requirements were specified, professors' responsibilities were formalized, and even a competition for a textbook on musical forms was announced only after detailed debates.[69] For instance, on 4 April 1883 the theoretical branch of the Artistic Council (Rimsky-Korsakov, Iogansen, Zike, Rubets, Lyadov and Sacchetti, among others) discussed four items on their agenda:

1) dividing the general harmony course into two years;
2) starting instruction in practical composition at the same time as classes in counterpoint;
3) establishing requirements in piano skills for composers;
4) opening a chair in History of Russian Music (not implemented, unlike the previous three items).[70]

On 18 February 1885, the same quorum decided to divide all the composition students among three professors (Rimsky-Korsakov, Iogansen, and Solovyov); assign each professor a class in orchestration; require successful graduation from classes in solfège and elementary theory before entering a specialized class in theory; and divide the general course of theory into short and comprehensive courses.[71] In 1886 the curriculum was again revamped.[72] Evidently, the council sought to create by trial and error the most effective theoretical curriculum possible.

By contrast, their attitude to music history was laissez-faire. The records of the Council meetings reveal that except for the class in aesthetics in 1883 and the specialized two-year course in music history in 1885, no changes were introduced to the curriculum in the 1880s that did not concern composition theory or performance. Nor did anything of the sort come under discussion in the 1890s. The "science of music" was mentioned extremely rarely, and to no avail.[73] Even the word *nauchnïy* (scientific) was reserved almost exclusively to denote such general subjects as geography, physics, and languages, which were mandatory for Conservatory students. Rarely was the word applied to the study of music. From this it is not hard to infer that music history and aesthetics were not understood as independent academic disciplines. They may well have opened wider intellectual horizons to Conservatory graduates, allowing them to assimilate better in elite social contexts and thus add to the prestige of the profession. However, these disciplines remained subservient to performance and composition, necessary only so long as they helped produce a well-rounded musician. Unlike music theory, music history and aesthetics were not practically applicable, and their role was correspondingly less important, and a lower priority for the Artistic Council.

One of Sacchetti's letters to the St. Petersburg Directorate of the Imperial Russian Musical Society, which oversaw the Conservatory, provides further evidence that the objective of music history courses was purely practical. Asking to reverse his pay cut, Sacchetti justified the necessity of his Conservatory courses as follows:

> Anton Grigoryevich [Rubinstein] . . . gave me an opportunity to concentrate on my work on history and aesthetics. These subjects Anton Grigoryevich regarded as the foundation of a sensible musical education, and voiced this opinion to the audience of my lectures, which he sometimes attended. According to Anton Grigoryevich's views, I try to teach music history as a science that can protect the younger generation from fashionable, haphazard trends, which do not always agree with the true progress of art, and to aid the Conservatory students not only in acquainting themselves with the exemplary works of the past eras, but also in understanding them. By reading lectures on aesthetics I mean to open the students' eyes to the meaning and significance of art in general and music in particular, in order to protect future artists from mere virtuosity, which lowers art to the level of musical craft.[74]

The opposition of art and craft was also crucial for Anton Rubinstein, the first director of the Conservatory who returned to his directorial position in 1887. He viewed this institution as a "temple of art" to be purged of amateurs whom he considered "ballast," resenting the Conservatory's dependence on student tuition payments, which turned it into a mere factory churning out mediocre artisans. According to him, the few talented students were to be given the kind of education that would allow them to become artists, not artisans.[75] The Directorate's resolution in response to the letter above—"Ask the director to find the means to grant Professor Sacchetti's request"—shows that his petition resonated well with the official Conservatory position: the objective of music history and aesthetics was to cultivate artists who understood the meaning of art and could distinguish true progress from fashion.

Consequently, efforts to legitimize the professional identity of a scholar would have been alien to the agenda that preoccupied the conservatories at the time: to legitimize the profession of musician. In 1892, after fourteen years of teaching at the Conservatory and six years of being a professor, Sacchetti wrote:

> I am writing my composition on aesthetics in order to help my successor to continue my work; if such a person does not

appear, then I hope that this book can replace lectures on this subject for the future pupils of the Conservatory and the Academy of Arts.[76]

Not only was Sacchetti unaware of any other Russian scholar he deemed able to carry out a similar job; he also doubted he would ever have a successor at any of these two institutions.

For the first two decades of the twentieth century debates about the nature of Russian music scholarship and the quest to institutionalize it happened almost entirely outside the framework of higher education. All the while, music theory and history at the conservatories remained entirely subservient to music making. Nikolai Rimsky-Korsakov, it appears, was a staunch proponent of this status quo. That he strongly believed in the nineteenth-century hierarchy that deemed composition to be, in his own words, the "highest branch of activity in the art of music"; that the faculty meetings he attended at the Conservatory concerned themselves predominantly with the composition and theory curriculum; and that he had nothing but disdain for Sacchetti (whom he called a "mediocrity")—all point to his understanding of theoretical knowledge as a mere practical tool for composition. As we have seen, such understanding did not aid, but actually hindered, the development of musicology as an academic discipline.

It was not until 1916, the year Sacchetti died, that the venerable music critic Nikolai Dmitriyevich Kashkin (1839–1920) filed an official memorandum on the necessity to develop academic research at the St. Petersburg Conservatory. According to him, it was the responsibility of an institution that wielded so much authority in musical matters, to reinvigorate contemporary musical life, purging it of decadent elements—which he claimed stemmed from ignorance about the nature of music and its laws of development.[77] Kashkin suggested establishing chairs in contemporary harmony, rhythm (along with formal analysis), Russian music, and applied aesthetics. However, it was not until a decade later that such a change was really implemented at the St. Petersburg Conservatory, when in 1926 Boris Asafyev was tasked by the Soviet educational administration with establishing a department of musicology. By that time, musicology had already been flourishing for five years at the three musicological research institutions in Moscow and St. Petersburg.

In the opinion of the brave new Soviet musicologists, both Sacchetti and Findeisen were hopelessly outdated, and now it was Findeisen's turn to be taken to task by a scholar born sixteen years after him. Asafyev, however, would realize Findeisen's vision for a Russian musicology that had a solid foundation in primary sources and concerned itself primarily with studying Russian music, including the "richest examples of Russian musical creativity" and the "treasury of folksongs."[78] The research plan of the music department for the year 1924 reads:

> The objectives of the [Historical] Section lie primarily in the sphere of studying Russian music; naturally, [the Section does not] reject scholarly inquiry into the history of Western European music, since there are appropriate materials and primary sources for such an inquiry in Russia.[79]

Findeisen's criticism of Sacchetti helped define the identity of a musicologist in Russia. It took an independent scholar to lay the foundation for the institutionalized musicology that emerged during the 1920s. Sacchetti's career, however, had not fostered the kind of interdisciplinary, humanistic-oriented musicology that flourished in Russia from the early 1920s into the 1930s.

Once the research activities of the St. Petersburg Institute of Art History were curtailed during the Cultural Revolution of 1928–32, musicology was left with no institutional base other than the conservatories—where it has continued to reside until the present day. The Soviet ideological crackdown of the 1930s meant that conservatory-based musicology never had the chance to develop a historiographical methodology untarred by ideological control, or build a robust scholarly exchange with Western musicologists. The conservatory-style theory so deplored by Asafyev and Finagin became the safest space for musicological thought. Repercussions of such an institutional arrangement continue to be felt today, especially in the deep conceptual misunderstanding between Russian conservatory-based musicology and the university-based musicological traditions elsewhere in the world.

# NOTES

1. Richard Taruskin, *Russian Music at Home and Abroad: New Essays* (Oakland: University of California Press, 2016), 80.

2. The syllabi are kept at the Central State Historical Archive of Saint Petersburg (hereafter TsGIA); some of them are published. See Anna Lvovna Birkengof et al., *Iz istorii Leningradskoy konservatorii: Materialï i dokumentï 1862–1917* (From the History of the Leningrad Conservatory: Materials and Documents 1862–1917) (Leningrad: Muzïka, Leningradskoye otdeleniye, 1964), 99–100, 107–9.

3. Central State Archive of Literature and Art of St. Petersburg (hereafter TsGALI): F. 82, op. 1, d. 103, l.18

4. TsGALI: F. 82, op. 3, d. 1, l.1-1v.

5. Alexey Vasilyevich Finagin, "Obzor deyatel'nosti R.I.T.M. za pyat' let ego sushchestvovaniya " (Survey of the Work of the Music Department During the Five Years of Its Existence), in *De musica: Vremennik Razryada istorii i teorii muzïki Gosudarstvennogo instituta istorii iskusstv* (Leningrad: Academia, 1925), 100.

6. TsGIA: F. 361, op. 11, d. 155, l. 80.

7. Lynn M. Sargeant, "A New Class of People: The Conservatory and Musical Professionalization in Russia, 1861–1917," *Music & Letters* 85/1 (2004): 41–42.

8. Alexander Vucinich, *Science in Russian Culture: 1861–1917* (Stanford, CA: Stanford University Press, 1970), 96–97.

9. Biographical dictionary "Employees of the National Library of Russia: Scientists and Cultural Figures," ed. G. V. Mikheyeva and G. A. Khotuntsova (St. Petersburg: Rossiyskaya natsional'naya biblioteka, 2013). http://www.nlr.ru/nlr_history/persons/info.php?id=156

10. Richard Taruskin, *Defining Russia Musically: Historical and Hermeneutical Essays* (Princeton: Princeton University Press, 1997), 190.

11. Davidov later became conservatory director.

12. On Sacchetti's promotions see: TsGIA: F. 361, op. 11, d. 101, l. 67; F. 361, op. 11, d. 155, l. 8; F. 361, op. 11, d. 155, l. 80.

13. This biographical note is primarily based on Sacchetti's personal file in the conservatory archive, kept in the Central State Historical Archive of St. Petersburg. TsGIA: F. 361, op. 9, d. 48.

14. Published in Liveriy Antonovich Sacchetti, *Iz oblasti estetiki i muzïki* (From the Realm of Aesthetics and Music) (St. Petersburg: Izdatel'stvo L. Turïginoy, 1896), 96–111.

15. Vladimir Konstantinovich Frolov, "Ob otnoshenii muzïki k tekstu: Lektsiya prof. L. A. Sacchetti" (On the Relationship of Music and Text: A Lecture by Prof. L. A. Sacchetti), *Nashe vremya* 9 (1893): 155.

16. Ibid.

17. Ibid.

18. Ibid.

19. "Obituary: Frolov, Vladimir Konstantinovich," *Russkaya muzïkal'naya gazeta*, 9–10 (1915 ): col. 180.

20. Liveriy Antonovich Sacchetti, "Ob otnoshenii muzïki k tekstu," in *Iz oblasti estetiki i muzïki* (St. Petersburg: Izdatel'stvo L. Turïginoy, 1896), 111.

21. Mikhail Mikhailovich Ivanov, "'Iz oblasti estetiki i muzïki' L. Sacchetti, professora S.-Peterburgskoy konservatorii" ("From the Realm of Aesthetics and Music" by L. Sacchetti, Professor of the St. Petersburg Conservatory), *Novoye vremya* 7534 (1897).

22. Ibid.

23. See Sacchetti's personal file. TsGIA: F. 361, op. 9, d. 48, ll. 36, 39, 40, 44, 75.

24. Liveriy Antonovich Sacchetti, *Kratkaya istoricheskaya muzïkal'naya khrestomatiya s drevneishikh vremyon do XVII veka vklyuchit'no* (Short Historical Anthology of Music from

Ancient Times Up to and Including the Seventeenth Century) (St. Petersburg: M.M. Lederle, 1896).

25. August Wilhelm Ambros et al., *Geschichte der Musik*, 5 vols. (Breslau: F. E. C. Leuckart, 1862); Wilhelm Langhans, *Die Geschichte der Musik des 17., 18., und 19. Jahrhunderts*, 2 vols. (Leipzig,: F. E. C. Leuckart, 1884).

26. For instance, music critic Sergei Kazansky published an article titled "Place of Music Among the Arts" in 1892. See Sergey Pavlovich Kazansky, "Mesto muzïki sredi iskusstva," *Artist* 25/26 (1892).

27. Sacchetti, *Iz oblasti estetiki i muzïki*, 1–43.

28. Nikolai Davidovich Bernstein, *Kratkiy ocherk zhizni i Deyatel'nosti prof. Liveriya Antonovicha Sacchetti* (A Short Sketch of Prof. Liveriy Antonovich Sacchetti's Life and Work) (St. Petersburg: S.R. Baum, 1903 ), 7.

29. TsGIA: F. 408, op. 1, d. 296, l.1.

30. Nikolay Fyodorovich Findeisen and Marina Lvovna Kosmovskaya, *Diaries, 1902–1909* (St. Petersburg: Dmitriy Bulanin, 2010), 236; TsGIA: F. 361, op. 9, d. 48, l. 42; *III Kongress der Internationalen Musikgesellschaft Wien, 25 bis 29 Mai 1909: Bericht vorgelegt vom Wiener Kongressausschuss* (Vienna: Artaria, 1909 ), 11.

31. National Library of Russia, Manuscript department, F. 667, d. 79: Sacchetti, Liveriy Antonovich, letters (6) to Prof. Guido Adler, Vienna, 13ff., 1909–1910; F. 667, d. 85; Adler, Guido, Professor of the Institute of Music History in Vienna, letters (14) to Liveriy Antonovich Sacchetti, 29ff., 1909–1911.

32. Even in appearance, Sacchetti's publications differed from other Russian music-historical writing of the time; unlike most writers on music, he meticulously cited his sources.

33. Nikolay Fyodorovich Findeisen and Marina Lvovna Kosmovskaya, *Diaries, 1892–1901* (St. Petersburg: Dmitriy Bulanin, 2004); Findeisen and Kosmovskaya, *Diaries, 1902–1909*; Nikolay Fyodorovich Findeisen and Marina Lvovna Kosmovskaya, *Diaries, 1909–1914* (St. Petersburg: Dmitriy Bulanin, 2013).

34. Nikolay Fyodorovich Findeisen and Marina Lvovna Kosmovskaya, *Iz moikh vospominaniy* (From My Memoirs), Rukopisnïye pamyatniki, vyp. 8 (St. Petersburg: Rossiyskaya natsional'naya biblioteka, 2004), 55–56.

35. Ibid., 57.

36. Adolf Bernhard Marx and Aleksandr Sergeyevich Famintsïn, *Vseobshchiy uchebnik muzïki: Rukovodstvo dlya uchiteley i uchashchikhsya po vsem otraslyam muzïkal'nogo obrazovaniya* (The Universal School of Music: A Manual for Teachers and Students in Every Branch of Musical Art), 2nd ed. (Moscow: P. Yurgenson, 1881); Emil Naumann and Nikolai Fyodorovich Findeisen, *Illyustrirovannaya vseobshchaya istoriya muzïki: Razvitiye muzïkal'nogo iskusstva s drevneishikh vremyon do nashikh dney* (Illustrated Music History) (St. Petersburg: F. V. Shchepansky, 1897–1899).

37. Marina Lvovna Kosmovskaya, "Nikolai Fyodorovich Findeisen (1868–1928) i yego vospominaniya," in *Iz moikh vospominaniy* (St. Petersburg: Rossiyskaya natsional'naya biblioteka, 2004), 33.

38. Nikolay Fyodorovich Findeisen, *Ocherki po istorii muzïki v Rossii s drevneyshikh vremyon do kontsa XVIII veka* (Studies of the History of Music in Russia from Ancient Times to the End of the Eighteenth Century), 2 vols. (Moscow and Leningrad: Gosudarstvennoye izdatel'stvo, 1928–1930).

39. Diary entry, 20 November 1896, *Diaries, 1892–1901*, 180.

40. Findeisen and Kosmovskaya, *Diaries, 1892–1901*, 123–24, 244, 251, 282.

41. National Library of Russia, Manuscript Department, F. 816, op. 2, d. 2155, letter and card (H. Riemann's photo) to N. F. Findeisen (1901, 1909).

42. Findeisen and Kosmovskaya, *Diaries, 1902–1909*, 220.

43. Diary entry, 5 October 1898, Findeisen and Kosmovskaya, *Diaries, 1892–1901*, 232.

44. It lasted from the first entry concerning Sacchetti (1896) until the last one in the published portion of the diaries (1914).

45. Nikolay Fyodorovich Findeisen, "Liveriy Antonovich Sakketti: biograficheskiy ocherk" (Liveriy Antonovich Sacchetti: Biographical essay), *Russkaya muzïkal'naya gazeta*, no. 8 (1898): col. 722–26.

46. Diary entry, 21 April 1909, Findeisen and Kosmovskaya, *Diaries, 1902–1909*, 234. Emphasis in the original.

47. Diary entry, 5 July 1909, ibid., 241.

48. Diary entry, 23 January 1908, ibid., 201.

49. Diary entry, 17 October 1909, Findeisen and Kosmovskaya, *Diaries, 1909–1914*, 80.

50. Diary entry, 24 September, ibid., 77.

51. Birkengof et al., *Iz istorii Leningradskoy konservatorii*, 275.

52. Ibid.

53. Ibid, 276.

54. TsGIA: F. 361, op. 11, d. 101, l. 69.

55. Published in: Birkengof et al., *Iz istorii Leningradskoy konservatorii*, 109–17.

56. TsGIA: F. 361, op. 11, d. 155, l. 128.

57. The "country of savages" was one of the dominant stereotypes for the United States in Russia in the eighteenth and nineteenth centuries. Characteristically, Count Fyodor Tolstoy received his nickname "The American" on account of his "savage" tattoos, which he got while living among the Aleut people. Thus Sacchetti's classification of American indigenous populations was completely in line with the ideas of his time. See Ivan Ivanovich Kurilla, "Tïsyachelikaya Amerika" (Thousand-Faced America), *Otechestvennïye zapiski* 4/61 (2014): 56–70.

58. See Ambros et al., *Geschichte der Musik*, xxviii–xxxii, Table of Contents.

59. The only other author on Sacchetti's list of major music historians in the beginning of the syllabus was Emil Naumann, who treated the antiquity extensively. Emil Naumann, Ferdinand Christian Wilhelm Praeger, and F. A. Gore Ouseley, *The History of Music*, special ed., 5 vols. (London and New York: Cassell, 1886).

60. TsGIA: F. 361, op. 11, d. 155, l. 128.

61. Dommer, Brendel, and Naumann were added to the parenthetical listing of music historians in another version of this syllabus (TsGIA: F. 361, op. 11, d. 155, l. 128). Birkengof et al., *Iz istorii Leningradskoy konservatorii*, 111.

62. TsGIA: F. 361, op. 11, d. 155, l.8.

63. Birkengof et al., *Iz istorii Leningradskoy konservatorii*, 117.

64. See Sargeant, "A New Class of People." The following paragraph recapitulates her argument.

65. Aleksandr Nikolayevich Lushin, "Imenitïye i pochetnïye grazhdane v Rossii v XVII–nachale XX veka: Stanovleniye i razvitiye pravovogo statusa" (Eminent and Honored Citizens in Russia in the Seventeenth–Early Eighteenth Centuries: Establishment and Development of the Legal Status), *Vestnik Nizhegorodskoy akademii MVD Rossii* 18 (2012): 25–26.

66. Sargeant, "A New Class of People," 50, 56.

67. Ibid., 44.

68. Birkengof et al., *Iz istorii Leningradskoy konservatorii*, 278.

69. See TsGIA: F. 361, op. 11, dd. 9, 49, 64, 72, 101, 139, 155, 251, 293A, and other journals of meetings of the Conservatory Council and Artistic Council.

70. TsGIA: F. 361, op. 11, d. 155, l. 53-53v.

71. TsGIA: F. 361, op. 11, d. 155, l. 65-65v.

72. TsGIA: F. 361, op. 11, d. 155, l. 110.

73. I came across only two such instances, in 1878 and 1916.

74. TsGIA: F. 361, op. 9, d. 48, l. 41-41v.

75. Lynn M. Sargeant, *Harmony and Discord: Music and the Transformation of Russian Cultural Life* (New York: Oxford University Press, 2011), 99.
76. TsGIA: F. 361, op. 9, d. 48, l. 42.
77. Birkengof et al., *Iz istorii Leningradskoy konservatorii*, 305.
78. TsGALI: F. 82, op. 3, d. 1, l.1v.
79. TsGALI: F. 82, op. 1, d. 152, l.2.

# How Stravinsky Stopped Being a Rimsky-Korsakov Pupil

### YAROSLAV TIMOFEEV
### TRANSLATED BY JONATHAN WALKER

Rimsky-Korsakov taught more than two hundred students during the course of his career at St. Petersburg Conservatory, making him the grand old man of composition at that institution. Even so, the greatest of his pupils was nurtured outside the Conservatory walls.[1] From the outset, Rimsky-Korsakov's quirky relationship with Igor Stravinsky went beyond the normal bounds of academic instruction. Not only did Stravinsky inherit various professional skills and aesthetic precepts from his teacher, but also various personal mannerisms, like perching one pair of spectacles on top of another.

After Rimsky-Korsakov's death, Stravinsky's opinions on his teacher were likewise rather odd. His comments were contradictory, his evaluations widely diverging, doubtless stemming from the fact that it was not always clear whether he was writing under the influence of Rimsky-Korsakov or in reaction to him. On the one hand, we can, with a little effort, uncover certain features of Rimsky-Korsakov's musical thought and compositional technique even in Stravinsky's late works. On the other hand, we can equally well argue that none of Rimsky-Korsakov's other pupils departed from his master's artistic ideals so rapidly and profoundly as did Stravinsky.[2]

Stravinsky's active departure from his teacher's ways required no more than five years, and the end of this period was marked by a decisive full stop: Rimsky-Korsakov's completion of Musorgsky's unfinished *Khovanshchina* was pushed aside when Stravinsky, together with Diaghilev and Ravel, issued a new version designed to correct all of Rimsky-Korsakov's "errors."[3] Focusing on this project, I will try here to analyze the process of Stravinsky's departure from Rimsky-Korsakov's circle, during which time Stravinsky ceased to be a pupil and instead became an independent creative agent who had set out on a very different path.

The Funeral Song[4] and *The Firebird* were the first works Stravinsky produced after the death of his teacher, and they can quite legitimately be regarded as the music of a Rimsky-Korsakov pupil. And perhaps we could have categorized many more of Stravinsky's works in the same way if it were not for that unexpected turning point when Diaghilev entered his life.

On 24 January 1909, just seven months after Rimsky-Korsakov's death, Diaghilev happened to attend a concert conducted by Alexander Siloti, where he heard Stravinsky's *Scherzo fantastique*. Diaghilev sensed the talent behind this short piece, and immediately gave Stravinsky a commission—albeit a cautious first step. It was the young composer's responsibility to orchestrate two Chopin pieces for the Paris premiere of the ballet *Les sylphides*. After passing this test with great success, Stravinsky received an offer of a quite a different order: he was now to write a complete ballet, to be called *The Firebird*.

The relationship between Stravinsky and Diaghilev also went beyond the bounds of a normal partnership between composer and impresario. Stravinsky found a new mentor in Diaghilev, and though in a sense this was a further stage in his apprenticeship, he was now more mature and independent.

Thanks to Diaghilev and *The Firebird*, Paris became the new pole of attraction in Stravinsky's life as an artist. From this moment on, a kind of "jeu des cités rivales" began for the young genius: both Paris and St. Petersburg were connected for Stravinsky with a significant set of people and events, but the balance was gradually changing. This game lasted for about three years, and we can mark out its three phases in Stravinsky's three celebrated ballets.

All three premieres took place in Paris, of course, but for our purposes, the public reaction in both capitals to these events is very important. *The Firebird* was received enthusiastically in both locations, whereas *Petrushka* won over the Parisians but not the St. Petersburgers. In January 1913, when Koussevitzky conducted three fragments from *Petrushka* in St. Petersburg, Stravinsky wrote that he "found the newspapers all said my ballet sounded like crockery being smashed up."[5]

Between *Petrushka* and *The Rite of Spring*, Stravinsky was at last given an opportunity to establish himself as a stage composer back in Russia: Moscow's new Free Theatre offered to premiere his opera *The Nightingale*. But the arrangement fell through, mainly due to interference from Diaghilev, who liked to maintain exclusive control over the members of his entourage, and could not have them dealing with other agents and companies.

In 1913, *The Rite of Spring* was greeted with incomprehension in both Paris and St. Petersburg, and so this particular round of the "jeu des cités rivales" ended in a draw. Even so, the few individuals who immediately appreciated the status of the *Rite* were nearly all to be found in the Paris camp.

The Paris premiere of the *Rite* is notorious as the greatest upheaval in the history of music. So much so, that another grand premiere just two days later is now all but forgotten. This was the Diaghilev version of Musorgsky's *Khovanshchina*, with some of the orchestration and a new finale provided by Stravinsky (Musorgsky had left the opera unfinished, and the existing finale was Rimsky-Korsakov's work). From our perspective today, the second event pales into insignificance beside the first, but in 1913, things looked rather different.

The prehistory of Diaghilev's *Khovanshchina* began back in 1907, when Act 5, in Rimsky-Korsakov's version, was given its first airing in Paris during that year's concerts of the Saisons Russes (with Rimsky-Korsakov himself in attendance). The following year featured another Rimsky-Korsakov version of Musorgsky, the complete *Boris Godunov*, which drew even more attention, and prompted a wave of demands in the press for the French public to be given a chance to hear the authentic Musorgsky. Historically, this was the first public debate on the issue of authenticism in the treatment of Musorgsky's music. The French were in advance of the Russians in detecting a genuine originality in what had previously been written off as Musorgsky's "untutored" and "barbarian" passages.[6] Diaghilev had already been thinking along these lines: in his preparations for the production of *Boris*, he had studied Musorgsky's original score.[7] Now he decided that the public mood in Paris called for action.

The planned action was intended for the 1910 season, although it was a somewhat oblique response: instead of turning to the original *Boris*, Diaghilev decided to bring the original *Khovanshchina* to Paris. During the winter of 1909–10, he returned to St. Petersburg in order to study Musorgsky's manuscripts, which convinced him that the gamble could pay off:

> I spent all of last winter poring over the autograph manuscript of *Khovanshchina*, and I was able to see that in the only existing edition of this opera, published as revised by Rimsky-Korsakov, there was no living flesh to be found, that is, not a single page of the composer's manuscript was let through without several substantial corrections or changes by Rimsky-Korsakov.
>
> Regarding *Boris*, people usually say, "Yes, but it *does* exist in the original version, too." What about *Khovanshchina*, though? Is this forever doomed to be a work of Rimsky-Korsakov's? So it seems, but the fact has caused outrage across nearly all of the French press, which is now speaking out, demanding that they should finally be able to hear some "genuine Musorgsky, left unamended by Professor Rimsky-Korsakov."[8]

As early as 11 February 1910, Diaghilev announced the Paris production of *Khovanshchina* in his own version: "I allowed myself to restore several scenes to the score of the opera which were all absent from the Rimsky-Korsakov edition, preserved only in Musorgsky's original manuscript."[9] In addition to the claim that an authentic score was now being offered to the French public, Diaghilev also stressed in his publicity material that *Khovanshchina* was "a Russian opera of genius that had never run on any of the Imperial stages in Russia."[10]

Diaghilev had one more card up his sleeve, Fyodor Chaliapin, whom he hired in early 1910 to sing the role of Dosifey, which Diaghilev envisaged as the principal role in *Khovanshchina*. In the end, unforeseeable financial problems forced Diaghilev to abandon all opera productions that year: the Tsar, who had allocated a 25,000-ruble subsidy for the Saisons Russes on 9 April, canceled the payment a week later. According to rumor, the sudden change of mind resulted from some deft maneuvering behind the scenes by the ballerina Mathilde Krzesinska.[11]

It was not until the 1913 season that Diaghilev presented *Khovanshchina*, with preparation dating back to the previous autumn, when Fyodor Fedorovsky was commissioned to produce the sets.[12] In the meantime, Russian opera houses had finally mounted their own productions of *Khovanshchina*, in what seemed very much like a conspiracy to overtake Diaghilev: in 1910, it was staged by the Zimin Private Opera in Moscow; in 1911, at the Mariinsky; and in 1912, at the Bolshoi. Since Diaghilev could no longer claim to be reviving a forgotten masterwork, his advertising now focused on the restoration of Musorgsky's original text and the composition of the new finale (replacing Rimsky-Korsakov's finale). And of course, he made his treasured protégé Igor Stravinsky the chief executor.

There is no record of Stravinsky's first reactions to this highly unexpected offer, but we can imagine that he would have felt caught between Scylla and Charybdis. He was hardly in a position to refuse Diaghilev, on whom he still depended for his European career, but at the same time, he must have realized that this project was by its nature a challenge to his teacher's memory. Five years earlier, or even more recently, he could not have contemplated such a move, because he was still personally in awe of Rimsky-Korsakov, and still moved in circles that venerated his memory. But now the lure of his Paris triumphs and of Diaghilev's approbation enabled him to overcome his scruples. This, however, was not the only reason. There was nothing rash or light-minded in his eventual agreement. Stravinsky consciously entered into competition with the authority of Rimsky-Korsakov, still inviolable back in St. Petersburg, not because of mere opportunism, but because his aesthetic views had changed radically. This change was brought to a head when he counterposed Musorgsky to Rimsky-Korsakov.

In his *Conversations*, Stravinsky presents his own views on the change he underwent after his period of study with Rimsky-Korsakov:

> At that time, being influenced by the master who recomposed almost the whole work of Mussorgsky, I repeated what was usually said about his "big talent" and "poor musicianship," and about the "important services" rendered by Rimsky to his "embarrassing" and "unpresentable" scores. Very soon I realized the partiality of this kind of mind, however, and changed my attitude towards Mussorgsky. This was before my contact with the French composers who, of course, were all fiercely opposed to Rimsky's "transcriptions." It was too obvious, even to an influenced mind, that Rimsky's Meyerbeerization of Mussorgsky's "technically imperfect" music could no longer be tolerated.
>
> As to my own feeling (although I have little contact with Mussorgsky's music today) I think that in spite of his limited technical means and "awkward writing" his original scores always show infinitely more true musical interest and genuine intuition than the "perfection" of Rimsky's arrangements.[13]

This was Stravinsky's view on the issue of authentic Musorgsky (in line with the consensus of today's scholarship), and he maintained it for the rest of his life, since over the years he repeatedly denigrated Rimsky-Korsakov's edition of *Boris Godunov*. In his many comments on the matter, we find that he favored at least three striking images when referring to the Rimsky-Korsakov version: "false-Boris," punning on "false-Dmitri";[14] the allegation of "Meyerbeerization" mentioned above; and, wittiest of all, "Boris Glazunov."

It is difficult to put a date to Stravinsky's wholesale aesthetic re-evaluation, not least because of his tendentious denial of any French influence. Stravinsky's letter of 26 November 1910 to Rimsky-Korsakov's son Andrei allows us to deduce that the turning point had not yet been reached: "They also performed *The Commander* by Musorgsky, a work of genius. It is wonderfully conveyed through Nikolai Andreyevich's [R-K's] orchestration."[15] By this stage, the premiere of *The Firebird* and numerous encounters with French composers were already behind him. These encounters notably included a conversation with Debussy about Musorgsky and Rimsky-Korsakov, Debussy referring to the latter as "a voluntary academic, the worst kind."[16] But even if we were to grant the truth of Stravinsky's claim that his French colleagues had somehow failed to influence his opinions, we are still free to suppose that he could have been swayed by Diaghilev, who had long since arrived at the opinion that Musorgsky's original ideas were superior, and his powers of persuasion were well known. In any case, the turning point must have come somewhere in the period between the autumn of 1910 and the beginning of 1913, when Stravinsky was already prepared to put his name to the new *Khovanshchina* project.

The first news of Diaghilev's plans surfaced in the Russian press on 12 January 1913, sparking off a vigorous debate that raged in the papers during the second half of the month. The first to declare his hostility to the project was none other than one of its key participants, Fyodor Chaliapin. As reported in the *Obozrenie Teatrov* (Theater Review), he expressed his dissatisfaction that "S. Diaghilev has entrusted the composer Stravinsky with the task of reorchestrating some of the scenes from *Khovanshchina* and adding two new scenes." The report continued, "Since Diaghilev is still insisting on the restoration of *Khovanshchina*, F. I. Chaliapin declared that he refuses to perform in this year's Russian Season in London and Paris. F. I. does not consider Rimsky-Korsakov's work to be in any need of renovation and protests categorically against the remaking of *Khovanshchina*."[17]

The *Obozrenie Teatrov* was backed up by the St. Petersburg *Vechernee Vremya* (Evening Times): "F. I. Chaliapin, ... having discovered the planned mutilation of *Khovanshchina*, refused to participate in such a remake and insists that *Khovanshchina* must run in the same form that has been seen in Moscow.[18] This refusal, as well as the very issue of the opera's restoration, is cause for worry in our artistic world."

The journalist also interviewed the female singers who had participated in the Bolshoi production of *Khovanshchina*, and they gave their unanimous support to Chaliapin's demarche. Yevgeniya Zbrueva, who sang Marfa, declared:

> It seems to me, and in fact a whole group of musicians headed by the violinist Prof. Auer talked about this, that there is very little music in Stravinsky's works, and if this is the music of the future, it must be a very far-removed future. And it is this composer who is entrusted to remake what had already been done by Rimsky-Korsakov. Naturally, F. I. Chaliapin will not go along with this.[19]

The soprano Alexandra Gvozdetskaya also entered the fray—she had to sing the roles of the Lutheran Emma and the Old-Believer Susanna, different in all aspects other than their extremes of emotion. Here is her objection:

> I consider Mr. Diaghilev's plan quite pointless. Why must we show the French and English something that we have not yet seen ourselves? If we [Russians] have seen fit to stage Musorgsky's opera in Rimsky-Korsakov's edition, with his orchestration, why impose extra work on Chaliapin for the sake of Paris and London? He would need to start afresh, and as we know, Fyodor Ivanovich does not like to present the public with roles that have been hastily prepared and which are not fully polished.[20]

On 22 January 1913, the newspaper *Birzhevïye vedomosti* published a selection of quotations from eight significant musical figures on the project for *Khovanshchina*'s restoration: César Cui, Nikolai Solovyov, Stanislav Gabel, Liveri Sacchetti, Nikolai Sokolov, Nikolai Dubasov, Leonid Nikolayev, and Iosif Witol. In their expert opinion, they found the notion of reorchestrating Rimsky-Korsakov's final chorus grating (this was part of the ending that Musorgsky had not supplied), and one of them, Sokolov, pointed out what was required for the sake of consistency, hitting on what was actually planned: "Why reorchestrate this chorus? It would be more proper to rewrite it, since it was Rimsky-Korsakov's own composition, using only a tiny scrap of a theme by Musorgsky."[21] Nobody objected directly to the restoration of scenes that had been cut, although Nikolayev said that since Rimsky-Korsakov had made those cuts, the scenes in question could be considered unnecessary.

On the whole, Diaghilev's "marketing campaign" was a catastrophic failure: the debate drifted from the grounds he had intended—of Musorgsky's inviolability—to the idea of Rimsky-Korsakov's inviolability. As Gabel put it:

> The reorchestration of Rimsky-Korsakov is a task that could only be undertaken by someone who was his equal in talent. To anyone else, we can only say, "Hands off!"[22]

It was not forgotten, of course, that Stravinsky had been Rimsky-Korsakov's pupil, and so he found himself in an even more precarious position than Diaghilev. The latter, impulsive as ever, had not taken into account the difference between the Parisians, who revered the name of Musorgsky, and the Russians, who worshipped Rimsky-Korsakov, less than five years after his death.

Diaghilev now became aware of the crucial difference between his Russian and French audiences, and made his own contribution to the debate in an open letter to the editor of *Birzheviye vedomosti*:

> Dear Sir,
> Regarding the questionnaire your paper presented, on the restoration of *Khovanshchina*, I feel that it is only right that I respond to the attacks on my dear friend Stravinsky.
>
> It is not Stravinsky's intention to rework or reorchestrate Rimsky-Korsakov's own music, and everyone is quite aware that the final chorus of this unfinished opera was written by Rimsky-Korsakov on a theme by Musorgsky. Stravinsky is actually writing a new finale of his own on that same theme. The public will then be able compare the two finales for themselves and judge which of them is the better. As for the orchestration of those pages from *Khovanshchina* that have never previously been published (or orchestrated), it surprises me that it could ever be considered lamentable, from any point of view, for people to familiarize themselves with the work of a composer of genius.[23]

Diaghilev was not being entirely honest, since his plans did indeed include the reworking of Rimsky-Korsakov's own music—not in the final chorus, true, but in various other fragments of the opera.[24] This is clear from an examination of Diaghilev's own working vocal score for *Khovanshchina*, which is covered with his own notes (published by Bessel in 1983, the original held at the British Library).[25] On the basis of this working score, the musicologist Robert Threlfall was able to reconstruct in detail Diaghilev's plans for the revision.[26]

As for the polemics around *Khovanshchina*, this turned out to be the first mass attack from the press in Stravinsky's career. Knowing how much attention he always paid to his image in the media, and knowing also how badly he took published criticism, we might well suppose that his first encounter with a perpetual fount of critical negativity was a serious test for him. It is important to remember that St. Petersburg was still his home, and that St. Petersburg musicians still formed his social circle. At this stage, Stravinsky could not have foreseen that the outbreak of war was imminent and that he would soon emigrate.

The spring of 1913 brought a second wave of polemics in St. Petersburg that must have been still more painful for Stravinsky, because Andrei Rimsky-Korsakov now stepped forward to join battle for the honor of his father, signaling the abrupt end of what had been a close friendship with Stravinsky. Although he was the heir of Rimsky-Korsakov, he was not in a position to veto Diaghilev's project, because Russia had not yet signed the Berne Convention for the Protection of Literary and Artistic Works.[27] On 23 March, he published an extended article in *Russkaya molva*, primarily to argue that Stravinsky had no right to "disfigure" the Rimsky-Korsakov edition:

> I believe that the issue under contention is not so much whether Rimsky-Korsakov performed his task well or badly, but *whether anyone has the moral and artistic right to interfere with the* Khovanshchina *that is, in fact, the summation of both composers' work.*[28]
>
> I think that this can only be answered in the negative. Of course, every composer who considers himself the equal of Musorgsky's genius, or who at least imagines that his talent brooks some comparison with Musorgsky's, is *free to create his own edition* of *Khovanshchina*. It would indeed be fascinating if a significant composer carried out the task in his own manner. But *to maim someone else's version*, as Mr. Diaghilev intends to do, to lop pieces off it and to recompose what had been added by Rimsky-Korsakov to his edition, even if the ultimate purpose is to restore the genuine Musorgsky—all this I regard as absolutely inadmissible.
>
> I consider any attempt to destroy the artistic whole that is *Khovanshchina* in Rimsky-Korsakov's version an act of *vandalism*; I think it would be *tasteless* to mix original Musorgsky with Musorgsky that has passed through the hands of Rimsky-Korsakov, and then, on top of that, to add Ravel and Stravinsky, Diaghilev's amanuenses . . .[29]

Curiously, Andrei Rimsky-Korsakov fails to mention Stravinsky for most of his expansive article; only at the very end does his resolve falter. Even then, he places Stravinsky's name *after* the names of Ravel and Diaghilev (the latter having appeared earlier in the article). By contrast, Stravinsky bears the brunt of the accusations alongside Diaghilev in all the other critical essays on *Khovanshchina*. Caught between friendship and filial loyalty, Andrei was slow to pick a row with Stravinsky. The depth of the moral dilemma is made clearer when we realize that Stravinsky thought so highly of Andrei that he had made him the dedicatee of *The Firebird* ("To my dear friend") and several other works. The rift between them began to appear only after the premiere of *Petrushka*, when Andrei published a review that was by no means a demolition, but not laudatory either, given its characterization of Stravinsky's new ballet as "a kind of Russian home brew, all too blatantly adulterated with French perfume," and a piece of "conscious and refined pseudo-nationalism." This last epithet suggests that before it became acrimonious the rift between Stravinsky and the Rimsky circle arose not merely from the novelties of Stravinsky's musical language, but from more general aesthetic disagreements.

Through 1912, Stravinsky complained that he was being snubbed by Andrei, and in 1913, the cooling friendship degenerated into hostility. While Andrei's published review of *The Rite of Spring* showed some reserve, his letters to his mother after the premiere made his disgust clear: it was "the most revolting nonsense . . . monstrous filth." He even expressed *Schadenfreude*: "I am very happy to see that the piece is failing."[30] His mother, in turn, said that she was "absolutely delighted with Andrei's reaction."[31]

In 1914, Andrei and Igor met again in London. After a "strained" conversation, Andrei wrote to his mother the following day: "By the way, he still worships Rimsky-Korsakov's memory (or so he says) and will not admit (openly, at least) that his actions (*Khovanshchina*) might place a question mark over this 'worship.'"[32]

The story of the friendship has an unhappy ending. In 1932, Andrei turned again to Stravinsky, inviting him to participate in a collaborative biography of Rimsky-Korsakov. He even addressed Stravinsky as "cher maître." But Stravinsky did not reply.

It seems that both composers saw the other as a Judas. Andrei considered Stravinsky a traitor to his father's memory, and Stravinsky must have felt that Andrei had betrayed him personally through his public criticisms of *Petrushka* and *Khovanshchina*.

Stravinsky suffered a further loss in the estrangement of his friend Maximilian Steinberg. When the St. Petersburg newspapers exploded in outrage at Diaghilev's project, Steinberg appealed to Stravinsky: "It would be very good indeed if you yourself could present an explanation, to *Russkaya molva*, for example, since Andrei writes for this publication.[33] Personally, I do not credit the slanderous rumor that there was an instruction to 'correct' the orchestration of Nikolai Andreyevich. Such an explanation is *exceedingly* to be desired, and I beg you that you will see to it."[34]

Stravinsky replied with a mild refusal, adducing the fact that Diaghilev had already come to his defense in the St. Petersburg press. He also refused to react to Andrei's aggressive article, leaving the job to Ravel, his collaborator in Diaghilev's *Khovanshchina* project. It seems likely that Stravinsky preferred to avoid making any public statement of his own, as his work on the opera did indeed place him in a dubious position. On the one hand, he did not feel strong enough to fight in open battle with his former friends in the St. Petersburg circle, who could not forgive him his interference with Rimsky-Korsakov's score. On the other hand, the actual Paris production of *Khovanshchina* failed to live up to Diaghilev's original ambitions, leaving Stravinsky less than proud of the results. In his *Chronicle of My Life*, Stravinsky later described the production as a "mixture even more incongruously heterogeneous than Rimsky-Korsakov's version."[35]

In a sense, Stravinsky had painted himself into a corner, and the complexity of his feelings at the time is illustrated by the following story. On 8 November 1913, six months after the premiere of *Khovanshchina*, he wrote to Boris Jurgenson about his Symphony in E-flat Major: "I think my Symphony will soon see the light of day, so I hope you won't forget to add my dedication to Rimsky-Korsakov. It would be better placed on a separate page in large letters, as it was on the manuscript: 'To my dear teacher Nikolai Andreyevich Rimsky-Korsakov,' *en toutes lettres* [word for word]."[36] The letter's deferential tone indicates that Stravinsky had no desire to become a prodigal son, and the dedication shows that he still wanted the St. Petersburg public to think well of him.

But it is striking that the blame for this "motley" production, which diverged so far from the ideal of recovering authentic Musorgsky, fell not only on Diaghilev and the capricious Chaliapin, but also on Stravinsky himself.[37] The few extant manuscripts from Diaghilev's *Khovanshchina* project reveal some paradoxical details that highly complicate the psychological aspect of the whole story, and at the same time explain why Stravinsky did not wish to stake his reputation on this project by defending it publicly.

When he began working on *Khovanshchina*, one of Diaghilev's first ideas (which he was determined to implement) was the transferral of the aria "The Streltsy's nest is sleeping" from the role of Shaklovity (baritone) to Dosifey (bass). For Diaghilev, naturally, it was of no little moment that in this production Chaliapin was to take the role of Dosifey. The change would give him an additional showpiece aria, one that had much in common with Chaliapin's favorite repertoire pieces. Stravinsky's task, as orchestrator, was to free this aria from Rimsky-Korsakov's insouciant corrections and cuts in order to bring it closer to Musorgsky's original musical conception (leaving aside the question of the role and the vocal range!)

Stravinsky's orchestration, however, was consigned to the desk drawer—a rare occurrence in Stravinsky's career. Given Stravinsky's authority and popularity, the aria would often have been performed in concert if only the manuscript score had survived. But the fate of this manuscript, as well as the fate of the score of the Final Chorus, recedes into the darkness after 1913.

In every book, every catalogue, every piece of research that mentions the orchestration of Shaklovity's Aria, we are told that nothing remains of Stravinsky's work apart from two sketches that take up six pages, now held at the Paul Sacher Foundation in Basel. I have analyzed these manuscripts, and have been fortunate to discover a third source: some sketches for the coda of the aria, which were made by Stravinsky on page 8 of the sketchbook otherwise devoted to the Final Chorus (also held at the Paul Sacher Foundation).

The three manuscripts contain a total of forty-five corrections in a span of just fifty-one measures, and only a few of these are corrections of mere slips. The majority are of great value in helping us understand Stravinsky's editorial practices.

In Manuscript 1 at the beginning of Dosifey's part, measure 48, "Prestala," a natural sign at the third beat is stroked out (see Example 1). It is clear that Stravinsky intended to write a note at that point which actually arrives only on the fourth beat (and does so in the last version known to us). And this was no random error, because Rimsky-Korsakov's version had Shaklovity entering on the third beat.

Then, in the same fragment, on the third beat of measure 50, the half note that was originally present was filled in by Stravinsky to make it a quarter note (in accordance with the Musorgsky original). This also is unlikely to have been a slip of the pen, because once again, Rimsky-Korsakov's version has a half note at that point.

Although the first of these examples might be written off as the result of Stravinsky's memory of the Rimsky-Korsakov version getting the better of him, the second example cannot be explained in this manner, and conclusively demonstrates that while Stravinsky worked on the orchestration, he had the vocal score of the Rimsky-Korsakov version in front of him as well as Musorgsky's original.

The point I am making here is not just to mention the mistakes Stravinsky made and then corrected. They are only the visible part of the iceberg. A careful look at the manuscripts of the orchestration would bemuse any defender of Diaghilev's *Khovanshchina*, for it turns out that Shaklovity's Aria was orchestrated by Stravinsky not "from Musorgsky's original" (as he wrote

Example 1. Mm. 47–52. (1) measure 48: a natural sign at the third beat is stroked out; (2) measure 50: follows Rimsky-Korsakov completely; (3) measure 50: a half note was originally present, but Stravinsky filled it in to make it a quarter note.

in the titles of his manuscripts) but from the two originals, one Musorgsky's and one Rimsky-Korsakov's.[38]

The most significant of the compromises affects the large-scale form of the aria: following Rimsky-Korsakov's version, Stravinsky removed two fragments from the aria, namely the local reprise in the exposition (mm. 28–35) and five measures from the middle section (mm. 42–46). It is clear why Rimsky-Korsakov removed them: the first was a complete and almost exact repetition of the main theme that had appeared near the beginning of the aria, and the repetition had weighed down the form unnecessarily; the second passage was actually deleted by Musorgsky himself in his manuscript, but he changed his mind, and added the comment "needs to be performed." Rimsky-Korsakov most likely decided that the deletion was the better decision. A few dubious details in the lyrics may also have played a role.

It is hardly feasible that Stravinsky would have accepted Rimsky-Korsakov's cuts on his own initiative. Instead, we should look to the ultimatum that Chaliapin had laid down: when he met with Diaghilev on 9 March 1913, Chaliapin agreed to sing in the new production of *Khovanshchina* only on condition that his part remain the same, which is to say that it had to follow Rimsky-Korsakov's version (with the exception of the extra aria he had been given). Chaliapin had never sung Shaklovity's part, so he would not have had to relearn the aria. Perhaps he was just stubborn—if Dosifey's entire role was to be sung according to the Rimsky version, then let Shaklovity's Aria comply with this rule as well. We cannot exclude the possibility that Diaghilev did not discuss the fate of Shaklovity's Aria with Chaliapin in any detail, but simply instructed Stravinsky to orchestrate all of Chaliapin's material in accordance with the Rimsky-Korsakov version. The larger puzzle here, though, is in the bare fact that Stravinsky orchestrated this music, given Chaliapin's ultimatum. After all, once Diaghilev had acquiesced to the demands of his operatic star, he could simply have used Rimsky-Korsakov's own orchestration—what was the point of the reorchestration if there was no "original" Musorgsky at stake? That Stravinsky's orchestration was commissioned and carried out provides us with further evidence in favor of the hypothesis that Diaghilev simply had no time to think through the issues surrounding this aria.

Alongside these cuts, it is surprising to see that a dozen or so passages in the aria (shown below) follow or approximate the Rimsky-Korsakov version. Although this still leaves the larger part of Stravinsky's version of the aria faithful to Musorgsky, the situation is more or less reversed when we take his cuts into account, because here, Stravinsky did indeed follow Rimsky-Korsakov.

Following are Stravinsky's deviations from Musorgsky's manuscript, showing which passages coincide with or resemble the Rimsky-Korsakov version:

In Example 2, measure 10, there are repeated eighth notes in the strings instead of a single whole note. In Rimsky-Korsakov, there are also repeated eighth notes, although in unison rather than in chords. Here both Rimsky-Korsakov and Stravinsky correct Musorgsky according to the norms of orchestral development: the repeated notes, once they have begun, cannot end at any arbitrary point, but must run their course to the end of the phrase.

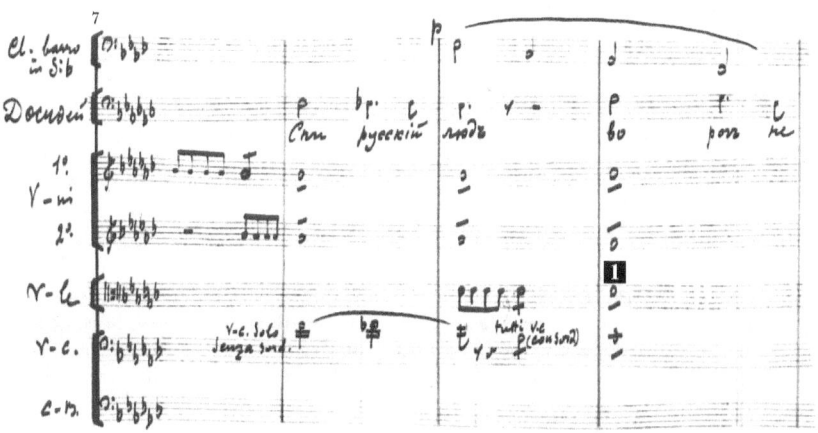

Example 2. Mm. 7–10. (1) measure 10, strings: repeated eighth notes instead of a single whole note.

In Example 3 the half-note rest at measure 12 follows Rimsky-Korsakov, perhaps to allow Chaliapin a beautiful solo sigh, but more likely to avoid a monotonous repetition of this motive in the second phrase, but the placing of the chord on the third beat follows Musorgsky. Stravinsky's original intention was to do everything according to Musorgsky's score—this is what the deleted third on the first beat tells us.

In measure 14, the first chord is Musorgsky's, but the second chord is Rimsky-Korsakov's, with the only difference that the D is shortened from a quarter note to an eighth note. In measure 15, Stravinsky wrote his own countermelody, one note of which coincides with the Rimsky-Korsakov version.

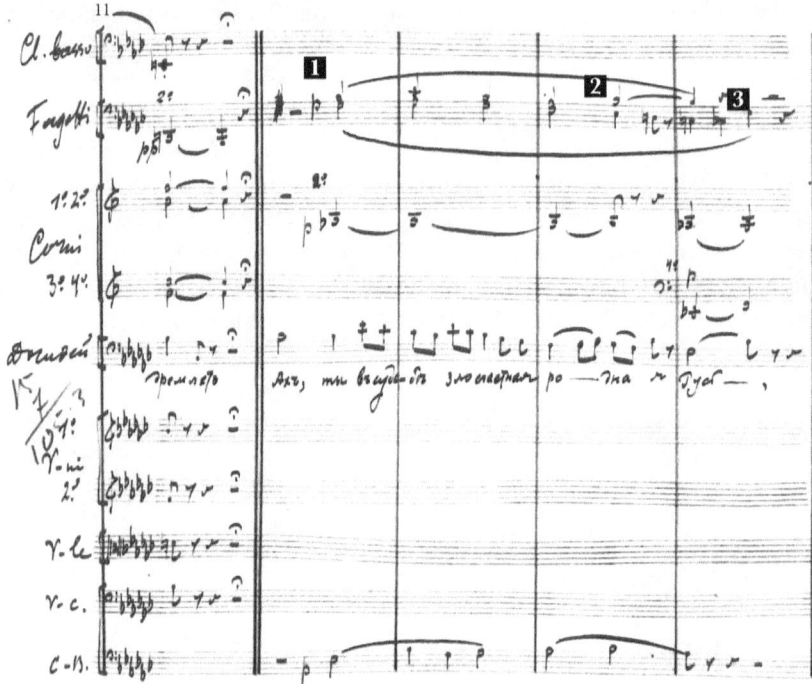

Example 3. Mm. 11–15. (1) measure 12, orchestra: the half-note rest follows Rimsky-Korsakov, but the placing of the chord on the third beat follows Musorgsky; (2) measure 14, orchestra: the first chord is Musorgsky's, but the second chord is Rimsky-Korsakov's; (3) measure 15, orchestra: Stravinsky's own countermelody.

In Example 4, the orchestra follows Musorgsky (measure 19),[39] but the vocal part follows Rimsky-Korsakov. The only difference is that the note E♭ in the vocal part is one-eighth shorter than in Rimsky-Korsakov.

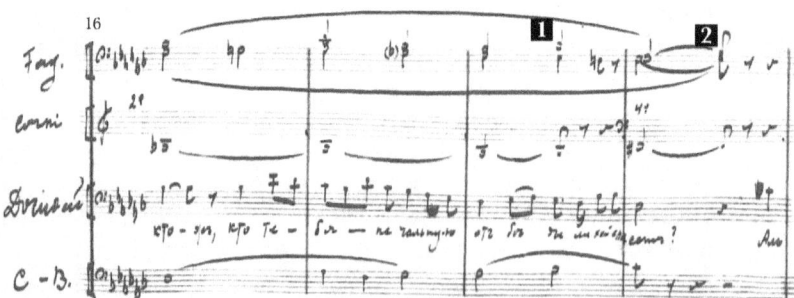

Example 4. Mm. 16–19. (1) measure 18, orchestra: as in measure 14; (2) measure 19: orchestra follows Musorgsky, but the vocal part follows Rimsky-Korsakov.

In Example 5, in Musorgsky there is a bare sixth functioning as a dominant (with doublings); Stravinsky (measure 21) supplies an extra note to the chord, making it a second-inversion chord V. Rimsky-Korsakov also has a full second-inversion chord but without Stravinsky's doubling of the root. In the vocal part in the same measure the way the syllable "-zhit" is sung follows Rimsky-Korsakov.

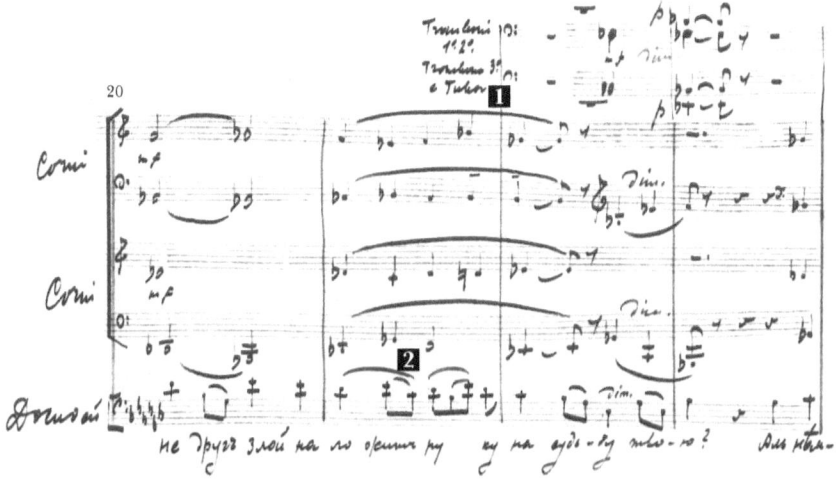

Example 5. Mm. 20–23. (1) measure 21, orchestra: on the fourth beat there is a second-inversion dominant chord instead of a doubled dominant sixth in Musorgsky; (2) measure 21, vocal part: the way the syllable "-zhit" is sung follows Rimsky-Korsakov.

In Example 6, the chord on the third beat (measure 24) is close to the Rimsky-Korsakov version, but does not fully coincide with it. Stravinsky repeated here the analogous fragment of the previous phrase, where exactly the same chord was in both Musorgsky and Stravinsky. Measure 25, like measure 21, is on the fourth beat. Measures 28–35 were cut altogether, following Rimsky-Korsakov. In measure 27, vocal part: the note on the third beat is deleted because it belongs to the next episode, which was cut by Stravinsky following Rimsky-Korsakov.

In Example 7, measure 40 follows Rimsky-Korsakov in all respects. It differs from Musorgsky's text in details of harmony (dominant seventh instead of a first-inversion dominant triad), in rhythm (there is no eighth-note rest on the second beat), and in texture (no doublings, and B♭ is held as a pedal note). Measure 38 follows Rimsky-Korsakov, but differs radically from Musorgsky's original in harmony, rhythm, and texture. Measures 42–46 are cut completely, following Rimsky-Korsakov. Measure 50: follows Rimsky-Korsakov completely, differing from Musorgsky in harmony and texture, and with a different final note in Dosifey's part.

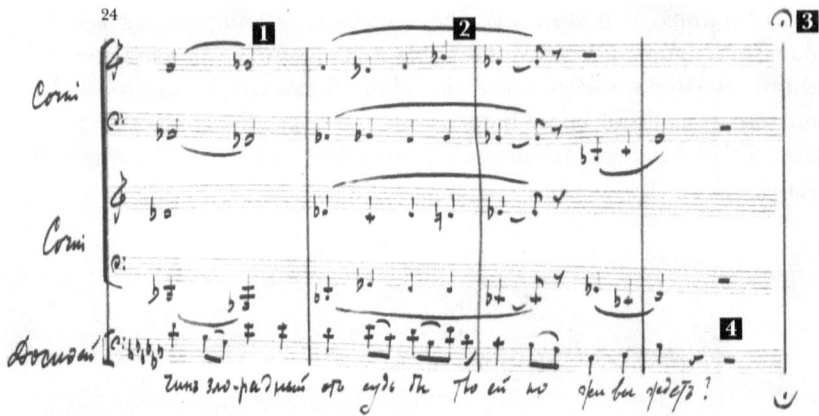

Example 6. Mm. 24–27. (1) measure 24, orchestra: the chord on the third beat is close to the Rimsky-Korsakov version, but does not fully coincide with it; (2) measure 25, orchestra, fourth beat, as in measure 21; (3) measures 28–35 cut altogether, following Rimsky-Korsakov; (4) measure 27, vocal part: the note on the third beat is deleted.

It would be very hard to find a rationale for all of Stravinsky's betrayals of Musorgsky's original in favor of Rimsky-Korsakov and vice versa. At times, these alterations are so insignificant that Chaliapin would not have noticed them. The hypothesis that Stravinsky had intended to orchestrate Musorgsky's original only to run up against Chaliapin's veto simply does not stand up to scrutiny. However plausible this might seem as an explanation for the cuts and for some of the deviations from the original, the hypothesis altogether fails to explain the selectiveness of these deviations, since in the many divergences between the two versions, Stravinsky still resolved a significant portion of them in favor of Musorgsky. Neither can that hypothesis explain the presence of passages that diverge from both Musorgsky and Rimsky-Korsakov. Finally, if Stravinsky, obeying Chaliapin's demand, actually had been orchestrating on the basis of Rimsky-Korsakov's vocal score, he would hardly have mentioned "Musorgsky's original" in the titles of both his manuscripts.

Having analyzed all the differences between Stravinsky's text and Musorgsky's original, we can conclude that his many excursions into the enemy camp have no justification beyond his personal aesthetic decisions made on a piecemeal basis (including the canons of good orchestration).

All these misdemeanors, small and large, were perpetrated by Stravinsky with such panache that every desire to judge him melts away. If we forget for a moment the ideals of Musorgsky himself and simply listen to this music without regard to authorship, we are forced to admit that in

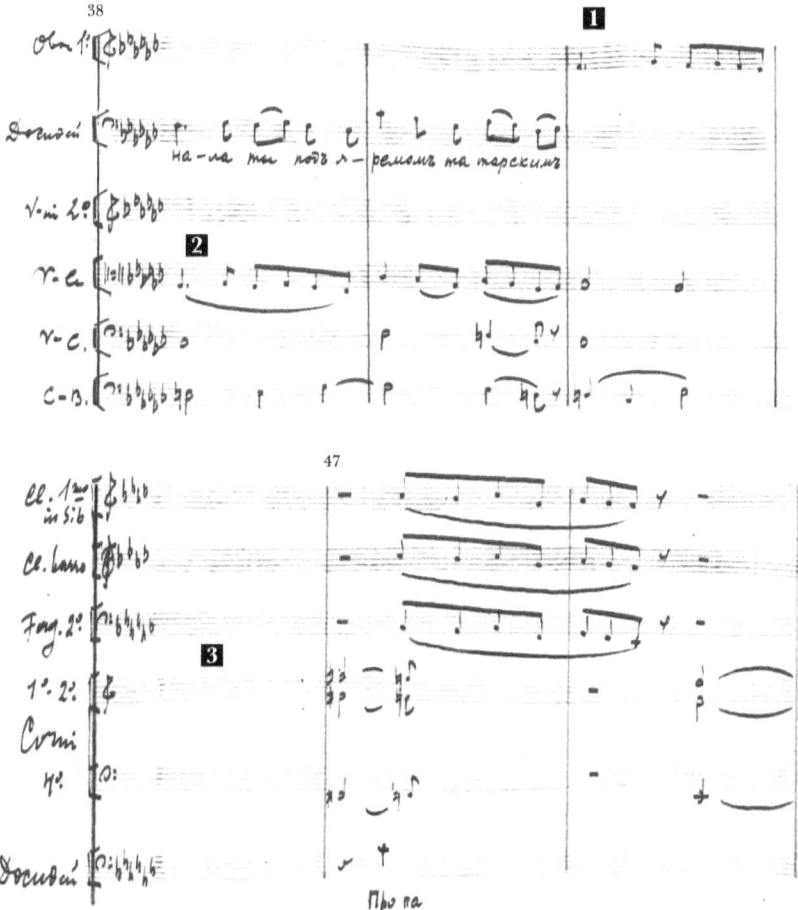

Example 7. Mm. 38–40, an empty measure, then mm. 47–48. (1) measure 40, orchestra: follows Rimsky-Korsakov in all respects; (2) measure 38, orchestra: follows Rimsky-Korsakov; (3) measures 42–46 cut completely, following Rimsky-Korsakov.

Stravinsky's version—and with the Rimsky-Korsakov/Stravinsky cuts—the music hardly loses anything of value, and gains much in formal balance.

Despite his negative opinion of Rimsky-Korsakov's work as an editor, Stravinsky paid ever closer attention to his teacher's solutions to each problem as he immersed himself deeper in the task, and in some cases he even admitted that his teacher had been right. This compilation not only contradicts the notion that Diaghilev brought about a "restoration," but also contradicts the theory that Chaliapin's demands determined the details of the new version, and even contradicts the express views of

Stravinsky himself. Indeed, the record of Stravinsky's orchestration of Shaklovity's Aria is a unique document: effectively a dialogue between pupil and teacher written into the score, a competition on the same playing field.

There is nothing comparable to be found elsewhere in the oeuvres of Rimsky-Korsakov and Stravinsky. Perhaps the only counterpart is to be found in the orchestration assignment Rimsky-Korsakov had once given Stravinsky while they were still teacher and pupil, asking Stravinsky to orchestrate the Polonaise from *Pan Voyevoda* (by Rimsky-Korsakov) from the vocal score. Once the task was completed, Rimsky-Korsakov showed Stravinsky his own orchestration and explained why it was more effective. Here, in Shaklovity's Aria, the story repeated itself, but more or less in reverse.

Obviously, Stravinsky would never have admitted to his friends in St. Petersburg, or to any of his opponents, that he did not always reject the Rimsky-Korsakov edition while producing his version of *Khovanshchina*. And he would have been particularly anxious to maintain silence on the fact that he had simply followed his own tastes as he wove various Rimsky-Korsakov passages into Musorgsky's original of the Shaklovity Aria. Andrei Rimsky-Korsakov, had he known about this, would surely have felt vindicated, since he had vehemently argued that Diaghilev's project was not really a restoration of the genuine *Khovanshchina*, but only a deformation of his father's score. To some extent, he was right. The claims of Ravel, "not a single note of the original was changed";[40] Diaghilev, "Stravinsky is not intending to rewrite or reorchestrate Rimsky-Korsakov's work";[41] and Stravinsky himself, "According to Diaghileff's plan, our work was to be amalgamated with the rest of the score,"[42] were indeed false.

Should we say then that Stravinsky lost the battle on the terrain of Shaklovity's Aria? Did he lose to Chaliapin, to his newspaper critics, and above all to the teacher whose reputation he had challenged? Yes, he did, but only in a certain sporting sense. In essence, Stravinsky the diligent editor of Shaklovity's Aria was a wiser man than Stravinsky the blowhard who later denigrated Rimsky-Korsakov's editorial work. He set out with a positivistic ideology of authenticism in mind: the task was only to uncover Musorgsky's decisions and to eradicate any revisions made by another hand, since these were defined, a priori, as blemishes. But in the course of his work, he set this ideology aside in order to uphold beauty, thereby providing us with a convincing affirmation that ideology must fall short when it is applied in real life. Nature has no straight lines or temperature limits, and in much the same way, there is no reason why Rimsky-Korsakov's interventions should be nothing but despoliation, and an absolute "faithfulness to the real Musorgsky" would (supposedly) guarantee the best musical result. In this sense, the aria "The Streltsy's nest is asleep" by Musorgsky/Rimsky-Korsakov/Stravinsky, for all its incorrectness, is a natural, living thing.

Every editor well knows what is meant here: in their profession, unalloyed success and distilled precision are unattainable. It is, we might say, a profession of compromises. In the best-case scenario, these compromises arise from aesthetic considerations, in the worst case, from the pressure of external circumstances, whether the editor's ambitions, the spell of an ideology, or various limitations in quality or quantity. In his work on the aria, Stravinsky encountered both the worst and the best of this profession, the former through Chaliapin's interference, the latter through his own free aesthetic choices. Under the strain, he developed a dislike for editorial work.[43]

As for the many cases of Stravinsky's work on other composers' scores, his liberal treatment of Shaklovity's Aria always characterized his approach thereafter. Beauty, and the *rightness* of the sound, would always be more important to him than mere loyalty to the letter of the text or the authorial conception of others.

*The Rite of Spring* was given its premiere on 29 May 1913. A week later, on 5 June, came the premiere of *Khovanshchina*. Two days before the second premiere, Stravinsky was diagnosed with typhoid and had to convalesce in the hospital for over a month. Generally, Stravinsky's biography does not offer much room for over-mythologizing, but this illness, one of the most serious in his life, seems to be symbolic.

Both the *Rite* and *Khovanshchina* place sacrifice at the center of their conception. The element of sacrifice in the *Rite* is obvious, and although in *Khovanshchina* the spectrum of ideas is broader, the climax in the finale is nothing other than a sacrifice in which the Old World annihilates itself (an event reflected in the closing chorus that Stravinsky supplied). In neither case are we talking about a Romantic sacrifice of heroism or protest, but one that is legitimate and preordained. At that time many sensed an impending catastrophe. The year 1913, Europe's last peaceful year, was the year of Malevich's *Black Square*, Rachmaninov's *Bells*, Mikhail Matuusjhin's and Aleksei Kruchenykh's *Victory over the Sun*, and Scriabin's "Black Mass" Sonata.

This list would, of course, be incomplete without *The Rite of Spring*, which was exactly where European music broke through into the twentieth century. Yet for Stravinsky himself, the premiere of *Khovanshchina* was no less crucial a watershed. If Stravinsky's great ballet became a symbol of the birth of new art, *Khovanshchina* turned out to be a symbolic "farewell to Petersburg," and particularly to the Rimsky-Korsakov circle in which Stravinsky had still so recently felt at home.[44]

Leaving behind the gravitational pull of Rimsky-Korsakov's influence, and changing his attitude to Musorgsky, Stravinsky cut his remaining ties to Rimsky-Korsakov. Then external events such as the press scandal and Diaghilev's conflict with Rimsky-Korsakov's heirs distanced him further from his teacher. Diaghilev accepted *The Rite* from the very outset, while Stravinsky's inner Rimsky-Korsakov did not. Diaghilev initiated the *Khovanshchina* project while "Rimsky-Korsakov" damned it. The St. Petersburgers attacked Stravinsky, while in Paris, Ravel and Diaghilev defended him. Stravinsky's own revaluation of values was concluding.

In artistic and intellectual terms, Stravinsky had emigrated a year before he finally quit his homeland. The "jeu des cités rivales" was over, and Paris laid claim to the genius. History lacks the conditional mood, but it is clear that even if the war had not taken place, Stravinsky's career would still have unfolded in Europe. War and revolution were only external confirmation of Stravinsky's internal evolution. He fell ill symbolically, offered up his own "sacrifice" before the premieres of two works about sacrifice, and was then symbolically restored to health as a new man. Stravinsky's spring was over, and his summer now began.

# NOTES

1. The second genius to emerge from Rimsky-Korsakov's composition classes was Sergei Prokofiev, who was his student in a more formal and impersonal setting. In his autobiography, Prokofiev wrote: "I didn't manage to get close to [Rimsky-Korsakov]: there were a lot of students in his class, and he didn't single me out for special treatment." See S. S. Prokof'yev, *Avtobiografiya* (Moscow: Sovetskiy kompozitor, 1973), 390.

2. Even so, Stravinsky's inner dialogue with his teacher undoubtedly continued for the rest of his life, not only on the level of his thoughts and views, but also on the level of texts and scores. Stravinsky's memoir is titled *Chronicle (khronika) of My Life*, which is almost the same as Rimsky-Korsakov's *Chronicle (letopis') of My Musical Life*. Stravinsky simply chose the more modern Russian word for chronicle over Rimsky-Korsakov's traditional word. See also Roman Nasonov's study on the 'antithetical relationship between *Les noces* and the *Tale of the Invisible City of Kitezh*, "Po sledam 'narodnoy verï': 'Skazaniye o nevidimom grade Kitezhe i deve Fevronii' N. A. Rimskogo-Korsakova i 'Svadebka' I. F. Stravinskogo," *Nauchnïy vestnik Moskovskoy konservatorii* 3 (2013): 121–35.

3. This version of the opera was never produced again after 1914, while the large body of associated documents was dispersed across the globe, buried until recently in private archives.

4. This orchestral piece was written as a memorial tribute for Rimsky-Korsakov and it was performed on 17 January 1909 in the first of a series of "Russian Symphony Concerts in Memory of N.A. Rimsky-Korsakov." There were no subsequent performances before the Revolution, and the score was deemed irretrievably lost afterward. Stravinsky thought very highly of the piece, and even in his later years he still expressed his deep regret over this misfortune. The Funeral Song was considered the most significant lacuna in his oeuvre until the orchestral parts were discovered in the St. Petersburg Conservatory library in 2015. The score was soon compiled from the parts, and after the work's "premiere" in 2016, it has been performed regularly on concert stages across the globe.

5. *Stravinskiy: Publitsist i sobesednik*, ed. V. Varunts (Moscow: Sovetskiy kompozitor, 1988), 12.

6. See A. A. Gozenpud, "*Boris Godunov* M. P. Musorgskogo vo Frantsii (1876–1908)," *Vospriyatiye russkoy kul'turï na Zapade* (Leningrad: Nauka, 1975), 236–37.

7. In a letter to Rimsky-Korsakov, Diaghilev wrote: "I am keeping Musorgsky's old score because I tend to submit everything that interests me to exhaustive research." Quoted in ibid.

8. S. P. Diaghilev, "Otvet N. N. Rimskoy-Korsakovoy," *Rech* 248 (10 September 1910).

9. Teatral, "Predstoyashchiye gastroli russkoy operï i baleta v Parizhe, Bryussele, Londone," *Peterburgskaya gazeta* 41 (11 February 1910). "Teatral" was a pen name for Diaghilev.

10. Ibid. *Khovanshchina* had been produced only by amateurs or in private theaters; in St. Petersburg at the Musico-Dramatic Circle of Amateurs, 1886; Russian Operatic Society, 1893; in Kiev, I Ya. Setov Enterprise, 1892; and in Moscow at the Mamontov Private Opera, 1897.

11. Matilda Krzesinska (1872–1971), the Mariinsky's prima ballerina, was close to several members of the Imperial family, enabling her to exert some influence on state cultural policy.

12. I. Vershinina, "Musorgskiy i Stravinskiy (O dyagilevskoy postanovke 'Khovanshchinï')," in *M. P. Musorgskiy i muzika XX veka* (Moscow: Muzïka, 1990), 196.

13. Igor Stravinsky and Robert Craft, *Conversations with Igor Stravinsky* (London: Faber & Faber, 1959), 43–44.

14. The Tsarevich Dmitri, youngest son of Ivan the Terrible, was generally thought to have been assassinated at the age of eight in 1591. Over the seven years following the

death of Boris Godunov in 1605, no less than four men in their twenties claimed to be Dmitri, who had supposedly survived and escaped. The first of these, possibly the genuine, actually reigned as tsar for just under a year.

15. I. F. Stravinskiy, *Perepiska s russkimi korrespondentami: Materialï k biografii*, 3 vols., ed. V. P. Varunts (Moscow: Kompozitor, 1998–2003), 1:451.

16. Igor Stravinsky and Robert Craft, *Expositions and Developments* (Los Angeles: University of California Press, 1981), 138–39.

17. "Russkaya opera dlya Yevropï," *Russkoye slovo*, 12 January 1913; "S. P. Dyagilev v Moskve," *Utro Rossii*, 12 January 1913. The latter newspaper reported Diaghilev as follows: "For some reason, Rimsky-Korsakov did not make use of the huge crowd scene in Act 1 or the scene with Kuzka in Act 2 [sic]; both of these will be reintroduced into the opera, and I have entrusted their orchestration to Stravinsky. He will also reorchestrate the final chorus of the Old Believers, for which Musorgsky notoriously wrote only the theme." But the journalist was incorrect in reporting that Diaghilev and Stravinsky intended to "reorchestrate" the final chorus written by Rimsky-Korsakov, and although this might seem like a trifling detail, the error had grave consequences.

18. This is a reference to the Bolshoi production, 12 December 1912, when Chaliapin was artistic director in addition to singing the role of Dosifey.

19. Ibid.

20. Ibid.

21. M. Dvinskiy, "Restavratsiya *Khovanshchinï*," *Birzhevïye vedomosti*, 22 January 1913, evening issue.

22. Ibid.

23. S. Dyagilev, Letter to the Editor (Otkrïtoye pis'mo redaktoru gazetï), *Birzhevïye vedomosti*, 4 February 1913.

24. It is curious how Cui changed his opinion about the project after learning about the interference with Rimsky-Korsakov's version. On 22 January, answering a question from *Birzhevïye vedomosti*, he said: "I think that if some new material by Musorgsky has been found, then what could be wrong with including it? I find that Diaghilev's decision to entrust the orchestration of this material [to Stravinsky] is completely logical. The latter is a pupil of Rimsky-Korsakov's and an excellent orchestrator." However, a few months later, Cui was to write: "*Khovanshchina* is being manhandled terribly in Paris: Stravinsky and Ravel (a French modernist) are reorchestrating it (after Korsakov!), while Stravinsky, moreover, is recomposing it and adding his own stuff!" Cui to M. S. Kerzina, 6 June 1913, cited in Stravinskiy, *Perepiska s russkimi korrespondentami*, 2:83.

25. Later, Diaghilev recalled: "Before presenting this opera in Paris, I started to check the vocal score as arranged by Rimsky-Korsakov against the manuscript vocal score kept in the St. Petersburg Public Library. . . . While comparing the two, I was astonished by the number of cuts, harmonic changes, etc., made by Rimsky-Korsakov. I started marking the changes in my own vocal score with red ink. The pages began to look as if they were smeared with strawberry jam." Bibliothèque de l'Opéra, Fond B. Kochno, pièce 121, 41 fiches de S. Diaghilev, quoted in Yu. De-Klerk, "*Dernier cri*," *ili Posledniy krik modï v iskusstve XX veka: Moskva–Parizh–Peterburg* (Moscow: P. Yurgenson, 2013) 4:37.

26. Robert Threlfall, "Stravinsky, *Khovanshchina* and Ravel: A Postscript," *Studies in Music* 17 (1983): 112–14. A reconstruction of the plan for *Khovanshchina* was carried out again by Richard Taruskin, who also examined Diaghilev's working vocal score. See Taruskin, *Stravinsky and the Russian Traditions: A Biography of Works through "Mavra"* (Berkeley and Los Angeles: University of California Press, 1996), 1041–42. The results of both studies were summarized by Viktor Varunts, in Stravinsky, *Perepiska s russkimi korrespondentami*, 2:25–29.

27. In 1914, the following year, when the relevant agreement between Russia and France had already been signed, Rimsky-Korsakov's widow, the mother of Andrei,

demanded that the French authorities ban Diaghilev's production of *The Golden Cockerel*. The newspapers had already printed cancellation notices, but the matter came to a close when Diaghilev paid a 3,000-franc fine to the bailiff who had been sent out. De-Klerk, "*Dernier cri*," 5:243.

28. All italics in the quotations are the original author's.

29. A. Rimskiy-Korsakov, "*Khovanshchina* M. P. Musorgskogo i S. P. Dyagileva," *Russkaya molva*, 23 March 1913. Suspension points in the original. "But he's just moaning about Stravinsky!" wrote Vladimir Derzhanovsky to Nikolai Myaskovsky on the day when this article appeared. "Although maybe he's partly right. But how superficial this is (how little is said about *Khovanshchina* and the new edition), even though he's an intelligent man and there are some intelligent thoughts in there." Manuscript in VMOMK, f. 71, no. 159, quoted in De-Klerk, "*Dernier cri*," 4:22.

30. Stravinsky, *Perepiska s russkimi korrespondentami*, 2:89.

31. Ibid., 90.

32. Ibid., 264.

33. At this stage, Andrei had not yet challenged Stravinsky. From his recommendation, it would appear that Steinberg believed Andrei would actually defend Stravinsky.

34. Stravinsky, *Perepiska s russkimi korrespondentami*, 2:21.

35. Igor Stravinsky, *Chronicle of My Life* (London: Victor Gollancz, 2004), 79.

36. See Stravinskiy, *Perepiska s russkimi korrespondentami*, 2:172–73.

37. On the unraveling of Diaghilev's original plans, see Ya. I. Timofeyev, "Etyud v basovïkh polutonakh: Ob eskizakh arii Shaklovitogo v orkestrovke Stravinskogo," *Nauchnïy vestnik Moskovskoy konservatorii* 1 (2013): 60–91.

38. Richard Taruskin was the first to suggest that Stravinsky "was tacitly eclectic in his editorial method, choosing at pleasure between Musorgsky's wares and Rimsky's," using two instances in which the Rimsky-Korsakov and Stravinsky versions coincided. See Taruskin, *Stravinsky and the Russian Traditions*, 1069. For Taruskin, however, this is only an "alternative explanation"; his main hypothesis is that there must have been another Musorgsky manuscript for Shaklovity's Aria that was used by both Rimsky-Korsakov and Stravinsky. Taruskin suggests that this manuscript would have been seen by Diaghilev, but must then have disappeared, mysteriously, from the collections of the Public Library, because Pavel Lamm, who painstakingly analyzed the complete collection of *Khovanshchina* manuscripts, does not mention it. But almost every deviation from the only original known to us (which was probably the only one in existence), betrays the hand of Rimsky-Korsakov, such as the unusual harmonic progressions corrected by his hand in measures 38 and 50. Musorgsky, who relished such idiosyncrasies, was unlikely to have "corrected" them himself.

39. Hereafter, "orchestra" means the aggregate of orchestral parts, rather than orchestration.

40. Further context for Ravel's claim: "We are also obliged to Monsieur Stravinsky for the orchestration of Shaklovity's Aria, which was restored to its original form." M. Ravel, "O 'parizhskoy' redaktsii *Khovanshchinï*," *Muzïka* 129 (14 May 1913): 339. "When we were orchestrating [the fragments of the opera] so that not a single note of the original was changed, neither Stravinsky nor I believed that we were involved in an act of 'vandalism'"(342).

41. S. Dyagilev, Letter to the Editor, *Birzhevïye vedomosti*.

42. Igor Stravinsky, *Chronicle of My Life*, 79. This quotation looks rather like a Freudian slip, because it implies, strictly speaking, that Stravinsky's and Ravel's task was to merge their work stylistically with Rimsky-Korsakov's score—because, of course, no Musorgsky score existed. But we can interpret this remark more charitably in the following way: Diaghilev selected for reorchestration only the fragments most distorted by Rimsky-Korsakov, and therefore the remainder of the opera would have been seen by the co-authors of the new

version as more or less authentic. Thus the newly orchestrated episodes had to fit with their context.

43. "Apart from the work mentioned above, I had no share in the arrangement of this version. I have always been sincerely opposed to the rearrangement by anyone other than the author himself of work already created, and my opposition is only strengthened when the original author is an artist as conscious and certain of what he was doing as Moussorgsky." Stravinsky, *Chronicle of My Life*, 80.

44. Wolfgang Dömling was perhaps the first to propose that *Khovanshchina* played a part in Stravinsky's decision to remain in the West. Dömling, *Igor Strawinsky* (Hamburg: Rowohlt, 1982), 42.

# Stylistic Turbulence: The Experience of the Rimsky-Korsakov School

## LIDIA ADER
## TRANSLATED BY JONATHAN WALKER

Professional music education in Russia won official recognition in 1862, when classes began at the new St. Petersburg Conservatory for the first intake of 179 students. Nine years later, the Conservatory's staff was bolstered by the arrival of an ambitious young musician, a very promising composer whose symphonic works had already made a mark on the concert stage—Nikolai Rimsky-Korsakov. During his career of some three decades at the Conservatory, he managed to bring together many talented young performers and composers who soon became mainstays of Russian musical life.

In this essay, we will look at the legacy of Rimsky-Korsakov's pedagogical work, a legacy that bore greatest fruit in the 1920s and '30s, well after his death, when musical life was rebuilt and pre-revolutionary ideas reassessed. During those years, a major reform of the Conservatory system was undertaken, and new pedagogical strategies emerged. The Rimsky-Korsakov school, and the composer's own oeuvre continued to influence musical tastes and teaching in this period, generating lively polemics. We shall follow the composers of the school, who took a leading role in the musical life of Leningrad, and see how they fared during the anti-formalist campaign.

## The "School" Phenomenon

The Rimsky-Korsakov school, broadly defined, consisted of approximately 230 of his former composition students, a good number of whom turn up in music reference books today with epithets such as "outstanding," "well-known," and "talented." Rimsky-Korsakov's area of influence spread far beyond the limits of St. Petersburg, since his students not only worked there and in Moscow, but also in Kiev, Riga, Vilnius, Minsk,

Tallinn, Tbilisi, and Yerevan. They also figured prominently in the establishment of new musical institutions. What, then, was so special about the Rimsky-Korsakov school?

Rimsky-Korsakov, in his own teaching career, developed a distinctive approach to the teaching of composition. He placed a heavy emphasis on theoretical understanding, and the main two subjects were counterpoint and orchestration. Students were only allowed to proceed to "practical," that is, free composition, after three years of prior study, the time required for the foundational course. This approach was followed until a new composition professor, Vladimir Shcherbachev, made far-reaching changes in the academic year 1925–26. Shcherbachev was himself a pupil of two major Rimsky-Korsakov pupils, Anatoly Lyadov and Maximilian Steinberg, and indeed all the leading figures at the Conservatory were connected directly or indirectly to Rimsky-Korsakov. Working alongside the prominent critic and musicologist Boris Asafyev, who did not teach composition but lectured in music history to student composers, Shcherbachev insisted that students should be able to work on free composition from their first year of study onward.

Returning to the original course, the foundation consisted of six subjects: harmony, counterpoint, fugue, orchestration, form, and score-reading. Rimsky-Korsakov's less illustrious predecessor, Nikolai Zaremba, had already established this framework (he had been invited into the Conservatory in the early planning stages).[1] The harmony course was accelerated in the case of very able students, and one student, Alexander Glazunov, had such a high level of musicianship that Rimsky-Korsakov was happy to waive all the normal rules, allowing him to skip basic exercises, merge several subjects, and work through the most complicated material in the course of just a few meetings.[2] Rimsky-Korsakov considered the course on musical form to be the keystone, since it drew together all the other disciplines. Counterpoint and fugue were considered essential for their contribution to a fully professional technique. The theory of orchestration was obligatory, and composers were strongly advised not only to attend orchestra rehearsals but also to take up conducting themselves.

Each subject was taught with a substantial theoretical element, and mastery of each newly acquired technical device would be demonstrated by students through practical work. The coursework involved the analysis of various pieces: students were shown the distinguishing feature of each piece, and details of form and orchestration were explained. This process of familiarization with compositional models and the examination of useful examples was introduced early in the course, and was a component of all of the subjects studied.

In his orchestration classes, Rimsky-Korsakov used scores, but he also had his students look over composers' drafts and sketches, since he had access to such material from his Russian predecessors and contemporaries.[3] By this means, the students could see how the initial impulse was channeled and planned out. In his treatise on orchestration, Rimsky-Korsakov had categorically rejected the practice of orchestrating works that were originally intended for another medium, dismissing it as a lower, secondary form of orchestration.[4] Even so, this rejection was hardly borne out in his Conservatory teaching, and orchestral arrangement became foundational for his students (and so it remained for students of the following generations).

The teaching tradition initiated by Rimsky-Korsakov took the Viennese classics as the most appropriate material for orchestration. We can, indeed, trace the roots of this approach beyond Rimsky-Korsakov to his own teacher, Mily Balakirev. In 1868, at Balakirev's behest, Rimsky-Korsakov orchestrated Schubert's *Grande marche heroïque* (for piano duet), and the result was performed at a free concert. Rimsky-Korsakov later recalled that back in 1868, "I had some degree of imaginative flair for orchestration, which served me well in my own works, but I had no experience." Fifty years later, we find the Rimsky-Korsakov protégé Maximilian Steinberg setting the young Dmitri Shostakovich the very similar task of orchestrating one of Schubert's Military Marches, confirming for us the stability of the curriculum over the decades. In the Conservatory archives, there is a folder with 242 pages of students' orchestration submissions, and the composer who appears most frequently is Schubert, the chosen works including his String Quintet, the C-Minor Piano Sonata, the A-Minor Piano Sonata, and, again, the *Grande marche heroïque*.[5]

Rimsky-Korsakov focused on practical sessions to develop students' skills, but talent was the *sine qua non*. He held that such a course would have been an artificial and futile pursuit if students did not display a manifest gift for composition.

## A Decade of Reaction

The year was 1918. In the ten years since the death of Rimsky-Korsakov, Russia had weathered a world war and two revolutions. Institutions around the country were being transformed to justify their continued existence in the new Soviet state. The Petrograd Conservatory was no exception.

Let us take a look at the panorama of musical life in St. Petersburg/Petrograd. The Conservatory was still strong in creative talent. The two most prominent figures were both former students of Rimsky-Korsakov: Maximilian Steinberg teaching composition, and Leonid Nikolayev teaching piano. In the few years following the Revolution, Steinberg's composition students included Dmitri Shostakovich, together with his close friend, the critic and composer Valerian Bogdanov-Berezovsky, as well the older Alexander Veprik. Lesser lights included Avenir Monfred, Vladimir Andreyev, Mikhail Mikhailov, and Pyotr Ryazanov. Nikolayev's piano students included the leading Russian pianists of that generation, Vladimir Sofronitsky and Maria Yudina, as well as Pavel Serebryakov, Elena Skryabina, Galina and Marianna Gramenitsky, Yuri Zander, Alexander Kamensky, Iosif Shvarts, German Bik, and Isay Renzin.

Let us fill in the picture with the names of other professors who had studied with Rimsky-Korsakov. Alexander Ossovsky, a music historian and critic, taught at the Faculty of Composition. The conducting course was taught by the internationally renowned Nikolai Malko. Theoretical subjects were structured and taught by Aleksei Petrov, whose books on the elements of music became the daily bread of music students through the 1920s. Counterpoint was studied using the (unpublished) textbook of another Rimsky pupil, Nikolai Sokolov, who was well known among students for his rigorous approach.[6] The director of the Conservatory from 1905 to 1928 was Alexander Glazunov, one of the best loved and most loyal of Rimsky-Korsakov pupils. His own pious attitude to his former teacher shaped the ethos of the institution. Under Glazunov, it was the tradition for the director himself, the leading professors, and the senior students to attend graded recitals. Glazunov had absolute authority—he was the final arbiter when student recitals and other exams were discussed.

The Conservatory's personnel and practice provide overwhelming evidence that Rimsky-Korsakov's school dominated teaching. Let us look at the curriculum of the 1920s in more detail.

The assessment of students depended to a great extent on the tastes of the professor. For many students the decision taken by the exam board would come as a surprise, but next to every mark there was a report from the professors and the director of the Conservatory. Pyotr Ryazanov, who was a student in the 1920s and became a pedagogue and a critic in the next decade, complained about this: "The possibility of any individual composerly conception in the composition submissions . . . somehow never occurred to the exam boards, or if it was ever noted, it still wasn't taken into account in the final evaluation of the virtues or shortcomings of a given composition."[7]

The curriculum of the Faculty of Composition was strictly regimented, and concessions such as a shortened period of study were no longer made to individuals. Rimsky-Korsakov's general wishes were followed, but they were set in stone, with strict discipline and biannual teaching plans. Composition assignments were officially limited to small-scale didactic pieces, and any work beyond these limits depended on the amenability of individual professors to private requests by their students. As the theorist Yuri Tyulin recalled, some professors were unhappy about being expected to provide extramural assessment.[8] Students in their harmony classes were officially restricted to the composition of miniatures in simple binary and ternary forms; only after they had gained experience with these were they allowed, in Year 4, to write sets of variations, and it was not until Year 5 that they were officially permitted to submit pieces in sonata form.

The counterpoint teacher, Nikolai Sokolov, treated his subject less dogmatically than his colleagues (Aleksandr Zhitomirsky, Vasilii Kalafati, Mikhail Chernov), and tried to provide his students with more creative assignments that fully acknowledged the harmonic dimension—in this, he was following in the footsteps of Rimsky-Korsakov. Steinberg also endorsed such an approach, stressing that compositional skills were best developed when counterpoint was linked with harmony.[9]

By the time of the Revolution, Rimsky-Korsakov's *Practical Manual of Harmony*[10] had been used by several generations of students, and the works of the Rimsky-Korsakov school were now established in the Conservatory's concert programs. Shostakovich studied the textbook, working through most (perhaps all) of the exercises. One extant manuscript contains a chorale harmonization whose melody was taken from the appendix to Rimsky-Korsakov's textbook.[11] Shostakovich spoke later of the textbook in grateful terms, saying that its lucid and uncluttered presentation of the material enabled him, for example, to achieve fluency in modulation and to develop a sensitivity to the problem of parallel perfect consonances.

Rimsky-Korsakov deserves particular attention as a teacher of orchestration. He started compiling his treatise on orchestration in 1873 and continued, off and on, until his death.[12] Aside from offering his own insights, his intention was to collect and present in a systematic form all the advice contained in previous treatises. He made many changes to the structure and content of the work over thirty years as he accumulated experience both in orchestrating his own and others' works, and in teaching the art to his students. Given this large time span, he also had to take account of rapid changes in the technology of orchestral instruments and in the practice of orchestration in the hands of other major composers. His *Principles of Orchestration* still remained incomplete at the time of his death.

Steinberg edited and completed the orchestration treatise, and it was published in 1913. The extent of Steinberg's personal input is unknown, but it was certainly substantial, since Rimsky-Korsakov had left only one chapter in a complete, publishable form, namely, the "General Overview of Orchestral Groups." Steinberg had to select and classify all of Rimsky-Korsakov's drafts written over the previous three-and-a-half decades. He assembled the score examples, which had been written out on separate sheets of paper, piecing together an intricate mosaic, and he organized into a logical form the many scraps of text containing isolated thoughts. He shortened the introduction that had been written for the planned (but aborted) edition of 1891, and added his own table of examples devoted to the topic of tutti orchestration. L. Butir, who painstakingly compared Rimsky-Korsakov's sketches with Steinberg's edition, found that Steinberg had added many of his own score examples to other sections as well.[13] Steinberg's work had in fact begun even before Rimsky-Korsakov's death, and by 1905, he had already brought together much of the material for a preliminary version. Even though Rimsky-Korsakov's own opinions carried great authority, he retained a certain modesty that enabled him to listen to the advice of musicians who had earned his respect. Steinberg shared in this humility: considering the amount of work he had to carry out, he could perhaps more easily have published an orchestration treatise under his own name, but as his teacher's leading pupil, he was well aware that his ideas stemmed from his thorough assimilation of Rimsky-Korsakov's system, which underpinned his own approach in both composition and teaching.

Steinberg did not continue the tradition of attending orchestra rehearsals with his students, but they continued to attend the Philharmonia's open and private rehearsals regularly, and many, like Shostakovich, acquired much of their craft in this way. The opportunity to watch conductors in action, to follow the way textures were built up in the score, to discover new details they had not previously noticed, and to see for themselves which passages were effective (or not) was excellent schooling in orchestral technique.

Programs at the Leningrad Philharmonia in this period included Bach, Mozart, Beethoven, Schubert, Schumann, Brahms, Franck, Bruckner, Mahler, Richard Strauss, Casella, Schoenberg, Krenek, Milhaud, and Poulenc, together of course with the Russians: Tchaikovsky, Rimsky-Korsakov, Prokofiev, and Stravinsky. Malko was the most prominent of the conductors (1921 and 1924–29), but others appearing on programs also included Hermann Abendrot (1925, 1928–29), Bruno Walter (1927), Albert Coates (1927), Otto Klemperer (1924–29), and Ernst Ansermet (1928–29). Since the Conservatory library did not yet possess all of these scores, the students had to listen all the more carefully. With hindsight, the students remarked that the main emphasis in their coursework was on the great German composers. But they do mention Russian composers who were studied in class: Musorgsky, Tchaikovsky, Borodin, Glazunov, Taneyev, and Scriabin. Some of Rimsky-Korsakov's works were also presented, such as the Spanish Capriccio, the Symphony No. 3, the Sextet, and *Sadko*, but these were normally introduced when there was some kind of link or comparison with a work by another composer. Rimsky-Korsakov's Spanish Capriccio, for example, turned up during a discussion of Tchaikovsky's *Italian Capriccio*. Similarly, some of Glazunov's symphonies were introduced in discussions of Beethoven and Tchaikovsky.

There was certainly no diminution of interest in Rimsky-Korsakov in the two decades after the composer's death, and performance of his music flourished. He became "holy writ" for a part of the Russian intelligentsia, although there was a backlash, from two different directions.[14] The modernists were displeased with such a conservative trend, and certain musical factions in the Communist Party (although not the leadership) objected on the grounds that this was a promotion of petit-bourgeois values. In the opera seasons of 1920–22, for example, no less than seven of Rimsky-Korsakov's fifteen operas were staged: *May Night, The Tsar's Bride, The Tale of Tsar Saltan, Kitezh, The Maid of Pskov, The Snow Maiden,* and *Sadko*.

In sum, higher music education in the 1910s and '20s alike saw no real challenge to the dominance of the Rimsky-Korsakov school. His name became a beacon for many graduates, who then used their knowledge and methods in their own teaching. Curricula were fine-tuned and standardized. The methods of assessment changed and the official duration of the course was more strictly upheld, but composers' education was still based around the Rimsky-Korsakov school. Hence the official pronouncement in the 1930s, when further change was afoot: "There is no denying the depth of the Rimsky-Korsakov trend at the Conservatory."[15]

## Arguments of the 1930s

The mood in the Conservatory began to shift when the Russian Association of Proletarian Musicians (RAPM) grew in power and influence from the autumn of 1928 onward, up to the point when the organization was disbanded by government order in 1932. Just before that period, in 1925, Vladimir Shcherbachev (a former pupil of Steinberg's) had attempted to launch some reforms of the curriculum. The composition course now began straightaway and continued throughout the period of study, which helped to bring theory and practice closer together. A course in melodic writing was added, which was constructed in a progression from simple to complex, with analytical thinking encouraged. Shcherbachev also sought to remove any strict regimentation of the boundaries, so that the concept of composition became more open. The momentum of his reforms, however, was eventually overcome by the inertia of the prior tradition.

RAPM's chief interest in composition was the creation of a repertory of revolutionary mass songs, and in music pedagogy they called for a democratized, mass music education. RAPM also campaigned against "contemporary" (modernist) music and what they called "West European bourgeois formalism," which they saw as inimical to their own goals. By "formalism" RAPM meant the elite teaching practice that emphasized the German musical heritage of Bach, Beethoven, Liszt, Wagner, Brahms, Bruckner, Mahler, Richard Strauss, and Reger. The organization sought to replace this with a simpler, more "democratic" approach—of the kind they used in mass songs. In composition, they decried the "contemporary" trend (*sovremennichestvo*) in the music of Hindemith, Berg, and Krenek in Germany, or of the music of Stravinsky and his followers in France, which they saw as a negation of all tradition. As models for composers who already wrote in a sophisticated manner they favored Beethoven, Schubert, and Musorgsky.

During the years of RAPM's ascendancy, criticism of the Rimsky-Korsakov school came out into the open. The year 1932 saw the disbandment of RAPM by order of the Party in a resolution that introduced sweeping changes to the arts,[16] but some of RAPM's ideas, in a less extreme but more authoritative form, nevertheless turned composers' values upside down. The 1932 resolution was followed by a series of critical articles in the official press, and finally, in 1936, by a clear directive from above. "Muddle Instead of Music," the editorial that appeared in *Pravda* on 28 January 1936, shortly after Stalin attended the Moscow production of Shostakovich's acclaimed opera *Lady Macbeth of the Mtsensk District*, was the climax of the increasing tension. The editorial strongly criticized Shostakovich's work, contrasting its modernism with the traditionalism and patriotism of Dzerzhinsky's opera *Quiet Flows the Don*.

In 1933, Anatoly Lunacharsky, the former Minister for Arts (with Education and Science) had marked the twenty-fifth anniversary of Rimsky-Korsakov's death with an article for *Izvestiya* titled "A Critical Fantasy." Addressing the composer in the style of dialogue from *Mozart and Salieri* (Rimsky-Korsakov's opera of 1898), Lunacharsky made a passing comment on the "high level of skill" that characterized the composer's work. Lunacharsky wrote that the main virtue of Rimsky-Korsakov's art was its beauty, a beauty that was lacking in art inspired by the "proletarian muse." Lunacharsky defined the main goal of Rimsky-Korsakov's creative work as "decorating the world around him"—using the Italian verb *ornare*. "The true decoration of ourselves and the environment we live in cannot fall into falsehood but must draw from an understanding of that environment. The ornament, i.e., what a human being adds to the found object, must reach a high degree of accord with this object."[17] But Lunacharsky was a spent force. Although he had been a government minister since the Revolution, he was demoted in 1929 to a diplomatic post. Thus Pyotr Ryazanov, who would become the main critic of formalism during the 1936 crisis, felt free to ignore Lunacharsky's nuanced appeal, and instead condemned the old musical culture as a "hedonistic savoring of music as if it were delicious food."[18] Rimsky-Korsakov was denounced as an academicist, and his school as propagators of the academic trend.

The 1932 dissolution of RAPM may have given a temporary boost to the nuanced ideas described by Lunacharsky. However, the force of the "Muddle" editorial and the subsequent follow-up campaign confirmed that the aesthetic ideas of Lunacharsky and his like had lost influence in the Soviet Union. At the Leningrad Union of Composers, and then at the Leningrad Conservatory, wide-ranging and intense discussions were held in the weeks following the Shostakovich critique. The transcripts of the Conservatory's "Discussion on Issues of Formalism in Musical Education" have been preserved in the Central State Archive for Literature and the Arts (TsGALI); the discussion took the form of a series of meetings from 16 February to 17 April (with a further isolated meeting on 4 June). The professors had close connections to Shostakovich, who was now being denounced, so they had to distance themselves from his "musical muddle." The speakers competed in eloquence, freely interpreting the points of an article that now served as their new rulebook.

All the speakers tried to justify themselves by appeal to a noble cause: the raising of teaching standards.[19] But the professors had good reason to be worried about the extent of the change that might be required, for beyond the official criticism of Shostakovich lay an implicit criticism of the schooling he had received. He had, after all, been a diligent student, absorbing all the advice of his professors, and remaining a postgraduate student until 1930 (well after the Shcherbachev reforms), and thus his "muddle" was liable to be construed as the direct result of his course of study. And indeed, one of the very first resolutions, passed at the meeting of composers and musicologists on 15 February, said as much: "In the music of some young composers, students of the Conservatory, we can see evidence of formalism, which is manifested in a neglect of the issues of musical content, in fascination with pure technique and ideology-free experimentation."[20]

Rimsky-Korsakov's pupils struggled to make sense of such slippery terms as formalism and academicism and then had to puzzle over the problem of how these aesthetic and ideological vices could be avoided in music. Sometimes compositions by Rimsky-Korsakov's pupils were proclaimed as being of "foreign outlook."[21] "Gaetan's Song," by Mikhail Gnesin (from the incidental music to Blok's *The Rose and the Cross*) was held up as a bad example on several occasions. He had studied with both Rimsky and his pupil Lyadov, but since he was one of the more recent arrivals on the teaching staff, it was considered important to direct him onto the correct path. Academicism was detected not only in Glazunov's music (as we have seen), but also in Lyadov's. On occasion Rimsky-Korsakov's younger pupils were also condemned as leading exponents of academicism.

Defensively, Gnesin identified a pattern: the most expressive passages in *Lady Macbeth of Mtsensk* all relied on a traditional harmonic system, whereas "cacophony" prevailed wherever linearity prevailed.[22] A certain desperation is evident in Gnesin's words: "While he was at the Conservatory, Shostakovich perfected this [linear] type of writing and made it his mainstay. And if that were so, then the Conservatory would also have to shoulder the blame, and we would have to fix something in our training, but it is not so."[23] (Shostakovich had indeed created his linear style while still at the Conservatory.) In any case, Gnesin's rationalization came too late, since the idea that the Conservatory's teaching was at least partly to blame had already taken root.

The changes brought about by the 1936 upheaval could not have failed to affect conservatory curricula. Rimsky-Korsakov's first- and second-generation pupils were all liable to be labeled as formalists, whether they upheld and developed the elite, Germanic heritage of the nineteenth century, or instead favored the tradition-denying modernists. Professor Gnesin (an original member of the Rimsky-Korsakov school) noted that students were no longer attracted to traditional courses in classical harmony.[24] Professor Yuri Tyulin (a second-generation member, taught by Nikolai Sokolov) began offering students unusual juxtapositions of keys, and more abrupt modulations in order to attract the new generation of composers—although he did exercise some moderation, saying that he did not wish to corrupt their as yet unformed tastes.[25] The musicologist Pyotr Ryazanov, once a pupil of Steinberg and Sokolov, soon came to the fore as a critic of the Rimsky-Korsakov school. In his teaching, he chose a radically different course of action: through many repeated listenings to *Pelléas and Mélisande*, he strove to cure his students of Impressionism once and for all, and to "liquidate shortcomings in harmonic thinking."[26] Among the self-professed beneficiaries of this "therapy" were Georgy Fardi, who went on to produce many works on revolutionary and war themes, and Ivan Dzerzhinsky, composer of the opera appropriated by Stalin as a counter-example to *Lady Macbeth*. Ryazanov also argued that the harmony course should be speeded up so that students could master the more sophisticated modulations earlier. In their efforts to keep clear of formalism, composers adjusted their focus, examining Musorgsky's harmonic innovations or searching for functional harmony in the folk music of Armenia or Chuvashia.

The practice of evening composition classes was criticized—it was thought that both teachers and students would be too tired. Students of Rimsky-Korsakov's time had been required to attend rehearsals, but students of the 1930s tended to think of them as extracurricular and therefore optional. Steinberg now insisted that student composers had to attend rehearsals at the Mariinsky at least once a month, because this kind of study was, in his opinion, indispensable. The students were expected to be there by 9 a.m., and were to follow the proceedings closely with the help of their professors' explanations.

The professors tried to prevent this conformity to official cultural doctrine from driving their institution to absurd conclusions, but it was a difficult undertaking. They had to defend themselves against charges of formalism, and at the same time defend all genres of texted music that had come under attack. Symphonic music proved to be in a stronger position, principally because the "content" of such music was harder to discern, especially when no program was provided. Complex counterpoint, however, was a common trigger for charges of formalism, partly because it characterized substantial stretches of Shostakovich's *Lady Macbeth*.

Without blaming Rimsky-Korsakov directly, Ryazanov laid out the objectionable features of the pre-revolutionary approach to music education, which we can summarize in the form of the following eight points:

1. a hedonistic attitude to the art of music (which led to a fascination with French Impressionism)
2. weak training of composers, emphasis being placed on the training of music theorists instead
3. a formalist system of education, with insufficient attention to the nurturing of musical creativity
4. a study of musical craft and technique, rather than a holistic creative practice
5. a gap between theory and artistic practice
6. a fascination for idealist philosophical conceptions (the objective idealism of Glazunov or subjective idealism of Scriabin)

7. academicism—a blind following of existing pedagogical traditions
8. deviations from the rules depending on changes in personal artistic taste and creative direction[27]

Another aspect of the course subjected to criticism was the three-year delay before students began classes in practical composition, with the first three years devoted to mastery of the theoretical disciplines: "If we are to speak of academicism as an outlook, then it is foreign to Soviet music theory."[28] Composition classes of the Rimsky-Korsakov type were diagnosed as academicist, and his school of composition-teaching was proclaimed "harmful."[29]

Rimsky-Korsakov's pupils stood up to defend their teacher's name, as they were entitled to as faculty members. Mikhail Gnesin, for example, argued that Rimsky-Korsakov's teaching method could hardly be further removed from the "chaos," or "muddle" (as in the *Pravda* editorial) that had just been condemned:

> The principle of artistic creation is opposed to "muddle," and [in Rimsky-Korsakov's teaching] it was almost pedantically pursued. That was his main goal: there could not be any "muddle."[30]

The new forces in the Conservatory articulated a contrasting position thus:

> They say that in the Conservatory the leading roles are played by Rimsky-Korsakov and Glazunov. That's all very well, but we should not forget the directives of Lenin and the Party, and we should not forget their slogans on this issue. We have Schubert and Mozart, who are now rising in importance, and we have Beethoven and many other composers who need to be adapted to our needs and brought forward in our practice.[31]

The more enthusiastic critics of the Conservatory declared that Rimsky-Korsakov's pupils "have been nourished by the traditions in composition and pedagogy that stem from the masters, with all of their positive and negative sides."[32] Glazunov's loyalty to conservatory and pedagogical work had earned him the reputation of Rimsky-Korsakov's most direct heir. Now he was criticized for his allegedly negative influence on his own students. His critics cited pedantic tendencies, an ossified view of music, stylistic contradictions and limited horizons, all comparing poorly with the qualities of his teacher.[33] Ryazanov, looking back over his education in the 1920s, remarked that Glazunov's music was featured in many courses for student composers and that his style influenced professorial demands: they valued organ-like sonorities, color, and transparency, and chromatic, sometimes Scriabinesque harmony that could obscure otherwise straightforward harmonic progressions. At the same time, Rimsky-Korsakov's own music was not often studied in the 1920s or 1930s, and Glazunov's was favored instead. According to Ryazanov, Glazunov also harbored formalist tendencies, which he had passed on through his teaching to Steinberg.[34]

Much of this criticism was contradictory. The 1920s interest in French Impressionism was frowned on, as we have seen, but when it surfaced in Glazunov, it was curiously presented as evidence for his academicism, which was remote from the original criticisms of Impressionism. Another pupil of Rimsky-Korsakov, Vasily Kalafati (of Greek extraction), was discussed in similar terms. Like Glazunov, Kalafati was seen as a preserver of tradition, in contrast to Shcherbachev and Asafyev. And even Steinberg, the pupil Rimsky-Korsakov regarded most highly (who became Rimsky-Korsakov's son-in-law), had to justify himself, arguing that he had disregarded Impressionism from the late 1920s onward, and that he had not imposed it on his pupils. In his defense, Steinberg cited the names of his students—Shostakovich, Rubtsov, Zeydman—who had all proven immune to the charms of Impressionism.

One aspect of the composition course that was actually praised by the critics was the evident continuity of the pedagogical system and composerly practice with the Russian tradition that could be traced all the way back to Glinka. Rimsky-Korsakov's teaching practices were praised where they were founded on Glinka's harmonic and voice-leading practices. In Rimsky-Korsakov's own works, his preservation and extension of Glinkian voice leading was lauded.[35]

Not long before the discussion of February–April 1936, there was a symphony concert of works by the Rimsky-Korsakov school, with programs compiled by the well-known pianist and chamber musician Mikhail Bikhter, who was himself a pupil of Lyadov, Glazunov, and Steinberg. "The concert convinced me that there is no deep optimism here, but rather that the composers had in some manner cordoned themselves off from life in their personal experiences. Was it not possible to select some rather different works for this program?"³⁶ Among the works played was Steinberg's Symphony No. 4 ("Turksib"), which was criticized for its formalism and surface pictorialism, vices which the critic traced back to Rimsky-Korsakov.

Back in 1929, the critic Lev Lebedinsky referred to Rimsky-Korsakov's works as quite "acceptable," together with works by Beethoven and Musorgsky (with some exceptions, like Musorgsky's vocal cycle *Sunless*), and also Dargomyzhsky, whose music was supposed to be "promoted." But in 1936 the position was made very clear: even if Stalin and Molotov loved *The Snow Maiden*, they still considered it *critically*.³⁷ It is interesting that *Kitezh*, so beloved of 1920s audiences, was treated with indifference when it was restaged in 1935, receiving neither praise nor censure. The 1935 production of *Pan Voyevoda* at the Leningrad Conservatory Opera Studio even received negative reviews, and was greeted with some bemusement from the professors: "There is no music and nothing to sing." This opera confounded both students and teachers: it contained no stand-alone numbers that could showcase a singer's voice, and so they considered it unsuitable for didactic purposes.³⁸

Even *The Snow Maiden* became a target for criticism on grounds of academicism, although it was steeped in the folksong elements that were supposed to be highly desirable at the time. Rimsky-Korsakov's academicism, in the words of the critics, was to blame for infusing folksong with a more personal lyricism, which was at odds with the song's collective essence.³⁹

The "Discussion on Issues of Formalism" arrived at the opinion that the Rimsky-Korsakov school's earlier representatives were more ordered in their voice leading, whereas later representatives were much less so (because of their modernist propensities), and this had brought about the "muddle" and "trivialization" that was condemned. Concluding, they noted: "Today we are still dealing with the same recipe, only slightly altered, beyond which there are no rules."⁴⁰

Rimsky-Korsakov's harmony textbook and orchestration manual were also subjected to criticism: "We see Rimsky-Korsakov's textbook as a relic of a bygone time that the new realities have overturned. We have to rethink much in this respect, because that was capitalism, and now we have socialism. That was in the 1890s, and now we are in 1936."⁴¹ Rimsky-Korsakov's precepts were seen as the shackling of a composer's talents, and basing courses of study on his own artistic work was also seen as wrong. There were vociferous calls for a broadening of the study of orchestration and stylistic comparison, since major figures, including Beethoven, Glinka, Wagner, Mahler, and Debussy, had receded to the margins of coursework. Rimsky-Korsakov had compiled several sets of score examples from such composers in the drafts for his orchestration manual. Steinberg's editing had of course been essential—there was no publishable manual until he prepared it—but his modesty and his reverence for his teacher had given the manual a bias toward Rimsky-Korsakov's works, which was not present in the drafts. Admittedly, many of Steinberg's extracts from Rimsky-Korsakov were effective in demonstrating various orchestral devices. And it is quite possible that as the years passed and Rimsky-Korsakov was seen as an important, but less overwhelmingly a great figure, this bias toward the composer's work might well have been seen as too restrictive.

Israel Gusin, who criticized the general state of affairs at the Faculty of Composition, declared that most of their students were talentless. He found only three deserving of some modest praise among all those who graduated in the years from 1930 to 1936: Brusilovsky, Ivanshin, and Zeydman. Their work he found acceptable. The work produced by the others wearied him: he found it "neuropathic, exhausted, and flustered," "neurasthenic, frazzled, and decadent."[42] Shostakovich, who had graduated back in 1926, was described by Gusin as "a symphonic trickster."[43] These epithets reflected a loss of confidence on the part of the Conservatory professoriate. They feared everything: Impressionism and Expressionism, and any overabundance of dissonance, because Rimsky-Korsakov himself, through his "colossal efforts,"[44] had attempted to avoid decadence, to hold fast to tonal development, and to avoid "trivialization."

In the wake of the "muddle" editorial, articles and public gatherings displayed a growing tendency toward withdrawal and self-flagellation as a means of survival and adaptation to the new conditions. For this, a valid reference point in history needed to be found, and once again it proved to be Rimsky-Korsakov. "There was a gap between Rimsky-Korsakov's teaching and his composition. His operas are not of a piece." Regarding his attitude to composition: "In these letters we can see a deeply self-critical attitude, here we see the searching mind of the composer." By contrast, "In one of the letters he says of teaching: 'Follow orders and all will be well.'" In conclusion, "Rimsky-Korsakov the composer was superior to Rimsky-Korsakov the pedagogue—and that was his strength."[45] It was noted that in Rimsky-Korsakov's letters and articles, there was evidence of a certain pessimism toward the prospects of Russian music culture: "There was a lack of belief that the school he had worked within could remain productive in the future."[46] Moreover, "Rimsky-Korsakov had no faith in the trend that he himself had inspired and we could cite both progressive and reactionary critiques of the problem of 'fathers and sons.' He used to say that sons take only the worst from their fathers, and gave proofs, so we have to pay a heavy price in order to learn from this."[47] Pyotr

Ryazanov concluded thus in the Leningrad Conservatory discussion of 31 March: Rimsky-Korsakov's aesthetic and pedagogical views were unstable, and he changed the principles of his work several times. Ryazanov, though, still confessed that he loved Rimsky-Korsakov's music, in spite of his reservations.

The participants did not manage to avoid contradictions. Steinberg, when it was his turn to show his repentance, pointed to the heterogeneous character of the Rimsky-Korsakov school. His own pedagogical views, he claimed, were formed without any influence from Glazunov. And Gnesin, who, in his own words, had not yet had a chance to harm the Conservatory, admitted, "I have great shortcomings. I take everyone's individuality very seriously and listen to the students; this means that I sometimes go against the demands of the course. I see them struggle, see how much they have to do and sometimes let them off. This is definitely a defect."[48] Every year, the Conservatory system added new subjects, leaving composition students with less and less free time to compose. Gnesin also had to admit to a further shortcoming: using improvisation in class, which he had thought would help his students to compose.

## Conclusion

"The present times are quite different from the era of Rimsky-Korsakov," said Gusin, with a note of regret, during the discussions on formalism in musical education.[49] In the 1930s, Soviet composers had to read official literature before composing. Starting in 1932, they had to learn to read Party resolutions, and from 1936 they also had to work out how to interpret them. The result of all this reading was the establishment of Soviet repertoire in the curricula, an active encouragement of topical pieces, and a strict adherence to the plan of study. The Rimsky-Korsakov school could not be eradicated while his pupils and second-generation pupils were still teaching at the Conservatory. But the professoriate managed to drop one of his main precepts in composition teaching, which was that work on large-scale forms should only be permitted once students have mastered all the theoretical subjects.

The stylistic turbulence of the 1930s failed to produce any great names at the Conservatory. There was a sense of general decline after the previous decade, when it could boast a whole constellation of stars: not only composers, but also musicologists, performers, and conductors. Although there were no doubt ancillary factors, at the center of the problem was the upheaval inflicted on a teaching tradition that had grown organically from Rimsky-Korsakov's practices and experiences. Those committed to radical change tended to be blind to the oral traditions, to the ad hoc adjustments and leeway offered to students, and saw the Conservatory only in terms of the written regulations and curriculum and some sloppy departures from it. From this point of view, it seemed reasonable to assume that the regulations and curriculum could be changed at will according to the doctrines of the day, and that the resulting perfect system would work best if it was adhered to strictly. They could then honor Rimsky-Korsakov as much as they liked, but they had lost a part of his legacy in the administrative upheaval.

Student composers at the Conservatory after 1936 did take music-history courses for a broader acquaintance with the repertoire, and these included a course on Russian/Soviet music. In the 1940–41 academic year, Year 4 students studied composers of the fin de siècle through to the end of the 1920s. Glazunov was prominent, alongside Lyadov, Taneyev, Kalinnikov, Rachmaninov, and Scriabin. The Prokofiev works listed for study were *fugitives*, *Sarcasms*, the Second Sonata, *The Ugly Duckling*, and the Classical Symphony. Stravinsky's *Firebird* and *Petrushka* were also listed. There were mainstream Soviet works by Dzerzhinsky, Kabalevsky, Uspensky, and Brusilovsky, together with works by various "national" composers from the outlying republics who had studied in Moscow or Leningrad: Lysenko, Paliashvili, Spendiarov, and Tigranian. Listed separately (presumably for reasons of prestige) were Soviet works by Shostakovich (Symphonies 1, 5, and 6) and Myaskovsky (Symphonies Nos. 5, 6, and 16). Khachaturian and Asafyev were also featured, although not prominently. New operas were ideologically fraught, and were thus fading from the curriculum, with the exception of "national" operas such as Victor Uspensky's *Farkhad and Shirin*, and Brusilovsky's *Kyz-Zhibek*. This kind of material generally remained ideologically unimpeachable, and was considered important for wartime efforts.

The centenary of Rimsky-Korsakov's birth, in 1944, had a panegyric character, but with one notable blemish. Aron Ostrovsky (a Conservatory graduate of 1931), broke ranks at the concluding meeting of the celebrations. Rimsky-Korsakov, he said, was being treated superficially and even disdainfully by the curriculum.[50] "This was the sad result of our education inside and outside of the Conservatory walls, because Rimsky-Korsakov is hardly present in our musical life."[51] Ostrovsky mentioned the productions of *The Tale of Tsar Saltan*, *The Snow Maiden*, *The Golden Cockerel*, *The Maid of Pskov*, and *Vera Sheloga*. The centenary celebrations became practically the first public discussion of Rimsky-Korsakov's oeuvre. Six months later, Professor Mikhail Druskin gave a lecture on Rimsky-Korsakov, characterizing him in a reserved and respectful manner that set the tone that was retained by later biographers: "We are commemorating a remarkable public figure, a musician and scholar who wrote a number of textbooks that are still being used today, particularly his harmony and orchestration manuals. We have before us the image of a man of crystalline purity, whose life was dedicated to meeting the extraordinary demands placed on himself and on his art. We remember a musician who defined almost half a century of Russian musical culture—he was its executor."[52]

Great names of the past are brought back to the foreground of public consciousness when an anniversary comes around. For Rimsky-Korsakov, 1958 was the 50th anniversary of his death, and the following year was the 115th anniversary of his birth. A new collection of articles and documents was published by the Leningrad Conservatory, titled *N. A. Rimsky-Korsakov and Musical Education*, compiled under the editorship of the musicologist Semyon Ginzburg. The contributors were all members of the Conservatory Council, and they wrote about Rimsky-Korsakov's multifarious activities and his reception, even including (posthumously, and probably for ironic effect) Ryazanov's old critical assessment of the Rimsky-Korsakov School. The tone of the book is set by the statement that the Rimsky-Korsakov school "played the most important role in the development of Russian music."[53]

Rimsky-Korsakov, the book declared, was among "the most outstanding representatives of the art of music." His pedagogical tradition would "continue to enrich the construction of a multinational Soviet musical culture for a long time to come"; his theoretical works had taken "a very prominent place" in the world's music theory and practice; musicology, meanwhile, was successfully covering the composer's life and work.[54]

# NOTES

1. A. Alekseyev-Boretskiy, "N. I. Zaremba—professor klassa spetsial'noy teorii," *Sankt-Peterburgskaya konservatoriya v mirovom muzïkal'nom prostranstve: Kompozitorskiye, ispolnitel'-skiye, nauchnïye shkolï, 1862–2012* (St. Petersburg: Izdatel'stvo Politekhnicheskogo universiteta, 2013), 302.

2. E. A. Fatykhova, "N. A. Rimskiy-Korsakov—Prepodavatel' teorii muziki (po uchenicheskim tetradyam A. K. Glazunova)," in *Rimskiy-Korsakov: Sbornik statey* (St. Petersburg: Kompozitor, 2008), 177.

3. Here, he could draw on his own experience from his completions of works left unfinished by Borodin and Musorgsky.

4. See N. A. Rimskiy-Korsakov, *Osnovï orkestrovki s partiturnïmi obraztsami iz sobstvennïkh sochineniy*, ed. M. O. Shteynberg, vol. 1 (Berlin, Moscow, St. Petersburg: Rossiyskoye muzïkal'noye izdatel'stvo, 1913), 3.

5. String Quintet D 956, C-Minor Piano Sonata D 958, A-Minor Piano Sonata D 537, *Grande marche heroïque* D 885.

6. N. A. Sokolov, *Imitatsiya na Cantus firmus*, manuscript, NIOR SPbGK (Manuscript Department of the Library of the St. Petersburg Conservatory), No. 6395.

7. "Discussion on Issues of Formalism in Musical Education" at the Leningrad Conservatory (*Diskussiya po voprosam formalizma v muzïkal'nom obrazovanii*), 31 March 1936, transcription, Central State Archive for Literature and the Arts, St. Petersburg, henceforth TsGALI SPb, f. 298, op. 4, d. 31, ll. 147–48v.

8. Yu. N. Tyulin, "Ot starogo k novomu," in *Leningradskaya konservatoriya v vospominaniyakh* (Leningrad: Muzgiz, 1962), 96. Shostakovich was fortunate to have Steinberg as his professor, since the latter was active as a composer, and allowed Shostakovich to show him anything he was working on, including the Eight Preludes, Op. 2; the Suite for Two Pianos, Op. 6; and the First Trio, Op. 8.

9. M. O. Shteynberg, "Vospominaniya o N. A. Rimskom-Korsakove i A. K. Glazunove," in *Leningradskaya konservatoriya v vospominaniyakh*, 41.

10. N. Rimskiy-Korsakov, *Prakticheskiy uchebnik garmonii*, ed. I. I. Vitol' and M. O. Shteynberg, 12th ed. (Petrograd: M. P. Belyayev, 1918).

11. From Example 1, [Compositional] Assignment No. 35, sec. 8, Shostakovich Archive (Moscow), f.1, r.1, yed. khr. 319.

12. Steinberg's introduction to N. A. Rimskiy-Korsakov, *Osnovï orkestrovki*, vii.

13. L. Butir, "Problemï instrumentovki v neopublikovannïkh materialakh N. A. Rimskogo-Korsakova (90–ye godï)," in *Orkestrovïye stili v russkoy muzïke: Sbornik statey*, ed. V. I. Tsïtovich (Leningrad: Muzïka, 1987), 50.

14. M. Rakhmanova, "K bïloy polemike vokrug 'Kitezha,'" *Sovetskaya muzïka* 10 (1984): 82.

15. "Discussion on Issues of Formalism in Musical Education," 3 March 1936, l. 78.

16. "On the Restructuring of Literary and Artistic Organizations," Resolution of the Communist Party Central Committee, 23 April 1932, trans. Marina Frolova-Walker and Jonathan Walker, *Music and Soviet Power 1917–1932* (Woodbridge, UK: The Boydell Press, 2012), 324–25.

17. A. V. Lunacharskiy, "N.A. Rimskiy-Korsakov: Muzïkal'no-kriticheskaya fantaziya k 25-letiyu so dnya smerti," *Izvestiya*, 20 July 1933.

18. "Discussion on Issues of Formalism in Musical Education," 31 March 1936, l. 152v.

19. Gusev's remarks in ibid., l. 71.

20. "Resolution of the General Meeting of Composers and Musicologists," 15 February 1936, *Sovetskaya muzïka* 2 (1936), n.p.

21. "Discussion on Issues of Formalism in Musical Education," 3 March 1936, l. 75.

22. Ibid., l. 87.

23. Ibid., l. 88.

24. Minutes of the 27 February–9 June 1936 Meetings of the Department for Scholarship and Composition, session of 26 April, TsGALI SPb, f. 298, op. 4, yed. khr. 35, l. 4.
25. Ibid., l. 4v.
26. Ibid.
27. Ibid., ll. 142–45.
28. Gusin's remarks, "Discussion on Issues of Formalism in Musical Education," 3 March 1936, l. 71v. This demonstrates that Shcherbachev's attempted reform of 1925 had long since faded from the scene, with a return to the status quo ante.
29. Gnesin's remarks, citing accusations against the Rimsky-Korsakov school, ibid., l. 88.
30. Gnesin's remarks, ibid., l. 89.
31. Gusin's remarks, ibid., l. 76.
32. Gusin's remarks, ibid., ll. 72 and 72v.
33. "Discussion on Issues of Formalism in Musical Education," 31 March 1936, l. 148.
34. Ibid., l. 145.
35. Ibid., l. 139.
36. Ibid., 3 March 1936, l. 75v.
37. Ibid., l. 76v.
38. Ibid., 31 March 1936, l. 166.
39. Yet by 1939, *The Snow Maiden* and *May Night* were deemed comfortable for the voice, and the parts were distributed among the students.
40. "Discussion on Issues of Formalism in Musical Education," 3 March 1936, TsGALI SPb, f. 298, op. 4, d. 31, l. 73.
41. Ibid.
42. Ibid., l. 75v.
43. Ibid., l. 78.
44. Ibid., l. 93.
45. Ibid., l. 75v.
46. Ibid., l. 77v.
47. Ibid., l. 78.
48. Ibid., l. 96.
49. Ibid., l. 78v.
50. Transcript of a conference in memory of Rimsky-Korsakov, 29–30 May 1944, TsGALI SPb, f. 298, op. 4, yed. khr. 397.
51. Ibid., l. 28.
52. Mikhail Druskin, "Rimskiy-Korsakov: Zhizn' i tvorchestvo," transcript of lecture, 30 January 1945, TsGALI SPb, f. 298, op. 4, yed. khr. 451.
53. *N. A. Rimskiy-Korsakov i muzïkal'noye obrazovaniye: Stat'yi i materialï* (Leningrad: Gosudarstvennoye muzïkal'noye izdatel'stvo, 1959), 5.
54. Ibid.

# Afterword

# In Search of Beauty: Autocracy, Music, and Painting in Rimsky-Korsakov's Russia

## LEON BOTSTEIN

"The tyranny of the St. Petersburg bureaucracy is more dramatic, but less omnipresent and probably less fatal to the capacity to enjoy art than the tyranny of our respectable, self-satisfied, and property-loving middle class." Aylmer Maude, Leo Tolstoy's English friend, translator, and biographer penned this observation in the 1899 introduction to his translation of Tolstoy's 1897 slender but blunt book, *What Is Art?*[1] Maude paid tribute to the unexpected and astonishing prominence the arts and letters held in Russia. To the average English reader at the turn of the century, Russia was exotic, alluring, possibly barbaric, and not viewed as an equal among civilized nations. Its system of government—monarchical absolutism—was regressive and despotic. Russia's humiliation in the Crimean War helped solidify the image of Russia as a backwater colossus when compared to England, the model of a democratic constitutional monarchy with an enviable cultural heritage.

Nonetheless, Russia's Imperial autocracy, despite its rigid and intricate bureaucracy, its agrarian economy only slowly experiencing modernization, and not much of a middle class, managed to cultivate a flourishing aesthetic sensibility within its elites. As a result, spectacular achievements in the arts came out of Russia in the nineteenth century. The English mix of materialism and individualism spurred on by thriving commerce and relative prosperity failed to inspire a comparable appreciation of the arts, Maude implied, the political rights, economic well-being, and civic influence of its citizens notwithstanding. Smug complacency and indifference undermined England's conceit of cultural superiority.

Maude's ironic observation helped explain to English readers why Tolstoy believed that *What Is Art?* was pertinent to his Russian readers. It also explained why it was uniquely Tolstoy who could spark a worldwide debate about the nature and purpose of art. Perhaps it was no accident that an eccentric, wealthy Russian nobleman (who now embraced a disciplined, radically ascetic, and anti-modern Christian ethic) had emerged, at the turn of the century, not only as the West's most celebrated living novelist, but also its most prominent spiritual critic. Tolstoy, in his last years, had become an inspiring symbol of a fundamental critique of values and mores associated with ideas of progress and modernity, including property and war. That placed him in a position to question a key truism inherited from the Enlightenment: that democratizing appreciation for the aesthetic dimension of life encouraged ethical behavior and the progress of civilization.

In *What Is Art?* Tolstoy went public with ideas he had been struggling with since the late 1870s and early 1880s. He firmly repudiated his earlier achievements as a writer and challenged the idea that art and the cultivation of some sort of "refined" taste was, if not essential, then at least helpful to the spread of morality and justice in history. Tolstoy argued that art should not be viewed as an autonomous form of life, but as wholly subordinate to morality. Claims on behalf of "pure art" or the validity of aesthetic criteria independent of any overriding ethical imperatives were false. If art were to play a role in the long overdue betterment of humankind, it would be only as "an organ of human life transmitting man's reasonable perception into feeling." Art was subordinate to science (the "true" kind that does not pervert nature) and religion ("Christian teaching in its true meaning"), but owing to its unique power over human emotions it could ultimately replace the role of violence in society. Art's legitimate purpose was to encourage the voluntary "peaceful cooperation of man," without lawyers, courts, the police, or prisons, all as the result of the "free and joyous activity" art inspired. Art was a key instrument in the task of realizing a nonviolent, universal "brotherly union of mankind."[2]

Tolstoy's targets were the assumptions and conceits of a wide swath of middle-class society in Europe and North America that by the end of the nineteenth century had cultivated an engagement with reading and writing, making music in the home and in public, attending the theater, and viewing visual art in galleries and museums. These activities were widely acknowledged markers of self-improvement. But was the growth of the market for fiction, poetry, paintings, sculpture, symphonic concerts, piano recitals, plays, ballet, and opera a sign of progress in terms of moral betterment? For Tolstoy, the answer was no. The enthusiasm for these pastimes masked a decline in virtue and decency.

Humanity's conscience could perhaps be strengthened and uplifted using the evident emotional allure of the arts. But Tolstoy, in 1897, considered what was deemed "art" by practitioners, critics, and consumers to be "counterfeit" art. Art, potentially an ally to virtue, had become a "prostitute," distorting its special and not inconsiderable power to spread the love for humanity by debasing empathy, sympathy, and generosity instead. For Tolstoy, neither Beethoven's Ninth Symphony nor Wagner's *Ring* qualified as true art; they exemplified the corruption of the potential of the aesthetic realm. Guided by his simplified but exacting construct of Christianity (for which he was excommunicated in 1901 from the Orthodox Church), Tolstoy excoriated contemporary norms and taste in the arts.

Tolstoy's attack on conventional wisdom about the arts did not go unnoticed in Russia.[3] Vasili Yastrebstev, Nikolai Rimsky-Korsakov's faithful Boswell, recalled several occasions when Tolstoy's radical views on art were discussed at gatherings in Rimsky's home. In September 1901, when Tolstoy's "absurd" book was mentioned, Rimsky-Korsakov became "so agitated that for one hour he paced back and forth across the room." Yastrebstev (evidently no expert on the dynamics of long marriages) was baffled that Rimsky's wife had been eager to bring up the subject, since she knew "perfectly well how irritating the very mention of this book is to Rimsky-Korsakov." Three years earlier, just after the book appeared in the spring of 1898, another "lively" discussion had taken place at the Rimsky household with Rimsky's collaborator and librettist Vladimir Belsky and the painter Mikhail Vrubel, husband of Nadezhda Zabela-Vrubel, the composer's favorite soprano, all in attendance. The consensus was that the book was, in Yastrebstev's words, "devoted to a total rejection of everything usually considered art, and, above all, beauty."[4]

For Rimsky, the fatal error in Tolstoy's thinking was his dismissal of the idea of an inherent quality of beauty in art. Although Rimsky ranked writers below painters and sculptors (and certainly beneath composers), Tolstoy was among five writers he admired most, the others being Turgenev, Gogol, Lermontov, and Pushkin. Why did Tolstoy's polemic against beauty in art and the independent value of aesthetic norms so irritate the composer? Rimsky met Tolstoy only once, in January of 1898, in Moscow. An argument between them ensued (from which the critic Vladimir Stasov quickly fled). It was, predictably, about the idea of beauty, which Tolstoy declared an "ulcer" on art, something "putrid" and "stinking." Tolstoy abhorred Beethoven and berated himself for not being able to "give up" Chopin. Rimsky, who venerated Chopin as an ideal, and thought Beethoven's greatness unimpeachable, challenged him, and suggested that through beauty, "art ennobles and elevates man's soul." Rimsky cited the value and impact of Tolstoy's prose, observing that Tolstoy's novels were "not simple" and yet "filled with beauty." Tolstoy responded that he considered his novels "worthless"; he "despised" himself for having written them. What irritated Rimsky especially was Tolstoy's ignorance of music. He had no idea who Balakirev was, had no interest in contemporary music—including Rimsky's—and confessed to not being able to sit through *Siegfried*, which he regarded as "revolting."[5]

Tolstoy's criteria for assessing the value of a work of art did not include beauty, understood as a formalist attribute, one contrasted—particularly in late eighteenth- and early nineteenth-century philosophy—with the sublime. The only proper aesthetic criteria by which works of art needed to be judged, according to Tolstoy, were individuality, clarity, and sincerity. Genuine art had to be simple and comprehensible by all, noble and plebian, aristocrat and peasant. Aesthetic value was reduced to a sweetener, or the emotionally appealing coloring of moral medication. As a powerful stimulus to feeling, art had to be personal and genuine.

Consequently, Tolstoy dismissed the idea that art, apart from its moral utility, could be seen as a desirable product of human activity or the imagination. He denied that art could generate a valuable aesthetic experience of beauty (or the sublime) that was disconnected from nature and the human community. In Tolstoy's view, a cult of beauty in art actually undermined the power of art to inspire virtue. Tolstoy had no interest in the potential of music, or any art, to transfigure and elevate the commonplace, and to transcend the mundane by creating a realm of the unreal, the unimagined, and the fantastic. Rimsky was persuaded that Tolstoy's book (which he once vowed he would not read) was bound to do harm. *What Is Art?* would further confuse a younger generation that seemed "generally speaking, not much interested in art."[6]

Rimsky's sharp reaction was rooted in more than Tolstoy's moralistic devaluation of his life's work. Tolstoy's refusal to acknowledge the inherent value of art, his skepticism about his own work and the state of the arts in modern life bore some uncomfortable resemblance to Rimsky's own internal dialogue during moments in his life when he experienced self-doubt and found himself unable to write. Rimsky, first during a period of discouragement between 1882 and 1887 and then in 1892 (after a foray into reading philosophy and musical aesthetics), struggled to formulate his own philosophical justification.[7] Tolstoy's views echoed his deep unease at modern trends from the West, which were increasingly visible at home. Rimsky declared Richard Strauss, a favorite bête noire (the music was "outrageous" and *Zarathustra*, "rubbish"), and Vincent d'Indy, "degenerate." The symptom of a dangerous "confusion" in Russia was the growing taste for Scriabin, whose music Rimsky thought "sick and disturbed." He worried about an excessive emulation of Wagner (whose harmonic ingenuity and dramatic genius he repeatedly acknowledged) among younger composers; it had led them to abandon proportion in musical form and to forget how to write a "melody" and "simple" music (an ideal Rimsky shared with Tolstoy). New music seemed awash in pretentiousness, marked only by harmonic cleverness and dazzling effects in sonority.[8]

Lyricism and poetic beauty, fundamental attributes of Glinka and Mozart (two composers Rimsky ranked above all others) as well as Chopin and Mendelssohn, defined great music for Rimsky.[9] Music, and all art, was, in the end, about beauty. Music inspired humans to "dream" through sounds in ways neither ornate nor "artificial," to find the "immutable" in the experience of musical forms and sounds. Beauty was absent in *verismo*, particularly Mascagni. Leoncavallo produced music that was "sheer trickery," a result of "creative impotence." These composers were as distant from Verdi as "they are from a star in the heavens."[10]

By the mid-1890s, beauty as Rimsky understood it seemed out of fashion. Rimsky felt "lonely and alienated." He hoped that future generations would rediscover classicist aesthetics, but he, like Tolstoy, feared the historic inevitability of a progressive "degeneration" in the arts. Music's "divine" character was born out of spontaneous human creativity. But its capacity to communicate a unique vision of beauty in nature and in the human character and experience was at risk, as was music's superiority to poetry and language. The threat was real. Beauty in music needed to transcend the mundane and conventional, but not become artificial, superficially alluring, "falsely" profound, and needlessly complex.[11]

Despite similarities in Tolstoy's and Rimsky's thinking as to what distinguished good from bad art—transparency, comprehensibility, authenticity, and simplicity—Rimsky had no doubt that music had value apart from moral utilitarianism. His project was to strengthen the role of music in Russia and assert its value as art. This required finding the right accommodation with the Russian state and the monarchy. And it led Rimsky on a career that paralleled and intersected with developments in Russian painting and with the work of Russia's leading visual artists. Indeed, painters and composers in Rimsky's generation confronted a vexing challenge: how could beauty, the realization of art's highest quality, be achieved and defended in the context of Russia's autocracy and radical social inequality?

## Art and Politics

Tolstoy's *What Is Art?* may have struck non-Russian readers as an idiosyncratic diatribe, but it was a late entry in a long line of Russian criticism of the arts, dating back to the 1830s, that explored the proper connection between art and reality. In this critical tradition, art and reality, often distinguished as fundamentally different, were fused together. Art, understood in the sense of "artifice," came under fire as being without value; it was just a diversion for the privileged—a merely formal exercise in entertainment and decoration. Critics began to demand that art, particularly literature, poetry, and prose, be connected to and drawn from reality. This was the view of the literary critic Vissarion Belinsky (1811–1848), who set the criteria by which all subsequent writers, painters, and composers in nineteenth-century Russia expected they would be judged.

Belinsky's generation widely shared the philosophical premise that the aesthetic was essential. The facts of the real world, no matter how grim, did not actually reveal the essence of reality. The spiritual essence of reality, for Belinsky, was embedded in the material. Particularly in the account of history, a "faithful presentation of the facts is impossible with the aid of erudition alone; imagination too is required."[12] The command of the aesthetic meant the capacity to transfigure—with an artistic vision and its formal means—the everyday; great art needed not to falsify or mask the real, but to evoke and reveal it so as to make it unforgettable. Art was "instrumental" in "opening society's eyes to itself" and "awakening its self-consciousness." For Belinsky, a nation's "education is the effect of our literature on the ideas and morals of society."[13]

Belinsky's outrage at the state of Russia's society, laws, and mores lay behind his call for the linkage of art to reality and his demand that art take its substance from the real world. In his famous 1847 letter to Gogol, whose "realism" in *Dead Souls* (1842) Belinsky had held up as a model, he wrote that Russia's "salvation" was in "civilization, enlightenment, and humanity." Art had to play a role in "awakening, in the Russian population, a sense of human dignity lost for so many centuries."[14]

After Belinsky, Nikolai Chernyshevsky (1828–1899) exerted the widest influence on Russian critical debates in the arts during the second half of the nineteenth century. He took one step beyond Belinsky, and in his writings in the 1850s on the relation of art to reality, declared art by definition subordinate to reality. Chernyshevsky, a populist, radical, and revolutionary for whom the reforms of the 1860s were a sham (the 1861 abolition of serfdom, and the 1864 reform of the judiciary guaranteeing public trials by courts), shed the remnants of Belinsky's belief in the existence of a Platonic metaphysical essence embedded in material reality. The only function of art was realism; its task was to reveal and transmit faithfully the evident facts in the world. The purpose of a painting or poem whose subject was cruelty and suffering was to expose the reality of cruelty and suffering.[15]

Rimsky may have belonged to a generation much younger than Belinsky and Chernyshevsky, but he and his contemporaries were keenly aware of the critical discourse they inherited. Nonetheless, unlike Vladimir Stasov (1824–1906), the dominant critic and ideologue on matters of music and painting, Rimsky was never entirely drawn to this line of criticism, whatever "liberal" political views he may have harbored. The radical call for a didactic realism in literature, directed at social reform, could readily be emulated in the visual arts, but its translation into music was far less straightforward, given how inherently problematic the appropriation of the criterion of realism or the promotion of radical social change was for music.[16]

The solution to the obstacle presented by the inherent artificiality of music, particularly instrumental music, was Stasov's notion that music's purpose in Russia was to assert and forge a new, distinctively Russian national sensibility. Realism became nationalism. In 1847 Stasov published his praise of Glinka's use of folk materials. Stasov shared Belinsky's belief that society "should be organic." Music written by Russians needed to "link" Russia's "multitude of people together."[17] Russian musical art could use Russia's past, its landscape, religion, and folk heritage in the service of defining a modern national sensibility. Music's participatory, temporal, and public character made it an ideal vehicle of national consciousness.

For the first two decades of his career, between 1862 and 1882, Rimsky-Korsakov pursued this goal and the idea that a distinctive Russian musical art could be developed from sources to be found in Russia's history, literature, and rural culture. He shared the conceit expressed by Maude about a special Russian affinity for the arts (Belinsky linked it to a Russian penchant for extremes). But Rimsky did not view the task of shaping a national voice as demanding the wholesale dismissal of the traditions of music developed in the West. Rather, much as Belinsky argued for literature, Russian music needed to take its place on the world stage as a distinctive equal. The imperative, for Rimsky, quickly acquired two aspects: to develop something uniquely Russian and at the same time achieve aesthetic preeminence in the world. Rimsky, toward the end of his career, feared an erosion of commitment to these twin goals; he detected a "decadence" that "wafted from Western Europe," infecting a new generation.[18]

By the time of his late encounter with Tolstoy, Rimsky had concluded that the content of Russian music ought to be national, but its form, its path to greatness, and therefore its beauty depended on an adherence to timeless norms of the art of music. Russian music needed to gain universal acceptance through a distinctly Russian augmentation of the ideal of the beautiful. The historic achievements from Western Europe ought not be imitated. They required appropriation and absorption, following the example of Glinka, in order to create a unique Russian synthesis of the national and universal that included the command of an international standard of compositional technique.

At the end of his career in 1907 Rimsky deconstructed the nationalist conceit of the Mighty Handful—the Kuchka—formed in the 1860s, and subsequently ardently promoted by Stasov as the genuine Russian "realist" protagonists in music: "In a certain sense Saint-Saëns and even Massenet are 'kuchkists,'" Rimsky observed, and "what's more, Tchaikovsky's *Queen of Spades* also conforms to the principles of the 'Kuchka.' And those principles are the following: 1) an intelligible and interesting libretto, 2) artistic truth, and 3) intelligent utilization of all the rich resources of today's orchestra and harmony, while at the same time giving primary importance (predominance) to the voice."[19] The achievement of Balakirev, Musorgsky, Borodin, and Rimsky himself was their contribution to a universal aesthetic criterion of judgment: musical beauty. Ultimately the national element had been a means to a cosmopolitan end. Rimsky took pride in the fact that he had written the music for *The Tsar's Bride* without a single authentic folk melody apart from "Slava," familiar to audiences on account of its presence in Beethoven's "Razumovsky" String Quartet, Op. 59, No. 2, and Musorgsky's *Boris Godunov.*

Rimsky's resistance to the intense Slavophile ideological fervor of Balakirev and Stasov—his tempered nationalism and his deeper respect for the craft of music composition from the West—all suggest that his patriotism had its roots in an earlier tradition of loyalty to Russia. His allegiance was to the monarchical state. His social status, lineage, family, and career as a Navy officer shaped his views. Rimsky understood that privilege, granted by birth, permitted him to cultivate a Russian sensibility for aesthetic values, and therefore to pursue a life in music.

In the thirty years prior to Rimsky's birth, in the decades following the Congress of Vienna, art and culture flourished among Russia's elite under the watchful control and patronage of the Imperial Court. After the defeat of the Decembrist mutiny in 1825, prospects for a successful agitation within the aristocracy, gentry, and *raznochintsy* (individuals outside the system of formal legal status) for political participation, rights, and social reform became remote. Art and culture thrived in its place. Art and an aesthetic sensibility became valued, even in the critical tradition of Belinsky and Chernyshevsky, as a means of promoting social change within an absolutist regime. At the same time, a tacit alliance between artists and the autocratic state emerged that used art to affirm the state's monopoly of authority over society.[20]

Russia's social and economic "backwardness" and the centrality of the Imperial bureaucracy—fundamental differences from the West—had two unintended consequences during the second half of the nineteenth century. Aesthetic values of refinement, taste, and creativity in the educated elite flourished at the expense of any change in broadening access within society to political power. At the same time, the social, political, and economic realities that outraged successive generations from Belinsky on—Russia's vast human suffering and history of oppression—were valorized as sources for art and culture. Not political change, but a consciousness about society, its ills and shortcomings—a discourse of self-analysis and criticism—became the goal. Within that discourse nationalism—the ambition to create, through the arts, a distinctive Russian national pride—became a dominant objective.[21] But by the late 1890s, a period of economic modernization, this symbiosis between the state and the arts was seen as increasingly fragile.

Rimsky also understood that Russia's entrance onto the world stage in the arts in the mid-nineteenth century drew unexpected strength from two unique national sources: 1) the conflict between Westernizers, who pursued the path symbolized by Peter the Great, and cultural nationalists or Slavophiles, who celebrated the distinction and superiority of Slavic culture in Russia, privileging pre-Petrine sources in Russian culture, particularly those from the East; and 2) the persistence of and challenge to centralized control by the monarchical state over public life and its institutions.

Rimsky positioned himself between Westernizers and Slavophiles. He was determined to assist Russian musicians to learn from the Italian, French, and German traditions. The acquisition of technique and skill by Russians needed to be competitive. Russian music had to integrate normative criteria of quality as part of its newly constructed national character. At the same time, such formal aesthetic aims required an allegiance to local traditions and history. Russia's arrival late on the international musical and cultural scene—its comparative innocence—and its traditionalist agrarian social structure as well as its distinct language and religious tradition lent it an advantage in the arts. Its national and folk roots remained rich, unexplored, and therefore not near exhaustion.

The second source that set Russia apart—the dynamics of the relation of the artist to the state—had a defining moment during the career of Russia's most venerated cultural figure: Pushkin. After the failed Decembrist revolt, Pushkin embraced the idea of a constructive, supportive alliance between artists and intellectuals and the autocratic monarchy. Nobility of birth and its privileges within state-mandated social hierarchies fostered an interior freedom characteristic of the spiritual nobility of the artist. Independence from politics, ceding to the monarchy a monopoly on political administration and control, and not citizen individualism could permit true freedom and independence, in art and thought. The "independent writer-nobleman" became an ideal made possible by autocracy.[22] Rimsky exploited this construct of the individuality and inner freedom of the artist. The composer Mikhail Gnesin recalled that his teacher Rimsky ended up pleasing no partisans of any school. "He tirelessly fought," Gnesin recalled, "against everything that weakens an artist and keeps him from working toward his purpose."[23]

The writer and critic Alexander Herzen, citing the influential philosopher Peter Chaadaev (1794–1825), put the matter less generously. Under the monarchy, in the early nineteenth century, "culture . . . had only given new means of oppression." The "worst" of outcomes could be imagined: a Russia defined by "enlightened slaves."[24] The Russian privileging of the aesthetic underscored an ideology in which spiritual and intellectual freedom alone was sufficient, and compatible with the absence of political freedom defined by legal egalitarianism and citizen rights. Before 1861, art was even compatible with serfdom. An aristocracy of taste was nurtured by rigid absolutism. The depoliticization of the concept of individual freedom was in part the legacy of early nineteenth-century German Idealism. Outside of German-speaking Europe, nowhere had there been as marked an enthusiasm for Fichte, Schelling, and Hegel as in Russia.

Tolstoy's challenge was therefore not only theological but political—a radical challenge to the way in which art and culture had legitimated despotism in his lifetime. The late nineteenth-century juxtaposition of autocracy, a pre-industrial communal agrarianism, and a particular Russian sensibility for beauty on the one hand, and citizen-based political freedom, the industrial, individualism, and disease (in the form of debased taste) on the other, was implicit in the debate surrounding Tolstoy's views on art. For Russians, America—the United States—played a small but significant role in this contrast. Herzen, in 1858 and again in 1866, compared Russia and America as "meeting on the other side" of a Europe in which civilization had "ground to a halt." A natural affinity existed between Russia and America even though these new powers were headed in opposite directions. Russia's path was toward "communal fusion" whereas America was breaking down into mere "individuals."[25]

The Russian fascination with the notion that it shared with America a historical destiny vis-à-vis Europe prompted Prince Sergei Mikhailovich Volkonsky (1860–1937) to give a series of eight lectures in the United States between February 1896 and May 1897. Given the apparent affinity between these two nations, Volkonsky sought to counter the insufficient "idea" Americans had of Russia or its people. "So little is yet known," he lamented, although America and Russia, beginning with de Tocqueville and Friedrich Kürnberger, had become points of comparison and objects of fear and envy with respect to Europe. Both nations were raw, youthful, and exotic powers. Volkonsky's purpose of promoting a sympathetic understanding of Russia among America's "intelligentsia" seemed imperative.[26]

The moment to fill the gap in mutual understanding had arrived. Volkonsky observed that during the "last twenty years" a "sudden interest" in Russian writers had "broken out": "I do not know whether in any country more splendor surrounds the wonderful figure of Leo Tolstoy than here in America."[27] Art, through literature, had emerged as Russia's most potent export, its most visible accomplishment. (Tchaikovsky's international fame, and his 1891 American tour, seems to have left little impression on Volkonsky.) The prominence of Tolstoy's polemic against beauty and autonomous aesthetic values therefore inspired Volkonsky to end his lecture series with a rebuttal. The significance of a distinctly Russian sensibility for beauty framed Volkonsky's effort to relieve American audiences of their fear and skepticism.

Volkonsky tempered the exoticism of Russia's nationalist distinctiveness. From Russia's "temporary and local" qualities he deduced "abstract" and "eternal elements of moral or artistic beauty." He cited Nikolai Danilevsky, who, in his 1869 *Russia and Europe,* celebrated the vibrancy and uniqueness of Russian civilization and warned, like Rimsky-Korsakov, against the influence of a tired and disintegrating Europe. "Beauty is the only spiritual quality of matter," Volkonsky asserted. Therefore "responsiveness" to beauty, to the aesthetic, represents the highest aim of human development. It was a key to peace, "one of the greatest powers which work at the destruction of those barriers which have been erected against human intercourse by national distinctions."[28]

The appreciation of beauty, a hallmark of modern Russia, could make Russia an ally in a worldwide effort to transcend the divisive politics of power, religion, and property. Since Tolstoy had challenged this conceit, Volkonsky predicted that "the philosopher shall not force out the artist.... The repentant author will not be able to erase himself from the list of the benefactors of humanity, for the artist in him has embodied in beauty too many great ideas."[29] Volkonsky took his own refuge in philosophy, citing Vladimir Solovyov's 1889 essay "Beauty in Nature," in which the aesthetic takes priority and assigns value to the quotidian and therefore lends moral and ethical value to life: "Beauty . . . is the better part of our real world, the one which not only exists, but is worthy of existence."[30] The essence of human freedom was therefore interior, within the realm of the mind. The exclusion from politics and the absolute power assumed by the state did not impede the flowering of the human spirit.

In 1899 Volkonsky took over as head of the Imperial theaters, much to Rimsky's delight, as Volkonsky had been a genuine admirer. He immediately arranged to have *Sadko* staged at the Mariinsky, with sets based on the work of painter Viktor Vasnetsov, and he went on to produce *The Tsar's Bride* in the 1901–1902 season. Volkonsky's appointment undid the damage that came from Tsar Nicholas II's striking *Sadko* from the list of new productions in 1897. The Tsar's refusal had led to Rimsky's somewhat reluctant but fruitful association with Savva Mamontov's private opera venture. Volkonsky (who wrote criticism as well) quickly sought to enlist Rimsky as an ally, commissioning a new work (which never materialized) and his membership on the artistic oversight committee for the opera. "You stand at the summit of our musical world and we cannot do anything without you," Volkonsky was purported to have told Rimsky.[31] The respect was mutual. Rimsky was not only grateful for Volkonsky's patronage, but during a high point in Rimsky's career—between the late 1880s and the political crises of 1905—Rimsky shared Volkonsky's views concerning the link between art and life and the place of the aesthetic within Russia's distinctive national self-image.[32]

In 1958, Vladimir Nabokov, in an effort to give Americans some notion of the conditions faced by Russian writers who achieved international prominence—Gogol, Tolstoy, Turgenev, Dostoevsky, and Chekhov—quipped that "nineteenth-century writers, composers, and painters" in Russia were "quite certain that they lived in a country of suppression and slavery." Comparing their lot to conditions in the Soviet Union, "they had the immense advantage . . . of not being compelled to say that there was no oppression and slavery." Nabokov identified two forces that had "struggled for the possession of the artist's soul" in pre-revolutionary Russia. The first was the state, the government. Its primary tool was censorship, which plagued everyone, including Rimsky and Alexander Ostrovsky, who wrote the play *The Snow Maiden*. The second force was the critics, the "anti-governmental, social-minded utilitarian criticism, the political, civic, radical thinkers of the day."[33]

Nabokov stressed the stupidity and ineptness of censors and the Russian bureaucracy, as well as their relatively small numbers. Censorship, which relaxed somewhat in the 1860s, was strengthened during the two decades before 1905. But it was porous, and inconsistent. The artist was therefore threatened and harassed, but in spite of that, still free. Nabokov understood the distinctive monopoly the Russian state had over the public sphere, economic growth, and social mobility. This persisted even after the humiliation of the Crimean War and the increasingly rapid industrialization under Alexander II and Alexander III. The composers in the Kuchka as well as Tchaikovsky and Anton Rubinstein were dependent on the state and Imperial patronage and consent, although Tchaikovsky and Rubinstein enjoyed income from royalties, commissions, and fees that stemmed from their international careers. Only toward the end of the century did private patronage, in opera and painting, begin to play a serious role in cultural life. Western observers were astonished at the absence of a mediating middle class, or any self-image among Russians as citizens.

After the 1861 emancipation of the serfs, an ideal rooted in a Russian agrarian culture of communal self-governance took hold. Neither the abolition of serfdom nor the renascence of traditional communal idealism challenged the state's bureaucratic stranglehold however. The state still categorized and controlled the population according to birth and occupation. The legal and administrative absolutism of the state and its agents as well as the privileges of status and wealth accorded to a landed aristocracy and the official bureaucracy gave Russian life and politics an exotic character. In world opinion, Russia's political and social structure seemed unique, as was its musical art—the studied "Orientalist" and Russian rural folk-derived devices employed by nationalist composers, audible in Balakirev's *Tamara*, Rimsky's *Russian Easter Overture*, Musorgsky's *Boris Godunov*, Borodin's music from the unfinished *Prince Igor*, Tchaikovsky's *Marche slave*, and last but not least, Stravinsky's three legendary ballets, *The Firebird, Petrushka,* and *The Rite of Spring*.

The assassination of Alexander II in 1881 and the reactionary policies of his successor increased the threat posed by anarchism and populism; so did the persistence of illiteracy and poverty, both urban and rural. Yet a state autocracy that separated social structure and economic life from politics, both legal and administrative, and ceded to a monarch and his operatives the monopoly on the control of public life not only survived, but tightened its grip. In Russia, there was little effective competition for power between society and state, no semblance of a Montesquieu-inspired political rule through a balance of competing constituencies and authorities, framed around notions of individual citizen rights (visible in England and France, and to a lesser extent in post-1870 Germany and the post-1867 Austro-Hungarian Empire). Art and the aesthetic thrived within this political inertia.

Between 1881 and 1905, writers, composers, and painters all exploited and benefited from the state's dominance and had little incentive to challenge or upend it. The three pillars of the official state credo crafted by Count Sergei Uvarov (1786–1855) and promulgated under Nicholas I in 1833, continued to frame the state's national ideology: orthodoxy, autocracy, and nationality.[34] The arts, particularly music, remained dependent on the state for funds, space, and the right to perform, and after 1862, the opportunity for musicians to train and gain official sanction and status. Painting also depended on state-approved training, public space, and official commissions and therefore the state. Only literature and printed materials could more easily elude the grip of a system that once earned the term, now in disrepute, "oriental despotism."

Max Weber, who studied the Russian social and political system in the wake of 1905, inspired Karl Wittfogel in 1957 to consider pre-revolutionary Russia as a case in point. After analyzing the "extraordinary staying power of the Tsarist bureaucracy," Wittfogel concluded that, given the state's control over the economy and public sphere, and "considering the role of the Tsarist bureaucracy in rural and urban society, it is difficult to avoid the decision that even at the beginning of the twentieth century the men of the state apparatus were stronger than society."[35]

Resistance, defiance, and criticism were never in short supply within the Russian intelligentsia, whether before 1861 or after 1881. These were met with censorship, imprisonment, and exile. But most exiles left either voluntarily (Turgenev) or with sanction (Herzen was able to access his wealth from abroad without interference), and most could return, as the painter Vasili Vereschagin ultimately did. Even the radical revolutionary populist Chernyshevsky, who fought openly against the autocratic regime and was sentenced to death, was in the end not executed, only exiled. Given that a large segment of the literary and artistic world was of noble or gentry origin, and of comparatively high status, harshness alternated with benevolence. In this contradictory manner of patronage, approval (often by the tsar himself), and suppression, the arts were inscribed into the autocratic system. Both composers and painters, Westernizers as well as Slavophiles, used foreign travel as a safety valve to seek relief from the oppressive aspects of government control, although Rimsky, who had circumnavigated the globe as a Navy officer before embarking on a musical career, was less enamored of sojourns in Europe than many of his colleagues.

The uneasy symbiosis between artists and the state brought its inevitable consequence in critical contempt, guilt, and resentment. Therefore, it is not surprising that Nabokov's second force fighting for the soul of artists was the critics. The intensity, virulence, and variety of printed criticisms were remarkable, even in music. Criticism assumed an important role precisely on account of the vulnerability of artists as clients of the state—whether as indirect (through the right to publish and perform) or direct beneficiaries (through patronage). Criticism represented the pressure from within society, distinct from, if not independent of, the state apparatus. However, the power exerted by critics was limited by the extent of literacy. According to the census of 1897, the literacy rate for the Russian Empire was 24 percent, most of it concentrated in the European West; the rural literacy rate was 19.4 percent. By comparison, in 1900 the literacy rate in the United States was 90 and in Brazil 35 percent. By 1870, England boasted a 76 percent literacy rate and France 69 percent.[36] Literary and aesthetic criticism in the Russian nineteenth century was contained within the narrow social and economic confines of the public sphere that included the state bureaucracy and the Imperial Court. Those same narrow confines defined the audience for painting, literature, and music.

As Nabokov pointed out, criticism of the arts from the mid-1830s on focused on the role of art in resisting autocracy and highlighting human suffering, social inequality, oppression, and cruelty. The leading protagonists demanded that art and literature in Russia concern itself with contemporary life. Realism and naturalism were the proper stylistic means for social criticism. Chernyshevsky, in his 1853 book on the relationship between art and reality, called for art to play a role in generating a populist national revolution that would lead to a uniquely Russian communal society. As Belinsky argued to Gogol, the public "looks upon Russian writers as its only leaders, defenders, and saviors against Russian autocracy, orthodoxy, and nationality"—Uvarov's three pillars of the Russian state.[37] Tolstoy, in 1897, knew that Belinsky's hopes had been dashed, not only by its writers but also by its composers and painters.

In the late 1860s and 1870s, Rimsky and his contemporaries were familiar with the competing arguments about how art might play a decisive role in political and social change: one that argued for reform, the emulation of the West, and the integration of liberal ideals, and one that sought the spread of a specifically Russian populist nationalism. Both favored realism and naturalism. Stasov, the dominant voice in music and the visual arts who first named the Kuchka, insisted on an aesthetic nationalist realism drawn from Russia's Eastern roots, its religion, and its unique agrarian society. He avoided Western liberalism and the call for radical political change. Music's role should be focused on redefining only one of Uvarov's trinity: nationality, leaving autocracy and orthodoxy untouched. None of the kuchkists sought to undermine the state or its autocratic hold on art and society.

But the criticism of art, whether in the Westernizing direction or the Slavophile, never went as far as Tolstoy to deny that art possessed value on its own terms, and that the aesthetic should be judged apart from its impact. From the start of Rimsky-Korsakov's career, however, the focus on art as a medium of social criticism through realism exerted only a modest influence. He honored his family lineage. He took his place, like his brother, in the service of the monarchy. He maintained his connection to the Navy, albeit through the medium of its regimental bands. As he matured, he distanced himself from Stasov's narrow notion of a national music without abandoning his interest in Russian folk music, the Russian landscape, Russian history and mythology. Rather, he saw in them unique and purely artistic sources.

Rimsky's atttidue to Uvarov's three pillars was marked by a growing detachment. Although he served in the Imperial Chapel, he was never possessed of a deep mystical or ritual attachment to religion and orthodoxy. He was not a rebel, but neither was he an enthusiast for autocracy. He sought Imperial patronage. He resented censorship, but was content to work around it. He worked for the professionalization and economic independence of musicians. He came to value the private support of the arts offered by the merchant wealth of Mitrofan Belyayev and Mamontov, even though he preferred the official venues and status of the Imperial theaters.[38] He devoted himself to a state-sponsored conservatory, and state-sanctioned organizations, the Russian Musical Society, and the Free School.[39]

Rimsky consistently displayed national pride. He smarted against the smug assumption of superiority by German, Italian, and French musicians, while acknowledging the achievements and even the superiority of many visiting performers. He held up Haydn, Mozart, and Chopin as models, but as models equal to Glinka.[40] Toward the end of his career he drifted further away from the quest for Russian uniqueness. He questioned the validity of declaring the existence of a specifically Russian school, and subordinated the idea of a national art to a cosmopolitan, transnational, universal definition of great music. Music should not be "national" but "universal" in form, leaving only the material, music's content, to be national and folk.[41]

Rimsky believed in immutable aesthetic principles governing tonal music and its forms. Aesthetic beauty in sound and the effective control of time and duration through music were ends in themselves. He valued form, along with the expressiveness made possible by the musically beautiful. A unique sensibility was achieved by the inspired use of melody, rhythm, and harmony. Opera ultimately gave Rimsky the widest berth to realize his musical ideals and augment a traditional genre of compositional practice tied to the Russian language. Rimsky was unexpectedly receptive to new influences. He took what he wanted from Wagner but never "liked" the music or lost the sense that "there was something wrong with" it owing to its "lack of real form and necessary proportion."[42]

In his pursuit of a distinctly Russian compositional achievement worthy of a successor to Glinka, and remaining a more explicit cultural nationalist than Tchaikovsky, Rimsky gave tacit consent to the peculiar privilege afforded him by his genteel origins and the monopoly of the autocratic state. As an artist, he could exercise his freedom to communicate to the elite public as composer and teacher. His goal was to express musical beauty with a distinctive Russian character, music that was original and intimate, contemplative and lyrical. He sought to convey the imagined rather than the historical, the personal rather than the heroic, even when the subject or context of a composition was historical.

## Politics and the Fairy Tale

As the euphoria and expectations of the 1860s inspired by the abolition of serfdom wore off, Rimsky-Korsakov's retreat from history as source of national inspiration gained momentum. He expressed enthusiasm for the ideal of "wonderful, poetic beauty"—the words he used to describe his impression of Alexander Ostrovsky's play, *The Snow Maiden*, on his second reading in 1880. Finding beauty within the pre-Christian, pagan, and early Christian Russian fairy-tale world became increasingly attractive. The 1860s reforms had turned out to be more limited than had been hoped (for example, censorship continued, particularly to the exasperation of Ostrovsky). Disappointment emboldened both radicalism and a conservative reaction. Between the assassination of Alexander II in 1881 and the accession of Alexander III, and the military humiliations Russia experienced during the Russo-Japanese War (Port Arthur and Tsushima), autocracy reasserted itself. The conservative, liberal, and radical reactions all sought inspiration from a distant Russian past that foregrounded a vision of community solidarity over the Western ideal of a society of property-holding individuals.

Within the post-1881 context of a search for sources of national ideals, Pushkin's fragile truce between art and despotism did not lose its relevance. Artists, composers, and writers were faced with two contrasting models from Russian literary Romanticism. As Friedrich Bodenstedt, who was the first to translate Lermontov into German, observed in 1852, following Herzen's view, Pushkin found a "bridge" of understanding and reconciliation by separating "art from life." Lermontov, on the other hand, understood art as "inseparable" from life, and brought the two together.[43] After 1881, under the watchful eye of a state that reasserted its monopoly on political power, Pushkin and Lermontov became reference points for future aesthetic interpretations and inventions of a national heritage for contemporary audiences. Lermontov, a favorite of Belinsky's, drew his "substance" more closely "from the life of his nation."

Rimsky had begun his career as a composer under the domineering guidance of Mily Balakirev. Stasov and Balakirev's strident assertion of a unique national voice was focused on a rural folk heritage and the distinct attributes of the Russian language. The latter was exemplified in music of Dargomyzhsky's *The Stone Guest* in which a distinct approach to recitative and word setting closely aligned with the Pushkin text was audible.[44] This aesthetic nationalism implicitly affirmed the political status quo. Their rejection of Western (German and French) compositional practice was more rhetorical than actual, since all of the kuchkists looked carefully at Beethoven, Schumann, and even Meyerbeer. Nonetheless, their acceptance of an aristocratic amateurism, and their contempt for efforts to professionalize music and composition (represented by Anton Rubinstein) masked a critique of European liberalism and a defense of Russian aristocratic habits.

Rimsky, however, clung to the example set by Glinka, in which the Russian found a voice in the context of a cosmopolitan and international musical culture. Before 1862, as César Cui observed, composers were self-educated, playing through everything, passing harsh judgments, disparaging Mozart and Mendelssohn, praising Berlioz and Liszt, and debating forms of instrumental music, the song, and opera. Ambitious and strikingly self-critical, Rimsky struck out on his own. He accepted a teaching post at the new Conservatory and befriended Tchaikovsky and taught himself the craft of composition—harmony, counterpoint, and orchestration. Rimsky, consistent with his notion that composers needed to absorb and respond to shifting influences around them, was skillfully eclectic, integrating strategies he had gleaned from Bach, Mozart, Chopin, and Liszt. He noted that "my newly sprung tendency toward cantabile and rounded forms found little favor" with his Kuchka comrades.[45]

Rimsky remembered that when Ostrovsky's *The Snow Maiden*, a "spring-time fairy tale," was first published in 1873, he had read it but it had left no impression. He asked, "Were the ideas of the sixties still alive in me, or did the demands, current in the seventies, to be taken from so-called *life* hold me in their grip? Or had Musorgsky's naturalism carried me away on its current?"[46] But in 1880, fantasy and allegory, the simplicity of a folk-style myth without Christian symbols offered a way forward, bypassing history and classic Russian literature as sources. A spiritual realism rooted in an imagined national consciousness could assert the autonomy of the aesthetic in a distinct Russian manner.

The opera Rimsky wrote based on Ostrovsky's *Snow Maiden* became the composer's favorite work. Its subject matter, a fairy tale set in an imaginary kingdom in the Russian landscape in which nature gods and human love interact, contrasted sharply with Musorgsky's and Borodin's use of historical subject matter in opera, or with the adaptation and use of revered poetic texts by Tchaikovsky (Pushkin) and Rubinstein (Lermontov). *The Snow Maiden* was non-naturalistic, fantastic, and yet contemporary. Whatever "realism" in terms of its inherent political argument and its Slavophilism existed was cloaked in universal symbolism. *The Snow Maiden* was also a departure for Ostrovsky and unique in his body of work. His fame and career resulted from a theater of naturalist social criticism and realist drama. He had pursued the Lermontov path. And he returned to it after *Snow Maiden*, which was not a real success on stage; even Tolstoy derided the work, which surprised Ostrovsky.[47] Rimsky's opera fared little better at its premiere in St. Petersburg in 1882. The first performance in Moscow in 1885 was a modest success.

Ostrovsky's seemingly innocent fairy tale suggested the autonomous magic of visual imagery, simple human emotion, and poetic expression and readily found its champions in music. Rimsky knew that Tchaikovsky had composed the incidental music for the play in 1873 (his Opus 12). Tchaikovsky's patron Nadezhda von Meck, writing in 1878 after declaring that true Russian music had only two exponents, Glinka and Tchaikovsky, and urging a more aggressive effort to sell Tchaikovsky's music abroad, expressed her delight at a forthcoming performance of the work. Tchaikovsky replied that his *Snow Maiden* may not be his "best" music, but it "was one of my favorite offspring." Despite the lasting rapprochement between Rimsky and Tchaikovsky that occurred in the 1870s, in 1882 Tchaikovsky resented that his younger colleague had written an opera on the play, and avoided seeing it. When Tchaikovsky finally studied the score of Rimsky's opera, he expressed "amazement" and was "ashamed to confess, envied him." The 1873 success of Tchaikovsky's incidental music, and the composer's own attachment to it may have inspired Rimsky. Both he and Tchaikovsky had recognized in Ostrovsky's play a synthesis of traditionalist Russian national sentiment with a contemporary assertion of the autonomy of the aesthetic, a recognition that led both composers to use folk material in their settings.[48]

Rimsky was attracted to the formal potential of Ostrovsky's play, its ceremonial, ritual elements as well the "fantastic" aspect, overtly distant from modernity but resolutely Russian, and in its evident allegorical but not explicitly nostalgic character. The pagan element surrounding sun worship and the didactic innocence of the protagonists inspired Rimsky to use an orchestral palette reminiscent of Glinka's *Ruslan*. He experimented with his own approach to leitmotifs. In the opera, he fused Glinka-like set pieces together in, as he put it, a Wagner-like manner. *The Snow Maiden* made Rimsky feel like "a fully matured composer who had finally come to stand on his own feet."[49] He had achieved a Mozartian transparency using a Russian subject matter defined by human simplicity and innocence.

Rimsky's direction in *The Snow Maiden* would lead Richard Strauss to comment, in 1907, that "this is all very well, but unfortunately, we are no longer children." He was unintentionally perceptive. In the 1880s, Rimsky viewed the loss of a classical sense of proportion—a feature of Wagner— and therefore musical beauty, as a sign of decline and a dangerous if seductive loss of innocence. Rimsky found in the modern fairy tale a new route to the reassertion of classical values. That Russia didn't have "Bachs and Palestrinas" was an advantage, since it lent Russian music based on folk practices a contemporary vibrancy. With *The Snow Maiden* Rimsky was repeating the example of Glinka, who appeared, totally unexpectedly, "like the Greek Minerva . . . fully equipped with all the artistic ideas and compositional techniques of his time," making him "unique."[50] Indeed, Glinka's first great opera had been historical and his second a Pushkin fairy tale.

Strauss's 1907 quip revealed his own defensiveness. The contrast between the cultural politics of Russia and Wilhelmine Germany was less pro-nounced than Strauss's cultural chauvinism allowed him to acknowledge. Rimsky's critique of Strauss's music—that it was decadent, pretentious, ugly, overblown, and bereft of genuine musical beauty— echoed similar attacks at home. Many critics in turn-of-the-century Germany envied the comparative vitality of the folk traditions in Slavic cultures. German reactionary nationalists, beginning in the 1880s, decried the atrophy of pre-industrial cultural continuities in their nation. The path encouraged by this cultural pessimism and invented nostalgia (one Strauss chose to avoid) was pursued by more than one post-Wagnerian German composer. German nationalist composers sympathetic to the vogue of "*völkisch*" culture and the chauvinism of William II's imperialist and autocratic monarchy sought to reconnect contemporary music with a German folk tradition, its history and legends.

Engelbert Humperdinck's *Hänsel und Gretel*, whose premiere Strauss conducted, made its sensational debut in 1893, and Max von Schillings's first opera, *Ingwelde*, premiered in 1894.[51] In 1903, Friedrich Klose succeeded with *Ilsebill*, another fairy-tale opera. In 1906, Strauss's closest rival Hans Pfitzner premiered his *Christ Elflein*, a Christmas tale. In symphonic music, tone poems of Siegmund von Hausegger such as *Barbarossa* (1899) and *Wieland der Schmied* (1904) seemed perilously similar to Russian works such as Balakirev's *Russia* (1889) and Glazunov's *Stenka Razin* (1885). The collapse of the dream of an English-style constitutional monarchy in post-1870 Germany and the evisceration and co-optation of the aspirations of liberalism led to the spread of a depoliticized concept of freedom not dissimilar from that nurtured in Russia. After the accession of Wilhelm II in 1888, the relationship of the individual to state resembled trends in Russia. These diverged sharply from Anglo-American and French traditions. Russia shared with Germany the currency of the notion that individual freedom is spiritual, subjective, interior, and aesthetic and not political, a conception that assigned the arts a privileged role consistent with monarchical power. Modern fairy tales set in some distant past emerged as an ideal medium to reconcile art and autocracy among proponents of a reactionary, conservative German cultural chauvinism.

The darker side of Rimsky's accommodation with the monarchical system, his liberal sympathies (including the absence of anti-Semitism) notwithstanding, was that until 1905, he accepted the role of art and culture as an instrument of legitimation, as an overt defense of tradition. At best, the fairy tale contained a critique buried under the surface of distant unreality. Rimsky's visceral rejection of Tolstoy's extreme radicalization of the notion that art needed to be justified by its role in improving society and promoting social justice was motivated by an understanding that the defense of art as autonomous was never, in the end, apolitical. The ideology of beauty contains within it claims about harmony, consonance, balance, and universal virtues closely aligned with claims to truth and reason. The cultivation of beauty, as a stable ideal immune from historical progress, provides in its aesthetics both a concealed critique and a disregard of the social and political status quo. The assumption of timelessness and universality in the ideal of musical beauty undermines the idea of progress, both in art and in human affairs, rendering the political subordinate.

For Rimsky, beauty in art and the innocence and simplicity of fairy tales and the focus on the personal lives of historic figures, as in *The Tsar's Bride*, constituted ethical parallels to classicism—the assertion of "healthy" traditional human values that were at the same time "realistically" and evidently Russian. This explains his skepticism and annoyance—his allegation of decadence—with respect to Scriabin and Strauss, who saw themselves as protagonists of a new modern age. Rimsky's music rarely displayed the attributes Herzen described as the three "chief strings of the Russian lyre" in its literature: "melancholy, skepticism and irony."[52] Nor did Rimsky harbor self-aggrandizing illusions; he saw himself more as a craftsman, committed to restraint and clarity. He was like Salieri, and not exceptional, like Mozart. Gnesin remembered Vyacheslav Karatygin's comment that Rimsky thought he had the "soul" of Mozart and the "mind" of Salieri.[53] He feared he would be forgotten; he never lost his self-critical modesty.

Rimsky's ambition, to fashion a Russian ideal of poetic beauty in music, led him away from a conventional approach to finding equivalents to naturalism or realism in music. The historical and national took shape within the realm of the fantastic and the decorative, moderated by Rimsky's own brand of classicist restraint. He therefore kept his distance from symbolism, a direction that became visible at the end of the nineteenth century alongside the radical aestheticism of Serge Diaghilev's *Mir isskustva* (World of Art) circle. Rimsky's drift away from the ideology of Stasov, the overt musical nationalism that defined the legacy of the Kuchka, and his deepening retrospective criticism of Musorgsky's lack of craft during the 1890s, particularly after the deaths of Tchaikovsky and Rubinstein—the Russian composers with the greatest international reputation—brought him nearer to Tchaikovsky's closest musical colleague (and friend of Tolstoy and his wife), Sergei Taneyev.

Rimsky was deeply impressed by the beauty and craft in Taneyev's opera *Oresteia* (1894), which he got to know in the late 1890s.[54] Rimsky's Prelude-Cantata *From Homer* (1901) was inspired by Taneyev's turn to Greek classical material as a promising source for dramatic music written by a Russian. Taneyev had set Greek tragedy brilliantly, in Russian and with distinctly Russian music. He had shown a different route to national assertion through the arts, by avoiding the exotically Russian and promoting the Russification of a shared canon of Classical literature and myth.

Rimsky's foray in this direction signaled a rapprochement between the St. Petersburg- and Moscow-based composers closely associated with Tchaikovsky, Taneyev, and a Westernizing sensibility. This made Rimsky the dominant national musical personality at the fin de siècle. Rimsky consistently sought to gain the favor of the state and its bureaucracy, and was proud to serve it. He shared with Rubinstein the ambition to lift Russian musical culture and practice to a level that equaled not only the status and professionalism of music in Western Europe, but the more advanced status and prestige enjoyed in Russia by the visual arts. By 1900, the accomplishments of Russian composers (including Tchaikovsky's growing fame and Rubinstein's legendary stature as a pianist) made it possible for Russian concert music and opera to challenge the stature of Russian fiction and poetry, at home and abroad, and represent a compelling new Russian culture, nurtured under absolutism. Had Volkonsky's lectures been delivered a decade later, music might have assumed a larger role.

A distinct liberal impetus certainly underlay the fight to establish musical institutions. Before 1861 many domestic serfs were also artisans, craftsmen, and artists; their contribution to pre-1861 art, theater, and music was considerable.[55] But the importance of serfdom to music and the theater in Russia before 1861 outdistanced its significance in the visual arts. Not only were serfs more indispensable to the performing arts, but in music there was no state-sanctioned path of training and certification by which to educate professionals and provide an opportunity to grant a musician a status that guaranteed civil freedom and exemption from taxation and restrictions, as there was in the visual arts.

Rubinstein's controversial 1855 essay on Russian composers in the Viennese *Blätter für Musik, Theater und Kunst* revealed more than his skepticism regarding the potential of Russian folk music to generate a repertoire of high art music (a thought Rimsky echoed decades later).[56] Willfully misunderstood by Alexander Serov, Balakirev, and Stasov (owing in large measure to Rubinstein being, in racialist terms, Jewish), the essay was a well-timed call for social, political, and educational reform. The polemic appeared first in April 1855, one month after the accession of Alexander II. Rubinstein sensed the opportunity for liberalization. The creation of musical institutions that required state approval and patronage seemed suddenly possible. Furthermore, without a state-sponsored infrastructure to sustain musical life, the Russian aristocratic patronage of musical culture would not survive the inevitable abolition of serfdom. A legitimate institutional path to musical careers was essential. Rubinstein's critique was not one of aesthetic criticism; his intent was to influence Imperial policy, now ripe for change under a new emperor. He would repeat his foray in journalistic advocacy again six years later, this time in a Russian journal.

## The Ideology of Beauty

Rimsky's turn away from a primary commitment to music's role in shaping Russian national sentiment and toward a focus on musical beauty per se revealed his acute sensitivity to the winds of change around him. The path he took after the completion, in 1888, of his three most celebrated orchestral works—*Sheherazade*, the *Russian Easter Overture*, and *Capriccio espagnol*, coincided with emergence of early twentieth-century Russian symbolism. In symbolist theory, music defined the nature and potential of art and the aesthetic realm. Andrei Bely (1880–1934), writing in 1903, claimed that "musical ideas are generic with respect to the ideas of all the other arts . . . that is why one may speak of the musical origin of all the arts . . . it is in music that the depths of the spirit approach most closely the surface of consciousness." For Bely, "The entire essence of a man is grasped not through events but *symbols of the other*. Music ideally expresses the symbol, and for this reason the symbol is always musical." Therefore, "he who is not musical understands nothing."[57] In 1906, Bely reaffirmed the notion that "music is the common trunk of all creation,"[58] and in 1909 he concluded, "Either life must be transformed into art, or art must be made living."[59]

This ideological foregrounding of music as "the very soul of all the arts," as "the latent energy of creation," whose "images are already perfect and complete," inverted the relationship between art and reality.[60] Art qua art became life's goal and the essence of reality.

This conceit was shared by the World of Art circle, and emblematic of the entrepreneurial ventures of Sergei Diaghilev.[61] Rimsky's operatic work before *The Golden Cockerel*, and after his most prominent neoclassical venture, *Mozart and Salieri*—including and particularly *Kitezh*, the orchestral suites drawn from earlier operas, and the vocal settings of Pushkin and Alexei Tolstoy—were ventures close to the Symbolists' notion of music. This affinity was in part the legacy of Russian autocracy that had survived rapid industrialization and the growth of a merchant, commercial, and professional middle class; it tacitly encouraged in the exclusive world of Russian arts and letters an ideology of the primacy of the aesthetic. Art had become "life," a superior reality for the literate public, one framed by political powerlessness. An aesthetic—defined by music, one entirely detached from naturalism and realism—dominated a public realm circumscribed by an increasingly incompetent and despotic state apparatus.

The limits to Rimsky-Korsakov's journey from the reductive nationalist ethos with which he started—and therefore his distance from Bely's Symbolism and its musical equivalent, Scriabin—can be gleaned in his decision never to write for the ballet separate from its place in the opera-ballet form he utilized. Rimsky chose not to follow Tchaikovsky's path as a composer for the art form most valued by the Imperial Court.[62] He was quite critical of the *Nutcracker*; for him, the ballet was a medium too glaringly aligned with absolutism. Nor was the ballet specifically Russian, or connected to the Russian language. Using a narrative without language, ballet tied music to movement alone, abstracting a key link between human experience and musical form central to Rimsky: language. He delighted in composing songs and romances. Dance as part of opera, where it was subsumed by context derived from the literary framework, made sense.

It would be left to Rimsky's pupil, Igor Stravinsky, to pursue the possibilities of a wordless synthesis of movement and music. Dance's embrace of formal constraints and its non-linguistic character (in addition to the opportunities presented by Diaghilev) attracted Stravinsky. Using Russian fairy tale, folk scenarios, and designs, his achievement rescued the ballet from its own history as an art form associated with arbitrary and absolute monarchical power. Improbably, dance emerged in Russia in the forefront of a modernist ideology that privileged what Tolstoy feared: the embrace of art for its own sake. The Russian element in Stravinsky's ballets, a direct link to Rimsky, had become the means to a purely aesthetic end.

Without Stravinsky's three great early ballets, it is hard to imagine a twentieth-century history of dance, including the sustained popularity of Tchaikovsky's major ballet scores. That being said, Stravinsky's flirtation with reactionary politics in the 1930s revealed residues of the pre-revolutionary symbiosis between art and absolutism. Stravinsky's aesthetic credo deviated from Rimsky's; it went further than art for art's sake by challenging the nineteenth-century discourse on beauty. Ballet's control over individual movement beneath a surface of visual and temporal spectacle mirrored an aesthetic legitimation of total control. The range of individual expression was circumscribed, notably in the corps de ballet. There were few real opportunities for a display of individual expression comparable to that given solo instrumentalists or singers in concert or opera.

In his 1936 *An Autobiography*, Rimsky's most famous pupil asserted that "expression has never been an inherent property of music" and that "the phenomenon of music is given for the sole purpose of establishing an order in things, including, and particularly, the coordination between *man* and *time*. To be put into practice, its indispensable and single requirement is construction. Construction once completed, this order has been attained, and there is nothing more to be said. It would be futile to look for, or expect anything else from it. It is precisely this construction, this achieved order, which produces in us a unique emotion having nothing in common with our ordinary sensations and our responses to the impressions of daily life."[63] For Stravinsky, the conception of music derived from its objective formal essence as an art form, its capacity to control, through sound, time, and space, using movement and gesture, rendering language and the ideal of subjective expression superfluous.

Rimsky's evolution never entirely transcended Romanticism. But it ended at a place well beyond the halfway mark between Stasov and the Stravinsky of the *Autobiography*. Rimsky retained Romantic conceits of music as a medium of subjective expressivity in response to nature and nation. He charted a path different from the symphonic practices of Western instrumental music and the Wagnerian techniques of inscribing drama into musical form in opera. Rimsky's rich and variegated musical painterliness emerged from the unique nineteenth-century symbiosis between art and autocracy under Alexander III and Nicholas II. That symbiosis led Rimsky to distill and evoke a distinctive, exportable, Russian-derived ideal of beauty in music, inverting the midcentury Russian advocacy of a link between art and reality. Art ceased to mirror reality. It redefined and supplanted the privileged place assigned to external reality by Belinsky and his successors.

By the 1930s the notion of beauty that Rimsky sought to uphold took on a new and terrifying significance with the renewed link between art and the state in communism.[64] The Soviet state carried to an extreme the patronage practices of the pre-revolutionary Imperial Court. In the 1920s, art needed to be reconciled explicitly with the modern by integrating into its character revolutionary elements adequate to a utopian vision of an egalitarian mass society. The potential of mechanization as an aesthetic device was explored, as an antidote to history and as a break from the bourgeois conceit of complexity and individuality. The "machine, the genie that man has thoughtlessly let out of the bottle," as George Orwell put it, became aestheticized.[65] Although Stalin returned to a retrospective aesthetic far from revolutionary experimentation, the control by the state became more relentless, prescriptive, and efficient than under the Romanovs, as Nabokov suggested.

In his 1923 dystopian novel *WE*, Yevgeny Zamyatin characterizes ballet as "square harmony." Witnessing the movements of the machine, the diarist "saw the entire beauty of this grand machine's ballet flooded with the light blue sky. I then asked myself: Why is that so beautiful? The answer was: Because the motion is unfree, because the whole deep meaning of the dance is about absolute and esthetical dependence, about perfect unfreedom. If it is true that our ancestors would give themselves up for dancing in the most inspired moments of their lives (religious mysteries, military parades), it means precisely that the instinct of unfreedom is organically inherent in human beings."[66]

This dehumanized oppressive detachment of the aesthetic from nature and the subjective human experience was a consequence different from the "degeneracy" Rimsky feared in the late 1890s. But the static aspects of the lush, colorful celebrations of the human experience of time and intimacy, audible in *Sheherazade*, *Kitezh*, and in Rimsky's contemplative tableaux of sound, contained seeds of inspiration, exploited brilliantly by Stravinsky, that pointed the way to Zamyatin's nightmarish vision.

## The Pictorial in Art and Music

The history of music and the history of painting and sculpture do not coincide as neatly as implied by the shared use of labels denoting stylistic periods, such as "Baroque," "Classical," and "Romantic." But the trajectory taken by Rimsky-Korsakov after 1862, when he resumed his engagement with music after his Navy service, suggests instructive parallels between music and painting in Russia.[67] In 1903, Rimsky expressed the thought that his best music strived to be "pictorial" and "to deal with themes drawn from the life of the folk." Even when he took a "sharp turn" to the symphonic, the pictorial intent, the emulation of the frame of a canvas, was audible.[68] Rimsky's distinctive Russian resolution of the ideal of musical beauty took the form of the canvas, the frame of the static painting.

Glinka's 1836 opera *A Life for the Tsar*, as well as his subsequent *Kamarinskaya* and *Ruslan and Lyudmila*, set the stage for future generations by heralding the emergence of a distinct Russian musical tradition. Glinka assumed a key symbolic role. *A Life for the Tsar* in particular demonstrated the patriotic function of the artist; it celebrated the monarchy and Uvarov's guiding ideology. A comparable new beginning occurred in painting during the 1830s. Karl Briullov (1799–1852), a friend and contemporary of Glinka's, astonished critics in Europe and Russia with a massive canvas, *The Last Day of Pompeii*, completed in 1833 (and, curiously enough, inspired in part by a Pacini opera).[69] Briullov had spent a decade in Rome after graduating from the Academy of Fine Arts in St. Petersburg. Just as the Italianate frame of Glinka's 1836 opera failed to obscure the work's distinctive Russian aspect, Briullov's masterpiece seemed distinctly Russian, "inspired by the atmosphere of St. Petersburg," Herzen declared, despite its Classical subject matter and its stylistic debt to Romantic historicism.[70]

Briullov returned to Russia in 1835 in triumph and established himself as St. Petersburg's leading portrait painter. He then undertook a major task in direct emulation of Glinka.[71] On a commission from Nicholas I, he began a massive historical painting. Like the composer, Briullov chose a legendary Russian subject, the 1581 Siege of Pskov (Figure 1). Stefan Bathory, the Polish King and Duke of Lithuania, undertook an unsuccessful siege. Russia, under Ivan the Terrible, repelled the invaders. The Russian victory established Russia's boundaries in Europe. It was a historical landmark of monarchy's triumph, similar in stature to the story of Ivan Susanin's courage in *A Life for the Tsar*. Not surprisingly, Rimsky's first opera, whose multiple revisions occupied the composer for the greater part of his career, was set in Pskov during the reign of Ivan the Terrible, a decade before the siege.

Figure 1. Karl Briullov, *The Siege of Pskov* (1837).

Briullov sought to emulate Glinka. He adapted techniques of historical and religious painting developed in France and Italy to assert a distinct Russian patriotism. But he did not quite succeed. Like Glinka, he ultimately returned to Western Europe, and died in Rome in 1852. (Glinka died in Berlin in 1857.) Briullov, having abandoned his painting on the Siege of Pskov, failed to create a major narrative canvas on a Russian subject. At the same time, his 1849 *Sweet Waters Near Constantinople* and the 1850 sketch *A Political Demonstration in Rome 1846* suggest a new direction in his stylistic evolution, and a break with neoclassicist composition. The gestural realism, the turn away from historical subjects and from the neoclassicist refinement of his probing portraits, indicate a shift that mirrors the direction Glinka took between *A Life for the Tsar* and *Ruslan*.

Despite parallels between Karl Briullov and Glinka, their careers highlight the marked contrast between the status of painters and that of musicians in the era before the founding of the St. Petersburg Conservatory in 1862. Glinka was born to a noble wealthy family. Briullov's father was a Russified scion of long line of Italian painters. Karl and his brothers all graduated the Imperial-sponsored Academy and, despite their non-noble foreign origins, gained the status of a free artist, a recognized category in the byzantine bureaucracy of post-Napoleonic Russia. A state-sanctioned institution, the Society for the Promotion of Artists, founded in 1821, sponsored Karl's first trip abroad. Glinka, in contrast, required no patronage. He attended no music school but was determined, on his own, to get training worthy of his gifts in the West, in Italy and Germany. He was not officially recognized by the state as a musician, suggesting that Anton Rubinstein's 1855 critique of Russian musical life was not off the mark.

Briullov's failure to follow up on his 1837 masterpiece was compensated for by a younger contemporary, Alexander Ivanov (1806–1858), who, like Briullov, was the son of a painter and a graduate of the St. Petersburg Academy.[72] True to the pattern followed by artists before 1861, Ivanov went west, to Rome, where he befriended Friedrich Overbeck, the leading German painter among the so-called Nazarenes. Following Overbeck's lead, Ivanov looked to Raphael as an ideal, and devoted himself to executing paintings on biblical and religious themes. Like the Nazarenes, Ivanov insulated himself against the hallmarks of contemporary Romanticism, particularly its subjectivism, mundane imagery, less hard-edged use of paint, and its pointed rejection of classical ideas of order and harmony.

In pursuing a biblical narrative Ivanov unexpectedly found a way to inject a stark element of contemporary Russian realism. He devoted his energies to one massive canvas, *The Appearance of Christ Before the People*, which he began in 1837 and finished twenty years later (Figure 2). Ivanov returned to St. Petersburg where the finished work was exhibited. Innumerable sketches for the work point to Ivanov's nearly obsessive concern to depict, realistically, varied and differentiated human personalities. In the painting, there are, apart from Jesus, thirty-three figures, each naturalistically portrayed. Ivanov practiced a form of unvarnished realism entirely novel within the context of religious painting. It earned him opprobrium from religious authorities. But he also won the enthusiastic admiration of Chernyshevsky, Herzen, and Stasov. Among the most ardent admirers of Ivanov's canvas was Gogol, whom Ivanov had befriended in Rome.

It was *Appearance of Christ* that would have an impact on Russian art comparable to Glinka's on subsequent composers. Ivanov was seen as realizing the promise of a new pictorial realism while retaining a classical sense of form. He had placed ordinary people in the center, Christ at the periphery; he did not idealize faces, figures, or poses. The expressions seemed utterly contemporary and Russian. The theology of the painting was not doctrinal, and the biblical became a vehicle by which to realize a realistic portrayal of ordinary people. Ivanov's realism was interpreted in a manner consonant with the ideology of the criticism of the late 1850s. The evocation of sympathy and empathy for ordinary people and a heightened sense of social responsibility were seen as Ivanov's objectives.

Figure 2. Alexander Ivanov, *The Appearance of Christ Before the People* (1837–57).

If Briullov and Ivanov mark the beginning of a distinctly Russian school of painting and occupy a role similar to Glinka in music, the closest parallels to Rimsky among Russian painters in terms of career and aesthetic ambitions were his contemporaries Vasili Vereschagin (1842–1904) and Ilya Repin (1844–1930), as well as two younger painters who played a direct role in Rimsky's later work, Viktor Vasnetsov and Mikhail Vrubel.

Two factors connected Rimsky and the Kuchka to Vereschagin and Repin. First, they shared, for better or worse, Stasov. The son of a well-known architect, Stasov was perhaps best known in Russia as a critic of art and architecture. Only in the West is his fame linked exclusively to music.[73] Although music started out in the nineteenth century as the Cinderella of Imperial patronage and state support, by the outbreak of the First World War, and largely through the ventures of Diaghilev, Russian music competed with literature as emblematic of the country's unique character. As a consequence, the international recognition of the achievements of nineteenth-century Russian painters has lagged far behind literature and music to this day.

The second connecting factor is Repin's membership in a group of artists that bears close comparison to the Kuchka.[74] These artists, eventually dubbed "the Itinerants" (*peredvizhniki*), initially consisted of fourteen students who decided in 1863 to leave the Academy. By 1870, the group, having established an artists' cooperative in the capital, formally created the Association of Traveling Exhibitions. This organization put together exhibitions not only in St. Petersburg and Moscow but also in provincial cities. By the 1890s, the Association had become closely allied with the Academy, rendering this once radical secessionist group a part of the ruling establishment and a target of criticism for followers of the aestheticist *Mir isskustva* movement.[75]

A cursory glance at the Itinerants reveals one major difference with the Kuchka. All the members were professionally trained. None of them balanced art and science on a daily basis, as did Borodin, or art and the military, as did Musorgsky and Cui. Nearly all of them sought instruction outside of Russia. The Itinerants spurred a nationalist and realist movement in Russian art, but they began with an exceptional level of technical mastery, which they sustained. What did link the two groups were the idealization of Russian subject matter, particularly history, a deep attraction to the rural, agrarian world and its traditions (and not especially to the urban landscape and city life), and the desire to render religion accessible and modern through art.

The Itinerants' heyday, from 1870 to the early 1890s, was also that of the Kuchka. They were determined to depict the unique character of the Russian landscape. The customs, sufferings, and circumstances of ordinary people, as well as their idealized goodness, demanded a natural and realistic representation. Russian history, contemporary life, and myth became the material of art. The Itinerant artists found their own private merchant patron, the visual arts' counterpart to Byelayev, who published Russian composers and sponsored performances, in Pavel Treytyakov. And both painters and composers benefited from Savva Mamontov's largesse. His private opera used Russian artists in its productions.

Among the most memorable Itinerants were Isaac Levitan, the finest landscape painter of the nineteenth century (and a Jew); Vasili Surikov, whose ornate historical canvases capture moments of action with riveting dynamism; Ivan Shishkin, who spent most of his career depicting the Russian forest; and Nikolai Ge, about whom Stasov produced a massive monograph in 1904 and whose work bridges that of Ivanov and Repin.[76]

Ge (1831–1894) descended from Russian nobility of French origin (de Gay). He first came to St. Petersburg to study science but switched to the Academy of Arts. Graduating in 1857, he went abroad and settled in Rome. His *Last Supper*, painted in 1861 under the influence of Ivanov, was bought by Alexander II. He would return to Italy in the mid-1860s but in 1870 found himself again in Russia. But success with the public eluded him.

Ge befriended Tolstoy. In his radical depictions of religious themes, the suffering and inequality of ordinary people were portrayed powerfully, with unsentimental realism. The paintings he made at the end of his career earned him sharp criticism from the state. The contrast between Alexander II and his son—between the years of reform and those of reaction after 1881—is made clear by the father's purchase of Ge's *Last Supper* and his son's censure and banning of the same painter's *Crucifixion* (Figure 3).

Equally clear in Ge's work is the tension between his vision and the artist's dependence on two of Uvarov's three principles: orthodoxy and autocracy. Ge mirrored the range of styles and genres championed by the Itinerants. His masterpieces include the 1871 historical painting of Peter I interrogating his son; the 1884 portrait of Tolstoy; an 1893 landscape, *The Road in the Forest*; and the nearly surrealist 1893 *Golgotha*, with its experimental quasi-Symbolist use of color. More startling is Ge's eloquent realist depiction of the confrontation between aristocratic power, conceit, and privilege on the one hand, and the poverty, wisdom, and simplicity of the ordinary man on the other in the 1890 canvas *What Is Truth?* In the spirit of Tolstoy, a nominally religious narrative of Pilate facing Christ becomes a critique of an inescapable social and political Russian reality. Aristocratic despotism and the simple humanism of Christianity are pitted against each other.

The Itinerant presenting the closest parallel to Rimsky was Ilya Repin, whose long career bears comparison with Rimsky on several accounts.[77] Repin was close to Stasov. He, like Rimsky, was deeply involved with teaching and the institutional structures that dominated his art form. His portraits—among them those of Rubinstein, Rimsky, Musorgsky, Balakirev, Cui, Borodin, and of course his mentor Stasov—remain among his most familiar paintings. He was a regular at the musical soirees at Stasov's home. However, Repin, like Ge, revered Tolstoy, the man as well as the artist, and spent considerable time at Yasnaya Polyana.

Repin was unusual in that he was born into serfdom, of the military variety, and trained initially as an icon painter. Graduating and winning a prize at the Academy in 1865 entitled him to become legally exempt from taxes and duties. Repin was drawn to contemporary life more than myth, literature, or history, and from the start of his career, he was politically engaged (he sketched the execution of Dimitri Karakozov, who attempted to assassinate Alexander II in 1866).

Upon seeing Ivanov's masterpiece when he was twenty-two, Repin wrote, "This is the greatest work in the entire world, by a giant who was born in Russia!"[78] Between 1870 and 1873, he worked on one of his most enduring masterpieces, *Barge Haulers on the Volga*, one of the

Figure 3. Nicolai Ge, *Crucifixion* (ca. 1892).

paintings that electrified Stasov and the public with its impassioned depiction of pain, resignation, despair, and inhuman exploitation. By his early thirties, Repin had achieved prominence as a painter of exceptional talent and ambition and as a social critic motivated by nationalism. Stasov commented after seeing the *Barge Haulers on the Volga* (Figure 4) that "Repin was a realist like Gogol, and equally deeply a nationalist."[79]

In 1867, the twenty-three-year-old Rimsky witnessed the premiere of his orchestral work *Sadko: A Musical Picture* that brought public attention to

Figure 4. Ilya Repin, *Barge Haulers on the Volga* (1870–73).

his talent and made a favorable impression, even on Tchaikovsky. Repin's alluring, decorative *Sadko in the Empire of the King of the Sea* was completed in 1876. Despite such evident overlaps and parallelisms—in age, subject matter, and social circles—Rimsky's skepticism about realist nationalism as an aesthetic ideology prevented him from unalloyed admiration. In 1894, after seeing one of Repin's most celebrated historical paintings, the depiction of Ivan the Terrible holding the corpse of his son (whom he had just murdered), Rimsky commented, after pointing out the "striking colors and amazing realism," that he did not like the painting, because of the overwhelming visual presence of blood. Repin had overstepped "the bounds of pure art."[80]

Repin, on the other hand, admired Rimsky and sketched him conducting in 1882. He even claimed that one of his great canvases from the 1880s, *They Did Not Expect Him*, depicting the return home of an imprisoned revolutionary, had been inspired by the capacity of Rimsky's music to evoke a moment, a mood, a feeling. Repin's painting captured human vulnerability and powerlessness, and evoked shock and outrage. Repin's painterly spontaneity made the canvas vibrate with life and succeeded in generating sympathy for the plight of Russia's disenfranchised would-be citizens.

Repin went on, in his long career, to mirror a Rimsky-like eclecticism. He produced society portraits, and accepted Imperial commissions.[81] His later canvases—the massive 1891 *Reply of the Zaporozhian Cossacks*; portraits of Sergei Volkonsky in 1899 and Nicholas II—include even the occasional religious work. His monumental collective portrait of the State Council (1902–1903), when juxtaposed against his depictions of the 1905 demonstrations, reveals political ambivalences similar to Rimsky. Repin took on official administrative duties in 1890, and, like Rimsky, stood by the 1905 demonstrators. Like Rimsky, he was committed to forging a vibrant world of Russian art by assisting a younger generation.

Repin was the dominant visual artist in St. Petersburg at the turn of the century. He also studied Western art, as Rimsky had—Rembrandt, French Impressionists—in search of techniques by which to render a canvas alive using the visible markers of the act of painting. Repin developed a dynamic naturalism capable of visualizing contemporary reality, and bringing history to life. His realism was accessible, and alternatively both affirmative and critical, but it was always national, and patriotic. Repin's emphasis, particularly in his portraiture, was specificity and individuality, and therefore the evocation of human sensibility and a distinct personality.

When asked, Rimsky admitted gladly that he preferred his 1898 portrait by Valentin Serov (1865–1911), the son of the composer and critic Alexander Serov, to the 1893 portrait by Repin.[82] Serov would become the dominant St. Petersburg portraitist in the generation after Repin, after the turn of the century. Serov's style and approach reflected the influence of Repin and Ge, but also late Impressionism, Adolph Menzel, and Arnold Böcklin. The Serov portrait of Rimsky is less restrained and more luminous. Rimsky is at his desk, concentrating, lost in thought. Repin's features the composer on a beautiful couch, holding a cigarette. But it was the beauty of the paint and color, the freedom of their application, and the quiet sensuality of Serov's canvas that impelled Rimsky to say that it far surpassed Repin's.

Although Repin became the most remembered nineteenth-century Russian painter in the twentieth, Vereschagin was by far the most famous and widely exhibited Russian artist during the nineteenth.[83] Never associated with the Itinerants, Vereschagin's biography was closest to Rimsky's. The son of landed gentry, he graduated from the Navy Cadet School in St. Petersburg and at age sixteen served on a voyage that took him as far as Egypt. In 1863 he turned to art, entered the Academy, and after finishing with distinction, went to Paris for further studies. He then elected to fight in Turkestan in 1868 and was awarded the Cross of St. George. In the 1870s, Vereschagin settled in Munich. The outbreak of the Russo-Turkish War in 1877 inspired him to rejoin the military. He served with distinction and was wounded. But Vereschagin was forced to leave Russia and go back to Munich where he became astonishingly prolific. In the 1880s he traveled to India and Palestine and he finally returned to Russia, to Moscow, in 1893. Among his last forays into history painting were illustrations for Tolstoy's *War and Peace* on the subject of

Napoleon's invasion of Russia. An inveterate traveler, in the later 1890s Vereschagin visited Manchuria, the Philippines, Cuba, and the United States. Finally, in 1903, he went to Japan. He died, along with a relative of Rimsky's wife, when the ship *Petropavlovsk* was sunk at Port Arthur in April 1904 during the Russo-Japanese War. Rimsky was deeply disturbed by what seemed a senseless loss.

War became Vereschagin's obsession. So was controversy. Despite the astonishing hyperrealist precision of his canvases, he was accused of falsifying reality, particularly in his 1884 *The Suppression of the Indian Revolt by the English*. His lifelong attraction to oriental subjects mirrored Rimsky's and the Kuchka's. But Vereschagin was not circumscribed by an exclusive interest in defining a Russian national culture. Indeed, except for his late foray into historical painting, he was more concerned with using realism to critique Russia's imperial ambitions and the politics of war. He kept his distance from internal debates about Russia's national character. Vereschagin's late portraits, genre scenes, and landscapes, whether Russian or Japanese, and his narrative hospital scenes from 1901 reveal extraordinary versatility and technical competence. But his depictions of war and its aftermath, for example, the 1879 *Defeated, Requiem* (Figure 5), and his renderings of Islamic dress and architecture from the 1870s (*The Doors of Tamerlane*) suggest brilliance and genius. They transcend any initial suggestion of mere journalism and illustration.

Vereschagin possessed virtuosity in the use of color and the depiction of detail. The realism of his canvases was calculated to shock the viewer. Yet the scenes, for all their pictorial refinement, are theatrical and staged, even when they presume to capture an historical moment (the 1888 *Shipka Sheinova*). Vereschagin's visual compositions are economical and purposeful; they intentionally transform reality using aesthetic values.

Vereschagin used art to reveal to his audience, an elite who stayed at home while others died, the horror and brutality of war. This was art with a clear social and political message. But in line with Rimsky's claim that whatever the content, the normative demands of compositional practice needed to prevail, each of Vereschagin's best canvases displayed the dominance of formal concerns. Art could heighten the sense of the real. The imagery was delivered with a static simplicity that riveted viewers or a theatrical sense of motion and space that overwhelmed them. The artifice of the aesthetic—the control of the formal elements—heightened the illusion of an unvarnished realism of death.

The brutality Vereschagin depicted was shorn of sentimentality; the aesthetic element, including the decorative, did not distract from the content. Consequently, in the 1880s, several of his canvases, particularly *The Apotheosis*

Figure 5. Vasili Vereschagin, *Defeated, Requiem* (1879).

*of War*, an iconic image of a mound of skulls, were banned, in Russia as well as in Vienna and Berlin. Vereschagin remained an outsider within Russia, even though his *War and Peace* illustrations became popular and were widely reproduced. The irony was that this painter was at one and the same time a critic and a patriot. His paintings from the Balkan War offended Alexander II and led to his exile. Yet Vereschagin elected to serve on the battlefield. The risks to his life did not seem to deter his determination to unmask cruelty, oppression, and injustice.

Before the 1880s, Russian art displayed its equivalence to Western Europe in terms of technical refinement and mastery. What made it Russian was the subject matter—landscape, genre scenes, historical narratives, social injustice, violence, and religious mysticism. Its manner and style remained rooted in European Classicism, Romanticism, and later Impressionism however. But the visual arts in Russia reacted to the retreat from social reform in Russia after 1881. National sentiment moved away from contemporary life and history toward a romanticized allegiance to Russia's rural agrarian culture. Toward the end of the century, that agrarian world was threatened by industrialization and the growth of cities. Inspired by William Morris and John Ruskin in England, as well as subsequent movements in Vienna and Munich, Russia witnessed a revival of interest in traditional folk art, design, and architecture. Colorful, decorative ceremonial attire, carvings, and the organic shapes that characterized village architecture evoked the communal ethos of the *zemstvo*, a Russian alternative to the rational capitalism of scientific agriculture and industry, in which a cash economy triumphed over communal rights and barter. These attributes seemed "healthy" (in Rimsky's sense of the word) sources of a particular Russian visual aesthetic, one that was fully in harmony with Russia's natural landscape.

Mamontov, the backer of the private opera that produced many of Rimsky's later works, was a major driving force in this Russian arts and crafts revival. A new rural, agrarian, and provincial (in the literal use of the word) nationalism in the arts flourished at the end of the nineteenth century, overtly divorced from the single-minded engagement with social progress and reform.

In music, the situation was different. Before 1881, Stasov and the Kuchka sought to stem the tide of Western influence on the content and form of Russian music. Stasov opposed a conservatory and music's emulation of the pattern of training established by the Academy of the Arts. What Glinka did, more than Briullov or Ivanov, was to point the way to a Russian approach to form through content. If Haydn and Mozart put down the foundations for normative musical practice in the West, then Glinka was, as Rimsky never tired of arguing, not a composer better at what others in the West were doing, but an innovator, a builder of a Russian approach to singing, setting words to music, rhythm, instrumental sound, repetition, and pitch relationships. His sources were Russian, and the consequences were inventive extensions of local musical practices. They were "realistic" in the sense that they were adequate to the Russian language, religion, history, contemporary politics, and social structure. Stasov was not bothered by primitivism and the absence of conventional technique. Liszt and Berlioz were embraced in Russia precisely because they presented role models for a different resolution of how to forge a musical narrative.

Self-critical, entirely disciplined, and organized, Rimsky, well before 1881, came to the conclusion that Russian special pleading about the lack of technique in harmony, orchestration, and counterpoint was needlessly defensive. Could Russian music, like Russian painting, be able to harness an astonishing legacy, from Bach to Meyerbeer, Schumann, and Mendelssohn and on as far as Wagner and Verdi, on behalf of a distinctive Russian musical tradition, one less reliant on exotic content and various types of Orientalist markers? Russian composers could create major works that absorbed the Western traditions, just as the Russian painters had done. The material—rhythm, melody, and harmony, and the character of the Russian language—could generate new aesthetically valid forms that were uniquely Russian. Chopin was in this sense a model for Rimsky of a synthesis of pure art and beauty, national character, and originality in form and expression. Russian music could itself be the object of international imitation.

This was Rimsky's project, and he felt he had achieved it in *The Snow Maiden*. All the elements were there. The elapsed time of the opera was not defined in terms of Italian opera, German Romantic opera, or even Wagnerian music drama, but by the logical elaboration of Russian elements. Musorgsky and Borodin had tried this using history and classic Russian poetry, emulating Glinka's first opera, and had created a distinctly Russian affirmation of the political and cultural tradition of the Russian monarchy. Rimsky succeeded differently, using Ostrovsky's (and Glinka's) reinvention of the Russian fairy tale rooted in a speculative and remote pagan past. The use of fairy tales and the mores and myths of a preliterate world, more closely bound to nature, offered a non-degenerate, clear, and simple opportunity to create a modern Russian music that realistically evoked the Russian language, a traditional Russian sense of nature, and a pre-industrial sense of time.

Rimsky's awareness of contemporary developments in art, his growing distress at musical developments in Europe, and his disillusionment with the reductive nationalism of Stasov, who clung to a musical equivalent of critical realism, led him to appreciate Vasnetsov and Vrubel, painters with whom he would collaborate. Mamontov's private opera company put Rimsky in direct contact with them. The sources used, as well as the approach to art of these two visual artists, were resolutely Russian, influenced neither by Rome nor Paris. Vasnetsov and Vrubel sought to develop a unique modern aesthetic out of ancient Russian visual sources. The character and ideology of this effort did not bring them into conflict with the state; it represented an aestheticized nationalism much in line with Rimsky's pursuit after *The Snow Maiden*. Vasnetsov and Vrubel pursued a direction already implied in Repin's *Sadko*. Its fairy-tale decorative imagery, fully integrated into a fantastic visual landscape, prefigured the taste for the art and architecture that accompanied the conservative reaction under Alexander III.

The period in Rimsky's career between 1882 and 1907, the year *Kitezh* reached the stage, corresponds exactly with the construction and completion of the Church of the Ascension in St. Petersburg, built to mark the assassination of Alexander II, and a *locus classicus* of late nineteenth-century Russian Slavophile architecture.[84] The contrast between the neoclassical 1811 Kazan Cathedral on the Nevsky Prospekt and the Church of the Ascension mirrors a shift in aesthetic ideology to foreground the rural, pre-modern Russian sanctioned and supported by the state. That shift is apparent when the canvases of Bruillov and Ivanov are compared to those of Vasnetsov in the 1880s. Vasnetsov's design for the sets of *The Snow Maiden* (with Levitan) for the Mamontov Moscow production of 1885 is a brilliant improvisation on traditional rural

Russian architecture and its Byzantine origins. In its studied simplicity and affected innocence, there are no evident evocations of Western models, Renaissance, Baroque, Gothic, or Classical.

Vasnetsov was, not surprisingly, the son of a rural priest.[85] His first ambition was to follow his father and he attended seminary. At age twenty, Vasnetsov changed course and entered the Academy in St. Petersburg. After finishing he took the obligatory trip abroad to Paris. Upon his return, he wrote to Stasov, "We will contribute to the treasury of world art only when we concentrate wholly on developing our own Russian art, in other words, when we depict and convey the beauty, strength and meaning of our national images with the utmost perfection and completeness."[86]

From Rimsky's point of view, Vasnetsov's emphasis on "utmost perfection and completeness," not the Slavophile content, located the affinity between the two. It signaled a welcome vindication of his departure from the habits of the Kuchka. A commitment to things Russian required the will to fashion perfect and complete works of art. Like Rimsky, Vasnetsov was curious and experimented with styles and techniques. He also readily tried his hand at making art that was not strictly speaking evocative of his primary commitment to create in a distinct Russian manner, just as Rimsky chose to write *Capriccio espagnol*, *Servilia*, and *Pan Voyevoda*. Vasnetsov, in addition to his most famous Slavophile works, produced realist paintings of contemporary life, including portraits, Romantic landscapes, and clever imitations of eighteenth-century genre paintings. His Daumier-like satirical character sketches and cityscapes, including a memorable one set in Paris, are remarkable. Vasnetsov reserved his signature visual style and technique for his Russian projects. In his other canvases, he easily reverted to the conventions of late nineteenth-century genre and realist painting.

But Vasnetsov's finest and most original work is to be found in paintings in which the content is evidently Russian, his narrative canvases and architectural decorations. Between 1885 and 1896, he produced fifteen paintings, thirty figures of saints, decorative inlays and innumerable smaller images for the neo-Byzantine Cathedral of St. Vladimir in Kiev, completed in 1882. His costumes and sets for Rimsky's *Snow Maiden* date from 1885; in 1899 he painted a beautiful, more Symbolist portrait of the main character standing alone in nature in winter (Figure 6).[87] Beginning in 1880 Vasnetsov produced a series of massive, meticulously executed canvases based on ancient Russian history and myth, beginning with 1880's *Prince Igor's Battle* and ending with the more surrealist depictions of the *Galloping Knight* and *The Frog Tsarevna* executed between 1914 and 1926.

Using fairy tale, religion, and the distant Russian past, Vasnetsov came closest to creating a visual parallel to the mature Rimsky. He flattened

Figure 6. Viktor Vasnetsov, *The Snow Maiden* (1899).

the plane of the canvas, approximating an antique two-dimensionality though one brilliant in its colors. Almost childlike distillations and exaggerations of the human figure predominated, stripping the subjects of anything resembling a Romantic sense of individuality and personality. The human and mythic subjects became increasingly symbolic, the compositions disciplined in their formal control of the space, and the color and decorative elements spectacular. A deceptive simplicity and static stillness pervade Vasnetsov's canvases, lending them a sense of symbolic realism, created by petrified poses and captured action. The element of the fantastic and eerie is rendered persuasive through an explicit appeal to a sensual sense of beauty. All the visual elements, transformed and invested with human symbolic meaning, are resolutely Russian.

The youngest painter whose work intersected with Rimsky was Vrubel,[88] the link being the composer's second favorite opera, *The Tsar's Bride*. Vrubel, who designed the curtain for Mamontov's Private Opera Theatre, did the sets and costumes for the 1899 production of the opera; he did the same for a 1900 Moscow production of *Tsar Saltan*. Vrubel also designed the sets for Mamontov's 1895 production of *Hänsel und Gretel*.

Vrubel's opera designs show the distance traveled from Vasnetsov. His designs penetrate and upend the illusion of any naturalist or symbolic realism; objects and spaces are recognizable but transformed by playfulness and freedom in the use of line and color. A delicacy and self-conscious richness of form and decoration are visible through a prism that softens the gaze of the viewer. Reality is approximated, dismembered, and aestheticized. The flatness of Vasnetsov is simplified and intensified and the awareness of the transfiguration of external reality through artistic means is sustained. Nature is reimagined, abstracted, and the formal resolutions are lent new meaning, often as symbols.

At the same time, the historic Russian elements are unmistakable. For Vrubel, realism as a vehicle for forging a distinct Russian school is a mere starting point. He drifts toward the fantastic and ethereal. The content is Russian, but now so too is the form, through a unique, totalizing aesthetic transformation inseparable from the content. This could serve as a description of the structure of the large-scale works Rimsky wrote between *The Snow Maiden* and *Kitezh*. Vrubel's costumes and sets display a stylization and formal abstraction of clearly recognizable Russian dress and jewelry, crowns and swords, analogous to Rimsky's celebrated handling of orchestral textures and sonorities.

Vrubel is often associated with Art Nouveau, but his distinctive aesthetic fingerprint is the insistence on preserving the act of painting in an expressionist manner, providing an awareness of the action associated with the application of color. There is little sentimentality, particularly when the subject is from Lermontov. Vrubel also breaks the surface of reality into almost geometric fragments, in the spirit of a mosaic. Not surprisingly, he also made sculpture. *Nightfall*, from 1900, takes this strategy of geometric dismemberment of reality toward pure abstraction.

A different tendency is Vrubel's periodic foray into a Vereschagin-like cultivation of refined, decorative detail. But in his hands, reality becomes fantasy. In *The Swan Princess* from 1900 and *The Pearl Oyster* from 1904, Vrubel produces a shimmering, seductive, but clearly Russian luminosity. The roots of his imagination remained Russian. His sources were his own ecclesiastical paintings for St. Vladimir's in Kiev from the 1880s. Evocations of Russia's link to Byzantium, evident in his 1898 *The Bogatyr*, made a decisive impact on his highly idiosyncratic painterly style.

One source became an obsession for the painter: Lermontov's *Demon*, the subject of Rubinstein's neglected opera from 1871. Vrubel's *Demon* canvases, from paintings to illustrations, became his most famous works. But he also drew inspiration from Lermontov's *A Hero of Our Times*. Vrubel's concentration on aesthetic form and his ambition to transform the conventions by which the illusion of a realistic perspective is conveyed is most visible in the portraits of his wife, Nadezhda Zabela-Vrubel.[89] The unfinished 1901 *Lady in a Violet Dress*, as well as the completed portrait from three years before, reveals Rimsky-like formalist instincts. The painterly strokes assembled in layers and fragments create an integrated surface, with the subject of the painting subordinated to the composition. A sensual beauty of color and form overwhelms the act of depiction. Not only are human subjects aestheticized, but so too is nature, as in *Lilacs* from 1900. Vrubel's totalizing of the canvas through structural and gestural abstraction can be compared to the strategy employed in Vienna by Gustav Klimt and later Oskar Kokoschka in their portraits.

In Vrubel, the imagination of the artist breaks the boundary between the real and the fantastic, and yet he always references a Russian sensibility, as in the 1904 *Six-Winged Seraph* (Figure 7). Without embracing a philosophical symbolism in the manner of Bely, Vrubel, like Rimsky, stepped away from everyday reality and history and found in legend and Russian fairy tale a vehicle by which to realize Vasnetsov's ambition—the creation of a world-class but self-evidently Russian art.

The Russian content of Vrubel's work did not, however, impress Stasov, who in a review from 1903 excoriated the new generation of "decadent" artists. Stasov, who had no use for the World of Art or Alexander Benois, its chief protagonist, singled out Vrubel as a "cripple." (Stasov knew that Vrubel struggled with severe mental illness.) There might be, he conceded,

Figure 7. Mikhail Vrubel, *The Six-Winged Seraph* (1904).

something to Vrubel's "insane absurdity." But apart from the flower paintings and the decorations for St. Vladimir's, Vrubel's work was marked only by "a disturbed imagination, meaninglessness, and revolting forms."[90]

The distance Rimsky traveled from his allegiance to Stasov's advocacy of the Kuchka as a model of a nationalist art is evident from the contrast between their views of Vrubel. Where the work stoked Stasov's ire, Rimsky recognized the gift, the talent, and the Russian aspect in Vrubel's work. Rimsky was well disposed to Vrubel personally on account of his wife. Stasov, on the other hand, could only express outrage at those who sought to lend Vrubel's art status as Russian.

Rimsky pursued in his music a path comparable to Vrubel—emancipating art from an obligation to commonsense realism—by investing music with the capacity to communicate the essence of a distinct Russian spirit in a manner that would garner worldwide enthusiasm without relying on the allure of exoticism. Vrubel abstracted from the achievements of the Russian painters who came before him but went in the direction of producing beauty, and sought to create "complete and perfect" works of art not through direct realism but through formal aesthetic means, just as Rimsky abstracted structures from realist strategies. (Between 1900 and 1904 Rimsky produced five orchestral suites from his earlier operas.)

The comparison between Rimsky and the painters Vasnestsov and Vrubel clarifies the composer's self-description as a "pictorial" composer. For Rimsky, the freedom to make art, through music, an art form most distant from any sort of direct link to reality and therefore realism, led him to tie beauty in art to beauty in life and nature, all the while striving for brilliance, individuality, clarity, and simplicity. A unique sense of the universal and divine had become possible in the space created by Russian autocracy. The result, in Rimsky's mature work, was a unique Russian poetic narrative in sound. What prevailed was not drama but a sense of musical space; not a directional dynamism but a nearly static aesthetic relief from the relentless passage of time. *Sheherazade*, Rimsky's most famous work, succeeds as a musical canvas to be contemplated and absorbed, rather than as a musical analogue to storytelling in poetry and prose. A world of daydreaming and reverie is created through music, arresting time. Rimsky's (and Vrubel's) debt to realism as a strategy is its path to the realm of the imaginary.

In his recollections, written decades after Rimsky's death, Rimsky's student Mikhail Gnesin, a fine composer and a founder of the St. Petersburg Society for Jewish Folk Music, formulated his mentor's achievement and his greatness. Gnesin persuasively focused on Rimsky's pictorial approach, his capacity to retard and halt time in music, and create the experience of beauty in stillness. He wrote:

> Without trying to characterize Rimsky-Korsakov's work in all of its many forms or its entire significance, it should be noted that he was endowed with two outstanding gifts, which made him such an extraordinary poet of nature in music. Everything that captured his imagination imprinted itself in his memory in the form of expressive and succinct musical impressions. An exceptional simplicity, a rigorous believability, and persuasiveness translate the sights of nature into music. The beauty and originality of the pages that Rimsky-Korsakov dedicated to musical reflection of stars and the atmosphere (*Christmas Eve*), the gentle ripples on the surface of a lake and the crashing of sea waves (*Sadko, Sheherazade, The Story of the Tsar Saltan*), and the unusual cogency of the images stem, in large measure, from a lack of superfluous detail, the ability to separate the essential from

the extraneous, and from everything that makes it hard to see the object in its most basic outlines.

The grander and farther away the phenomenon is from us, or the more regular its construction (both of which characterize a significant portion of natural phenomena), the less we require minor details to recognize it. A distant object is visible to us in "perspective." It is as it becomes lines converging at an angle, or waves that periodically crash into one another. This give us a complex picture out of intersecting broken or serpentine lines. An object moving very quickly seems to transform into an immobile, often more complex figure. This kind of perception and representation of phenomena can be called "graphic." In a musical work, however, discrete elements appear in succession, one after another, creating an impression of uninterrupted rotation. At the same time, music also has the means to reproduce stillness or relative stillness.

The "static" in music has come under attack without justification. . . . It should be apparent to all that *genuinely immobile* music does not exist. We are speaking exclusively of *relatively* static musical forms that reproduce our impressions of comparably immobile phenomena or elements of ongoing action. . . . This is precisely how artists and sculptors achieve, in great art, the impression of movement in otherwise immobile paintings and sculptures . . . great composers and musicians greatly enrich their art by finding means to reflect stillness in music. Rimsky-Korsakov's achievements in this area are exceptionally significant.

The special acuity of Rimsky-Korsakov's musical ear, which linked the pitch of a sound to color impressions and images, was another wonderful quality. The phenomenon of "color hearing" is common among musicians; however, no one else so distinguished himself by such keenness and completeness.

His possession and first-rate command of these two distinct abilities simultaneously—the persuasive representation of phenomena and the experience of color in musical form, always with a subtle, attentive, and sensitive relationship to the human experience—made Rimsky-Korsakov foremost among musicians as a *poet of nature and man in nature*.[91]

If Gnesin was right, the twentieth-century's debt to Rimsky may lie in his realization of musical time in a manner entirely distinct from the expectations created by the Western, and largely German, practices of thematic development and variation that emerged out of Viennese Classicism and subsequently were extended during the nineteenth century by Liszt and Wagner through expansion in harmonic usage driven by the ambition to link music explicitly with drama. Thematic development and narration in music were replaced in Rimsky by the creation of sequences of tableaux, a tapestry of human and natural fantasy and reality rendered in sound. The decisive roots of this achievement were Russian. No wonder Igor Stravinsky consistently, even under the guise of praise and boasting of his intimacy with his teacher, falsified Rimsky's influence on his own work, thereby helping to deflect future generations from recognizing Rimsky's greatness as a composer.[92]

# NOTES

I would like to acknowledge the help of Bryan Billings and Olga Voronina with the Russian-language materials, although the translations are, if not otherwise indicated, my own. Christopher H. Gibbs, Marina Frolova-Walker, and Irene Zedlacher made insightful comments on earlier drafts.

1. Aylmer Maude, "Introduction," in Leo Tolstoy, *What Is Art? and Essays on Art*, trans. Maude (London: Bloomsbury, 2016), 105–6. Tolstoy wrote the book in 1897, but the first publication was in English, in Maude's 1898 translation, owing to the censorship imposed by the Russian authorities.

2. Tolstoy, *What Is Art?*, 63–69, 151, 167–69. In particular, Tolstoy was prescient in his fulminations about bad science, such as the "artificial" processing of food.

3. All writing on Russian music in the nineteenth and twentieth century is indebted to the brilliant and pathbreaking work of Richard Taruskin. My debt to his contribution is evident throughout this essay. Likewise, Marina Frolova-Walker's work has been indispensable. For Taruskin, see his *Defining Russia Musically: Historical and Hermeneutical Essays* (Princeton: Princeton University Press, 1997); *On Russian Music* (Berkeley: University of California Press, 2009); *Russian Music at Home and Abroad: New Essays* (Berkeley: University of California Press, 2016); and his *Musorgsky: Eight Essays and an Epilogue* (Princeton: Princeton University Press, 1993). Taruskin's key essays on Rimsky are "The Case for Rimsky Korsakov" in *On Russian Music*, and "Catching Up with Rimsky-Korsakov," in *Russian Music at Home and Abroad*. For Frolova-Walker, see especially *Russian Music and Nationalism from Glinka to Stalin* (New Haven: Yale University Press, 2007). See also Gerald R. Seaman, *Nikolay Andreevich Rimsky-Korsakov: A Research and Information Guide*, 2nd ed. (New York and Oxfordshire: Routledge, 2014).

4. Vasily Yastrebtsev, *Reminiscences of Rimsky-Korsakov*, ed. and trans. Florence Jonas (New York: Columbia University Press, 1985), 291, 206.

5. Ibid., 197–98.

6. Ibid., 199.

7. The biographical material in this essay is drawn from Rimsky-Korsakov, *My Musical Life*, ed. and with an introduction by Carl Van Vechten, trans. Judah J. Joffe (London and Bosten: Faber & Faber, 1974), a remarkably candid memoir, and unusually humble and self-critical (in striking contrast to Wagner's autobiography). The Russian text used here *Litopis moye musicalnoye zhizn'* (St. Petersburg: 1910). See also Tatiana Rimsky-Korsakov, *Letters to His Family and Friends*, ed. Malcolm J. Crocker and Margarita Maksotskaya, trans. Lilia Timofeeva (Milwaukee: Amadeus Press, 2016).

8. Ibid., 188, 211, 254, 303, 342.

9. Yastrebtsev, *Reminiscences of Rimsky-Korsakov*, 290.

10. Puccini was, for Rimsky, the best of a bad lot. See Rimsky-Korsakov, *My Musical Life*, 329; and Yastrebtsev, *Reminiscences of Rimsky-Korsakov*, 35, 94, 220.

11. The particular word *divine* comes from the English translation of Yastrebtsev, *Reminiscences of Rimsky-Korsakov*, 188 and 414. It should be understood in a non-religious sense, since Rimsky was not conventionally religious. It suggests that music is a human attribute, a gift of human nature in a commonsense notion of natural religion, and therefore sacred as a universal, inborn human capacity.

12. Vissarion Belinsky, "A Survey of Russian Literature in 1847: Part Two," in *Belinsky, Chernyshevsky, and Dobrolyubov: Selected Criticism*, ed. Ralph E. Matlaw (New York: Dutton & Co., 1962), 34. See also Frederick C. Copleston, *Philosophy in Russia: From Herzen to Lenin and Berdyaev* (Notre Dame, IN: University of Notre Dame Press, 1986).

13. Belinsky, "Thoughts and Notes on Russian Literature," in *Belinksy, Chernyshevsky, and Dobrolyubov*, 8, 6.

14. Belinsky, "Letter to N. V. Gogol," in ibid., 84.

15. See Nikolai G. Chernyshevsky, "The Aesthetic Relations of Art to Reality" (1853), in *Selected Philosophical Essays* (Honolulu: University Press of the Pacific, 2002), 281–422.

16. For the writings of Stasov, I have used the three-volume 1952 edition, *Izrannie Sochineniya b trioch tamax* (Moscow: Isskustva, 1952).

17. Vladimir Stasov, "Twenty-five Years of Russian Art: Our Music," in *Selected Essays on Music*, trans. Florence Jonas (London: Cresset Press, 1968), 66–84, 92–110.

18. Rimsky-Korsakov, *My Musical Life*, 379; Yastrebtsev, *Reminiscences of Rimsky-Korsakov*, 365.

19. Yastrebtsev, *Reminiscences of Rimsky-Korsakov*, 415.

20. See Richard Pipes, *Russia Under the Old Regime*, rev. ed. (London: Penguin Books, 1997), 249–80; and Martin Malia, "What Is the Intelligentsia," in *The Russian Intelligentsia*, ed. Richard Pipes (New York: Columbia University Press, 1961), 1–18.

21. See D. Yu Struysky, "A Few Words about National Identity (*Narodnost'*) in Music," (1842), in *Russians on Russian Music: 1830–1880*, ed. and trans. Stuart Campbell (Cambridge: Cambridge University Press, 1994), 43–47.

22. See Oleg Proskurin, "Pushkin and Politics," in *The Cambridge Companion to Pushkin*, ed. Andrew Kahn (Cambridge: Cambridge University Press, 2006), 105–17.

23. Mikhail Gnesin, *Mislii i Vospominanie o N. A. Rimskom-Korsakove* (Moscow: Government Music Publishing House, 1956), 8.

24. Alexander Herzen, *My Past and Thoughts: The Memoirs of Alexander Herzen*, abr. Dwight Macdonald, trans. Constance Garnett, introduction by Isaiah Berlin (Berkeley: University of California Press, 1982), 299–300.

25. Alexander Herzen, *A Herzen Reader*, ed. and trans. Kathleen Parthé (Evanston, IL: Northwestern University Press, 2012), 303–5.

26. Sergei Volkonsky, *Pictures of Russian History and Russian Literature*, Lowell Lectures (London: British Library, Historical Print Editions), 3–4. Volkonsky's lectures included only two passing mentions of music—Tchaikovsky's setting of Pushkin's *Eugene Onegin* and Glinka's of *Ruslan and Lyudmila*.

27. Ibid., 5.

28. Ibid., 6.

29. Ibid., 262–70.

30. Citing Vl. Solovyov, in ibid., 270.

31. Rimsky-Korsakov, *My Musical Life*, 393; Yastrebtsev, *Reminiscences of Rimsky-Korsakov*, 280.

32. See Marina Frolova-Walker's essay in this volume on Rimsky's views after 1905.

33. Vladimir Nabokov, "Russian Writers, Censors, and Readers," in *Lectures on Russian Literature*, ed. Fredson Bowers (Orlando, Austin, New York: Harcourt, 1981), 1–12.

34. See Richard Pipes, *Russian Conservatism and Its Critics: A Study in Political Culture* (New Haven: Yale University Press, 2005), 98–100.

35. Karl A. Wittfogel, *Oriental Despotism: A Comparative Study of Total Power* (New York: Vintage Books, 1981), 181. For the relevant Max Weber analyses, see "Zur Lage der bürgerlichen Demokratie in Russland," and "Russlands Übergang zum Scheinkonstitutionalismus," in Weber, *Zur Russischen Revolution von 1905* (Tübingen: Paul Siebeck, 1989), 272–74 and 675–79 respectively.

36. Wittfogel, *Oriental Despotism*, 429.

37. Belinsky, "Letter to N. V. Gogol," 89.

38. See Murray Frame, "Culture, Patronage, and Civil Society: Theatrical Impresarios in Late Imperial Russia," in *Late Imperial Russia: Problems and Prospects*, ed. Ian Thatcher (Manchester, UK: Manchester University Press, 2005), 64–83, esp. 69–71.

39. See Lynn M. Sargeant, *Harmony and Discord: Music and the Transformation of Russian Cultural Life* (Oxford and New York: Oxford University Press, 2011), 53–120.

40. Rimsky's view of Glinka echoed earlier sentiments, particularly those of Prince Vladimir F. Odoyevsky. See the 1836 Odoyevsky reviews of *A Life of the Tsar* in *Russians on Russian Music: 1830–1880*, 1–13.

41. Yastrebtsev, *Reminiscences of Rimsky-Korsakov*, 212.

42. Ibid., 300. On Rimsky and Wagner, see I. A. Korzukhin, *N. Rimsky-Korsakov i Richard Wagner* (Berlin: O. Shtoleberg, Russische Bücherzentrale, 1922).

43. Friedrich Bodenstedt, ed., *Michail Lermontoffs poetischer Nachlass* (Berlin: Verlag der Deckerischen Geheimen Ober-Hofbuchdruckerei, 1852) 2:346–47.

44. See César Cui's 1872 discussion in "*The Stone Guest* of Pushkin and Dargomizhsky" (1872), in *Russians on Russian Music: 1830–1880*, 163–75.

45. Rimsky-Korsakov, *My Musical Life*, 222.

46. Ibid., 228.

47. Tolstoy's criticism prompted Ostrovsky to reply: "Shakespeare also had, next to his serious plots some fairy-tale subjects." This exchange is in Dushan Petrovich Makovitsky, "Yasnopolyanskiye zapiski," *Literaturnoe nasledstvo* 90/2 (1979): 350. Dushan Makovitsky was Tolstoy's personal physician.

48. *"To my best friend": The Correspondence between Tchaikovsky and Nadezhda von Meck, 1876–1878*, trans. Galina von Meck, ed. Edward Garden and Nigel Gotteri (Oxford: Clarendon Press, 1993), 216; David Brown, *Tchaikovsky: The Early Years: 1840–1874* (New York: W. W. Norton, 1978), 284–88.

49. Rimsky-Korsakov, *My Musical Life*, 242.

50. Yastrebtsev, *Reminiscences of Rimsky-Korsakov*, 254.

51. Rimsky commented in 1898 on the unbearable boredom of the Schillings opera and its self-conscious seriousness and complexity. Yastrebtsev, *Reminiscences of Rimsky-Korsakov*, 211.

52. Alexander Herzen, *Selected Philosophical Works*, trans. L. Navrozov (Moscow: Foreign Languages Publishing House, 1956), 493; see also the perceptive discussion of music and essentialist notions of national identity in Marina Frolova-Walker, "Music of the Soul?" in *National Identity in Russian Culture: An Introduction*, ed. Simon Franklin and Emma Widdis (Cambridge: Cambridge University Press, 2006), 116–31.

53. Gnesin, *Mislii i Vospominanie o N. A. Rimskom-Korsakove*, 11.

54. Rimsky-Korsakov, *My Musical Life*, 382–84.

55. See Sargeant, *Harmony and Discord*, and Richard Stites, *Serfdom, Society and the Arts in Imperial Russia: The Pleasure and the Power* (New Haven: Yale University Press, 2005), 53–129.

56. Anton Rubinstein, "Die Componisten Russlands," *Blätter für Musik, Theater und Kunst*, 11 and 25 May and 8 June 1855. See also Philip S. Taylor *Anton Rubinstein: A Life in Music* (Bloomington: Indiana University Press, 2007), 46–122.

57. Andrei Bely, "Symbolism as a World View," in *Selected Essays*, ed. and trans. Steven Cassedy (Berkeley: University of California Press, 1985), 77.

58. Bely, "The Principle of Form in Aesthetics," in ibid., 209.

59. Bely, "The Magic of Words," in ibid., 100.

60. Bely, "The Principle of Form in Aesthetics," 208.

61. See John E. Bowlt, *Moscow and St. Petersburg 1900–1920: Art Life and Culture* (New York: Vendome Press, 2008), 161–200.

62. Rimsky-Korsakov, *My Musical Life*, 393; Taruskin has explored Tchaikovsky's close relationship to Alexander III and his court, and his status as an "official" composer, a relationship far closer and more intimate with the state than Rimsky's. Taruskin has also discussed Tchaikovsky's concern with the attribute of beauty in music. See "Chaikovsky and the Human," in *Defining Russia Musically*, 239–307.

63. Igor Stravinsky, *An Autobiography* (New York: W. W. Norton, 1962), 53–54.

64. See Evgeny A. Dobrenko's fine and provocative essay, "Terror by Beauty: Russo-Soviet Perspectives," which pursues a parallel argument; in *Beauty: The Darwin College Lectures*, ed. Lauren Arrington, Zoe Leinhardt, and Philip Dawid (Cambridge: Cambridge University Press, 2013), 143–50.

65. George Orwell, "Introduction," to Yevgeny Zamyatin, *WE*, trans. S. Viatchanin (New York: Concept, 2018), v.

66. Zamyatin, *WE*, 5.

67. See a complementary effort to link Russian art and music in the nineteenth century in my "Music as the Language of Psychological Realism: Tchaikovsky and Russian Art," in *Tchaikovsky and His World*, ed. Leslie Kearney (Princeton: Princeton University Press, 1998), 99–144.

68. Yastrebtsev, *Reminiscences of Rimsky-Korsakov*, 329–30.

69. On Briullov, see Galina Leontyeva, *Karl Briullov* (Leningrad: Chudoshnik RSFSR, 1986).

70. Herzen, *Selected Philosophical Works*, 493.

71. See O. I Senkovsky, "Opera in St. Petersburg: *Ruslan and Lyudmila*, music by M. I. Glinka" (1842), in *Russians on Russian Music: 1830–1880*, 13–27, esp. 25.

72. On Ivanov, see Mikhail Alpatov, *Aleksandr Andreevich Ivanov* (Leningrad: Chudoshnik RSFSR, 1983).

73. See A. K. Lebedev and A. V. Solodovnikov, *Vladimir Vasilievich Stasov: Zhizn'i tvorchestvo* (Leningrad: Chudoshnik RSFSR, 1982). Stasov's extensive writings on Repin, Vereschagin, and Vasnetsov, and the other painters discussed in this essay can be found in the three-volume collection of his writings, *Izrannie Sochineniya*.

74. For reasons of space, one artist, well known to the members of the Kuchka but not discussed here is Vasili Perov (1834–1882), the realist painter who preceded Repin and was perhaps closest in ambition to Chernyshevsky's views on the connection between art and reality. Perov is best known in the West for his portrait of Dostoevsky. He taught in Moscow and even made sketches for Ostrovsky's *Snow Maiden*. Petrov's finest works are genre scenes of daily life, poverty, and suffering. See Vladimir Leniashin, *Vasili Grigoreivich Perov* (Leningrad: Chudoshnik RSFSR, 1987); and Marina Shumova, *Vasili Perov* (Leningrad: Aurora, 1989).

75. See Janet Kennedy "Closing the Books on the Peredvizhnichestvo: Mir isskustva's Long Farewell to Russian Realism," in *From Realism to the Silver Age: New Studies in Russian Artistic Culture*, ed. Rosalind P. Blakesley and Margaret Samu (DeKalb: Northern Illinois University Press, 2014), 141–52.

76. Vladimir Stasov, *Nikolai Nikolaevich Ge: Ego zhizn', proizvedeniia i perepiska* (Moscow: Kushnishev, 1904).

77. See Elizabeth Kridl Valkenier, *Ilya Repin and the World of Russian Art* (New York: Columbia University Press, 1990).

78. Ya. B. Bryuk, ed., *Ilya Eyfemovich Repin k 150 letnuyu co dnia roshdenya* (Moscow: Treytyakov Gallery, 1994).

79. Stasov, "Kartina Repina 'Burlaki na Volge,'" in *Izrannie Sochineniya*, 1:239.

80. Yastrebtsev, *Reminiscences of Rimsky-Korsakov*, 95. For all his affinities with the liberals of the 1860s, Rimsky remained more a patriot and a bit more at ease with the regime than Repin, and less motivated by the cause of social reform. Rimsky saw himself less as a rebel and more in a line of composers that had its roots in classicism. And, as was evident in his dispute with Tolstoy and his dismissal of Strauss's music, he believed in the primacy of normative qualities in art and beauty. Repin's first commitment was to progress, both in art and society.

81. Grigori Sternin, ed., *Ilya Repin: Malerei, Graphik* (Leningrad: Aurora, 1985).

82. Yastrebtsev, *Reminiscences of Rimsky-Korsakov*, 206.

83. The most recent monograph on Vereschagin is the Russian Museum's 175th anniversary catalogue, *Vasili Vereschagin* (St. Petersburg: Palace Editions, 2017). See also Andrei Lebedev and Alexander Solodovnikov, *Vasili Vasileivich Vereschagin* (Leningrad: Chudoshnik RSFSR, 1987).

84. George Heard Hamilton, *The Art and Architecture of Russia*, 3rd ed. (New York: Penguin, 1983), 392–94.

85. A. K. Lazuko, *Viktor Mikhailovich Vasnetsov* (Leningrad: Chudoshnik RSFSR, 1990).

86. Vasnetsov to Stasov, quoted in ibid., 196.

87. See the beautiful edition of Ostrovsky's play with Vasnetsov's illiustrations, A. N. Ostrovsky, *Snegurochka* (Moscow: Mescheryakov, 2017).

88. Nina Dimitriyeva, *Mikhail Alexandrovich Vrubel* (Leningrad: Chudoshnik RSFSR, 1984).

89. See the selected correspondence between Rimsky and Nadezhda Zabela-Vrubel in this volume.

90. Stasov on Vrubel, in Stasov, *Izrannie Sochinyenia*, 3:219–21.

91. Gnesin, *Mislii i Vospominanie o N. A. Rimskom-Korsakove*, 8–11. It is interesting that the young Alexander Tcherepnin compared Gnesin's early music to Vrubel (athough not in a flattering manner). See Ludmila Korbabelnikova, *Alexander Tcherepnin: The Saga of a Russian Emigré Composer*, trans. Anna Winestein (Bloomington: Indiana University Press, 2008), 19–20.

92. See, for example, Robert Craft and Igor Stravinsky, *Memories and Commentaries* (New York: Doubleday, 1960), 52–58; and Stephen Walsh, *Stravinsky: A Creative Spring: Russia and France, 1882–1934* (New York: Alfred A. Knopf, 1999), 68–69.

# Index

Note: page numbers followed by "n" indicate chapter endnotes; those in italics refer to figures and musical excerpts. Throughout the index, RK refers to Nikolai Rimsky-Korsakov.

*Index of Rimsky-Korsakov's Works of Music*

*Antar*, 145, 149–52, *151*, 168–69, 171n6
*Boyarinya Vera Sheloga, The*, 6, 7, 8, 15–17, 22, 23, 25, 27, 293
*Capriccio espagnol*, 283, 323, 340
*Christmas Eve, The*, 7, 12–15, 18–19, 56, 92n36, 103, 105, 345
"Eastern Melody," 159–62, *162*
*From Homer*, 47, 322
*Golden Cockerel, The*: augmented triad in, 172n27; ballet versions of, 177, 188, 190–92, *191*; Belsky libretto, 156–62, 168, 178, 180–85, 187, 192, 198, 204–8, 212; Bolshoi Theater production of, 185, 187; censorship of, 182–85, 197–98; Tsar character and trivialist image of RK, 88; death of RK and, 184; Diaghilev's staging of, 188, 190; ending, disagreement between Belsky and RK on, 216–17; Guidon, Alfron, and Polkan, 206–7; Metropolitan Opera production of, 188; musical language of, 188–90; political context and subtext of, 178–80; popular music and, 187–88; Pushkin's tale, 157, 177–78, 197–98, 204, 210, 218n4; Soviet era and, 293; three spheres of, 187; Zimin production of, 185–87
—oriental themes and, 145–69; Astrologer characterization, 162–63; Badmaev and, 163–68; Belsky and RK's contention over, 180; Belsky's Preface, interpretation of, 168; intention to offend, 155–56; musical language of, 155; Queen of Shemakha characterization, 152–53, *153*, 158–62, *160–61*, 180–82, 207–8; Russian attitudes toward the East and, 146–47, 155–58; Russo-Japanese War and, 155–56, 163; Tsar Dodon characterization, 156
—Russo-Japanese War and, 197–217; bitter note of the opera, 197; causes and events of the war, 198–204; Kubin's painting *Das Grausen* (The Horror), 172n32, 203–4, *205*; musical implications, 211–17; references in the opera, 204–11
"Hebrew Song," 172n27
*Kashchei the Immortal (An Autumn Fairy Tale)*, 10, 50, 51–52, 87, 92n41, 179
*Kitezh*. See *Legend of the Invisible City of Kitezh and the Maiden Fevroniya*
*Legend of the Invisible City of Kitezh and the Maiden Fevroniya*, 197, 326; in letters, 54, 56, 58; oriental theme in, 216; religious-philosophical aspects of, 109, 193n11; Soviet era and, 283, 290; Zabela in, 11
"Maiden and the Sun, The," 12
*Maid of Pskov, The* (*Pskovitanka*): in letters, 13, 15, 21, 23, 28–29, 40, 48; Lunacharsky in, 139n86; at MPO, 5, 8; revision of, 110; RK's aesthetic shift and, 63–64; RK's revision of, 72, 91n32; *Snegurochka* compared to, 83; Solovyov's theory of progress in, 66; Soviet era and, 283, 293; terrible past theme, 74; *Vera Sheloga* as prequel to, 6
*May Night*, 6, 24, 28–29, 72, 92n33, 283, 296n39
"Midsummer Night's Dream," 11, 58
*Mlada*, 171n6

*Mozart and Salieri*, 97–132; aesthetics of responsiveness and, 105–21; "Aha!," 101–2, 104, *106*, *107*; background, 97–99; Dargomyzhskian/Musorgskian recitative in, 215; Grave (Mozart improvisation), 117–19, *118*; in letters, 13, 21, 23–24, 35; at Mamontov's home, 7; Moscow Private Opera premiere, 122–24, *123*; at MPO, 8; Pushkin's *Mozart and Salieri*, 97–102, 104–6, 117–18, 124, 131; reception and reviews, 121–32; the "worth" of Mozart, 99–105
"Nightingale, Captivated by the Rose," 28, 147, 152, 172n27
"Nymph, The," 11, 24, 28
*Pan Voyevoda*, 51n101, 268, 290, 340
"Pine and the Palm, The," 147
"Quiet Evening," 28
*Russian Easter Overture*, 313, 323
*Sadko*, 116, 283, 333–34, 345; in letters, 13, 15, 22–23, 32–33, 35, 56; at Mariinsky, 312; Mariinsky's refusal of, 4, 103, 128; at MPO, 4–5, 7, 8; Nadezhda Nikolayevna Rimsky-Korsakov on, 9n21; revision of, 110; self-parody in, 208; "The Song of the Hindu Trader," 192; Tsar's reversal on, 9–10; Zabela in, 4, 11
*Servilia*, 340; in letters, 40, 43–45, 48, 50–51; plans for, 10; Russian style, departure from, 212; Zabela in, 11
Sextet, 283
*Sheherazade*, 145, 323, 326; clarinet solo, 153–55, *154*; Diaghilev's ballet version of, 168; oriental themes in, 147–48, *148*, *149*, 159, 168–69; pictorial approach and, 345; premiere almost canceled, 155
*Snow Maiden, The* (*Snegurochka*), 63–88; Act 1 monologue and arietta, 77–79, *78*, *79*; Act 3 arioso, 79–80, *80*; aria, final, 83–85, *84*; aria, "I've heard the singing of the larks," 81–82, *82*; aria, "To go out raspberry picking," 81, *81*; censorship and, 312; as "dead" opera, 85, 94n56; decreased conflict and increased emotion compared to Ostrovsky's *Snegurochka*, 75–86; fairy tale, politics, and, 319–20; Glinka's influence on, 91n33; *Kashchei the Immortal* and, 87; in letters, 13–14, 35; love duet, 82–83, *83*; Mikhailovsky, the populist ideal, and, 65–70; nostalgic utopia in Ostrovsky's *Snegurochka*, 70–75; reception of, 319; RK's aesthetic shift and, 64, 212; as Russian project, 339; Soviet era and, 283, 290, 293, 296n39; Vasnetsov's art for, 339–42, *341*; Zabela in, 6
Songs (Opus 50), 3, 12
Symphony No. 3, 283
*Tale of Tsar Saltan, The*, 8, 75, 342, 345; *Golden Cockerel* and, 212–13; in letters, 29–30, 32, 34–35, 39–43, 45, 52, 54, 56; march, 213; Musorgskian recitative and, 215; Soviet era and, 283, 293; voice typing, 92n33
"Thy Glance Is Radiant as the Heavens," 147
*Tsar's Bride, The*, 312, 342; classicism and, 321; Kuchka taboos and, 215; in letters, 15–17, 19–22, 27–29, 33–40, 50, 56; Marfa's concluding scene, 93n52; performances, 8–10; RK's aesthetic shift and, 12; Russian style, departure from, 212; Soviet era and, 283; Swan Princess, 36–38, *37*; voice typing, 92n33, 93n42; Zabela and, 7, *57*

## Index of Names and Subjects

Abbate, Carolyn, 189
Abraham, Gerald, 75, 156
absolutism, 313, 324–25
"academicism," Soviet critiques of, 285–90
Adler, Guido, 108, 225
aesthetic utopianism, 108–9, 136n45
Afanasev, Alexander, 65
Aikhenvald, Yuli, 100
"Akh, Dilav!" (Georgian song), 147, *148*
Alexander II, 313, 317, 332, 337, 339
Alexander III, 317, 326, 339, 350n62; Asia and, 163
Alix of Hesse (Alexandra Fyodorovna), 178–79
Allanbrook, Wye J., 117, 138n77
Ambros, August Wilhelm, 112–15, 136n59, 137n60, 229, 236
American Ballet Theater, 190–92, *191*
*ancien régime*, persistence of, 130–31
Andreyev, Vladimir, 280

*Index*

Arensky, Anton, 137n71
art, 301–47; agrarian ideal and arts & crafts movement, 337–38; autocratic politics, nationalism, and, 306–17; Briullov, 327–29, *328*; Ge, 331–32, *333*; ideology of beauty, 321–22, 323–26; the Itinerants, 330–35; Ivanov, 329, *330*; the pictorial in art and music, 327, 345–47; politics and the fairy tale, 317–23; Repin, 332–35, *334*; Tolstoy's *What Is Art?*, 301–6; Vasnetsov, 339–42, *341*; Vereschagin, 335–37, *337*; Vrubel, 342–45, *344*
Asafyev, Boris, 85, 162, 178, 242–43, 278, 289, 293
Association of Traveling Exhibitions, 331
augmented triads, 152, 172n27
autocratic politics, 301–26; art, reality, and nationalism, 306–9; the fairy tale and, 317–23; ideology of beauty and, 321–22, 323–26; tacit alliance between state and artists, 309–17; Tolstoy's *What Is Art?* and, 301–5; Uvarov's three pillars, 314, 315–16, 332

Bach, Johann Christoph Friedrich, 110
Bach, Johann Sebastian, 72, 110, 119, 282, 284, 318, 320, 338
Badmaev, Pyotr, 163–68, *164*
Bakst, Léon, 132
Bakunin, Mikhail, 89n11
Balakirev, Mily, 151, 171n17, 180, 323, 332; Caucasian sketchbook, 146, 147–48; "Oriental Song," 152; RK's relationship with, 149, 318; *Rogdana*, 152; *Russia*, 321; *Tamara*, 145, 148, *148*, 313; as teacher, 279
Ballets russes, 188, 191
Baskin, Vladimir Sergeyevich, 52, 54
beauty, 303–5, 308, 311–12, 321–22, 323–26
Beethoven, Ludwig van, 112–13, 119, 130, 290, 303, 308
Belgard, Alexei, 183–86
Belinsky, Vissarion, 100, 306–7, 315
Belsky, Vladimir, 116, 172n32, 215, 303; about, 193n11; *Golden Cockerel* libretto, 156–62, 168, 178, 180–85, 187, 192, 198, 204–8, 212, 216–17; *Das Grausen* proposal, 203; on RK's musical quotations, 180, 212
Bely, Andrei, 324

Belyayev, Mitrofan, 316k
Berlioz, Hector, 113, 318, 338
Bik, German, 280
Bikhter, Mikhail, 289
Bilibin, Ivan, 156, 162, 173n38, 179–80, 213; "Tsar Pea," *165*, 167, 179, *181*
Billington, James, 66, 70, 89n6
Bodenstedt, Friedrich, 317–18
Bogdanov-Berezovsky, Valerian, 280
Bolm, Adolph, 187, 188
Bolshoi Theater, Moscow, 4n5, 51; *Christmas Eve* at, 7, 14, 19–20; *Golden Cockerel* and, 185, 187; *Khovanshchina* at, 252; *Maid of Pskov* at, 48; performers at, 20nn42–45, 40n74, 41n79, 46n86; *Saltan* at, 10
Bolskaya, Adelaida Yulianovna, 46
*Boris Godunov* (Musorgsky), 8, 63, 102, 134n29, 135n39, 213, 214, 308, 313
*Boris Godunov* (Musorgsky/RK), 103, 214–15, 251, 253
Borisoglebsky, Sergei, 20
Bormann, Emil, 128–29
Borodin, Alexander, 180, 189, 319, 331, 332; *Prince Igor*, 75, 159, 216, 313
Botstein, Leon, 108
Bourgault-Ducoudray, Louis-Albert, 171n17
Brandt, Skylar, 190, 191
Briullov, Karl, 327–29, 339; *The Siege of Pskov*, 327
Brusilovsky, Yevgeni, 291, 293
Bryusov, Valeriy, 193n8

*Carmen* (Bizet), 21
Cavalli, Francesco, *Vermonda*, 193n3
censorship, 182–85, 312–13
ceremonial songs, 72–73
Cervantes, Miguel de, 178
Chaadaev, Peter, 310
Chaliapin, Fyodor, 46; in *Khovanshchina*, 252, 254, 262–63, 266–69; in *Mozart and Salieri*, 13, 24, 122, *123*, 139n85; at MPO, 4n3
Chernov, Mikhail, 281
Chernyshevsky, Nikolai, 306–7, 314, 315, 329, 351n74
Chigaryova, Evgeniya, 135n39
Chopin, Fryderyk, 119, 127–28, 250, 303, 305
Christianowitsch, Alexander, 150, 171n6, 172n22

• 357 •

Church of the Ascension, St. Petersburg, 339
Communist Party, 283
Cui, César, 39, 149, 152, 255, 272n24, 318, 331, 332
da Barberino, Andrea, 219n22
Daniel, Salvador, 171n6
Danilevsky, Nikolai, 311
Dargomyzhsky, Alexander, 104, 120, 172n22; Conservatory and, 290; dedication to, 134n29; *Finnish Fantasy*, 152; "Oh Rose-Maiden, I Am in Shackles," 152; oriental idioms and Algerian tune, 149–53, *150*; recitatives of, 215; *Rusalka*, 25; *The Stone Guest*, 102, 118, 134n29, 152, 215, 318
Darwin, Charles, 89n8
David, Félicien, 145
Davidov, Karl Yulievich, 2268
Debussy, Claude, 253, 286
Dehn, Siegfried, 111
Deisha-Sionitskaya, Maria, 20
Diaghilev, Sergei, 132, 324; ballet version of *Sheherazade*, 168; *Golden Cockerel* staging, 188, 190; *Khovanshchina* version, 250–62, 268, 270; Stravinsky, relationship with, 250; World of Art circle, 322
d'Indy, Vincent, 304
Dobrolyubov, Nikolai, 91n29
Dömling, Wolfgang, 274n44
*Don Giovanni* (Mozart), 103, 105, 116–18, *119*, 126
Donskoy, Lavrenty, 20
Dorzhiev, Lama Agvan Lobsang, 163, 166
Dostoevsky, Fyodor, 101
Druskin, Mikhail, 293–94
Dubasov, Nikolai, 255
Dzerzhinsky, Ivan, 284, 287, 2937

Emerson, Caryl, 105, 135n39, 138n85
Engel, Yuli, 189, 230
Expressionism, 291, 342–43

Fardi, Georgy, 286–87
Fedorovsky, Fyodor, 252
Finagin, Alexei, 224
Findeisen, Nikolai, 139n94, 224, 226, 230–35, *231*, 242–43
*Firebird, The* (Stravinsky), 208, 249–50, 257, 293, 313

Fleischer, Oskar, 232
Fokine, Michel, 177, 191, 192
folk traditions: *Boris Godunov* and, 214; *Golden Cockerel* and, 188, 190–92; nationalism and, 307; RK's aesthetic shift and, 63–64; in Russian art, 91n28; *Snow Maiden* and, 65, 70–74, 92n39, 290; as vulgar vs. noble, 194n29
formalism, Soviet critiques of, 284–90
Free Artist title, 238–39
Frolov, Vladimir, 226–29
Frolova-Walker, Marina, 98, 102, 133n9, 172n27, 179, 187–88, 194n29

Ge, Nikolai, *Last Supper*, 331–32; *Crucifixion*, 332, *333*
Germany, 320–21
Gershelman, Konstantin, 183–84
Gershelman, Sergei, 183, 184–85
Ginzburg, Semyon (ed,), *N. A. Rimsky-Korsakov and Musical Education*, 294
Gladkaya, Sofya, 7, 31
Glazunov, Alexander, 33, 43, 128, 156, 203–4, 286; "Arabskaya melodiya," 152; Conservatory and, 278, 280, 287, 288–89, 293; "The Fire of Desire Burns in My Blood," 152; RK reinstated at Conservatory by, 211; *Stenka Razin*, 321
Glinka, Mikhail, 316, 317; beauty and, 305, 308; Briullov and, 328–29; compared to Mozart, 111; *Golden Cockerel* and, 180, 212; *Kamarinskaya*, 327; *A Life for the Tsar*, 72, 213, 327; RK's *Snow Princess* and, 91n33; *Ruslan and Lyudmila*, 72, 92n33, 129, 180, 206, 213–16, 320, 327; Russian approach and, 338; Soviet critics and, 289; Stasov on, 307
Gnesin, Mikhail, 157, 286, 288, 292, 310, 322, 345–46
Gogol, Nikolai, 72, 92n36, 303, 306, 312, 315, 329, 333
Golburt, Luba, 130
"Golden Cockerel" (Pushkin), 157, 177–78, 182, 204, 210, 218n4
Goncharov, Ivan, 158
Goncharova, Natalia, 190
Gozenpud, Abram, 85, 88, 91n28, 135n39
Grabar, Igor, 157
Gramenitsky, Galina, 280

Gramenitsky, Marianna, 280
Greenleaf, Monika, 101
Grétry, André, 131
Guidi, Carlo, 53, 54
Guiraud, Ernest, 132
Gunke, Osip Karlovich, 235–36
Gusin, Israel, 291, 292
Gvozdetskaya, Alexandra, 254–55

Halbe, Gregory, 91n26
Haldey, Olga, 122
Handel, George Frideric, 110, 119
Hanslick, Eduard, 136n59, 225, 229
Harss, Marina, 190
Hausegger, Siegmund von, 321
Haydn, Joseph, 110, 121, 233–34, 316, 338
Hegel, Georg Wilhelm Friedrich, 64, 67, 90n17, 113, 114
Hermitage Theater, 53, 132, 140n115
Herzen, Alexander, 65, 310, 314, 322, 327, 329
Hudson, Richard, 190–91
Humperdinck, Engelbert, 320

Imperial New Theater, 52–53
Imperial Theatres Directorate, 94n56, 103, 132, 183–84, 312
Impressionism, 286–87, 289, 291, 335
Insarova, Maria, 10
International Music Society (IMS), 232
Iogansen, Yuli, 226, 240
Ippolitov-Ivanov, Mikhail, 38, 40, 50; *Assya*, 38
Iretskaya, Natalia, 31
Irving, Washington, 177, 188, 193nn2–3, 218n4
Itinerants (*peredvizhniki*), 330–35
Ivanov, Alexander, 329, 339; *The Appearance of Christ Before the People*, 329, *330*
Ivanov, Mikhail, 41, 229
Ivanov-Razumnik, Razumnik, 87

Jankélévitch, Vladimir, 189, 190
Japan and Japanese culture, 156–58, 210. *See also* Russo-Japanese War
*japonisme*, 157, 173n43
Johansen, July Ivanovich, 155
Jurgenson, P., 182, 184, 187

Kabalevsky, Dmitri, 293
Kal, Alexei, 234

Kalafati, Vasili, 281, 289
Kamensky, Alexander, 280
Kandinsky, Aleksei, 105
Karatygin, Vyacheslav, 322
Kashkin, Nikolai, 242
Kerzin, Arkadi, 29
*Khovanshchina* (Musorgsky), 86
*Khovanshchina* (Musorgsky/RK/Diaghilev/Stravinsky), 249–70; aria "The Streltsy's nest is sleeping," RK vs. Stravinsky version, 259–69; debate over Diaghliev/Stravinsky version, 254–59; early history of versions, 251–52; premiere of Diaghliev/Stravinsky version, 251, 269–70; Stravinsky's changing aesthetics and views, 252–54
Kiev Conservatory, 238
Kitaev, Sergei, 157
Klado, Nikolai, 203
Klimovitsky, Arkadi, 126–27, 140n100
Klose, Friedrich, 321
Kobayashi Kiyochika, *209*
Kompaneyskiy, Nikolai, 170n3
Koshelev, Vyacheslav Anatol'yevich, 91n31
Kruglikov, Semyon, 4–5, 6, 15–17, 27, 30, 32, 38, 39, 51, 92n39, 135n32
Krzesinska, Mathilde, 252, 271n11
Kubin, Alfred, *Das Grausen* (*The Horror*), 172n32, 203, *205*
Kuchka (the Mighty Handful): autocracy and, 315–16; Dargomyzhsky's *The Stone Guest* and, 102; *Golden Cockerel* and, 187–88; Kerzin and, 29n59; *The Maid of Pskov* and, 63, 72; *Mozart and Salieri* and, 98, 215; oriental themes, 152–53; principles of, 308; representational accuracy and, 170n3; RK's abandonment of, 63–64, 88; RK's purism and, 102–3; Rubinstein's influence on, 153; state patronage and, 313; *Tale of Tsar Saltan* and, 215; *The Tsar's Bride* and, 8–9, 215; Vasnetsov and, 340; Vrubel and, 344
Friedrich Kürnberger, 311
Kuropatkin, Aleksei, 167

Labiche, Eugène, 132
*Lady Macbeth of Mtsensk* (Shostakovich), 91n29, 284, 286, 287

Lamm, Pavel, 273n38
Langhans, Wilhelm, 229
Larosh, Gherman (Hermann Laroche), 125–27, 132, 140n101, 226, 236
Lavrov, Pyotr, 66–67, 89n11, 90n12
Lebedinsky, Lev, 290
Lenin, Vladimir, 70, 86–87, 288
Leningrad Conservatory, 285, 292, 294
Leningrad Philharmonia, 282–83
Leningrad Union of Composers, 285
*Le nozze di Figaro* (Mozart), 125–26
Leoncavallo, Ruggero, 305
Lermontov, Mikhail, 317–18, 319, 343
Leskov, Nikolai, 91n29
Levandovsky, Mikhail, 43
Levitan, Isaac, 331
Lewes, George Henry, 112, 114–15, 117, 136n59, 137n70, 137nn64–65, 138n77; *Problems of Life and Mind* (Lewes), 114, 137n64
librettos, self-fashioned, 73, 92n37
*Life for the Tsar, A* (Glinka), 72, 213, 327
Linyova, Yevgeniya, 188, 214
Lipaev, Ivan, 41, 123–24, 139n91
Liszt, Franz, 119, 284, 318, 338, 347
Lunacharsky, Mikhail, 122, 139n86, 284–85
Lyadov, Anatoli, 128, 188, 240, 278, 286, 289, 293
Lyle, Duncan, *191*
Lyubatovich, Tatyana, 13

Macaulay, Alastair, 190
Maes, Francis, 98
Malinin, Mikhail, 29–30
Malko, Nikolai, 280
Mamontov, Savva, 4, 13, 15–18, 22, 26, 122, 312, 316, 331, 338, 342
Mariinsky Opera: about, 4n5; in letters, 32, 46, 48, 50, 55, 58; rehearsals at, 287; Rubinstein's *The Merchant Kalashnikov* at, 33n66; *Sadko* turned down by, 4–5, 9–10, 103; *Servilia* at, 10, 50; *Snow Maiden* at, 75; Zabela and, 8, 10–11, 27n55, 55
Marx, Adolf Bernhard, 231–32
Marx, Karl, 66, 89n6
Mascagni, Pietro, 305
Massenet, Jules, 308
Maude, Aylmer, 301, 307
Maykov, Apollon, 3
Meck, Nadezhda von, 92n37, 157, 319

melodiousness, RK on, 126–27
Mendeleyev, Dmitri, 225–26
Mendelssohn, Friedrich, 305
Metastasio, Pietro, 194n26
Metropolitan Opera, 187, 188
Mey, Lev, 40
Mikhailov, Mikhail, 280
Mikhailovsky, Nikolai, 67–70, 86–87, 89n8, 90n13, 90n17; "What Is Progress?" 67–68
modernism, Soviet critique of, 284
Molas, Alexandra (née Purgold), 200, 218n10
Molas, Mikhail, 200
Molotov, Vyacheslav, 290
Monfred, Avenir, 280
Moscow Private Opera (MPO), 4–8, 17, 27, 29–34, 40–41, 43, 50, 53, 122–24, *123*, 342
Mozart, Wolfgang Amadeus: beauty and, 305; Beethoven and, 112–13; *Don Giovanni*, 103, 105, 116–18, *119*, 126; free style of, 110, 136n54; Glinka compared to, 111; *Le nozze di Figaro*, 125–26; as model for students, 115; Pushkin's *Mozart and Salieri*, 99–100, 104–6, 117–18, 124, 131; RK's *Mozart and Salieri*, 97–132; struggle over soul and meaning of, 108; Symphony No. 40, 126; Tchaikovsky and, 125–26, 128
Musikwissenschaftliches Institut, 225
Musorgsky, Modest, 149, 180, 189, 234, 319, 322, 331, 332; Alexandra Molas's performances of, 218n10; *Boris Godunov*, 8, 63, 102, 103, 134n29, 135n39, 213, 214–15, 251, 253, 308, 313; *The Commander*, 253; Conservatory and, 287, 290; *Khovanshchina*, 86, 135n32, 249–70; *Nursery*, 215; on *opéra dialogué*, 98; populism and, 85–86; recitatives of, 215; RK compared to, 223; RK's *Mozart and Salieri* and, 134n29; *Salammbô*, 152, 170n3
Mutin, Nikolai, 30
Myaskovsky, Nikolai, 273n29, 293

Nabokov, Vladimir, 312–15
Nápravník, Eduard, 40, 89n1, 94n56
nationalism, 307–9, 315–16, 318, 334
Naumann, Emil, 232, 236, 246n59
Nekrasov, Nikolai, 70–71

New Russian School, 232
Nicholas I, 314
Nicholas II: autocracy, art, and, 326; Badmaev and, 166–68; *Golden Cockerel* and, 185, 208–10; in Kobayashi woodblock print, *209*; Otsu Incident, 210; Rasputin and, 178–79; Repin portrait of, 334; Russo-Japanese War and, 163, 198–99; on *Sadko*, 4, 9–10, 103, 312
Nikolaev, Leonid, 255, 280
nostalgia, 70–75
Nozhin, Nikolai, 89n8

octatonic scale, 212
October Manifesto, 179, 193n8
Olenin, Pyotr, 185
*opéra dialogué*, 98
oriental themes and the Orient, 145–69; *Antar*, 145, 149–52, *151*, 168–69; Badmaev and, 163–68; Borodin's, *Prince Igor* and, 216; early influences on RK, 147–54; Glinka's *Ruslan* and, 215–16; *The Golden Cockerel*, 146–47, 152–53, *153*, 155–63, *160–61*, 168, 216; *Kitezh*, 216; Orientalism, 146, 171n12; RK's paraphrases and blatant quotations, 180, 189, 212; RK's self-evaluation on, 145–46; RK's world travel and attitudes on, 146, 157–58; Russian views of the East, 155–56, 201; Russo-Japanese War and, 146–47, 155–58, 163; *Sheherazade*, 145, 147–48, *148*, *149*, 153–55, *154*, 168–69
Orwell, George, 326
Ossovsky, Alexander, 230, 280
Ostrovsky, Alexander: *The Pretender Dmitry and Vasily Shuisky*, 74; at RK centenary, 293; *samodur* type and, 91n29; *The Snow Maiden (Snegurochka)*, 64, 70–85, 91n31, 312, 317, 318–20, 351n74; *Tushino*, 74
*Otechestvennye zapiski* (Notes from the Fatherland, journal), 70
Oulibisheff, Alexandre, 136n54
Overbeck, Friedrich, 329
Ovsianiko-Kulikovsky, Dmitri, 100–101

Paliashvili, Zacharia, 293
Paperno, Irina, 108
Paskhalova, Alevtina, 6, 23
Perov, Vasili, 351n74

*Persian Songs* (Rubinstein), 153–55, *154*, 159
Petipa, Marius, 132
*Petropavlovsk*, sinking of, 200–201, 336
Petrov, Aleksei, 280
Petrovsky, Evgeni, 124, 139n92, 139n94
*Petrushka* (Stravinsky), 192, 194n29, 250, 257–58, 293, 313
Pfitzner, Hans, 321
Pisarev, Dmitri Ivanovich, 89n8, 90n12
populism (*narodnichestvo*), 65–70, 85–86
Port Arthur, 199–201, 205
*Prince Igor* (Borodin), 75, 159, 216, 313
Prokofiev, Sergei, 188, 203, 271n1, 293
Proudhon, Pierre-Joseph, 66, 89n6, 89n8
Pushkin, Alexander, 319; art vs. life and, 317–18; autocracy and, 309–10; "Golden Cockerel," 157, 177–78, 182, 197–98, 210, 218n4; *Mozart and Salieri*, 97–102, 104–6, 117–18, 124, 131; "Tale of Tsar Saltan," 156
Pyman, Avril, 193n8

*Queen of Spades, The* (Tchaikovsky), 125, 126, 129–32, 308

Rachmaninoff, Sergei, 4n3, 13, 30, 122, 139n85, 293
Rakhmanova, Marina, 105, 189
Rasputin, Grigoriy, 178–79
Ratmansky, Alexei, 190–92
Ravel, Maurice, 258, 268, 273n40
realism, 306–7, 315–16, 329–39, 342, 344–45
recitatives, Dargomyzhskian/Musorgskian, 215
Renzin Isay, 280
Repin, Ilya, 330, 332–35; *Barge Haulers on the Volga*, 332–33, *334*
Riemann, Hugo, 232–33
Rimskaya-Korsakova, Nadezhda Nikolayevna (née Purgold), 9, 14, 19, 29, 31, 32, 34, 36, 55, 185, 258, 303
Rimsky-Korsakov, Andrei, 9, 87, 253, 256–58, 268
Rimsky-Korsakov, Fyodor, 200
Rimsky-Korsakov, Nikolai: aesthetic shift of, 11–12, 63–64; birth centenary celebration, 293–94; on composition, place of, 242; death of, 184; diary of, 121; "formalism" and, 289; gatherings at home of, 303; as "man of the sixties" or "man of the

seventies," 88; on melodiousness, naturalness, and nobility, 126–27; Mikhailovsky's biography compared to, 86; on musical creativity, 239; naval trip around the world, 146; pictorial approach of, 345–47; political views of, 87; portraits of, 332, 335; as revolutionary, 87, 210–11; as trivialist, 87–88
—writings of: "Mozart and Glinka," 110, 113; *My Musical Life* (*Letopis' moyei muzïkal'noi zhizni*; memoirs), 64, 87, 104, 128, 136n59; *Practical Manual of Harmony*, 281, 290; *Principles of Orchestration*, 223, 281–82, 290–91; "Wagner and Dargomyzhsky," 113–14, 117
Rimsky-Korsakov, Voin, 158, 173n50
*Rite of Spring, The* (Stravinsky), 250–51, 258, 269, 313
Romanticism, 325–26
Rosenfeld, Paul, 88
Rossini, Gioacchino, 103
Rostovtseva, Alexandra, 28
Rozenov, Emily, 28
Rubinstein, Anton, 153, 239, 241, 313, 318, 319, 332; death of, 322; *The Demon*, 75, 343; *The Merchant Kalashnikov*, 33; *Persian Songs*, 153–55, *154*, 159
Runge-Semyonova, Alexandra, 19
Rusanov, Nikolai, 90n12
*Ruslan and Lyudmila* (Glinka), 72, 92n33, 129, 180, 206, 213–16, 320, 327
Russian Academy of Artistic Sciences, 223
Russian Association of Proletarian Musicians (RAPM), 283–85
Russian Musical Society, 39, 155, 229–30, 235, 238
Russian style, dehumanization of, 212–13
Russian Symphony Concerts, 15, 17, 23, 26, 30, 271n4
Russo-Japanese War, 197–217; about, 163; causes and main events of, 198–204; *The Golden Cockerel* and, 155–56, 197–98, 204–17; protests of 1905 and October Manifesto, 179, 193n8; sinking of the *Petropavlovsk*, 200–201, 336
Ryazanov, Pyotr, 280, 285–89, 291–92, 294

Sacchetti, Antonio, 226
Sacchetti, Liveri Antonovich, *227*, 255; appointment of, 225, 236, 237; on Artistic Council, theoretical branch, 240; background, 226; Findeisen's criticism of, 230–35; "Foundations of Music Criticism," 229; music history and aesthetics courses, 225, 235–38, 240–41; public lectures and Frolov's critique, 226–29; *From the Realm of Aesthetics and Music*, 229; RK's disdain for, 242; *Short Historical Anthology of Music from Ancient Times*, 229; Stasov as mentor to, 232–33; travels, 229–30.
Said, Edward, 171n12
Saint-Saëns, Camille, 145, 308
Sakharov, Ivan, 65
Salieri, Antonio, 98–101, 104–6, 120, 124–25, 133n12, 322
*samodur* character type, 72, 91n29
Samprovalakis, Yannis, 190
Sargeant, Lynn, 88, 238
Scherr, Apollinaire, 190
Schiller, Friedrich, 69
Schillings, Max von, 320–21, 350n51
Schubert, Franz, 279
Scriabin, Alexander, 189, 287, 293, 304–5, 321, 324
Sekar-Rozhansky, Anton, 5, 9, 30, 42
Senkovsky, Osip, 149–50
Serebryakov, Pavel, 280
Serov, Alexander, 180, 323, 335
Shcherbachev, Vladimir, 278, 283–84, 289, 296n28
Shcherbatov, Sergei, 157
Shein, Pavel, 65
Shishkin, Ivan, 331
Shkafer, Vasili, 13, 21, 24, 30, 33, 43, *123*
Shostakovich, Dmitri: Conservatory and, 279, 280, 282, 285, 286, 289, 293, 295n8; Gusin on, 291; *Lady Macbeth of Mtsensk*, 91n29, 284, 286, 287; linear style of, 286
Shvarts, Iosif, 280
Siloti, Alexander, 250
Skrinnikova, Olga, 178
Skryabina, Elena, 280
Slavophiles, 308–10
*Snow Maiden, The* (*Snegurochka*) (Ostrovsky), 64, 70–85, 91n31, 312, 317, 318–20, 351n74
Society for Private Opera, 4n3, 41n81
Sofronitsky, Vladimir, 280

## Index

Sokolov, Nikolai, 232, 255, 280, 281, 286
Solodovnikov, Gavrila, 40, 52
Soloviev, Vladimir, 109, 312
Solovyov, Nikolai, 255
Solovyov, Sergei, 63, 66, 67, 240
Spencer, Herbert, 237
Spendiarov, Alexander, 145, 293
Stalin, Joseph, 287, 290, 326
Stasov, Vladimir, 303, 307, 322, 323, 325, 329, 330, 332; on *Boris Godunov* revision, 103, 214–15; on *Mozart and Salieri*, 121–23, 135n31; nationalism and, 315–16, 338, 339; RK's relationship with, 318; Sacchetti and, 226, 232–33; on Vrubel, 343–44
Stavitskaya, Anna, 23
Steinberg, Maximilian, 258; Conservatory and, 278, 279, 280, 287, 289, 291, 292; RK's *Principles of Orchestration* and, 281–82; Shostakovich and, 295n8; Symphony No. 4 ("Turksib"), 290
*Stone Guest, The* (Dargomyzhsky), 102, 118, 134n29, 152, 215, 318
St. Petersburg Academy of Sciences, 225–26
St. Petersburg Conservatory, 223–45; arrival of RK, 277; curriculum, 1920s, 280–81; curriculum and figures, 1930s, 279–83; curriculum, 1940s, 293; decline of in 1930s, 292–93; first music history and aesthetics courses, 225, 235–38; Free Artist title, 238–39; Gunke memo, 235–36; Kashkin memo on academic research, 242; legitimization of music as profession, 238–42; Mozart as model composer for students, 115; musicology department established by, 242–43; practical focus of, 239–41; Rimsky-Korsakov school, legacy of, 277–94; RK birth centenary (1944), 293–94; RK's name on, 223; Sacchetti appointment, 225; scientific institutions compared to, 225–26; Soviet reforms and critiques of 1930s, 283–92; temporary dismissal of RK from, 179, 210–11; theory, RK's objections to, 111–12; see also Leningrad Conservatory
St. Petersburg Institute of Art History, 223–24, 243

St. Petersburg Private Opera, 52, 53, 54
Strauss, Richard, 304, 320–21
Stravinsky, Fyodor, 75, 93n42
Stravinsky, Igor, 249–70; *An Autobiography*, 325; *Chronicle of My Life*, 271n2; *Conversations*, 253; dance and, 325; Diaghilev, relationship with, 250; *The Firebird*, 208, 249–50, 257, 293, 313; Funeral Song, 249–50, 271n4; ill with typhoid, 269, 270; *Khovanshchina* orchestration, 252–53, 256–70; *The Nightingale*, 250; orchestration of Chopin's *Les sylphides*, 250; *Petrushka*, 192, 194n29, 250, 257–58, 293, 313; *The Rite of Spring*, 250–51, 258, 269, 313; on RK, 249, 347; *Scherzo fantastique*, 250; as student of RK, 249; Symphony in E-flat Major,
Suk, Vyacheslav, 41
Surikov, Vasili, 331
Symbolists, 182–83, 188, 189, 324, 340

Taine, Hippolyte, 237
Taneyev, Sergei, 283, 293, 322
Taruskin, Richard: on *Golden Cockerel*, 187–88; *Khovanshchina* and, 272n26, 273n38; on *Legend of the Invisible City of Kitezh*, 109; on *Mozart and Salieri*, 98, 135n39; on *Pskovityanka*, 63; on RK, 86; on *Snegurochka*, 64, 74, 83, 91n32; on Tchaikovsky, 125, 127, 140n100, 140n112, 350n62
Tchaikovsky, Pyotr Ilyich, 317, 319; death of, 322; *The Enchantress*, 43; *Eugene Onegin*, 126, 128, 129, 130; incidental music for Ostrovsky's *Snegurochka*, 92n36; Larosh and, 125; *The Maid of Orleans*, 41, 92n37; *Mazepa*, 75; Mozart and, 125–26, 128; *Mozartiana*, 126; *Nutcracker*, 324; *Oprichnik*, 103; *The Queen of Spades*, 125, 126, 129–32, 308; RK on, 128; RK's *Mozart and Salieri* and, 127–32; RK's relationship with, 318; Serenade for Strings, 126; on *Snow Maiden*, 319; state patronage and, 313, 350n62; St. Petersburg Conservatory and, 225; Taruskin on, 140n100, 140n112; *Vakula the Smith*, 92n36
Tcherepnin, Alexander, 352n91.
Telyakovsky, Vladimir, 48, 183–84

• 363 •

Tereshchenko, Alexander, 65
theory, RK's objections to, 111–12
Threlfall, Robert, 256
Tibet, 165–66, 168
Tigranian, Armen, 293
Tolstoy, Alexei, 324
Tolstoy, Lev, 69, 203, 311, 315; on art and beauty, 301–6, 310–11, 321; RK and, 303–4; on *Snow Maiden*, 319; *War and Peace*, 66; *What Is Art?*, 301–6
Trezvinsky, Stepan, 20
triads, augmented, 152, 172n27
"Tsar Pea" (Bilibin), *165*, 167, 179, *181*
Tsvetkova, Elena Yakovlevna, 13, 30
Tyulin, Yuri, 281, 286

Ukhtomsky, Esper, 163
United States, 246n57, 310–11
Uspensky, Alexander, 20
Uspensky, Gleb, 65, 71
Uspensky, Victor, 293
utopianism, 70–75, 108–9, 136n45
Uvarov, Sergei, 314, 315–16, 327, 332

van Zandt, Marie, 22
Vasilenko, Sergei, 54
Vasilyev, Mikhail, 75
Vasnetsov, Viktor, 312, 330, 339–42; *The Snow Maiden*, *341*
Vechten, Carl van, 188
Veprik, Alexander, 280
Vereschagin, Vasili, 314, 330, 335–37; *Defeated, Requiem*, 336, *337*
Vinter, Klavdiya Spiridonovna, 40
Vlasov, Stepan, 20
voice typing, 75, 91n33
Volkonsky, Sergei Mikhailovich, 311–12, 323, 334
Vrubel, Mikhail, 4, 15, 25–26, 30, 46, 352n91; mental illness of, 10, 49, 53, 54, 55; *Mozart and Salieri* and, 139n87; MPO and, 4, 7–8; RK and, 5, 330, 339, 342–45; at RK home gathering, 303; *The Six-Winged Seraph*, 343, *344*
Vsevolozhsky, Ivan, 103

Wagner, Richard, 43, 108, 180, 233, 284, 290, 320, 338; *Ring*, 303, 304; RK on, 113–14, 116; RK's *Mozart and Salieri* and, 120–21; RK's study of, 135n35, 317; Tolstoy on, 303, 305

Weber, Max, 314
Witol, Iosif, 255
Witte, Sergei, 163, 166
Wittfogel, Karl, 314
World of Art circle, 124, 132, 322, 324, 343
Wortman, Richard, 68

Yastrebtsev, Vasili, 34, 87, 103, 139n91, 172n32, 303; on "coldness," 135n37; on *Golden Cockerel* censorship, 183; on *Mozart and Salieri*, 121, 139n94; on RK and Tchaikovsky, 127–29; on sinking of the *Petropavlovsk*, 200
Yudina, Maria, 280

Zabela-Vrubel, Nadezhda Ivanovna, 92n33, 122–23, 139n87; death of baby son of, 10; letters (1898), 12–27; letters (1899), 28–31; letters (1900), 31–44; letters (1901–1902), 45–52; letters (1903–1906), 52–58; portraits of, *37*, *57*, 343; relationship with RK, 4–12
Zamyatin, Yevgeny, 326
Zander, Yuri, 280
Zaremba, Nikolai, 278
Zbrueva, Yevgeniya, 254
Zhitomirsky, Alexander, 281
*Zhupel* (magazine), 179
Zimin, Sergei, 185–87
Zlatovratsky, Nikolai, 65, 71
Zubov, Valentin, 223

# Notes on the Contributors

**Lidia Ader** is a senior researcher at the Nikolai Rimsky-Korsakov Apartment-Museum, and an artistic director of the "Art-parkING" Center for New Technology in the Arts. She is also a curator of international art projects, and the organizer of several international musicological conferences and symposia. She is the author of more than forty articles, which have appeared in five languages, and a member of the editorial boards or editor-in-chief for seven books on Russian and Western music published in Russian or English.

**Leon Botstein** is president and Leon Levy Professor in the Arts at Bard College, author of several books, and editor of *The Compleat Brahms* (1999) and *The Musical Quarterly*. The music director of the American Symphony Orchestra and The Orchestra Now and conductor laureate of the Jerusalem Symphony Orchestra, he has recorded works by, among others, Szymanowski, Hartmann, Bruch, Dukas, Foulds, Ries, Toch, Dohnányi, Bruckner, Chausson, Richard Strauss, Mendelssohn, Popov, Shostakovich, and Liszt. In 2018 he became artistic director of the Grafenegg Academy in Austria.

**Emily Frey** is visiting assistant professor of Russian at Swarthmore College. She completed the PhD in music history and literature at the University of California, Berkeley, where her dissertation on opera and psychological prose in nineteenth-century Russia was supported by an Alvin H. Johnson AMS 50 Fellowship. Her articles have appeared in the *Journal of the American Musicological Society* and *19th-Century Music*, and she is currently completing a book entitled *Russian Opera in the Age of Tolstoy and Dostoevsky*.

**Marina Frolova-Walker** is professor of music history at the faculty of music, University of Cambridge, and Fellow of Clare College. She is the author of *Russian Music and Nationalism from Glinka to Stalin* (Yale, 2007), *Stalin's Music Prize: Soviet Culture and Politics* (Yale, 2016), co-author (with Jonathan Walker) of *Music and Soviet Power, 1917–32* (Boydell, 2012), and co-editor (with Patrick Zuk) of *Russian Music after 1917: Reappraisal and Rediscovery*. In

2015, she was awarded the Edward J. Dent Medal by the Royal Musical Association for "outstanding contribution to musicology."

**Adalyat Issiyeva** is affiliated with McGill University and holds degrees from Almaty State Conservatoire and McGill. She is the author of a number of articles exploring the subject of Russian Orientalism ("'Connected by the Ties of Blood': Musical Scales in the Quest for the Russian/Asian Identity," *Revue du Centre européen d'études slaves* 2 (2013); "The Origin of Russian Primitivism? Alexander Grechaninov's Arrangements of Asian Songs," in *Sacre Celebration: Revisiting, Reflecting, Revisioning* (2013); "Dialogue of Cultures: French Musical Orientalism in Russia, 'Artistic Truth,' and Russian Musical Identity," *Revue musicale OICRM* 3/1 (2016). She is currently working on a book, *Representing Russia's Orient: From Ethnography to Art Song*. Her studies are funded by the Social Sciences and Humanities Research Council (SSHRC) of Canada, the Fonds de recherche du Québec—Société et culture (FRQSC), and the Schulich School of Music.

**Simon Morrison** is professor of music and Slavic languages and literatures at Princeton University, specializing in Russian and Soviet music and ballet. He is the author of *Russian Opera and the Symbolist Movement* (2002), *The People's Artist* (2008), *The Love and Wars of Lina Prokofiev* (2013), and *Bolshoi Confidential* (2016). Last year he restored the music of Cole Porter's ballet-pantomime *Within the Quota* for performance by Princeton University Ballet and London's Penguin Café Orchestra. In 2008, he edited the Bard Music Festival volume, *Sergey Prokofiev and His World* (Princeton University Press).

**Anna Nisnevich** (PhD, University of California, Berkeley) specializes in Russian/Soviet music, opera, and film sound. She has taught at UC Berkeley and University of Pittsburgh, lectured for Cal Performances, San Francisco Opera, and Pittsburgh Symphony, and published in *Opera Quarterly*, *Russian Literature*, and other academic venues. She is currently working on a book, *How Chaikovsky Became Soviet*, which explores the paradoxical rise of the consummate nineteenth-century lyricist to the top of the Soviet cultural pantheon in the 1930s.

**Olga Panteleeva** is a visiting scholar at Princeton University and lecturer in musicology at Utrecht University. Engaging with different periods of Russian and Soviet music culture, her research focuses on the relationship between music and power, intersections between musical and scientific discourses, knowledge production under authoritarianism, and postcolonial perspectives. She is currently completing her first monograph, *The Making of Soviet Musicology*, which is under contract with Indiana University Press. As a music critic Olga Panteleeva has written for the Russian daily *Vedomosti* and the online magazine Colta.ru. She received her PhD in musicology from the University of California, Berkeley (2015).

**Yaroslav Timofeev** defended his PhD at Moscow Conservatory in 2014 (dissertation: "Borrowed Music in Igor Stravinsky's Oeuvre"). Laureate of international piano, composition, and campanology competitions, he is the author of more than 700 publications. From 2009 to 2015, he headed the musicology section of the Russian Composers' Union (MolOt) Youth Division. He has been script writer for the program *Absolute Pitch*, broadcast on the Kultura TV channel. Consultant and lecturer for the Moscow State Philharmonic Society, and a prolific music critic for national newspapers, in 2015 he won first prize at the "Resonance" All-Russian Young Music Critic Awards. He has served as consultant for the Olympic Games Music Program in Sochi (2014), and as a jury and board member of the Golden Mask National Theatre Award.

**Jonathan Walker** is a London-based freelance writer and private teacher of advanced piano students. He is co-author (with Marina Frolova-Walker) of *Music and Soviet Power* (2012). He studied at Edinburgh University, at the Liszt Academy, Budapest, and at Queen's University Belfast, where he defended his PhD thesis on the musical-work concept. He has taught at Queen's University Belfast and Cambridge University, performed on BBC2 television, given talks for BBC Radio 4, and published translations in French and Russian.

OTHER PRINCETON UNIVERSITY PRESS
VOLUMES PUBLISHED IN CONJUNCTION WITH
THE BARD MUSIC FESTIVAL

*Brahms and His World*
edited by Walter Frisch (1990)

*Mendelssohn and His World*
edited by R. Larry Todd (1991)

*Richard Strauss and His World*
edited by Bryan Gilliam (1992)

*Dvořák and His World*
edited by Michael Beckerman (1993)

*Schumann and His World*
edited by R. Larry Todd (1994)

*Bartók and His World*
edited by Peter Laki (1995)

*Charles Ives and His World*
edited by J. Peter Burkholder (1996)

*Haydn and His World*
edited by Elaine R. Sisman (1997)

*Tchaikovsky and His World*
edited by Leslie Kearney (1998)

*Schoenberg and His World*
edited by Walter Frisch (1999)

*Beethoven and His World*
edited by Scott Burnham and Michael P. Steinberg (2000)

*Debussy and His World*
edited by Jane F. Fulcher (2001)

*Mahler and His World*
edited by Karen Painter (2002)

*Janáček and His World*
edited by Michael Beckerman (2003)

*Shostakovich and His World*
edited by Laurel E. Fay (2004)

*Aaron Copland and His World*
edited by Carol J. Oja and Judith Tick (2005)

*Franz Liszt and His World*
edited by Christopher H. Gibbs and Dana Gooley (2006)

*Edward Elgar and His World*
edited by Byron Adams (2007)

*Sergey Prokofiev and His World*
edited by Simon Morrison (2008)

*Brahms and His World* (revised edition)
edited by Walter Frisch and Kevin C. Karnes (2009)

*Richard Wagner and His World*
edited by Thomas S. Grey (2009)

*Alban Berg and His World*
edited by Christopher Hailey (2010)

*Jean Sibelius and His World*
edited by Daniel M. Grimley (2011)

*Camille Saint-Saëns and His World*
edited by Jann Pasler (2012)

*Stravinsky and His World*
edited by Tamara Levitz (2013)

*Franz Schubert and His World*
edited by Christopher H. Gibbs and Morten Solvik (2014)

*Carlos Chávez and His World*
edited by Leonora Saavedra (2015)

*Giacomo Puccini and His World*
edited by Arman Schwartz and Emanuele Senici (2016)

*Chopin and His World*
edited by Jonathan D. Bellman and Halina Goldberg (2017)

GPSR Authorized Representative: Easy Access System Europe - Mustamäe tee 50, 10621 Tallinn, Estonia, gpsr.requests@easproject.com

www.ingramcontent.com/pod-product-compliance
Lightning Source LLC
Chambersburg PA
CBHW030431300426
44112CB00009B/945